WEST COUNTRY

CRUISING COMPANION

A yachtsman's pilot and cruising guide
to ports and harbours from Portland Bill
to Padstow, including the Isles of Scilly

MARK FISHWICK

Copyright text and photographs © Mark Fishwick 2004
Copyright charts and aerial photographs © Nautical Data Limited 2004
The Author has asserted his right to be identified as the author of this work
in accordance with the Copyright, Design and Patents Act 1988
Cruising Companion series editor: Lucinda Roch
Published by Nautical Data Ltd, The Book Barn,
Westbourne, Hampshire, PO10 8RS
ISBN I-904358-25-X

NAUTICAL DATA LIMITED

Cover picture: *Temptress* at Dandy Hole

Photographs by Mark Fishwick
Aerial photography by Patrick Roach
Aerial photograph on page 99 courtesy of Mayflower Marina
Aerial photograph on page 104 courtesy of Plymouth Yacht Haven
Aerial photograph on page 145 courtesy of Falmouth Premier Marina
Aerial photograph on page 156 courtesy of Mylor Yacht Harbour/John Such
Photograph on page 113 courtesy of Weir Quay Boatyard/Mike Hooton
Photograph on page 136 courtesy of Fowey Harbour Commission
Photograph on page 149 courtesy of NMMC/Bob Berry

Charts: Jamie Russell and Chris Stevens
Art direction: Chris Stevens

Colour reproduction: PPG Design & Print Limited, PDQ Digital Media Solutions Ltd

Published by Nautical Data Ltd,
The Book Barn, Westbourne, Hampshire, PO10 8RS. Tel: 01243 389352
Second edition of this Cruising Companion volume 2004
revised from the fourth edition of *West Country Cruising*,
originally published 1988 by Yachting Monthly

OTHER CRUISING COMPANIONS

This Cruising Companion is one of a series. Other titles include:

Channel Cruising Companion
Solent Cruising Companion
East Coast Rivers Cruising Companion
North France & Belgium Cruising Companion
North Brittany & The Channel Islands Cruising Companion
West France Cruising Companion
North West Spain Cruising Companion
South West Spain & Portugal Cruising Companion

 # PREFACE

With each new edition of this book I reflect with some dismay how rapidly the time has passed since the last edition emerged fresh from the printer three years ago! Major developments, for once, have been less notable – the extensive improvements to the harbour entrance at West Bay are still ongoing

and Torquay's at one time drying inner harbour has been transformed into a tidal basin.

Life afloat has become a tad easier on the navigational front with the conversion of all the Admiralty West Country charts to WGS84 datum, technology continues its impressive and onward march with the proliferation of electronic charts and plotters, and now you can even get the local weather forecast text messaged to your mobile phone!

Safety too has been much enhanced by the admirable expansion of the National Coastwatch Institution visual lookout stations around the West Country, details of which are now included in both the passages and harbour sections.

However, if there was one single thing that jumped out at me as I waded through all the mounting paperwork that each new edition attracts, it was the spectacular growth of websites. Now it seems no matter how small or large the company, club, pub or organisation they are all out there somewhere in the ether and where appropriate I have endeavoured to include this in the text.

There have been the inevitable changes on the human front. Reg Mathews retired as HM of Teignmouth, where Ian Hayward has taken on the mantle. In the Yealm Julian Stapley has retired, the new HM a face familiar in west country waters for Robin Page was for many seasons manager at the Mayflower Marina in Plymouth, where Charles Bush has duly replaced him. At

Sutton Marina Susan Tansy has succeeded Chris Price as manager, while John Osmond has taken over at Falmouth Marina. Steve Bassett is the new HM of St Ives following Eric Ward's retirement and Phil Ward has replaced Captain Ken Milburn as HM of Porthleven.

And finally, a minor, barely perceptible change which I rate as a sad reflection on the busy commercial times we now live in, the virtual disappearance of something that was still quite normal when the first edition of this book was published back in 1987 – early closing day! There are few places now, it seems, where traders can afford to enjoy this luxury and thus it has vanished from the Port Guide sections, I suspect for good.

I have done my best to ensure accuracy but apologise in advance for any mistakes or omissions that have crept in. Changes are continual and any assistance to keep this book up to date will always be much appreciated. It does however surprise me generally how little feedback I do get from readers. Any suggestions for improvements are also always most welcome and wherever possible, acted upon. To make it, hopefully, even easier, a simple e-mail to mfishwick@aol.com is all I would request.

To those who have helped in the past, my thanks, yet again. Enjoy your West Country cruising!

Mark Fishwick, February 2004

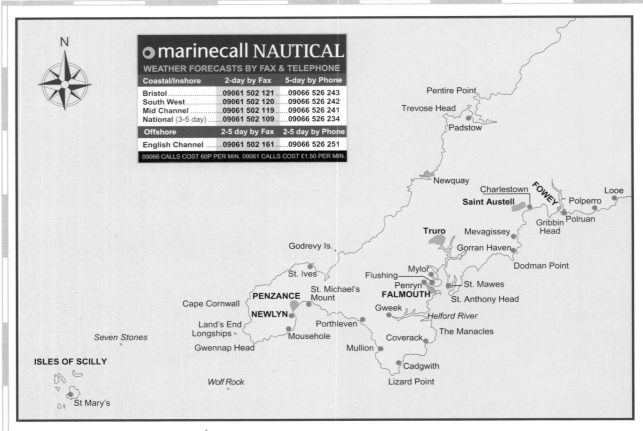

CONTENTS

Preface 3
Introduction 6
    General Information 8
    TidalStreamChartlets............................16

Chapter 1
Passages: Portland Bill to Start Point 18
    Portland Bill tidal tactics 19
    West Bay (Bridport).............................21
    Lyme Regis 23
    Axmouth 24
River Exe 30
    Exmouth 33
    The Bight 34
    Starcross 35
    Lympstone 35
    Exeter Ship Canal 36
    Topsham 37
River Teign 42
    Teignmouth 43
    Shaldon 44
Torquay 45
Brixham 50
River Dart 55
    Dartmouth 60

    Kingswear 62
    Dittisham...63
    Stoke Gabriel and Bow Creek 64
    Totnes...65

Chapter 2
Passages: Start Point to Rame Head 68
Salcombe 74
    Kingsbridge 82
Bigbury Bay 84
    Hope Cove 84
    River Avon 84
    River Erme 86
River Yealm 88
    Newton Ferrers 91
Plymouth 94
    Cawsand 97
    Plymouth marinas 98-104
    St German's River 107
    River Tamar.......................................110
    Cargreen 112
    Calstock 113

Chapter 3
Passages: Rame Head to the Manacles ..116
Looe and Polperro 124

ENGLISH CHANNEL

Fowey 130
Mevagissey and St Austell Bay 139
   Polkerris 139
   Charlestown 140
   Mevagissey 141
   Gorran Haven.....................................143
Falmouth 144
   Flushing..152
   Penryn 153
   St Mawes..154
   Mylor Yacht Harbour 155
   Restronguet..158
   Malpas 160
   Truro 161
Helford River 164
   Helford 169
   Port Navas 169
   Gweek 170

Chapter 4
Passages: The Manacles to Land's End 171
Coverack and Cadgwith 176
Mullion and Porthleven 179
Penzance 182
Newlyn 186
St Michael's Mount and Mousehole 190

Chapter 5
The Isles of Scilly 195
Passages: Mainland to Scilly 201

   Passage: S. Cornish coast to Scilly....201
   Passage: N. Cornish coast to Scilly ..206
St Mary's 208
   St Mary's Pool, Hugh Town 211
   Porth Cressa 215
   Watermill Cove 216
St Agnes and Gugh 218
   Porth Conger and The Cove 220
Tresco 222
   New Grimsby and approaches 225
   Old Grimsby 228
   Bryher 229
   Samson 230
St Martin's, Tean Sound and
St Helens Pool 231
   Tean Sound 233
   St Helen's Pool 235
   Eastern Isles 237
Isles of Scilly: anchorages at a glance ..238

Chapter 6
Passages: Land's End to Pentire Point ..239
St Ives and Newquay 244
   St Ives..244
   Newquay..245
Padstow 247
Index 253

 # INTRODUCTION

If I was given a brief to design a perfect cruising ground the West Country would not fall too far short of it, and I would be little inclined to make many changes. Year after year the magnificent coastline of Devon and Cornwall has attracted more and more visiting yachts to its ports and rivers – deep and mostly of easy access – and its rock bound coast, steep-to with few off-lying dangers.

If there could be one major change that we would all agree on it would inevitably have to be the weather, but what would English cruising be without its unpredictability? Generally speaking, well in the track of the prevailing south-westerly air stream and its accompanying depressions, the early summer can often provide some of the better spells of weather, and we can also be lucky in the early autumn. There does, however, seem to be a tendency for far more unsettled weather, often a blow or two, in August; not in itself a great problem once the long haul across Lyme Bay is astern, for a whole variety of harbours and safe anchorages abound, all within an easy day's sail of each other, and deep wooded rivers like the Dart and the Fal thread far inland to provide days of absorbing exploration in themselves.

Way back in 1957, *Yachting Monthly* produced a slim little book called *West Country Rivers*, written by D J Pooley, and it proved invaluable throughout my early explorations of my home waters back in the 1960s. Long since out of print, it was a very pleasant surprise when *Yachting Monthly* invited me to revamp the book in 1987 and my researches then soon confirmed that in those 20 years much had changed 'down west'; sailing, at one time the pursuit of the select few had become a big leisure business, and the changes reflected it. Once forgotten backwaters and creeks, the haunt of rotting hulks, whispering mud and seaweedy smells, had been cleared and dredged, and marinas had blossomed forth; anchorages that were easy of access under sail were diminishing fast and, as moorings encroached into every available space, a reliable auxiliary was no longer a luxury but a real necessity.

To my delight the resulting book, *West Country Cruising*, soon established itself as the cruising guide for the area, growing with each new edition and evolving in 2001 into the *West Country Cruising Companion*. But *tempus* really does *fugit*, another 20 years are already fast looming, and the changes have continued apace, not least the much increased numbers of boats that now visit these waters. However, in spite of it all, the essential beauty and atmosphere of the West Country continues to survive the onslaught well, and the sailing is as good as ever. Ashore, the varied and colourful villages and towns provide all the facilities a cruising yacht might need, from essentials like good ale and launderettes, to engineers and riggers. There is much of historical interest, and with vast areas fortunately preserved by the National Trust, many lovely walks.

There can be few visitors to these waters who sail away disappointed – hopefully this latest edition of the *West Country Cruising Companion* will help to make your cruise just that little bit more enjoyable. . .

Mark Fishwick

THE AUTHOR

Born in Exeter and brought up on the River Exe, Mark Fishwick began sailing at an early age and soon ventured further to explore the rivers, creeks and harbours of the West Country in his parents 18ft 6in Alacrity sloop *Vallette*. He moved to Cornwall in 1973 soon after buying his present boat, the 34ft 1910 gaff yawl *Temptress*, and since then has enjoyed a varied nautical life encompassing commercial fishing, charter skippering in the West Indies, yacht delivery, boatyard work, writing, photography and just occasionally sailing for fun!

ACKNOWLEDGEMENTS

Inevitably a book of this sort could not have been completed without a large amount of assistance from others, now too numerous to mention by name, but my heartfelt thanks again to all the harbour masters, marina managers, yacht club secretaries, readers and other diverse individuals who have generously helped with my requests for information and suggestions to keep this book up to date. My thanks also to my publisher *Nautical Data Ltd* for ensuring the ongoing continuity of this book, and last, but definitely not least, to my partner Sue for her tireless support.

GENERAL INFORMATION

EMERGENCIES

Rescue services within the coastal and sea area covered by this book are coordinated by Portland Coastguard (Tel: 01305 760439) – as far west as Topsham (River Exe). Brixham Coastguard (Tel: 01803 882704/5) – Topsham to Dodman Point, and Falmouth Coastguard (Tel: 01326 317575) – Dodman Point to North Cornwall. All maintain a 24 hour listening watch on VHF Channel 16 and normally work on VHF Channels 67 (Small Craft Safety), 10, 23, 73, 84 and 86 (Maritime Safety Information – MSI).

In emergencies only, VHF direction finding facilities can be activated by the Coastguard to locate a vessel in distress from Grove Point on Portland Bill, Berry Head, Prawle Point, Rame Head, The Lizard, Land's End, St Mary's and Trevose Head.

With the implementation of the Global Maritime Distress and Safety System (GMDSS) Portland, Brixham and Falmouth Coastguards all have VHF Channel 70 Digital Selective Calling (DSC) and a distress signal on this channel will be automatically received and recorded once the distress button has been activated on the shipboard VHF set.

All of the UK is an A1 GMDSS sea area – which means that throughout it there are Coast Radio

Stations with DSC receiver/transmitters within 40 miles of each other. In September 2003 UK Coastguard ceased to operate its dedicated headset distress watch on VHF Ch 16, but will continue to maintain a loudspeaker distress watch on Ch 16 until 31st January 2005. After this date ships at sea will no longer be required to maintain a listening watch on Ch 16.

NATIONAL COASTWATCH INSTITUTION (NCI)

Formed in 1994, the NCI is a charity that maintains Visual Watch Stations around the UK coast, many of which are located in former Coastguard Lookouts. They are manned by volunteer watchkeepers who monitor VHF channel 16 and provide a visual and verbal link with the Coastguard and RNLI during search and rescue operations. Passing small craft traffic is routinely logged, they can provide local weather information by telephone and in poor visibility some stations keep a radar watch up to 20M offshore. West Country NCI stations operational in 2004 are:

Portland Bill (Tel: 01305 860178) (Radar)
Exmouth (Tel: 01395 222492)
Prawle Point (Tel: 01584 511259) (Radar)
Rame Head (Tel: 01752 823706)
Polruan (Tel: 01726 870291)
Charlestown (Tel: 01726 817068)
Portscatho (Tel: 01872 580180)
Bass Point (Tel: 01326 290212) (Radar)
Penzance (Tel: 01736 367063)
Gwennap Head (Tel: 01736 871351) (Radar)
Cape Cornwall (Tel: 01736 787890) (Radar)
St Ives (Tel: 01736 799398)
Boscastle (Tel: 01840 250965)
Stepper Point (Tel: 07810 898041)

PASSAGE PLANNING

Since July 2002, Regulation 34 of the Safety of Life at Sea (SOLAS) Convention makes voyage planning on all vessels that go to sea a legal requirement. This is not really as onerous as it might at first seem as most sensible people afloat have doubtless long been doing this as a matter of common sense. Nevertheless, given that any passage, however short, must now be pre-planned, even in familiar waters, you should at the very least adhere to a simple check list covering the following areas:

1) Log the times of high and low water at relevent ports, and particularly those which might affect arrival and departure where there are tidal restrictions such as drying harbours, crossing bars or access into tidal locks.

2) Note the times of favourable and contrary tidal streams, with special regard to tidal gates.

3) Ensure that you have relevant charts and almanac and pilots to cover the intended route and alternative options should the passage plan need to be amended en route.

3) With recourse to the chart note down potential hazards to navigation and assess safe distances to clear them by.

4) Note down relevant pilotage detail – lights, buoyage etc – that will be encountered along your route, with particular attention to entering unfamiliar harbours.

5) Obtain and record the latest available weather forecast and outlook.

6) Take into due account the competence and strength of your crew.

BUOYAGE

All buoyage within the area of this pilot falls for the most part into IALA System A.

LATERAL MARKS, defining extremities of channels are red cans with a square red topmark and red light – to be left to port. Green or black conical buoys with triangular topmark and green light are to be left to starboard, in both cases when proceeding in the direction of the main FLOOD stream.

CARDINAL MARKS are used in conjunction with the compass, placed N, S, E, or W of a hazard. They are usually pillar buoys coloured with a combination of black and yellow, (see abbreviations) with quick flashing white lights, the significant feature being the double cone topmark. Two black cones pointing upwards mean the best water lies to the north (ie 'go north'); two cones pointing down mean pass to the south; points up and down (like **E**levator buttons) indicate safe water to the east, and two points together (**W**ineglass) likewise to the west.

Other marks likely to be encountered include ISOLATED DANGERS, black double spheres topmark, as on Black Rock, Falmouth. SPECIAL MARKS, yellow buoys, often with a yellow 'X' topmark, mark the limits of danger areas such as the firing ranges at the entrance to the River Exe.

Note that in the upper reaches of some of the rivers, several buoys are privately maintained and

Udder Rock buoy, between Polperro and Fowey

do not necessarily conform to these shapes or colourings. A variety of beacons from simple poles or stakes in the mud to complicated perches with wire stays and topmarks can mark narrower creeks.

DEPTHS

Depths mentioned in the text (eg least depth 2m, or Polca Rock 1.2m) are all in metres and 10ths of metres reduced to Chart Datum, the level of the LOWEST ASTRONOMICAL TIDE – LAT. This effectively gives the minimum depth you are likely to encounter but it should always be remembered that predicted tidal heights and depths can be much affected by the weather. Very low atmospheric pressure and strong winds may occasionally increase the predicted height by as much as 1m; conversely very high atmospheric pressure can have the opposite effect and a predicted height may be much less than anticipated. Remember too, to make due allowance for sea and swell, a rock or bar with 1.5m LAT will have considerably less water over it in the bottom of a 1m trough.

Heights above sea level (eg Ham Stone, an isolated rock (11m) are in metres and 10ths of metres above mean high water springs, MHWS.

Drying heights (eg dries 1.5m) are in metres and 10ths of metres above LAT.

DISTANCES

These are in nautical miles, (2,000 yds), cables, (200yds) or metres.

CHARTLETS

Are of necessity simplified to show the main basics a visitor will require and should always be used with caution. Green shading = dries LAT. Dark Blue = up to 5m LAT. Pale Blue = over 5m LAT. Soundings are shown in metres and tenths of metres showing depth of water above LAT. Underlined soundings show drying heights above LAT in metres and tenths of metres.

A back up of current/corrected Admiralty Charts is essential, or the Admiralty Small Craft Folios, which represent particularly good value (SC5601: East Devon and Dorset Coast, Exmouth to Christchurch), has various passage charts covering the coast between Start Point and the Needles and harbour plans for Christchurch, Poole, Swanage, Portland, Weymouth, Bridport, Lyme Regis and the River Exe. Small Craft Folio SC 5602 (The West Country, Falmouth to Teignmouth) has passage charts covering the coast between Teignmouth and the Lizard and harbour plans for Teignmouth, Torquay, Brixham, Dartmouth, Salcombe, Plymouth, Polperro, Fowey, Par, Charlestown and Falmouth, including charts of the tidal upper reaches of the rivers. Small Craft Folio SC5603 (Falmouth to Padstow, including the Isles of Scilly) incorporates passage charts and harbour plans for Helford, Cadgwith, Coverack, Porthallow, Porthoustock, Mullion Cove, Porthleven, Penzance, Newlyn, Mousehole, Isles of Scilly, St Ives, Newquay, Padstow and Port Isaac.

Imray also produces a West Country Pack (WCP), No 2400 in its '2000 Series' of smaller format charts. Covering the West Country from the Exe to Land's End, it comprises 11 harbour and passage charts for the area.

Stanfords' Chart Packs, CP 22 (The South Devon Coast) and CP 23 (The West Country), are another alternative. The company is also producing a new series of local charts (L) designed for smaller craft, with an increasing number being introduced for the West Country. Please note also that Stanfords Passage Chart 13, Start Point to Trevose Head, will be discontinued during 2004.

Electronic charts include: Arcs (Skipper): Folio 2 England South West Coast. Maptech: BACD01 England SW Coast. C-map:(all M-EW-C) 128 Scilly Isles to Portland, 019 English Channel Western, 017 Falmouth to Lundy, 072 Portland to Dartmouth, 073 Plymouth to Falmouth, 074 Falmouth to Scilly Isles.

BEARINGS

Are True from seaward except otherwise stated. Magnetic variation should be applied as shown on current Admiralty charts. Variation in the West Country (2004) ranges roughly between 05°00'W (Scilly) and 04°00'W, (Lyme Bay), decreasing about 8' to 10' annually.

WAYPOINTS

Waypoints, particularly when used with GPS, should be regarded with due caution and at all times a regular plot of your position – course, speed, set and leeway – should be maintained at hourly intervals in case of electronic failure. Particular care should be taken to avoid mistakes when loading lat/long coordinates into your GPS memory, and although accuracy is supposed to be within 20–25m, it is probably safest to assume 50m. Throughout this book GPS waypoints are referenced to WGS84 datum, now that all of the Admiralty charts for the West Country have been converted to this datum. Remember though, if using any Admiralty charts published before 2003, that they were based on the OSGB36 datum and a small correction – WGS shift – as indicated on the chart under a *Satellite Derived Position Note*, will have to be applied before plotting your GPS (WGS84) position to achieve full accuracy. If this is not applied, errors of up to 175m can be expected. The range of WGS shift in the West Country varies between 0'.03S, 0'.09E in the east and 0'.04S and 0'.06E in the west (0.05' approximates to 100m).

Although navigation in good visibility poses no problem, in close quarters situations and low visibility, great care should be taken and any other traditional back up, particularly soundings, needs to be taken into account when confirming your GPS position.

The harbour waypoints I have derived myself to give convenient arrival or departure points, and my thanks go to Peter Cumberlidge, author of the excellent *Waypoint Directory for the English Channel* (Adlard Coles Nautical) for his generous permission to include most of the waypoints selected for each Passage section. It should be noted that all lat/long positions used in this book are in degrees, minutes and hundreths of a minute – the last two figures adjoining the N or W notation – eg 50° 36'·45N / 04° 17'·88W to enable easy input into a GPS receiver.

TIDES

The maximum rate at springs is used throughout this book to give an indication of the worst, or if you're going with it, best rate you will encounter.

Generally, along the coast of the West Country, streams run parallel to the shore, but set in and out of the bays, and allowance should be made for this when crossing them. Within the bays, and

High and dry! Bull Hill Bank, River Exe

inshore, streams are generally weak but increase considerably in the vicinity of headlands where overfalls are often found. Streams are also much stronger within the confines of the rivers, and here it should be remembered that these are fed by the large gathering basins of the inland moors, Dartmoor, Exmoor and Bodmin, and after any period of rain, the amount of flooding fresh water can noticeably increase the rate of streams by up to two knots, particularly in the upper reaches. Explore upper reaches of rivers only on a rising tide and do not push your luck too close to high water at springs or you risk being neaped!

Spring tides occur a day or so after the full and new moon, approximately every 15 days. High water is usually 50 minutes later each day; low water approximately six hours after high water.

High water at springs occurs early morning and evenings, at neaps high water occurs towards the middle of the day.

Rise and fall of the tide is not at a constant rate, and the old *rule of twelfths* is always a good guide:
  Rise or fall during the 1st hour: 1/12 of range
  Rise or fall during the 2nd hour: 2/12 of range
  Rise or fall during the 3rd hour: 3/12 of range
  Rise or fall during the 4th hour: 3/12 of range
  Rise or fall during the 5th hour: 2/12 of range
  Rise or fall during the 6th hour: 1/12 of range

WEST COUNTRY WEATHER

As in most places in the British Isles, the weather in the West Country can be very changeable and, although it can deteriorate fast, with comprehensive forecasting and ports within easy reach of one another, there is little excuse for getting caught out.

However, in such an eventuality it is worth remembering that the exposed nature of much of the coastline and prevailing ground swell will produce seas considerably larger than elsewhere in the Channel, particularly with wind against tide. Remember, too, when negotiating the major headlands such as Portland Bill, Start Point, the Dodman and the Lizard, if the wind is forward of the beam a fair tide will also create a noticeable increase in its apparent strength.

If it is remotely possible to generalise, May and June can often provide a fine spell giving rise to all sorts of hopeful predictions that we're in for a long hot summer. July, alas, has a tendency to dispel such promise, and can often be very mixed. Although summer gales are rare, August often serves up at least one bad blow, such as the Fastnet disaster in 1979, and the tail end of Hurricane Charley in 1986. However, for once, it surpassed itself in 2003, with record breaking temperatures in the high 30s and a surfeit of sun! September, too, can be very unsettled although occasionally, the much vaunted Indian Summer can occur, if only briefly, as in 1994.

The prevailing south-westerly air stream and the warmer waters of the Gulf Stream which embrace the far west create the dominant feature of the weather – depressions which usually pass to the north of the area with associated trailing warm and cold fronts creating an unsettled but at least predictable sequence of wind and accompanying rain.

When the Azores High manages to push far enough north to keep these depressions at bay it should result in fine weather. Frequently it does – ashore – but the easterly airstream that usually results has a tendency to be unpredictable in its strength and is often fresh at sea, creating very hazy conditions, blowing hard during the day and easing at night.

As most of the West Country ports evolved to provide shelter from the prevailing westerlies, many can be very uncomfortable in easterlies –

Just about as good as it gets. Temptress at Dandy Hole

Falmouth inner harbour can be spectacularly rough in an easterly gale, while the Helford is a very miserable place to be – with justification borne of long experience, the 'beastly easterly' is a wind little loved by locals in west country havens.

The topography of the rivers creates its own localised effects, particularly those bounded by high steep shores like the Dart, Fowey and the Yealm, where baffling breezes are not only encountered in the entrance but also in the upper reaches, where frustratingly fluky winds often follow the river's course. The upper Fal is a classic example – a breeze will be dead ahead in one reach, you can then follow the next bend through 90 degrees and, instead of the expected freeing, you'll find it still doggedly on the nose!

In gales these same high shores, seemingly so protective, can often produce powerful, williwaw-like downdrafts that are very unpredictable in their direction – I recall one very restless night, anchored just below the Anchor Stone on the Dart, ranging wildly across the full scope of our chain as gusts hit us from every quarter, and on another occasion, tucked away in the perfect landlocked shelter of Yealm Pool during a south-westerly gale, the boat was laid over almost on her beam ends on several occasions!

Many places, and in particular Fowey and Salcombe, can become doubly uncomfortable in strong winds blowing contrary to the tide, but at least the misery only has to be endured for a few hours at a time!

In settled spells of fine weather land and sea breezes can be encountered anywhere, but one particular localised phenomenon I have often encountered, notably in the approaches to the Fal, Plymouth, Salcombe and also the Exe, is a fresh catabatic breeze funnelling seawards in the late afternoon, making for an interesting final thrash into port.

Fog, fortunately, is not overly frequent this far west, but in fine weather banks of low lying sea mist can occur without warning, often towards the end of a fine warm day. In settled weather, usually when high pressure prevails, early morning mist in rivers will often be surprisingly thick, but soon burns off as the sun rises. Poor visibility associated with the passage of fronts is far more frequent in the soft misty rain, known to the Cornish as *mizzle*.

Thunderstorms do not occur particularly frequently, as they tend to generate over the continent and drift across the channel further to the east. And, having woken on many a depressing morning to the sound of steady rain on the coachroof, let us not forget the old adage: 'Rain at seven, fine by eleven.' It's remarkable how often it turns out to be true!

WEATHER FORECASTS can be obtained from a variety of sources:

BBC Radio 4 (LW198kHz, MW 756kHz, FM 92.4 –96.1,103.5, 104.9MHz,) Shipping forecasts, weekdays, at local time 0048 and 0535 (LW, MW and FM, full shipping forecast, inshore waters forecast and weather reports from Coastal Stations). 1201 and 1754 (LW Shipping forecast only, no inshore water forecast or coastal station reports). On Saturdays the early morning forecast is at 0556 local time (LW, MW, FM), which includes a 'topical leisure' forecast after the coastal station reports. *Portland*, *Plymouth*, *Sole*, *Lundy* and *Fastnet* are the most relevent sea areas to the cruising grounds covered by this book.

BBC Local Radio Stations also issue Coastal Waters forecasts, but their times are subject to annual change.

BBC Radio Devon broadcasts on:
  FM 95.8, 990kHz (Exeter area)
  FM 103.4, 1458kHz (Torbay area)
  FM 103.4, 855kHz (Plymouth area).
BBC Radio Cornwall broadcasts on:
  FM 95.2, 657kHz (north and east)
  FM103.9, 630kHz (mid and west)
  FM 96.0 (Isles of Scilly).

The Coastguard repeat the Inshore Waters forecasts, strong wind/gale warnings, navigational warnings, gunfacts and subfacts every four hours, UT (which means you will have to add an hour during BST), commencing:
  Portland Coastguard 0220
  Brixham Coastguard 0050
  Falmouth Coastguard 0140

At the following broadcast times they also repeat the latest Shipping forecast:
Portland 1020 and 2220 (Sea areas:
  Plymouth, Portland, Wight)
Brixham 0850 and 2050 (Sea areas:
  Plymouth, Portland)
Falmouth 0940 and 2140 (Sea areas:
  Plymouth, Lundy, Fastnet, Sole)

In all cases it should be noted that the timing of these broadcasts can be affected if there is an ongoing emergency. When strong wind or gale warnings are in force these will be broadcast every two hours from the starting times. Following an initial announcement on VHF Channel 16, you will be advised to listen on one of the following channels: 10, 23, 73, 84 or 86. See introduction to each Passages section *Safety information and weather* for specific details.

The Coastguard will normally repeat the latest forecast on request, but this facility should not be abused. They will also provide the most recent forecast by telephone:
  Portland Coastguard (Tel: 01305 760439)
  Brixham Coastguard (Tel: 01803 882704/5)
  Falmouth Coastguard (Tel: 01326 317575)

By Navtex
The West Country is covered by Niton navtex station which transmits weather information on 518 kHz at 0840 and 2040 UT, with an extended outlook at 0040 UT. Inshore waters forecasts are transmitted on 490 kHz at 0520 and 1720 UT.

From Marinecall
There are a variety of telephone and fax services available through Marinecall, which works in partnership with the Met Office to provide telephone weather forecasts on demand. For a Local Area five day forecast, call 09066 526 plus the relevant area number: 241 (Selsey Bill to Lyme

Regis) or 242 (Lyme Regis to Hartland Point including Isles of Scilly).

For Marinecall current weather condition reports phone 09068 226 plus the relevant area number 457 or 458. All these calls cost £0.60 a minute from a landline; mobiles will be subject to operator charges.

By Mobile Phone (Short Message Service)
To obtain a forecast by text you will need the name of your Inshore/Coastal location. These will be found on the Marinecall website: www.marinecall.co.uk or in the Marinecall Marine Weather Services Handbook, which is available free of charge from its Customer Helpdesk (Tel: 0871 200 3985) or through its website. It also lists its weather services in full.

You can then create a TEXT MESSAGE, type MC and the name of the Inshore/Coastal location and send your request to 83141 – you will receive details of current weather conditions, (temperature, wind direction, wind

speed, visibility and likelihood of rain), and an outlook forecast for the same location for six hours later. These texts are charged at £0.25 per message.

By Marinecall Fax
A variety of fax services are now available, the most useful for the purposes of this book being the Marinecall Premium Fax (Inshore Coastal Areas), providing a detailed 48 hour forecast, including localised six hour forecasts for selected sailing points within the area and synoptic charts for the current and the next day. Fax: 09061 502, plus suffix 119 for the sea area Selsey Bill to Lyme Regis or 120 for Lyme Regis to Hartland Point, including the Isles of Scilly. These faxes are charged at £1.50 per minute.

Marinecall Standard Fax (Inshore Coastal Areas) is charged at £1 per minute, and gives a less

Exmouth Marina

detailed forecast without the six hourly predictions, but does include two synoptic charts. For this, fax 09060 100 plus suffix 457, Selsey Bill to Lyme Regis, or 458 Lyme Regis to Hartland Point, including the Isles of Scilly.

Other sources of weather information
Nearly all the marinas and harbour authorities within the area covered by this book display a daily forecast and synoptic weather map.

YACHT CLUBS
The once stuffy image of many yacht clubs has fortunately changed dramatically in recent years and most West Country clubs now welcome genuine cruising yacht crews to use their facilities on a temporary basis. It is, however, a privilege that visitors should not abuse, and on arrival at any new Club immediately introduce yourself to the Steward, Secretary or a member, ascertain if you are indeed welcome and ask for the visitors' book which should be signed not only by yourself but also your crew. For two or three nights, this will be sufficient, but should you wish to use the Club facilities for a longer period, check with the secretary as to the arrangements for temporary membership, which is often available. Remember at all times, you are their guest and should behave and dress accordingly.

CUSTOMS
As long as you are only moving between countries within the European Union (EU) there is no longer any need to make declarations to the Customs on departure from or re-entry into the UK, although Customs Officers do retain the power to search any boat at any time. However, if you are departing to or arriving from any port outside the EU, AND THIS INCLUDES THE CHANNEL ISLANDS, you will have to obtain a copy of HM Customs form C1331, either from your nearest Customs Office, by phoning the National Advice Service (0845 010 0900 Mon – Fri 0800 – 2000), or

via its website www.hmce.gov.uk. Copies can also usually be found at local yacht clubs and marinas. Part one of C1331 must be returned to the Customs prior to departure and part two retained for completion as soon as you re-enter UK 12 mile territorial waters when a Q flag must also be flown until all formalities are complete. On arrival contact the Customs immediately on its 24 hour *Yachtline* (Tel: 0845 7231110) for clearance, which can be usually effected over the phone.

Sadly, drug-smuggling has been increasing along the British coast and the West Country is no exception. Any suspicious activity, such as gear being unloaded from boats in isolated bays, or small craft alongside each other at sea, should be reported immediately to the Customs. Dial 0800 595000 and ask for DRUG SMUGGLING ACTION LINE.

As increasing numbers of pleasure boats are being used in this insidious trade, ultimately it can only bring the name of genuine cruising yachtsmen into suspicion and disrepute, so it is very much in our interests to do anything we can to help assist in stamping it out. It may be irksome at times to be asked, often frequently, who you are and where you have come from by Customs patrols; try not to forget that they are only doing their job.

HARBOURS AND MARINAS
VHF
The primary working channel between vessels and marinas covered in this book is Channel 80, or alternatively the secondary working Channel M (ex-37). Harbours, for the most part, maintain a listening watch on Channel 16 and you will then move to their working channel as advised; however, increasingly many will often respond if you call them in the first instance directly on their working channel.

Charges
To give an overall indication of the sort of charges you can anticipate, the price shown under *Overnight Charge* in the information for each port is the maximum you should have to pay for an overnight stay in a boat of 10 metres LOA (33ft) on Harbour Authority facilities, either alongside or on a mooring, or in other private commercial operations such as marinas. This includes Value Added Tax (VAT) and harbour dues, if applicable, and was, for the most part, correct for the start of the 2004 season. Most harbours tend to increase their charges annually in line with inflation, and this should be taken into due consideration.

All other charges within the main text are shown inclusive of VAT.

ABBREVIATIONS AND SYMBOLS

The following abbreviations and symbols may be encountered in this book; others may be found which are self-explanatory or are listed in the *Reeds Nautical Almanac*

AB	Alongside berth	⊕	Hospital	PHM	Port-hand Mark
	Boatyard	Ⓐ	Harbour Master	✉	Post Office
	Boathoist	IDM	Isolated Danger Mark	✕	Restaurant
Ca	Cable(s)	ℹ	Information Bureau	⇌	Railway station
	Chandlery	◯	Launderette	RNA	*Reeds Nautical Almanac*
⊹	Church	Ldg	Leading		Showers
	Diesel by cans	◆	Lifeboat	SCM	South Cardinal Mark
	Direction of buoyage	LAT	Lowest Astronomical Tide	SHM	Starboard-hand Mark
ECM	East Cardinal Mark	M	Sea mile(s)		Slip for launching, scrubbing
	Fuel berth	MHWN	Mean High Water Neaps	SWM	Safe Water Mark
FV(s)	Fishing vessel(s)	MHWS	Mean High Water Springs	TSS	Traffic Separation Scheme
	Fish Harbour/Quay	MLWN	Mean Low Water Neaps	SS	Traffic Signals
H+, H–	Minutes after/ before each hour	MLWS	Mean Low Water Springs	Ⓥ Ⓥ	Visitors' berth/buoy
		NCI	National Coastwatch Institution	WCM	West Cardinal Mark
H24	Continuous	Ⓑ	Bank	WPT ⊕	Waypoint
	Holding tank pumpout	NCM	North Cardinal Mark		
Ⓗ	Heliport	PA	Position Approximate		

BUOY COLOURS, LIGHTS AND FREQUENCIES

R	Red
G	Green
Y	Yellow
B	Black
W	White
RW	Red and white
YB	Yellow and black (South cardinal)
BYB	Black, yellow, black (East cardinal)
BY	Black and yellow (North cardinal)
YBY	Yellow, black, yellow (West cardinal)
BR	Black and red
FR	Fixed red light
FG	Fixed green light
Fl	Flashing light, period of darkness longer than light. A number indicates a group of flashes, eg: Fl (3). Colour white unless followed by a colour, eg: Fl (3) R. Timing of whole sequence, including light and darkness, shown by number of seconds (sec or s) eg: Fl (3) R 15s. The range of the more powerful lights is given in Nautical miles (M) eg: Fl (3) R 15s 25M
L.Fl	Long flash, of not less than two seconds
Oc	Occulting light, period of light longer than darkness
Iso	Isophase light, equal periods of light and darkness
Q	Quick flashing light, up to 50/60 flashes per minute
VQ	Very quick flashing, up to 120 flashes per minute
Mo	Light flashing a (dot/dash) morse single letter sequence, eg: Mo (S)

Dir   A light, usually sectored, RWG or RG, usually giving a safe approach within the W sector. Either fixed or displaying some kind of flashing characteristic

Plymouth Breakwater light (FlWR10s)

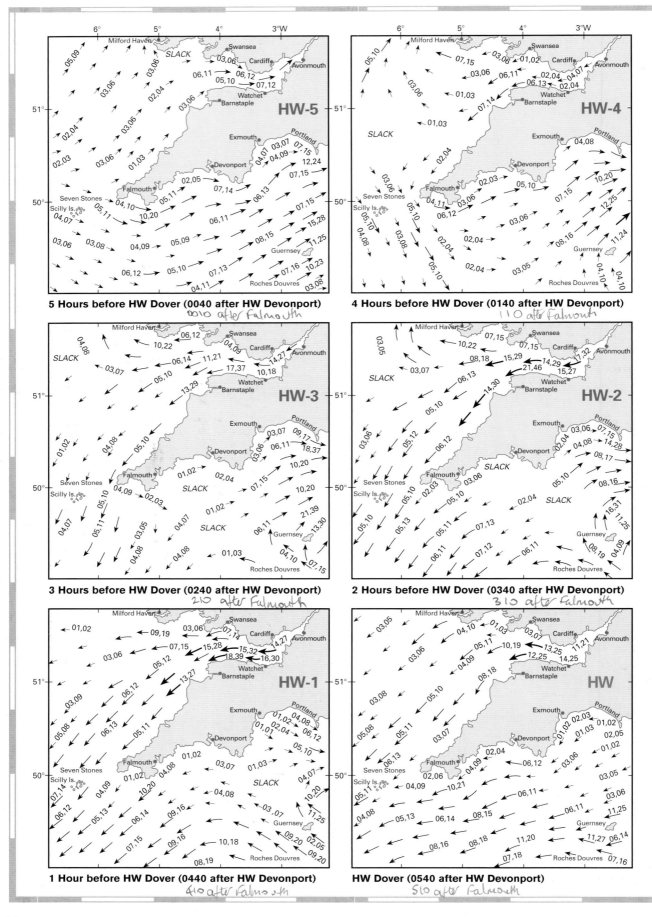

5 Hours before HW Dover (0040 after HW Devonport)
0010 after Falmouth

4 Hours before HW Dover (0140 after HW Devonport)
110 after Falmouth

3 Hours before HW Dover (0240 after HW Devonport)
210 after Falmouth

2 Hours before HW Dover (0340 after HW Devonport)
310 after Falmouth

1 Hour before HW Dover (0440 after HW Devonport)
410 after Falmouth

HW Dover (0540 after HW Devonport)
510 after Falmouth

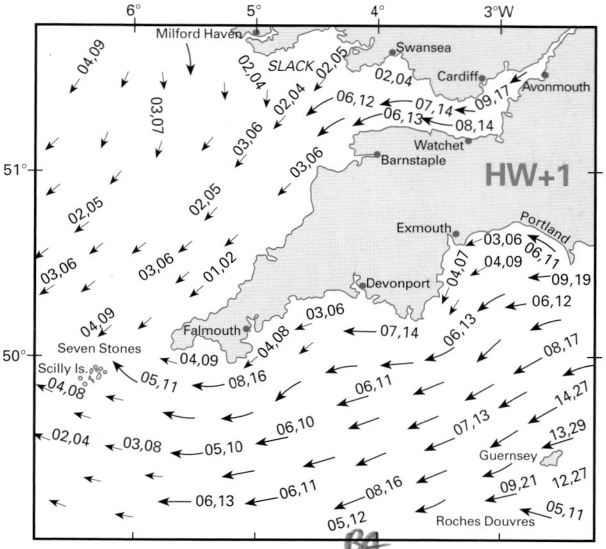

1 Hour after HW Dover (0545 ~~after~~ B4 HW Devonport)

515 before Falmouth

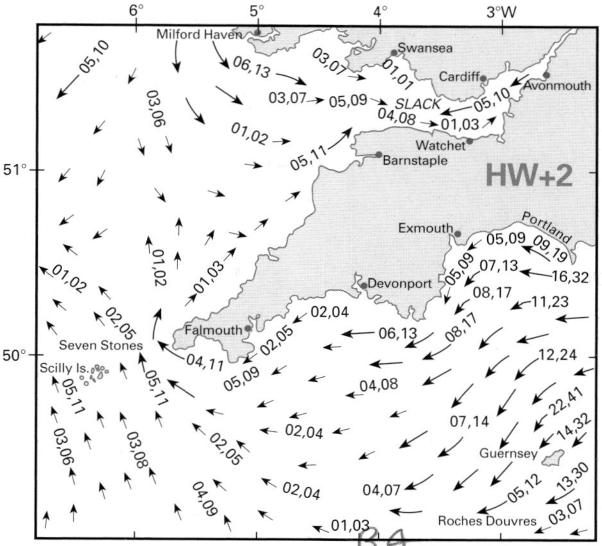

2 Hours after HW Dover (0445 ~~after~~ B4 HW Devonport)

415 Before Falmouth

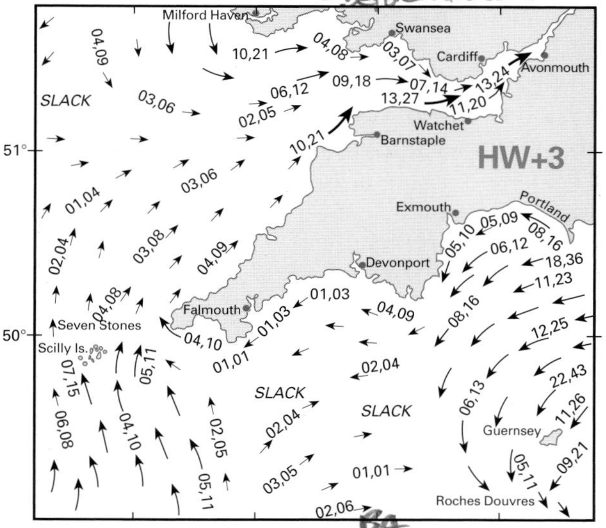

3 Hours after HW Dover (0345 ~~after~~ B4 HW Devonport)

315 B4 Falmouth

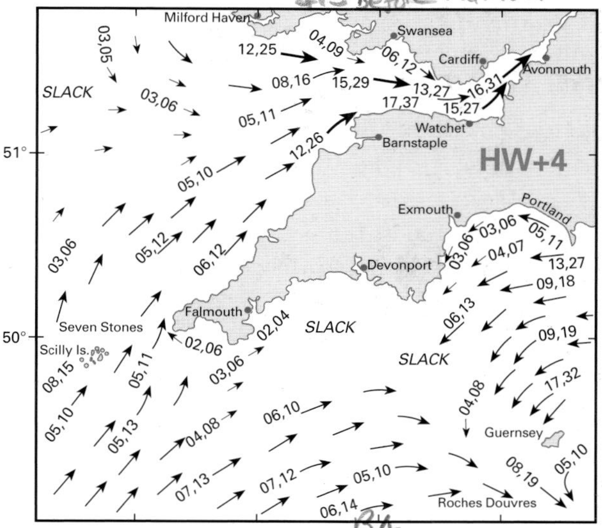

4 Hours after HW Dover (0245 ~~after~~ B4 HW Devonport)

215 before Falmouth

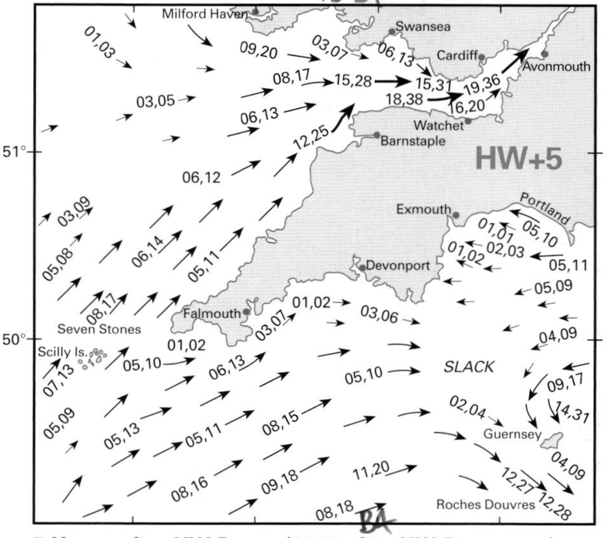

5 Hours after HW Dover (0145 ~~after~~ B4 HW Devonport)

0115 before Falmouth

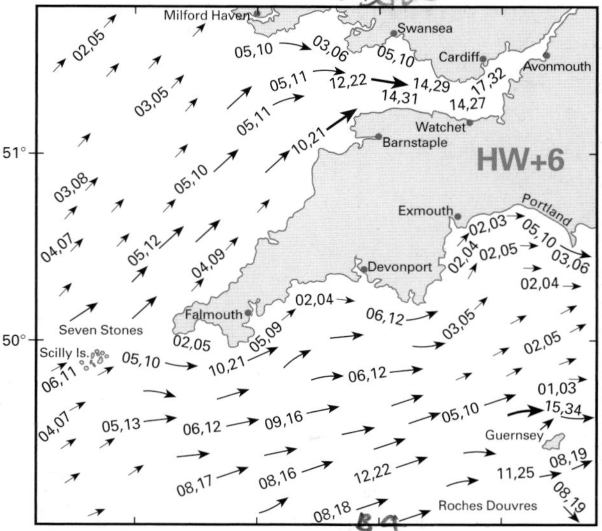

6 Hours after HW Dover (0045 ~~after~~ B4 HW Devonport)

015 before Falmouth

PASSAGES
PORTLAND BILL
TO START POINT

Favourable tidal streams

Portland Bill:
  Bound West: HW Dover
  Bound East: Five hours after HW Dover

Start Point:
  Bound West: One hour before HW Dover
  Bound East: Five hours after HW Dover

Passage charts for this sea area

BA: 2675 English Channel
             442 Lizard Point to Berry Head
             2454 Start Point to Needles
             3315 Berry Head to Bill of Portland
             1613 Eddystone to Berry Head
             1634 Berry Head to Bolt Head
             SC5601 East Devon and Dorset Coast

Imray: C5 Portland Bill to Start Point
             WCP2400.1 Exmouth to Salcombe

Stanfords: 12 Needles to Start Point

French: 4813 Du Start Point à Needles

Portland Bill from the south-east with tide flooding; the race and inshore passage are clearly visible

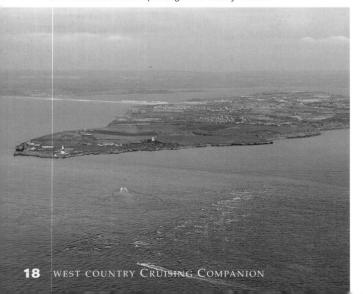

Safety information and weather

In all cases make an initial announcement on VHF Channel 16 then switch to:

Portland Coastguard: VHF Channel 73 (Weymouth Bay to Portland Bill), Channel 10 (south-east of Portland Bill), Channel 86 (Lyme Bay – Portland Bill to River Exe) at 0220, 0620, 1020, 1420, 1820, 2220 UT

Brixham Coastguard: VHF Channel 84 (Beer Head area), Channel 10 (Teignmouth and Exmouth), Channel 86 (Berry Head area), Channel 23 (in River Dart), Channel 73 (south and east of Start Point including Dartmouth) at 0050, 0450, 0850, 1250, 1650, 2050 UT

Portland Bill NCI station (Tel: 01305 860178)

Exmouth NCI station (Tel: 01395 222492)

Waypoints

1 **Portland Bill offshore clearing**
    (5M S of light)
    50°25'·83N / 02°27'·38W

2 **Portland Race clearing**
    (3.5M S of lighthouse)
    50°27'·35N / 02°27'·38W

3 **Portland Bill inshore approach from west**
    (1M NW of light)
    50°31'·55N / 02°28'·49W

4 **Tor Bay northern approach**
    (4ca due south of Ore Stone)
    50°26'·99N / 03°28'·31W

5 **Tor Bay south approach**
    (3ca due N of Berry Head light)
    50°24'·27N / 03°29'·01W

6 **Dartmouth outer approach**
    (4ca SE of Mewstone)
    50°19'·76N / 03°31'·50W

7 **Start Bay, Skerries buoy**
    50°16'·31N / 03°33'·78W

8 **Start Point** (2M SE of lighthouse)
    50°11'·92N / 03°36'·35W

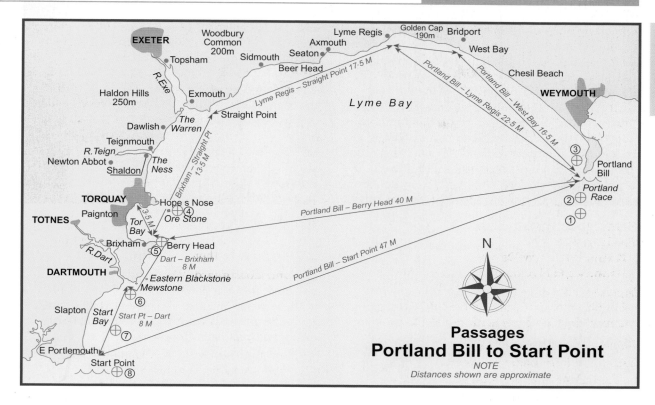

Passages
Portland Bill to Start Point
NOTE
Distances shown are approximate

'"Going West?" said the skipper of the pilot cutter. "Yes", we answered, and felt like adventurers. "And you?" He shook his head. We'd have a head wind, he reminded us, all across the bay. We knew it, but we had a good ship, too. The west wind still blew.

When we were clear of the harbour we backed the jib and let the boat lie while we hoisted the dinghy on deck, and lashed it. That done, we let draw, set the foresail and mizzen, and stood away for the Shambles Light.

Our voyage had begun. We were bound west, to visit a new country beyond the Bill . . .'

From Portland Bill to Berry Head it is exactly 40 miles, and 47 to the Start. It never seems less, and usually feels much further. The opening lines were written by Aubrey de Selincourt in 1948, and nothing has really changed – with the prevailing south-westerlies the odds are still just as much in favour of being on the wind most of the way. However, you will have barely started this passage before the first major hurdle is encountered – Portland Bill and its notorious tidal race. Depending on your port of departure, the time of day and the prevailing weather conditions, there are two options for negotiating this major hazard and tidal gate: the longer but safer offshore route, or the inshore passage.

PORTLAND RACE AND HOW TO AVOID IT

The race is formed by the considerable intrusion of Portland Bill into the main English Channel tidal stream, creating large eddies on both sides of its tapering point. These run southwards for over nine hours out of every 12 at springs and collide just to seaward of the Bill in an area that is already much disturbed by a shallower ledge (10.4m), which extends nearly half a mile south of the Bill and over which the main tidal stream tumbles east and west.

The situation is further exacerbated by the three-mile-long Shambles Bank (least depth 3.4m) to the ESE, which deflects the main stream towards the tip of the Bill at rates of up to seven knots at springs, and even more, up to 10 knots within the Race. And that is just the tide – add a bit of wind and sea and you get the general picture!

To avoid Portland Race completely you will have to pass well south of the Shambles, and a good five to six miles south of Portland Bill. In heavy weather an offing of 10 miles would be preferable and still very uncomfortable. It is easy enough to allow for this southerly offshore course if you are bound up or down Channel. Departing from the Needles (Bridge buoy) it is about 35 miles to a waypoint five miles due south of Portland Bill, a course that will also take you clear to the south of St Alban's race. However, if you break the passage with a stop in Weymouth, you will then be faced with a detour of about 15 miles to take the safe course east and south of the Shambles. Although it seems tempting to cut through to the west of the Shambles, in anything other than a high powered vessel this is asking for big trouble, except perhaps at neaps and in very calm weather; at any other time you will be in grave danger of being swept inexorably into the Race, or set onto the Shambles, so for me the extra miles are well worth the peace of mind.

It is seven miles from Weymouth to the East Shambles BYB east cardinal buoy (Q (3) 10s) and you will need to leave in time to get to the buoy at about HW Dover – 0030, just as the tide is beginning to turn westwards. At night Portland Bill has a powerful light of 25 mile range with interesting characteristics. Approaching from the east its single flash gradually increases to four every 20 secs between 221° and 244°, it shows four flashes every 20 secs through the southern sector between 244° and 117°, and to the west four flashes decreasing to one every 20 secs between 117° and 144°. In addition, it also has a very useful (FR 19m 13M) sector light (271° to 291°) covering the danger area to the ESE over the Shambles.

The alternative is the shorter but much more demanding passage inside Portland Race, which should only be attempted in daylight, moderate weather, and avoided at the top of springs. Although this inshore passage is often described as an area of relatively smooth water extending two to three cables from the shore, the key word here is relative, and that is relative to the far greater turmoil a short distance further to seaward!

The timing of the passage is fairly critical, but with the benefit of an engine it is easy enough to judge, although this too can be hazardous due to the many pot buoys in the inshore passage which are often submerged just below the surface by the strength of the tide. On one memorable occasion when I was berthed in Weymouth, no less than three disabled boats were towed in by the lifeboat with pot lines around their propellors in the course of two days.

Bound west, aim to be at the tip of the Bill at, ideally, HW Dover, certainly no earlier than half an hour before HW Dover and no later than two hours after HW Dover, which will normally mean a departure from Weymouth at about HW Dover –0100 (about two hours after HW Portland). You will then have a south-going stream right down the eastern side of the Bill. Aim to close the land off Grove Point, keep within 200m of the shore and as you round the tip of the Bill you should then run into the favourable north-west going stream to shoot you clear of the Race. The prominent isolated flat-topped Pulpit rock stands at the south western extreme of the Bill and you can start to bear away to the west once this draws abeam. If you attempt the passage any later than an hour after HW Dover, you will encounter a strengthening south-going stream on the west side of the Bill that will do its very best to force you back into the Race.

The Portland Bill inshore passage from the west is more complicated because of the problem of timing your arrival after the 40 mile crossing of Lyme Bay. Ideally you should be at the tip of the Bill at HW Dover +0530, but as you approach the Bill steer towards the high northern end of Portland to counteract the south-going stream along its western side. You should then hold close down the western shore and, as you approach the old High Light and the tip of the Bill, keep about 200m off.

If you have any doubts about the timing, or if the weather is deteriorating as you cross Lyme Bay, don't take a chance. Alter course in good time to pass well south of the Bill and the Shambles, where the main east-going flood will become favourable at HW Dover +0600.

If treated with the respect it deserves, given careful planning and in suitable weather, the reality of Portland Bill is rarely as bad as the anticipation. Hundreds of small craft safely pass this way in the course of an average season, but admittedly the first time is always the most daunting. Nevertheless, the sight of Portland dropping safely astern is always accompanied by a certain nervous relief, but for many that is soon replaced by other anxieties as the long haul across Lyme Bay, in normal visibility, is often the first opportunity to make a passage out of sight of land.

There is at first, the pleasant anticipation of the new cruising ground ahead, but as the hours pass, and there is still nothing to be seen, those first niggling doubts begin to set in. Is the compass really accurate? Did I allow for tidal set, and leeway? Is the GPS really telling the truth?

Always, an anxious eye on the weather, the slight greyness to windward, and the hint of an increase in the wind. And underlying it all, that hollow awareness that there are now no real harbours of refuge under your lee; both drying, neither West Bay or Lyme Regis can be regarded as such, although they can provide an interesting diversion in suitable offshore weather.

But then at last it is there – no longer a figment of wishful thinking although looking not the least bit as you imagined. A featureless, thin, low line, and no sign of the two bold headlands you expected to see. Berry Head and Start Point will be indistinguishable until you are much closer.

Berry Head is distinctively square and flat topped, and the Start is an unmistakeable jagged cockscomb with a conspicuous white lighthouse and two very tall radio masts close by. It is invariably much easier to make a landfall on a strange coastline at night, ideally just before dawn, for then the lights will take away the doubts.

Start Point (Fl 3 10s) has a 25-mile range and Berry Head (Fl 2 15s) has a 14-mile range. For first timers across the bay, the prospect of a night passage is probably not very appealing and it is more likely that your approach will be a race against daylight, which is no real drawback as

The major works to improve the entrance to West Bay are due for completion in 2005. Visitors should call ahead for the latest update

your probable first ports-of-call – Torquay, Brixham or the River Dart – are all well lit and easy to enter. Though tired, the excitement of landfall and arrival in the West Country should definitely carry you through.

INSHORE ACROSS LYME BAY

Given Lyme Bay's traditionally poor reputation, which to a great extent is a hangover from the days of sail when ships were regularly embayed here, most boats heading for the West Country wisely take the direct offshore route and get across as quickly as possible. However, with suitable quiet offshore weather, the longer inshore route along the coast can provide an interesting diversion with a couple of possible overnight or daytime stops along the way, and breaking this passage can be particularly useful when heading east to enable more accurate timing for the inshore passage at Portland Bill. Admiralty Chart 3315 covers the whole of Lyme Bay from Portland to Tor Bay, including harbour plans for both West Bay (Bridport) and Lyme Regis. Alternatively use its Small Craft Folio SC5601 (East Devon and Dorset Coast, Exmouth to Christchurch).

Running north-westwards from Portland, the spectacular low line of Chesil beach (the name derives from the Anglo-Saxon for stones) extends for nearly 15 miles as a steep and featureless shingle bank, its pebbles decreasing in size the

further west you travel to such an ordered degree that local fishermen were reputed to be able to locate their position in fog or darkness by their size! There are no offlying dangers and you can follow its length just a few cables offshore if conditions permit.

Towards its western end a line of high ochre cliffs begin to rise immediately to the east of West Bay, the small tidal harbour serving Bridport, which lies just over 16 miles NW of the Bill of Portland; there is a yellow can buoy (Fl Y 5s) marking a sewer outfall just under a mile SSW of the entrance. The traditionally poor reputation of the harbour's narrow 12m wide drying entrance (approach waypoint 50°42'·23N / 02°45'·86W) in any sort of onshore breeze which created dangerous seas between the two 180m long West and East piers, meant that it could only safely be considered in settled offshore weather two hours either side of local HW (HW Dover –0500) . However, in April 2002 work began on a new, much enlarged 230m long West Pier to the west of the existing entrance to improve the access and safety. Extending south eastward to a position due south of the old East Pier to create a protective overlap and a new 43m wide entrance with a depth of 5m MLWS, the new pier and other associated works, including the removal of the outer 100m of the old West Pier, are due for completion during 2005. If the anticipated improvement in shelter proves correct, it should increase the accessibility of the harbour by 50 per cent and two visitors'

pontoons are planned on the inside of the new pier. The berths on the East pier will be exclusively for local fishing boats and the drying inner harbour mostly given over to local craft. Here the flood rises fast for the first hour, slackens for the next hour then continues a fast rise to HW when there can be a stand of up to one hour. Lights are only displayed if a vessel is expected at night, FR and FG lights on the outer end of the breakwaters.

It is advisable to call ahead, (Tel: 01308 423222 or 07870 240644) to enable the harbour master, Tony Preston, to allocate a berth. An intermittent VHF watch is maintained on VHF Channel 16, call sign, *Bridport Radio*, working channel 11, but this cannot always be relied on.

The harbour dries extensively and most of the available space is taken up with local fore and aft moorings, but there is a pool at its head (least depth about 2–3m), which is scoured out by sluice gates that retain the River Brit, providing an all-tide floating berth at the inner end of the east quay. The overnight charge for a 10m boat works out at £10.50. If waiting for the tide, or as an alternative to entering the harbour, it is possible to anchor to the south-west of the western pier in about 2–3m.

Thinly diguised as *Bridehaven*, West Bay achieved national prominence as the location for the 1999 BBC TV series *Harbour Lights*! There are shops, cafes and pub, while diesel and petrol can be obtained in cans from the local Texaco garage. However, a much wider range of facilities, including banks, can be found in Bridport, a mile inland and reached by regular buses.

Bridport was a harbour during Saxon and Medieval times when vessels could still navigate the River Brit and the proximity of much hemp and flax growing saw it develop as a major manufacturing town for rope, nets and sailcloth, an industry that continues today, albeit with synthetic material. For many years too, there was another association with small craft, for the famous 'Brit' petrol engines were manufactured here.

Because of the continual silting problems in the river a new harbour – West Bay – was completed at the mouth of the River Brit in 1744 and, in spite of its exposed entrance, it was busy for well into the mid 1800s, both as an exporting port for the ropes of Bridport and as a shipbuilding centre. Elias Cox's yard flourished from 1779, building vessels as large as the 1,000 ton full-rigged ship *Speedy* in 1853 and the 800 ton barque *Nourmahal* in 1856 and, although the last ship was launched

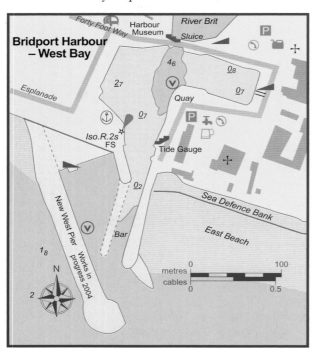

The drying harbour at Lyme Regis is protected by the famous Cobb. There are visitors' moorings just east of the entrance

in 1879, repair work continued until 1885. By then the port's demise was assured, for the Great Western Railway had reached Bridport the previous year and it was proving far more cost effective to transport the town's produce by rail. Despite commercial traffic eventually ceasing during the 1960s, the port continues to provide a base for a sizeable fleet of small craft and fishing boats.

Although it is just under seven miles from Bridport to Lyme Regis, there is plenty to see as the the coastline begins to take on a more dramatic aspect. The unstable coastal cliffs have been much effected by subsidence and landslip, creating many typical 'undercliff ' formations, with the reddish cliffs banked above each other, undulating and rising to over 155m in places before reaching a peak at Golden Cap three miles west of Bridport which, at 190m, is the highest point on the South Coast. Its name derives from the distinctive rounded summit of yellow tinged jurassic limestone, which is particularly evident when caught in sunlight, and it tumbles away in orange cliffs towards the seaside resort of Charmouth, rising again into another spectacular stretch of jumbled coastal landslips, cliffs, gorse and bramble forming Black Ven and The Spittles, an area renowned for fossil remains. Drying rocky ledges extend to seaward from Golden Cap westwards, but as long as you keep half-a-mile offshore there are no other dangers.

Lyme Regis, of much easier access, is a far more yacht friendly place than West Bay, although it too dries completely. Lying just to the west of the

town, the main shelter is provided by the famous Cobb, a robust and ancient sea wall immortalised in the film of John Fowles' novel *The French Lieutenant's Woman*. Built on top of a projecting reef, the Cobb dates from around 1284 and protects the artificial harbour from the prevailing south-westerly wind and sea, its outer end composed of a large rocky extension marked at its outer, eastern end by the Beacon Post – a reddish port hand beacon. The inner harbour wall, Victoria Pier, branches off the Cobb to

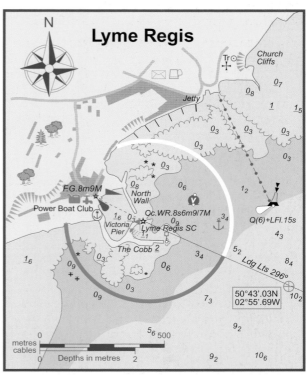

provide additional protection to the drying harbour, while the North Wall protects it to the north-east, affording good shelter within.

There is a YB south cardinal buoy 500m east of the end of the Cobb, marking the end of long outfall running northwards. About 100m east of the harbour entrance are eight red visitors buoys which can be used if waiting to enter the harbour. Lyme Regis is accessible about two hours either side of local HW (HW Dover –0455) and displays the same sort of tidal characteristic as described for Bridport. The visitors' buoys can also be used for overnight stops but if there is any underlying swell they are liable to be rolly and be warned – there is not much more than 1m here at LW springs. Deeper draught boats can anchor further to seaward but clear of the harbour entrance where there is good holding. By far the best bet is to contact the friendly harbour master, Mike Poupard, ideally the day before (Tel: 01297 442137 or mobile 07870 240645), otherwise call *Lyme Regis Harbour Radio* on VHF Channel 16 – he works on 14, 0800–2000 during the season – when you are about an hour away and he will endeavour to ensure there is a berth for you on arrival. His office is prominently situated in the NW corner of the harbour opposite the large launching slip.

Normally space can be found for boats up to a maximum of about 11m LOA (36ft), and deep draught boats will have to dry out on firm sand alongside the outer end of Victoria Pier, which dries between 0.3 and 1.3m – fender boards can be provided if needed. The overnight charge for a 10m boat alongside works out at £10.50, but there is a reduced rate if you remain outside on the buoys. Fresh water is available on the pier and fuel can be obtained in cans from the nearby garage.

At night a light at the seaward end of Victoria Pier (Oc RW 8s 9M) and one on the shore (FG 9M) form a leading line of 296°T, giving a safe approach into the harbour although a night approach is not recommended for a first time visit. A useful harbour approach waypoint 600m from Victoria Pierhead on the same leading line is 50° 43'·03N / 02° 55'·69W – the south cardinal outfall buoy (Q(6) +L Fl 15s) conveniently lies 300m north of this waypoint.

Between 200 and 300 yachts a year now visit Lyme Regis, but not quite as many as during the early 19th century when as many as 600 ships a year were recorded. The need for a port developed in the 13th century to export wool from Somerset, and by 1331 it was written that the town was 'inhabited by rich and powerful merchants owning fifteen great ships and forty boats'.

But commerce finally gave way to the more genteel 19th century pursuits and it soon became the popular seaside resort it is today. Jane Austen was a regular visitor and wrote *Persuasion* while staying here, and John Fowles lives here today. The town is a short walk along the promenade from the harbour past sandy East Beach and is a very attractive place with many fine Regency and Georgian buildings. Most normal requirements can be obtained, there are plenty of pubs and restaurants, a fascinating museum in the Guildhall, and the friendly Lyme Regis Sailing Club (Tel: 01297 442800 or try its very useful website: www.lrsc.org.uk) is in the quayside building on Victoria Pier overlooking the harbour entrance – when open visitors are welcome to use its bar and showers.

The shingle beach to the west of the harbour is remembered as the place where the Duke of Monmouth landed in 1685 to begin his Monmouth Rebellion with his march on London to assert his claim on the throne, an ill-fated venture that ended within weeks with his defeat and capture at Sedgemoor. He arrived in London to be executed, not crowned!

West of Lyme, the coast degenerates into another geological spectacle, the huge five mile scar of the Downlands Landslip, which became the Undercliffs National Nature Reserve in 1956. This stretch of very unstable land comprises porous chalk on top of greensand on top of clay, and is moving almost continuously, but never quite as spectacularly as in 1839 when over eight million tons – 20 acres of fields – slipped towards the sea creating a spectacular shattered landscape of deep chasms and general chaos. It attracted such great attention that Queen Victoria ordered a detour so that she could see this phenomenon from the Royal Yacht.

At the western end of Downlands the Haven Cliff falls away to where the River Axe emerges from behind the high sheltering bank of shingle that forms the eastern end of Seaton beach. Axmouth harbour is just within the mouth of the river, a small haven with a quay and moorings which can be accessed by small shoal draught craft (max 1.2m draught) capable of taking the ground. A prominent stone pier with a starboard hand beacon at the extreme eastern end of Seaton beach deflects the river seawards through the shingle bank. There is a bar which dries nearly 1m and access is only really feasible about half an hour either side of HW (Dover –0440) in offshore winds and settled weather; it should not be considered in any other circumstances.

Once inside the river you turn sharp to port and follow the wall lining the starboard bank. As the river widens there are drying berths alongside the quay at the inner end of the wall, but these are mostly used by local fishing boats. Opposite are a number of drying trot moorings, max 8.5m LOA, belonging to the Axe Yacht Club which might be able to provide an overnight berth. Due to the changing nature of the entrance, any stranger is advised to contact the Yacht Club in advance (Tel: 01297 20742), or to anchor off and investigate by dinghy first. It is also worth knowing that the ebb at springs can run at up to six knots within the river! However, those who attempt a visit are welcome to use the Yacht Club bar and showers and benefit from the services of a boatbuilder and Seaton Chandlery (Tel: 01297 24774). Seaton, another popular seaside resort, is within easy walking distance and all normal requirements will be found there.

In 1825 Thomas Telford was engaged on a feasibility study to create a canal from Axmouth to the Bristol Channel, but like many schemes it came to nothing. Later, the Axe's potential as a commercial port was diminished considerably with the construction in 1877 of the world's first concrete road bridge, which limits navigation just upstream of the harbour.

As you continue west of Seaton the coast trends more to the south to form Beer Roads, sheltered to the west by the last prominent chalk headland of Beer Head. The once busy fishing community of Beer still has a few of the typical East Devon full-bodied varnished clinker boats which are hauled up its steep shingle beach on wooden

Axmouth's small haven is hidden behind Seaton's long shingle beach

skids. It was also once home to Jack Rattenbury, one of Devon's most notorious smugglers who published his *Memoirs of A Smuggler* in 1837 after eluding the Excisemen for nearly 50 years! A good anchorage can be found here, well sheltered in winds through north to west if you sound in to the south of the main beach clear of the local moorings. Flanked by a stream, the attractive main street of the small town leads up from the beach. Most normal provisions are available and there is a good choice of restaurants, cafes and pubs, including the Dolphin Hotel. Chandlery and rigging is of course available from the redoubtable Jimmy Green Marine at The Meadows (Tel: 01297 20744).

It is 15 miles from Beer Head to Straight Point at the mouth of the River Exe, and from here onwards the coast is increasingly dominated by cliffs of deep red Devon sandstone topped with green and broken only by the seaside towns of Sidmouth and Budleigh Salterton, where beaches of large round pebbles rise steeply from the sea. There are no offshore dangers within half-a-mile of the shore and tidal streams are weak. Inland, Woodbury Common, an area of heathland and forestry plantations, rises to nearly 200m.

THE EXE ESTUARY

Straight Point (Fl R 10s 7M) forms the eastern side of the entrance to the River Exe, a low lying sandstone promontory with two prominent flagstaffs indicating if the rifle ranges are in use. Two yellow DZ buoys just under a mile south-east and east of the point mark the seaward limit of this range. Straight Point light has a range of seven miles, visible 246°–071°T.

The River Exe is a broad, drying estuary,

River Exe approach from the south-east – DZ buoy and Straight Point

navigable for six miles inland to Topsham, but less frequented by visitors, who are perhaps unnecessarily put off by the reputation of the bar. Although dangerous in strong east or south-easterly onshore winds, in favourable conditions the river is definitely worth a visit, and the entrance channel is well-buoyed, leading inwards from the East Exe BYB east cardinal buoy (Q(3)10s) just under half a mile SW of Straight Point. Although well lit, I would always recommend a first time approach in daylight.

The high red cliffs of Orcombe Point lead in to the beach and town of Exmouth on the eastern side of the entrance. Opposite, the Warren is a long sandy promontory which closes off the greater part of the wide mouth of the Exe from which shallow banks extend nearly a mile to seaward. To the west, the red sandstone cliffs reappear between the resort towns of Dawlish and Teignmouth, and beneath them the main London/Penzance railway line enjoys a spectacular run along the coast. Inland, the land rises to over 250m again into the Haldon Hills. There are no off-lying dangers except Dawlish Rock (2.1m), a mile ESE of the town, and a course half-a-mile from the shore can safely be followed if you wish to admire the weathered cliffs and sandstone pinnacles – like the fast disappearing Parson and Clerk.

Inshore, the tidal streams along this stretch of coast are generally weak and run parallel to the coast, the NNE going flood beginning five hours after HW Dover, and SSW ebb beginning just after HW Dover, attaining a maximum of one knot at springs. Channelled in the closer approaches to the rivers, however, rates increase considerably, attaining in excess of four knots at springs.

THE TEIGN ESTUARY

Immediately to the west of **Teignmouth**, which is easily located by the prominent church tower and long pier on the seafront, there lies the narrow entrance to the River Teign, bounded on the western side by the prominent high sandstone headland of the Ness and its sectored approach light (QWRG 7M). Strangers, however, should not approach at night, for here too a sandy bar renders the entrance dangerous in onshore winds.

Facilities for visitors within the river are severely restricted by a bridge which cuts off the upper reaches half a mile above the entrance. There is a yellow sewage outfall buoy (Fl Y 5s) 1.16 miles south-east of the Ness.

The coast remains steep from the Ness for the next four miles westwards, with no dangers except within a few boat's lengths of the shore. Topped with fields, trees and isolated houses, the red sandstone gives way to pale grey and ochre limestone off Babbacombe Bay, where there is a reasonable anchorage in westerly winds. Anstey's Cove to the west of quarry scarred Long Quarry Point is another good temporary anchorage, although care must be taken to avoid three drying rocks near the southern entrance point to the cove.

TOR BAY

In contrast to the high cliffs further to the east, Hope's Nose, the eastern boundary of Tor Bay, slopes gently down to the sea, its grassy turf and low rock ledges and cliffs home to the largest kittiwake colony in Devon.

Just under four miles away, the distinctive flat topped line of Berry Head marks the western limit of the bay, which takes a deep, sheltered bite into the Devon coast. Well protected in westerly winds, it was a traditional anchorage for the Navy prior to the development of Plymouth, and it has always been a popular venue for yacht racing, notably the magnificent J Class during their brief heyday in the 1930s. More recently the punishing Cowes/Torquay Race has been a long standing powerboat racing event.

To seaward, the low, flat Lead Stone and the 32m high Ore Stone, a mile offshore, are also popular with the seabirds and white with droppings. There is a deep passage between the two islands, but do not pass too close to the south-west of the Ore Stone where the Sunker lurks awash at LAT. In calm weather, with an absence of swell, it is possible to land on the Ore Stone, anchoring just north of the island on the rocky ledge which has 3m LAT. Pick anywhere on the rocky shore and lift your inflatable on to the rock platform. I would not, however, recommend leaving your mother ship entirely unattended.

The last of the Hope's Nose islands is Thatcher Rock, a jagged pyramid rising to 41m south-west of the point. Behind it, the concave sweep of the large hotel high on the cliffs is a foretaste of what will be seen as Torquay opens beyond the next point. Just under a mile west of Thatcher Rock lies Morris Rogue, a shoal with a least depth of 0.8m LAT. Keep the Ore Stone open of Thatcher Rock and you will clear this hazard, otherwise deep water extends safely right to Torquay Harbour entrance.

Although the actual harbour mouth is not easy to spot until close, **Torquay** is an unmistakeable proliferation of large buildings and tower blocks, with the large façade of the Imperial Hotel high on the cliffs just south of the harbour. It is easy to enter, both by day and night, and there is a large marina with ample berthing and excellent facilities for visitors.

The whole of the coast backing Tor Bay is one large urban sprawl. The English Riviera is an unbroken line of busy beaches comprising Preston sands, Paignton sands, Goodrington sands and Broad sands, with promenades, resorts and holiday camps in the hinterland. Along their length yellow speed limit buoys are positioned about two cables offshore during the summer, with '5 KTS' on square topmarks, restricting the areas for swimming. Inside these controlled areas you should proceed with extreme caution.

Paignton, just under half way across the bay, is a popular resort with a traditional pier; west of this is the sandstone bluff of Roundham Head, and a small drying harbour is situated on its northern side. Given over completely to local moorings and busy with tripper boats, the harbour is not recommended for visitors, except for very small boats which can sometimes find room to dry out against the walls. Rocky ledges extend eastwards from the south wall, marked by

a red beacon, and an approach should be made from a north-easterly direction close to HW.

On arrival berth on the south-east wall and seek out the harbour master to see if space is available. As there are heavy mooring chains across the harbour do not attempt to anchor. Facilities are limited, but there is a restaurant, pub and a small chandlery beside the harbour.

The once-peaceful anchorage of Elberry Cove in the extreme south-western corner of the bay is now busy with water skiing activity. East of it, the houses give way to the large expanse of Churston golf course, beneath it the cliffs, broken with many disused quarries, fall steeply into the sea with no dangers at their feet. Just west of the wide entrance to Brixham outer harbour is Fishcombe Cove, a quiet, secluded anchorage in westerly winds. Brixham, a busy fishing port, has a large deepwater outer harbour that is easy of access in all conditions and provides all weather shelter within its large marina. Visitors' berths are usually available.

BRIXHAM TO DARTMOUTH

With the exception of rocks extending a cable to the north of Shoalstone Point, the coast between Brixham and Berry Head is steep-to. The headland, 55m high, is an impressive sight, rising steeply and heavily quarried on its northern side . A coastguard lookout with latticed radio mast stands beside the lighthouse at the eastern end. This drops almost vertically into the sea and, though not recommended, you could sail to within a boat's length of the foot of the cliffs. Off the point the tide attains 1.5 knots at Springs, the north going flood begins five hours after HW Dover, south going ebb one hour before, the streams running parallel to the coast.

Half a mile south of Berry Head, off Oxley Head, which has a ruined fort and car park on its top, are the Cod rocks – two steep islets, with the largest, East Cod, being 9m high. Between them lie the

Long and flat topped, Berry Head from the south with Torbay opening beyond

Approach to River Dart from south: note daymark, right, and former Coastguard cottages conspicuous to left of entrance

drying Bastard Rocks and, although it is quite safe to enter the bay to the north to admire the impressive limestone cliffs overhanging a large cave, keep well to seaward when leaving and do not attempt the inshore passage between the rocks.

Various dangers and shallows extend for about half a mile to seaward for the rest of the four mile passage along this stretch of coast, and a sensible offing should be maintained. Mostly high, rolling turfy hills, sloping to low irregular limestone cliffs, it is interspersed with several beaches and coves backed by steep valleys. Mag Rock, drying 0.3m, lies one cable east of Sharkham Point, and to seaward, Mudstone Ledge, safe enough, with a least depth of 5.4m does, however, kick up an uncomfortable sea at times. It is also a popular spot for pots, and markers and buoys, the scourge of the whole Devon and Cornwall coastline, will be found in abundance from here

on. Many are barely awash and a careful lookout must be kept at all times, making inshore passages particularly wearisome and ill advised at night under power.

A course at least half a mile from the coast will clear both Druids Mare, a group of rocks (drying 2.1m) one cable SSE of Crabrock Point, and Nimble Rock, a particularly insidious outcrop (0.9m LAT), which lurks nearly two cables SSE of Downend Point. Start Point lighthouse open of Eastern Blackstone will clear the Nimble.

Eastern Blackstone, steep and 16.5m high, is not difficult to miss, nor too, the much larger, 35m high jagged outcrop of the Mewstone beyond it to the south-west. Pass to the south of the Mewstone YB south cardinal buoy (VQ(6) + LFl 10s). Do not be tempted to cut the corner from here into Dartmouth as submerged rocks extend nearly three cables to the south-west of the Mewstone, marked at their outer extremity by the West Rock YB south cardinal buoy (Q (6) + LFl 15s). Inshore, high on Froward Point is the prominent Dartmouth day beacon, a tower with a wide base that is particularly valuable for locating the Dart when approaching from the south or south-west, as the narrow entrance to the river is very difficult to distinguish in the high folds of the coastline.

START BAY

The wide sweep of Start Bay extends nearly eight miles south-west from Dartmouth to Start Point, and inshore the high cliffs undergo a dramatic transformation into Slapton Sands, a long low beach enclosing the fresh water lake of Slapton Ley, a valuable wildlife sanctuary. During the

Dart approach from north-east showing Mewstone and daymark

Second World War, this area was used extensively by the American forces practising for the D-Day invasions. There are no inshore dangers and, with an offshore breeze, a fine sail in calm water can be enjoyed along its length close to the shore.

West of Torcross, the cliffs begin to rise again, with the tiny fishing village of Beesands at their foot and its less fortunate neighbour, the ruined village of Hallsands. During the latter part of the 19th century nearly 700,000 tons of shingle were removed from this corner of the bay to build the new docks in Devonport. Without these vital natural defences the small fishing village met its fate on 26th January 1917 when an easterly gale and high tide destroyed the entire settlement, leaving just one ghostly ruin which remains today. In settled offshore weather, if time permits, or waiting for the tide west around the Start, this is a handy anchorage, though a trip ashore has a distinctly ghoulish fascination.

Ironically, it is further offshore that Start Bay poses problems, for it is here that you encounter the only real offshore bank in the West Country, the Skerries, which extends three miles in a NE'ly direction from a position six cables NE of Start Point. On old charts from the early 18th century a possible derivation of the name is found, for on these the bank is called *The Scary*, which it can be at times! Although the depths over the bank are adequate for most small craft, the shallowest point being the SW end with a depth of 2.1m LAT, it creates dangerous breaking seas in bad weather, when it should be given a wide berth. An approach to Dartmouth from the south

should not be attempted until the red Skerries can buoy at the NE end of the bank has been passed.

Deriving its name from the Anglo-Saxon word for a tail, Start Point is one of the more distinctive West Country headlands. Five grassy hillocks topped with rocky outcrops about 60m high range along its prickly spine, topped by two BBC radio masts (264m). Built in 1836, the white buildings and lighthouse (Fl(3)10s) perch neatly above the low cliffs at the eastern end, the fixed red sector of which covers the Skerries Bank (210°-255°T).

In fog or poor visibility, audible aids to navigation are restricted to the foghorn on Start Point (60s) and the bell on the Skerries Buoy and, as ships that are bound down Channel for Plymouth and Fowey close the land, at this point there is a noticeable increase in traffic.

Although weak in Start Bay, tidal streams now have to be reckoned with again, becoming much stronger off Start Point and attaining up to four knots at springs, creating a race which extends about a mile to seaward from the lighthouse. Three miles south of the point the streams are weaker, just over two knots at springs, the ENE flood beginning five hours after HW Dover, and the WSW ebb about one hour before HW Dover. Closer inshore the tide turns about half an hour earlier.

There is no inshore passage as such, but in fair weather less turbulence can be found closer to the point, taking care to avoid Start Rocks and the numerous pot markers. In bad weather, especially with wind against tide, the race should be taken seriously as it produces heavy overfalls, and the point should be passed at least two miles to the south.

Start Point from north-east with off-lying Start Rocks and Prawle Point in the distance

RIVER EXE

Tides	HW Dover −0445
Range	Exmouth MHWS 4.6m–MHWN 3.4m, MLWN 1.7m–MLWS 0.5m (HW Topsham approx 20 mins after HW Exmouth). Spring ebb can attain five knots off Exmouth docks
Charts	BA: 2290, SC5601.6. Stanford: CP 22. Imray: WCP2400.2
Waypoints	East Exe Buoy, 50° 36'·00N / 03° 22'·37W
Hazards	Pole Sands, Maer and Conger Rocks (lit by fairway buoys). River approach dangerous in strong east and southerly weather. Strong tidal streams in entrance. Large part of river dries
Overnight charge	Exmouth Marina £17.60. Exe Harbour Authority, river moorings £4.50, Topsham alongside £6. Trouts Pontoon £14

As most yachts heading west make a landfall on Berry Head or Start Point, the River Exe, lying inshore of the normal track across Lyme Bay, tends to be overlooked by visitors, which is a shame as it differs greatly from its deeper, wooded companions further west.

At low water it is but a meandering channel amidst a wide expanse of glistening mud and clean yellow sandbanks. Internationally renowned as a haunt of waders and seabirds, in the upper reaches summer fishermen still shoot their long seine nets on the last of the ebb in pursuit of wild salmon. At full flood it metamorphoses into a broad but shallow lake over six miles long and a mile wide; an atmospheric place of optical illusion and frequently changing light, Turner was but one of the many artists to succumb to its subtle drama. If transposed to the East Coast the Exe would slot very neatly into that shifting maze of swatchways and creeks and could easily be dubbed the Blackwater of the West.

Deflected eastwards by the long beach and

Exe approach 2½ hours after LW with Pole Sand just covered to left of centre. The Warren and Bull Hill Bank are beyond with Exmouth Dock entrance opposite on right

scrubby dunes of Dawlish Warren, the river's exit to the sea is flanked by drying sands to seaward and the extended, narrow approach channel along the Exmouth seafront has always engendered the myth that this is a tricky place to get into. However, the channel is well-buoyed and in the right weather it can provide a unique diversion from the better known cruising haunts. For many years this was my home patch, and my father's boat was based at Topsham. Though commercially far less busy than it used to be, in contrast the leisure boating has expanded dramatically. However, there are still several peaceful anchorages and plenty of places to explore – particularly mid-week – and it is unlikely that you will sail away disappointed with what you have found.

The 'East Exe' landfall buoy and Straight Point

APPROACHES

The entrance to the river is a long, narrow channel running parallel to the beach and foreshore at Exmouth, flanked to seaward by the Pole Sands, an extensive area of shallow water that dries in places. The tides can run hard, particularly on the ebb at springs and, in strong winds from the south or south-east, a first time visit to the Exe should not be considered as a confusing area of breaking sea soon builds up in the approaches, and the run in along an uncomfortable lee shore leaves little room for mistakes. Ideally an approach should be made from the south-west, in favourable weather and on the flood, preferably two hours after local LW when most of the drying banks can be seen. Although well lit, entry is not recommended at night without local knowledge.

Due to the frequently changing nature of the sands and buoyage within the Exe an up-to-date copy of Admiralty Chart 2290, SC5601.6 , CP22 or WCP 2400.2 is essential.

Exmouth Bar is two miles to the east of the town, which is best located by the conspicuous tower of Holy Trinity Church and, approaching from the south-west, the East Exe BYB east cardinal buoy (Q (3) 10s) marking the entrance to the buoyed channel lies just under a mile SW of Straight Point. This low headland is situated just south of the prominent white diamond shape of Sandy Bay caravan park with high red cliffs beneath it. There are two flagpoles on the headland, and in its vicinity are invariably large numbers of small local angling boats.

Straight Point is used by the Royal Marines as a firing range and its seaward limits are marked by two spherical yellow DZ buoys to the south-east and east, both Fl Y 3s. From March to October

Entering the Exe, Dawlish Warren, left, and Exmouth right. Note the impressive strength of tide!

firing can take place on weekdays between 0800 and 1600, and the danger area should be avoided. When firing is in progress a safety boat patrols the area, while red flags are flown from the flagstaffs on the point. No flags mean no firing, a flag on each pole indicates firing in progress and two flags on each pole means firing temporarily ceased. The range can also be contacted on VHF channel 08, call sign *Straight Point Range*.

From the East Exe buoy, the channel is well-marked with even numbered red cans to port and odd numbered green conical buoys to starboard, with the deeper water tending towards the starboard hand buoys. Once past the high red sandstone cliffs that end at Orcombe Point, the shallowest water lies between Nos 3 and 7 buoys where there is little more than 0.3m LAT in places. Exmouth beach and promenade run in close on your starboard hand, with brightly painted beach huts, followed by a long row of typical Edwardian seaside hotels as you near the real mouth of the river, situated between the Warren – a long, low, sandy promontory – and the entrance to Exmouth Docks. Do not be tempted to stray from the channel as there is little room outside of it and the Pole Sands are steep-to and surprisingly hard if you run aground.

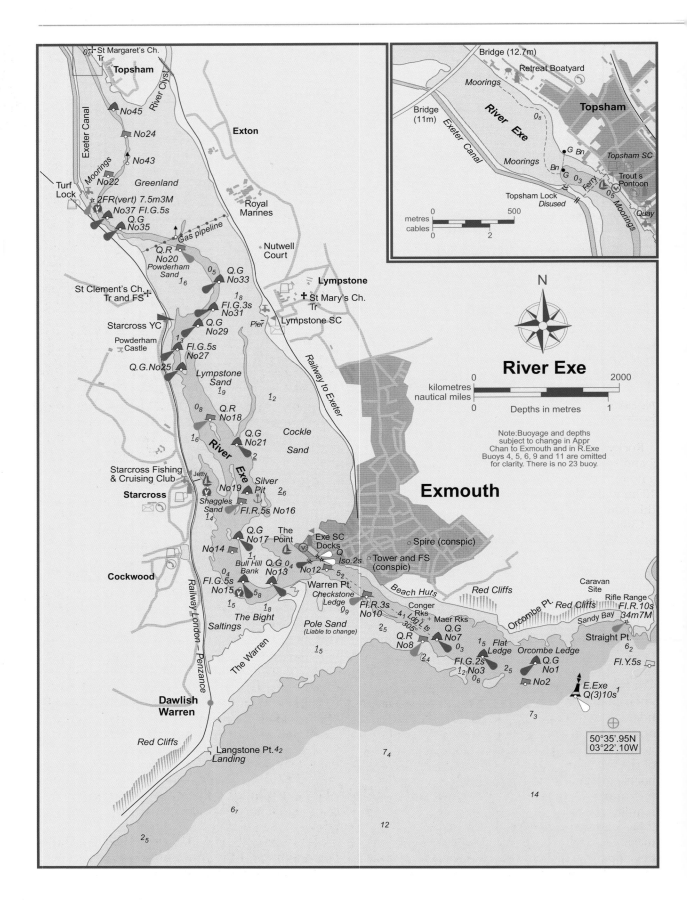

Topsham

St Margaret's Ch. Tr
No45
No24
No43
No22
Turf Lock
2FR(vert) 7.5m3M
No37 Fl.G.5s
Q.G No35
Q.R No20
Powderham Sand
Exeter Canal
Moorings
Greenland
Exton
Royal Marines
Gas pipeline
Q.G No33
St Clement's Ch. Tr and FS
Fl.G.3s No31
Q.G No29
Starcross YC
Powderham Castle
Fl.G.5s No27
Q.G.No25
Lympstone Sand
Q.R No18
Q.G No21
Cockle Sand
Starcross Fishing & Cruising Club
Jetty
River Exe
Silver Pit
No19
Shaggles Sand
Fl.R.5s No16
Starcross
Cockwood
Q.G No17
No14
Bull Hill Bank
Q.G No13
Fl.G.5s No15
The Bight
Saltings
The Warren
Dawlish Warren
Red Cliffs
Langstone Pt. Landing
Nutwell Court
Lympstone
St Mary's Ch. Tr
Lympstone SC
Pier
Railway to Exeter
The Point
Exe SC Docks
Q
Iso.2s
No12
Warren Pt.
Checkstone Ledge
Fl.R.3s No10
Pole Sand (Liable to change)
Spire (conspic)
Tower and FS (conspic)
Beach Huts
Conger Rks
Ldg
Maer Rks
Q.G No7
Q.R No8
Fl.G.2s No3
No2
Red Cliffs
Orcombe Pt.
Red Cliffs
Flat Ledge
Orcombe Ledge
Q.G No1
Caravan Site
Rifle Range
Fl.R.10s 34m7M
Sandy Bay
Straight Pt.
Fl.Y.5s
E.Exe Q(3)10s
Railway London – Penzance

Exmouth

N

River Exe

kilometres
nautical miles
Depths in metres

0   2000
0   1

Note:Buoyage and depths subject to change in Appr Chan to Exmouth and in R.Exe Buoys 4, 5, 6, 9 and 11 are omitted for clarity. There is no 23 buoy.

50°35'.95N
03°22'.10W

Bridge (12.7m)
Retreat Boatyard
Moorings
Bridge (11m)
Exeter Canal
River Exe
Moorings
Topsham
Topsham SC
G Bn
Bn
G
Ferry
Trout s Pontoon
Topsham Lock
Disused
Quay

metres   0   500
cables   0   2

The channel off Exmouth beach nearing low water, with Pole Sands drying to seaward

Rocky ledges extend southwards between Nos 5 and 9 buoys, forming **Maer** and **Conger Rocks**, a notorious grounding spot. Little more than 100m wide, the channel is at its narrowest at this point.

Checkstone Ledge, a rocky outcrop to the west of No 10 buoy, is also one to avoid, and at LW do not be tempted to cut the corner towards the low sandy promontory of Warren Point as this is continually extending south-east, forming a large area of gravelly shallows. Leave No 12 buoy well to port and hold a course towards the dock end before turning west across the river.

EXMOUTH

The tidal streams run strongly, in excess of three knots on the ebb at springs, creating a confused tidal lop in the narrows, and a very strong run across the entrance to Exmouth Dock – which is hidden until you draw abeam of it. Beware of the frequent passenger ferries and other boats emerging.

Exmouth Dock is privately owned and was regularly used by coasters until 1989, since when it has undergone a major transformation into a marina with a large surrounding housing development. Pontoons and alongside berths are incorporated within the dock, with an average maximum depth of about 2.0m MLWS. Although the berths are private, space can usually be found for visitors if berth owners are away. Call *Exmouth Dock* on VHF channel 14 or berth alongside the pontoon on the starboard side of the long dock entrance and see the dockmaster, Keith Graham, whose office is close by on the quay. The overnight charge for a 10m boat is £17.60 which includes the use of showers and toilets. The bridge across the inner end of the dock entrance lifts on request during normal working hours (VHF Ch 14) and remains open at night. Diesel can be obtained alongside during normal working hours in the entrance to the dock on the starboard hand side. Petrol is only available in cans from the garage near the town centre.

The pool to the north-west of the dock entrance off The Point is completely taken up with local moorings, including that of the Exmouth Lifeboat. Anchoring is not recommended due to the risk of fouling moorings and the strong run of the tide. There is a Harbour Authority buoy here marked *ECC Visitors* that can be used for short stays at £2.50 for a part day or if waiting to go into Exmouth Dock. This is normally serviced by the Exe water taxi that operates from Exmouth Dock to anywhere in the lower Exe; call sign *Conveyance*, VHF Ch M.

With sufficient water, a boat capable of taking the bottom comfortably can always anchor round the back of The Point. Here, out of the main

Exmouth Marina is entered through a lifting Bridge. The waiting pontoon and fuel berth is on the right. The Harbour Office is on upper floor of building with balcony

stream and clear of the moorings, you can dry out on hard sand on Shelly Bank, just off the Exe Sailing Club where visitors are welcome to use the showers, clubhouse and bar when open. This large new building was built several years ago after the previous clubhouse on the north side of the dock entrance was spectacularly destroyed when the quayside collapsed. There is a fresh water tap at the Sailing Club, while Peter Dixon's Chandlery (Tel: 01395 273248) is conveniently close to the dock entrance, and there are several small boatyards that can arrange engine and electronic repairs. Alternatively ask the dockmaster.

Exmouth, the oldest seaside resort in Devon, dates from the 1750s and is a typical busy holiday town in season, with its long sandy beach, amusements and traditional donkey rides. Attractive Georgian buildings rise along the elevated Beacon area and the adjoining seafront, but much of the newer town centre, about half a mile from the dock area, is fairly bland. It caters well for all normal requirements, having a large Gateway supermarket in the Magnolia Centre and cashpoint-equipped branches of all main banks. There are plenty of lively pubs and cafes as well as a small number of specialist restaurants including the Seafood Restaurant (Tel: 01395 269459), Italian food at Donatos

(Tel: 01395 279644) or exotic Mexican/Caribbean at 11a Restaurant (Tel: 01395 223195).

DAWLISH WARREN

Just a short distance across the water, the eastern end of the Warren always used to provide a peaceful contrast, but sadly the once popular anchorage is now very restricted by moorings which run parallel to the beach along the curve of the river known as the Bight, opposite No 13 buoy.

In the 1930s this end of the Warren was covered with a large number of bungalows and holiday homes, but the winter storms and shifting sands allow no such permanence. As a boy, I can remember the last few houses high on the dunes on the seaward side of the beach, and the fascination of seeing their broken remains after they had been undermined and began to collapse. The sea broke right through the Warren in the 1960s during a winter storm, although the massive repair works and new groynes on the seaward side have resulted in a steady re-growth ever since.

The western end of the Warren is a popular golf course, but is within an extensive 500 acre nature reserve and bird sanctuary protected under by-laws passed in 1983. These have been enforced with increasing vigour over the past few years, particularly with regard to access to the remoter eastern end of the Warren, which is regularly patrolled by wardens.

It used to be possible for bilge keelers to dry

out along the edge of the Bight, however this is now judged to be a protected area for birds. Avoid it at all times as your presence is not likely to be appreciated. The beach along the very eastern tip and part of the seaward end of the Warren – Warren Point – is now designated as very sensitive, being the only roosting area for birds when the tide rises over 3.2m. Wardens will clear it of people on these occasions. In other words, there's a lot less space for visitors of the human variety!

I am fortunate, I suppose, to have been able to enjoy it long before these restrictions were imposed. Then there was nothing more than the low sweep of the beach and the dunes behind – a wilderness of lupins and marram grass. At dusk it became the silent haunt of the rabbits and birds, while just across the water the cheerful glare of the lights along Exmouth sea-front emphasised the pleasant isolation of the place. Nothing, except the rumble of the main line trains along the western shore, disturbed its peace.

In complete contrast, a mile or so along the beach, the village of Dawlish Warren is a sprawl of amusement arcades, gift shops and even a betting shop, catering for the large holiday chalet villages nearby. Also located here are a grocery, newsagent, post office and pub.

STARCROSS

To avoid the encroaching edge of Bull Hill Bank do not steer directly for No 15 buoy – keep out towards the large mooring buoys in mid-channel. These are primarily for commercial vessels but can be used if you are not too worried about your topsides. Just to the NW are four yellow Harbour Authority visitors' buoys (up to 40ft, marked *ECC Visitors*) with white pick up buoys at £6 per day. To check availability one can try calling *Port of Exeter* or *Harbour Patrol* on VHF Ch12 during normal working hours, although a reply is not guaranteed.

Above No 14 and No 17 buoys a channel branches away to port towards the mass of moorings off Starcross, where there is a good Londis convenience store with off-licence, a baker, newsagent, post office, chemist, three pubs serving food, including the large Courtenay Arms, and a fish and chip shop. Starcross Garage can supply diesel and petrol in cans and they have a convenient all-tide pontoon (about 1m MLWS) moored just south of the end of the pier where you can secure while you go ashore. If you

contact the Garage (Tel: 01626 890225) it is often possible to lie here overnight, or they might be able to find a spare mooring for you.

The Starcross Fishing and Cruising Club (Tel: 01626 891996) has one visitors' mooring off the village, although more are available if members are away cruising. Visitors are welcomed to its fine clubhouse in the old Brunel Tower at the inner end of the pier. To access the village and club, use the small landing hard and underpass beneath the railway line at the inner end of the pier, clearly indicated by the large SFCC sign. Note that Starcross pier is private and only open when ferries arrive.

The main channel continues between No 16 Shaggles buoy and No 19 buoy, with the line of moorings to port marking the edge of the drying Shaggles Sand; to the east of the larger moorings on your starboard hand the whole area of Cockle Sand dries completely at LW. Just south of No 19 buoy and out of the fairway there is a deeper hole known locally as Silver Pit which provides a very useful anchorage in just over 2m.

LYMPSTONE

From the Shaggles buoy head for green No 21 buoy. The drying channel to Lympstone, a former fishing village nestling between two red cliffs on the eastern shore, branches off just above No 21 buoy and this can provide an interesting diversion, sounding in on a rising tide, for a quick dinghy ride ashore. Thatched cottages mingle with more elegant and substantial Georgian houses, and there are limited provisions, two pubs and a Sailing Club. A number of local boats have drying moorings off the small harbour but the bottom is mud, and it will be a messy walk ashore if you stay to dry out!

Back in the main channel there is **no** No 23 buoy. Leave No 18 buoy to port, and opposite No 25 (Powderham Perch) buoy, the extensive estate of Powderham itself lies behind the railway embankment. Through the trees and across an elegant deer park you can just glimpse Powderham Castle, which had been the seat of the Courteney family since the fourteenth century and is at present home of the Earl and Countess of Devon.

From the next buoy, No 27, the channel is well marked as it turns north-east past the buildings and slipway belonging to Starcross Yacht Club, which has the distinction of being one of the oldest in the country, formed in 1773. The moorings in the pool off the Club mostly dry at LW.

Next, steer for Nutwell Court, a large Georgian house set among trees on the eastern shore. Keep to the starboard side of the channel, past No 29 buoy and hold very close to No 31 (Lympstone Perch) buoy as the channel here is extremely narrow. Follow the outside curve of the channel to No 33 buoy, taking care not to cut across the shallow edge of Powderham Sand to port, then steer directly for No 20 (Nob) buoy.

During the summer months, as in several of the other West Country rivers, these upper reaches are frequently used by salmon fishermen who shoot long seine nets from small rowing boats, usually on the last of the ebb and first of the flood. They are likely to be encountered anywhere between here and Topsham.

The few licences granted for these fisheries are jealously guarded and passed down from father to son, but disease and pollution have seen a dramatic decline from the heady days when up to ninety-nine prime fish were caught in a single shot of the net. Nor, too, has a monster 61 pound salmon like the one caught close to this spot in March 1924 by netsman Dick Voysey ever been seen again. This was no fisherman's tale, for it was preserved and can still be seen in Exeter's City Museum.

The large incongruous blocks of flats on the eastern shore are accommodation blocks for the Royal Marine Training Camp at Lympstone, so don't be too alarmed if you hear the sound of gunfire along the shore!

Beyond No 20 buoy, the channel lies to port of the next unnumbered starboard hand buoy and not the beacon with a green triangular topmark and yellow Gas Pipeline sign. This carries North Sea Gas and runs east-west across the river, so anchoring should not be attempted anywhere in the vicinity. Also at this point the tributary of the River Clyst enters the Exe, winding away through the mudbanks to the distant railway bridge on the northern shore beyond which Tremlett's, builders of high speed powerboats, have premises at Odhams Wharf.

EXETER SHIP CANAL

The main channel, much narrower at this point, leads close to the western shore, under the high flood embankment past the green No 35 (Ranje) and No 37 (Barrel) buoys. The building half hidden right ahead – in the trees with a isolated tall pine – is Turf Hotel. The entrance lock of the

Looking upstream to Turf Locks and Hotel with Topsham in the far distance

Exeter Ship Canal is to the left of the buildings and the canal, which runs five miles inland to Exeter, is the oldest pound lock canal in England. It was opened in 1566 after the river passage to Exeter was blocked by the Countess of Devon by a weir in an attempt to force vessels to use her own port at Topsham.

The canal was originally entered above Topsham, although larger vessels resulted in the extension to Turf in 1827. Despite declining importance, the Port of Exeter remained active until the late 1960s for coasters carrying petrol, timber and coal. They appeared incongruously above the reed beds opposite Topsham and created havoc with holiday traffic on the once notorious Exeter by-pass when the swing bridge opened for them to pass.

Today the M5 motorway bridge sweeps across the wide Exe Valley just upstream of Topsham and, although this ended the traffic jams, the bridge's 10m clearance also finally sealed the fate of Exeter's waterborne commercial trade. Since then the canal has seen increasing amenity use for fishing and pleasure boating, and a fascinating trip to Exeter is quite feasible either by dinghy – with a bit of portage –

or boats below the 10m height limit.

Summer visitors are welcomed at reduced rates of £8.75 per day if they want to lie below the motorway bridge in peaceful non-tidal berths at Turf and opposite Topsham, or at £15 per day if they wish to proceed all the way to the heart of Exeter. In both cases they must stay in the canal for a minimum of two nights, but the charges include the cost of locking in and out, transit and a berth at Turf, Topsham Lock or the Exeter Canal Basin.

This fascinating excursion through a wetland conservation area is well worth the experience, and alongside berthing close to the centre of Exeter (where there are shoreside shower and toilet facilities) for sightseeing and shopping completes it. Arrangements to enter the Canal can be made by phone (Tel: 01392 274306) or by calling *Port of Exeter* on VHF Ch 12. You can lock in from 0730 – 1600 (weekdays), 0730 – 1230 (Saturdays). There is a surcharge at weekends.

Until late 1996 the Canal Basin was the home of Exeter Maritime Museum which had struggled against increasing odds to survive since 1968 when it was created by David Goddard. The collection of working boats, sold in early 1997, moved to Lowestoft, where they will eventually go on permanent display under the auspices of the International Sailing Craft Association (ISCA). Many of the smaller craft were transported by sea aboard a coaster which loaded its intriguing cargo alongside Topsham Quay.

Turf Hotel

Turf Hotel is a favoured local watering hole and a popular evening trip down river from Topsham. Anchor south-east of the pier on the edge of the channel clear of the local moorings, where there is about a metre of water and a soft mud bottom, or pick up the Harbour Authority's visitors mooring for £6 per night and pay at the hotel.

Landing is easy at the steps or the inside of the pontoon at the end of the jetty – but do not obstruct the outer end, as *Sea Dream*, the regular Topsham to Turf ferry, berths here during the summer. This is a great place for children, with a tree house, climbing frames, stranded boats and a huge grassy lawn leading up to the old slate hung Georgian building. Turf Hotel is open during normal licensing hours, has an excellent choice of imaginative bar food and DIY barbecues throughout the summer – they provide the food, you cook it!

Water containers can be filled up from a tap at the back of the building. The adjoining basin, a tranquil spot, is popular for laying-up and there is invariably an interesting assortment of boats. From here, the tow path along the canal provides a pleasant walk of just over a mile to Topsham Lock where another small ferry runs across to the town.

TOPSHAM

The final stretch of the river from Turf to Topsham is very shallow at LW, with less than a metre in many places, but (on the flood) a few groundings in the soft mud are no problem. The channel is not difficult to follow, leaving Nos 39 and 41 green buoys on your starboard hand, No 22 red can (Ting Tong) to port. As the channel curves northwards again, do not cut too close to the R/W pole with red topmark as this is a Topsham Sailing Club race mark and is outside the channel. Leave the perch with a triangular topmark (traditionally known as Black Oar) well to starboard and steer directly for No 24 red can buoy, leaving it close to port. Topsham lies ahead to starboard, and the last green channel buoy, No 45, is in the approach to the main bulk of the moorings. These have a clearly defined fairway between them.

Beyond the large modern block of flats that dominates the waterfront, Topsham Quay is easily located by the large brick built former warehouse, now an antiques market. Visitors can berth alongside the quay, where you will dry out in soft mud. Officially there is a charge of £6 a night levied by Exeter City Harbour Authority for lying alongside the Quay, but unless someone appears to collect your dues the odds are in favour of a free night or two. The authority is slowly upgrading the facilities, and toilets, water, refuse disposal and electricity are now available. Sails and Canvas sailmakers and marine engineers, Exe Leisure, are both based on the quay.

The alternative for berthing is alongside the private pontoons off Trout's Boatyard (Tel: 873044) if space is available. There is 1m at MLWS on the outside of the three hammerhead pontoons where visitors normally berth, making it best suited for bilge keels or centreboards; deeper draught boats and those with fin keels can sometimes lie alongside Trout's wall where they will sink into the very soft mud. The inside pontoons are all taken up with permanent drying berths for local boats. The overnight charge for a 10m boat is £14, and a refundable £5 deposit is charged for a key to the boatyard gate. A toilet block with a shower (£1 slotmeter) is situated in the boatyard, diesel and water are available alongside, (petrol can only be obtained in cans from the garage on the main Exeter road) and Trout's also stock Calor Gas. The yard has a mobile crane and services include engineering, general repairs and rigging. Further details and some good aerial pictures of the River Exe will be found on their website: www.troutsboatyard.co.uk

The only possible anchorage off Topsham town is just downstream of the quay in mid-channel, clear of the moorings on the eastern side of the fairway. There is about 1m here at LAT, but the bottom is gravel and the holding not good, particularly on the ebb when the current can run quite fast. Topsham Sailing Club might be able to provide a mooring if members are away cruising.

'. . . "not so small a Town as I find it represented in some Accounts' wrote an observer in 1754. 'It has not only one pretty long Street to its Kay (where there is a Custom House) and another below it to a fine Strand, the latter adorn'd with diverse handsome Houses, but several good Bye-Streets branching out several ways; and is, in short, a very pleasant, a considerable, and flourishing place, inhabited by many Persons of good Fashion and Politeness, as well as Ship-masters, Ship-builders etc etc . . . Its chief Market, Saturdays, is well supply'd not only with Shambles Meats of all sorts, but Poultry and other Fowls, Butter Cheese and Fruits, and here being Butchers and Fishermen resident, there's seldom a total Lack of Provisions of either Kind, neither of very good Bread, nor as good Beer, Cyder, Wine, Spirit, Liquors . . . It may be concluded that 'tis no despicable or mean Town." '

The same holds good two hundred and fifty years on, with just a few additions to the facilities. All provisions are available, including a Stop & Shop, which is open late and also on Sundays, Arthur's excellent butchery and

Topsham at high water. Visitors can often find a berth on the outside hammerheads on Trouts' pontoons

You will dry out in very soft mud alongside Topsham Quay

delicatessen, a bakery, a specialist cheese shop, a green grocer and two chandlers, The Foc'sle (Tel: 874105), which is also an Admiralty Chart agent, and Ash Marine (Tel: 876654) on the Exeter road. Other services include Westaways Hardware, branches of Lloyds TSB and Natwest (with cashpoints) and a traditional Saturday morning indoor market.

Ashore in Topsham

Though small, Topsham is both attractive and often surprisingly busy! It was once an important Roman and medieval port and was particularly prosperous in the mid-17th and early 18th centuries when it flourished as a shipbuilding centre. During the Napoleonic wars no less than 27 warships were built here for the Royal Navy by Davy's yards, and in 1850 John Holman opened a new yard with a plan to rejuvenate Topsham as a major port. Wooden vessels up to 600 tons were built, and a dry-dock capable of handling 1,000 ton ships was opened. But within 15 years Holman died and there the dream ended, the silting river finally sealing Topsham's fate in the late 1970s, when the last of the timber and lager ships regularly used the quay.

The link with the name remains, however, for John Holman's great grand-daughter, Dorothy, established Topsham Museum in her house at 25 The Strand, and left it to the town on her death. It is manned by volunteers, and is open Mon, Weds, Sat, Sun – 1400 –1700.

Architecturally Topsham has many gems, particularly its heritage of Dutch Style houses along the Strand, built by local shipowners inspired by their frequent trips to Holland – interestingly many of Topsham's houses are also built of clinkers, small Dutch bricks that were used to ballast empty ships. A rabbit warren of narrow streets runs inland from the elegant Strand – humbler cottages and houses, now smartly renovated and bedecked with overflowing window boxes and hanging baskets. Once the homes of the fisherfolk and watermen, property in Exeter's satellite town is much sought after today, and the new incumbents consider themselves more genteel!

The locals' favourite circular walk continues beyond the end of the Strand and along the raised foreshore footpath known as the Goatwalk with more expansive views of the river. The leafy road at its end skirts Bowling Green Marsh, owned by the RSPB, where you will find an informative bird hide, and continues to the top of Monmouth Street which leads back down to the quay.

Today there are no cargoes on the quay – just cars. Those who sit beneath the cheery umbrellas outside the Lighter Inn – formerly the Custom House – are a far cry from the hardened characters that frequented its once tiny and smoke filled bar! Despite its relatively small population, Topsham has always been renowned for an abundance of hotels and pubs. At one time there were over 20 and today 10 still remain, affectionately dubbed the *Topsham Ten* by Exeter University students for whom this challenge has become something of a rite of passage. Certainly a fascinating evening can be spent finding them, and don't miss the

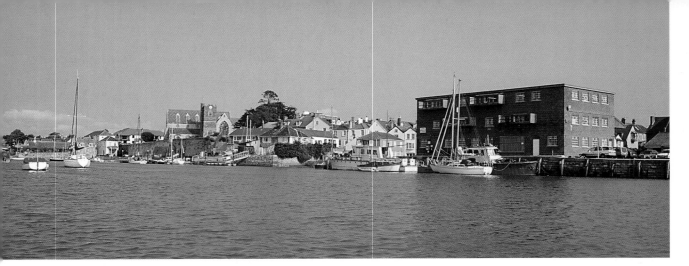

Approaching Topsham Quay – Trout's pontoon lies just to the left of the church

delightfully unspoiled Bridge Inn which gained nationwide fame in 1998 when HM the Queen dropped in en route to Lympstone Marine Camp!

Most of the pubs and hotels serve food, and restaurants abound. There is seafood at The Galley Restaurant (Tel: 876078) or The Passage House Inn (Tel: 873653) and french style cuisine at La Petite Maison (Tel: 873660). The Globe Hotel (Tel: 873471) offers traditional English cooking, with Italian well catered for at Marcello's Pizzeria (Tel: 879061) or Il Giardino (Tel: 877878). Otherwise, on the main Exeter road, try Denleys Wine Bar – the latter has live music on Wednesdays and Fridays – and you will find the Saffron Indian restaurant (Tel: 875675) on the same premises. Close by, the Bamboo Topsham Fryer (Tel: 876463) does takeaway Chinese or fish and chips!

The town has also become something of a focal point for antique collectors and, in addition to the Antiques Market in the old Tuborg warehouse on the quay, there are a number of other businesses – Bounty Antiques in Fore Street reveals an additional surprise at the back of the shop, 'The Cafe', which offers a particularly good choice of breakfasts and a varied lunch menu. Joel Segal's is a good secondhand bookshop, and even more used nautical books will be found for sale in the unlikely surroundings of Paul Properties estate agent's office just across the road!

Topsham is well placed for an excursion to the historic and attractive Cathedral City of Exeter, just three miles away. Frequent buses or half hourly trains go right into the centre.

Boating facilities

Topsham Sailing Club was founded in 1885 and today its very active cruiser fleet is one of the largest in the West Country; it is also home to a large fleet of Devon Yawls, (the GRP derivative of the Salcombe Yawl). Visitors are welcome, and those two cruising essentials, showers and a bar, are available on Wednesday evenings and at weekends. There is a convenient fresh water tap on its slipway, and an all-tide landing pontoon with a bridge to the shore immediately off the Clubhouse.

The Retreat Boatyard lies half a mile beyond Topsham. Nestling almost beneath the motorway bridge, the yard is accessible two hours either side of HW for an average draught boat. Diesel and water are available alongside and onshore services include a 36 ton crane, comprehensive chandlery, Calor and Camping Gaz, rigging, repairs and electronics. Staff at the yard are also appointed *Volvo Penta*, *Yamaha* and *Bukh* service engineers. Their website is: www.retreatboatyard.co.uk

To reach the Retreat, continue upstream through the moorings past the Sailing Club, leaving the old lock entrance on the port hand and the outfall beacon with green triangular topmark to starboard. Keep a few boat lengths off the shore and pick your way through the large number of local moorings. Beyond these the river mostly dries at LW leaving a large area of mud and reedbeds, with the narrow channel following the reed fringed edge of the playing field on the starboard hand. The next beacon with triangular topmark off a dinghy park is also left to starboard. From here, the channel holds tight to the right hand shore, overlooked by a number of substantial detached modern houses, and there is a large shallow bank to port, so don't be tempted to cut the corner. It is then a straight run past Retreat House, a large white Georgian building, towards the group of moorings and the pontoon off the boatyard. Do not try to anchor as the bottom is foul, but berth alongside its pontoon, rafting if necessary, as this is only used for short stay visitors. If you wish to stay longer, drying moorings are sometimes available off the yard.

River Exe Port Guide
Area telephone code: 01392

Harbour Master: Exeter, City Canal Basin (Tel:274306)

Exmouth Dockmaster: The Docks (Tel: 01395 269314)

VHF: Normal working hours only, Ch 12; call sign *Port of Exeter* or *Harbour Patrol*.

Exmouth Dock, Ch 14, call sign *Exmouth Dock*. Retreat Boatyard: Ch M (ex-37)

Emergency services: Lifeboat at Exmouth. Brixham Coastguard

Anchorages: Below No 19 buoy. Off Turf. Topsham. Various possibilities within river

Mooring/berthing: Exmouth Marina (Tel: 01395 269314). Harbour Authority visitors moorings in lower Exe and at Turf. Drying alongside quay or Trout's pontoons at Topsham, (Tel: 873044). Drying moorings at Retreat Boatyard. Lock into Exeter Canal

Dinghy landings: The Point, Exmouth. Starcross Pier. Turf. Public slipways at Topsham, ladders on Quay. Topsham SC. Trout's Pontoon

Water taxi: VHF Ch 80 or M, call sign *Conveyance*

Marina: In Exmouth Dock

Charges: Exmouth Marina: 10m boat per night £17.60. Harbour Authority visitors' moorings £4.50 per night. Exeter Canal (minimum 2 nights), berth below M5 bridge £8.50, Exeter Canal basin £15, including locking and transit. Trout's Pontoon, Topsham, from £10 to £14 per night, depending on size. Alongside Topsham Quay £6

Phones: Dock entrance, Exmouth. Starcross. High Street by Church, Topsham

Doctor: Exmouth (Tel: 01395 273001).Topsham (Tel: 874648)

Hospital: Exmouth (Tel: 01395 279684). Exeter (Tel: 411611)

Churches: Exmouth, Topsham, most denominations

Local Weather Forecast: None

Fuel: During normal working hours, diesel alongside in entrance to Exmouth Dock; at Trout's Pontoon and Retreat Boatyard, Topsham. Diesel and Petrol in cans from Starcross Garage, Starcross. Petrol in cans from Pretty's Garage, Topsham.

Gas: Calor and Camping Gaz, Hancock and Wheeler, Exmouth. Starcross Garage, Trout's and Retreat Boatyards Topsham

Paraffin: Westaways, Topsham

Water: Exe Sailing Club, Exmouth. Turf Hotel. Topsham SC. Trout's Boatyard and Retreat Boatyard, Topsham, Topsham Quay.

Banks/cashpoints: Exmouth: all main banks have cashpoints. Topsham: LloydsTSB, Natwest both with cashpoints. All main banks in Exeter have cashpoints

Post Office: Exmouth, Starcross, Topsham

Rubbish: Bins at Exmouth, Trout's Yard Topsham and Topsham Quay

Showers/toilets: Exe Sailing Club, Exmouth. Starcross Fishing & Cruising Club, Starcross Topsham Sailing Club. Trout's Boatyard, Topsham. Retreat Boatyard, Topsham. Public toilets Exmouth Dock and Topsham Quay

Launderette: Exmouth

Provisions: Exmouth: all facilities. Dawlish Warren: limited shops. Starcross: provisions/chemist. Topsham: good selection of shops

Chandlers: Peter Dixon's Chandlery, Exmouth (Tel: 01395 273248). Lavis & Son, Camperdown Terrace, Exmouth (Tel: 01395 263095). Foc'sle, Fore Street, Topsham (Tel: 874105). (Admiralty Chart Agents) Trout's Boatyard, Topsham (Tel: 873044). Ash Marine,Topsham (Tel: 876654). Retreat Boatyard, Topsham (Tel: 874720). John Bridger Marine, Haven Road, Exeter (close to canal basin) (Tel:250970)

Repairs: Lavis & Son, Camperdown Terrace, Exmouth (Tel: 01395 263095). Rowsell & Adkin, Camperdown Terrace, Exmouth (Tel:01395 279727). Trout's Boatyard, Topsham

(Tel: 873044). Retreat Boatyard, Topsham (Tel: 874720)

Marine engineers: Starcross Garage (Tel: 01626 890225). Trout's Boatyard, Topsham (Tel: 873044). Retreat Boatyard, Topsham (Tel: 874720). Exe Leisure, The Quay, Topsham (Tel:879055)

Electronic engineers: Retreat Boatyard, Topsham (Tel: 874720).

Sailmakers: Rowsell Sails, Camperdown Terrace, Exmouth (Tel: 01395 263911). Sails and Canvas, The Quay, Topsham (Tel: 877527)

Transport: frequent bus and train connections from Exmouth via Lympstone and Topsham to main line at Exeter, (Tel: 08457 484950). Buses and trains to Exeter from Starcross. M5 Motorway at Topsham. Exeter Airport 15 mins (Tel: 367433) UK, Ireland and continental connections

Car hire: Exmouth (Tel: 01395 278294). Exeter, Hertz (Tel: 207207). Budget (Tel:496555)

Yacht clubs: Exe Sailing Club, 'Tornado', Estuary Road, Exmouth, Devon EX8 1 EG (Tel: 01395 264607).

Starcross Fishing & Cruising Club, Brunel Tower, Starcross (Tel: 01626 891996).

Starcross Yacht Club, Powderham Point, Starcross, Exeter, Devon (Tel: 01626 890470).

Topsham Sailing Club, Hawkins Quay, Ferry Road, Topsham, Exeter, Devon (Tel: 877524).

Lympstone Sailing Club

Eating out: Exmouth: Pubs, restaurants, cafes and fish & chips. Starcross, pubs and fish & chips. Topsham: Good selection pubs and restaurants, cafes, fish & chips

Things to do: Swimming/walking at Exmouth and Dawlish Warren. Attractive Cathedral City and major shopping centre of Exeter within 15 minutes of Topsham

Teign entrance at half flood. Shaldon, left, Den Point centre and Teignmouth right, with the large Salty bank, centre

RIVER TEIGN

Tides	HW Dover −0450
Range	MHWS 4.8m–MHWN 3.6m, MLWN 1.9m–MLWS 0.6m. Spring rates can attain knots in entrance
Charts	BA: 26, SC5602.5 Stanford: 12. Imray: WCP2400.3
Waypoints	Abeam SW end Den Point, 50° 32'.39N / 03° 30'.07W
Hazards	Shifting bar, dangerous in east or southerly winds and swell, particularly on the ebb. Strong tidal streams in river. Large part of harbour dries. Low bridge across river one mile from entrance
Overnight charge	Harbour Authority pontoon: £10

Just over five miles west of the Exe, and in many ways similar, the River Teign has less immediate appeal from a visitor's point of view. Not only does it have a bar, but, sadly, the wide and drying upper reaches of the estuary are effectively closed to all but small boats by the 2.9m clearance of the road bridge just above the town of Teignmouth. The Salty, a large sand and gravel bank which dries 3.3m, fills much of the central part of the harbour, space is at a premium and within the main channel and the entrance the tides run fast, between four and five knots at springs. However, in spite of the difficult entrance, a considerable amount of commercial shipping uses the docks – vessels in excess of 2,000 tons and 100 metres overall, exporting clay (around which the harbour developed during the 19th century), and importing pulp and animal foodstuffs.

It is nevertheless an interesting small port and worth a visit if time and weather permit. The Harbour Authority has improved facilities for visitors in recent years, with the 20m *Jubilee pontoon* off the town which can take up to 10 rafted boats (max 20m LOA) and where you will remain afloat in 2.5m LAT. It is not possible to anchor anywhere due to the number of local moorings and the fairway, which must be left clear. Moorings can also sometimes be arranged with the harbour master if local boats are away cruising.

APPROACHES

The Bar has a justifiably unpleasant reputation and in fresh winds from the south or east, especially on the ebb, it can become a treacherous area of steep breaking seas and surf. In offshore winds, however, and after half-flood, with no likelihood of southerly or easterly weather in the offing, the river is not particularly difficult to enter, and once inside, perfectly sheltered. The approach should be made from a position east of the Ness and, although lit, I would only recommend a first visit in daylight. A yellow buoy 1.16M south-east of the Ness, marking the end of a sewer outfall, is useful to gauge your distance off. The Harbour Authority endeavours to maintain a dredged fairway running east/west into the river mouth flanked by the Ness Pole sand on the southern side and the Spratt sand to the north, both of which extend nearly half a mile to seaward. It should be noted

that this channel cannot be relied on, particularly after any strength of winds from the east, when it can silt up very rapidly. Small yellow, black or orange buoys are normally stationed along the south side of this channel to assist the pilots. These should usually be left on your port hand when entering and the larger yellow buoy should be left to starboard. However, due to the changing nature of the bar, it is always wisest to call ahead before entering either by phone or on VHF Channel 12 during office hours call sign *Teignmouth Harbour Master*.

There is a long row of terraced hotels at the south end of the Teignmouth seafront and closest to the second gabled building two prominent landmarks (note that a very tall black pole with a grey stone tower in front of it should NOT be mistaken for a leading line). These merely provide a transit of 334°T which clears the Ness Rocks, a rocky ledge extending north-eastwards from the Ness where the shore is littered with large boulders. Once into the river entrance the white Philip Lucette beacon (Oc R 6s) marks the south side of the channel. It stands on a training wall just off the shore which dries 2m – leave it several boat lengths to port and steer towards the beacon with a triangular topmark (Oc G 6s FG vert), which marks the end of Den Point, a low sandy

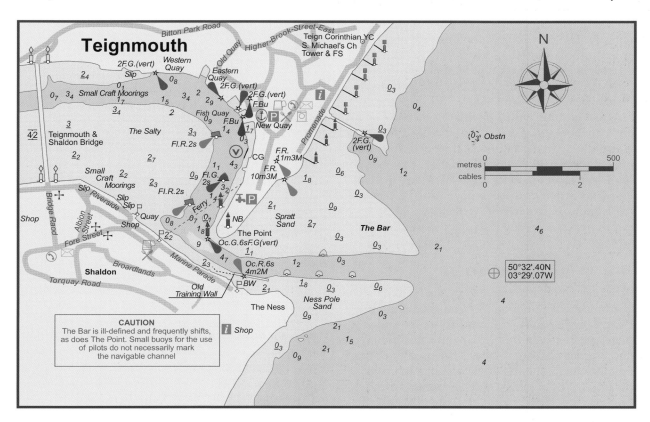

Dominated by the distinctive bluff of the Ness, the Teign mostly dries

spit. Shaldon and a large group of moorings in the pool lie ahead, but the main channel turns sharply to starboard, with the moorings and waterfront of Teignmouth opening before you.

BERTHING

Here the tide runs strongly – do not cut the corner, but keep in midstream. The eastern edge of the Salty is marked by the Lower Salty red can buoy (Fl R 2s), which should be left to port, with a conical green starboard hand buoy (Fl G 2s) further upstream on the opposite side of the fairway. The visitors' pontoon lies beyond this on your starboard hand and is clearly marked. The overnight charge for a 10m boat is £10. From here you will have to dinghy ashore and land on the nearby beach.

The Harbour Office is situated on New Quay, a bit further upstream on the starboard hand, and is usually open during normal weekday working hours. On arrival contact the harbour master, Mr Ian Hayward (Tel: 01626 773165), unless he has already spotted you – in season, during busy times and particularly at weekends a harbour patrol boat is often on duty. Its website is well worth a visit: www.teignmouth-harbour.com.

FACILITIES

A recorded port for nearly 1,000 years, today Teignmouth is rather an intriguing mixture. It is a typical beach resort with reddish sands, and was developed early in the 1800s with a traditional pier and elegant seafront. It boasts the usual modern accoutrements such as novelty golf, a seafront theatre, children's rides and amusement arcades. In marked contrast, behind the town, the jumble of

brightly painted fishermen's beach huts, slipways, alleyways and small quays along the shingly waterfront has its own particular charm.

Salmon fishermen work the river in season, often shooting nets right across the river mouth at low water. The famous Morgan Giles Shipyard was located here from before the war until it closed in 1969, once employing over 150 local people designing and building many fine wooden yachts – many still sailing today.

All usual facilities can be found in the town, with water available in cans from a tap in the lower car park on Den Point, and public showers and toilets on the Den open daily 0800 to 2200 in summer. Showers and bar, (Wed & Fri) can also be enjoyed at the Teign Corinthian Yacht Club (Tel: 01626 772734), which is situated on the main seafront to the north of St Michael's Church. Fuel is only available in cans from the local garage.Rubbish can be disposed of in bins at the Harbour Office, New Quay and on the Point. There is no shortage of shops including the Old Salty Chandlery (Tel: 01626 775754), launderette, pubs, restaurants, cafés, post office, branches of all main banks, marine engineers (Tel: 01626 879879 or 772324) and repairs (Tel: 01626 772324). The Tourist Information Centre (Tel: 01626 215666) is near the pier, while a local museum can be found close to the station. There are also regular main line rail connections to London and the North.

SHALDON

Shaldon is a much quieter place – an unspoilt waterside village – with a delightful central square surrounding a bowling green. There is less of a choice for facilities, but all the basics are obtainable at the Spar Waterside Village Stores (open daily 0800–2100, 1000–1300 Sundays). There are two chandlers, Mariners Weigh (Tel: 01626 873698), specialising in motorboat gear, and the extremely well-stocked Brigantine (Tel: 01626 872400) on the foreshore, which has just about everything, including Calor and Camping Gaz, although fuel is not obtainable. Eating places comprise pubs and fish and chip shops as well as several restaurants and tea-rooms.

A distinctive black and white ferry with painted gunports runs from Teignmouth river beach to Shaldon 0800–sunset in summer, and for the energetic the coastal footpath up to the summit of the Ness and beyond provides good exercise and fine views. There is also a curious tunnel through the Ness to Ness Cove and the Shaldon Wildlife Trust is located just by its entrance.

TORQUAY

Tides	HW Dover −0500
Range	MHWS 4.9m–MHWN 3.7m, MLWN 2.0m–MLWS 0.7m. Tidal streams weak
Charts	BA: 26, SC 5602.5. Stanford:12.CP22 Imray: C5, WCP2400.3
Waypoints	Haldon Pier Head 50°27'.43N / 03°31'.74W
Hazards	Narrow harbour entrance, often busy. Approach poor in strong SE'ly winds. Inner harbour accessed via half tide sill
Overnight charge	Harbour Authority £11.70 alongside. Marina £27

Centre of the self-styled English Riviera, visually Torquay is the nearest thing to Cannes or Nice you are likely to find on a West Country cruise. Once described by Tennyson as the 'loveliest sea village in England', he would see some considerable changes today from the small fishing

village that he knew as a fledgling resort.

Torquay's inhabited existence has a definite pedigree. Nearby, within an easy bus ride, in the famous underground caves at Kent's Cavern you can see spectacular stone age remains dating from circa 35,000 BC. By the 12th century Torre Abbey had been established and the small stone quay built by the Monks to serve it became known as

Torquay Harbour and Marina is set amidst an exotic backdrop of parks, gardens and elegant Georgian terraces

Torre Quay. However, its real growth and prosperity came during the Napoleonic Wars, when Tor Bay was much used by the Royal Navy as an alternative to Plymouth before its breakwater was built, being accessible and better sheltered in south and south-westerly weather. With the Fleet often anchored in Tor Bay for months at a time, the town soon found favour among Naval officers, with smart lodging houses rising beside the old thatched medieval cottages.

The unusually mild climate was another obvious attraction. Large hotels soon began to rise on the surrounding hills, palms and other sub-tropical plants flourished in the new parks and gardens and elegant Georgian terraces began to grow around the small harbour. To quote Macaulay:

'. . . a great watering place to which strangers are attracted by the Italian softness of the air; for in that climate the myrtle flourishes unsheltered . . . with white streets, rising terrace above terrace, and gay villas peeping from the midst of shrubberies and flower-beds.'

The final element in this transformation from humble hamlet into the West Country's premier seaside resort came with the arrival of the Great Western Railway in 1848, which inevitably unleashed a huge increase in holidaymakers.

At this time, though, there was still only a small drying harbour and it was customary for vessels to lie at anchor offshore. Here, in August 1868, RT McMullen had a very close shave with his 16 ton cutter *Orion* as he lay among the fleet of boats brought up in the bay for the annual regatta.

'. . awakened at 2am by the uneasy motion of the vessel, I immediately struck a match over the barometer, and, perceiving that its state was

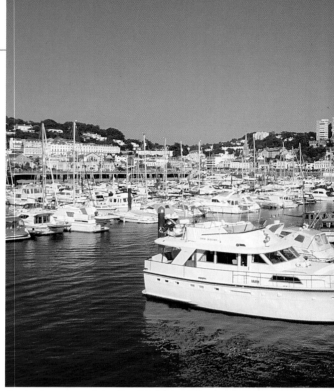
Set in the centre of the 'English Riviera', Torquay has a large marina with excellent facilities and plenty to do ashore

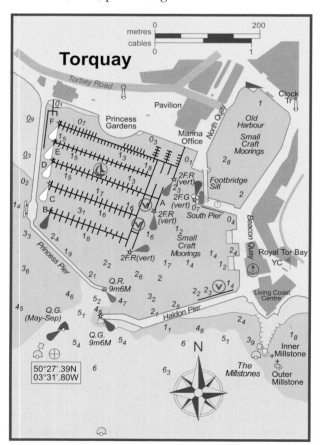

unsatisfactory, hastily dressed myself and called up the men to make snug, as a precaution . . . we first stowed the boat, then housed topmast, and hove the bowsprit short in. Meanwhile the rain was pelting down and the wind gradually backing to the SE, throwing in a nasty sea. The mainsail in very short time became so thick and heavy with the rain, that the labour of reeving the earrings and taking reefs down was very great indeed. At 4am it blew a heavy gale SE . . . 5am there was a terrible sea, all the yachts were pitching bows under, and most of them beginning to drag home. I was glad to see three or four yachts that lay in our way slip and run for the harbour, although it was only half-tide. Having unshackled our chain at 30 fathoms and buoyed it, we set mainsail with four reefs down, reefed foresail and storm jib and slipped at 5. 30am.'

Not exactly the perfect start to a day, but unlike several of the vessels that went ashore *Orion* and her crew managed to beat out to sea without mishap.

Torquay developed early as a popular yachting centre. The Royal Tor Bay Yacht Club was founded in 1875 and, with the completion of the large outer harbour in 1880, the fashionable resort soon became a firm favourite in the grand era of Edwardian yachting growth, but as Frank Cowper wryly observed in the 1880s:

'I find the prices a little prohibitive, and my tastes

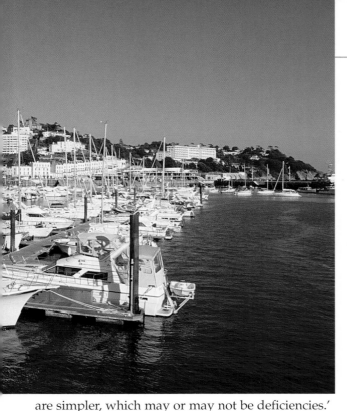

approximately 70m west of the end of Haldon Pier – leave this to starboard and keep to starboard between the pierheads. The yellow buoy situated to seaward and marked 5KTS is one of the limits of the controlled inshore swimming areas around Tor Bay, within which the speed limit of five knots must not be exceeded. Take care in the final approach as the entrance is invariably busy. If closed due to navigational hazards three vertical red balls are displayed on the pierhead (three vertical red lights at night), and no vessels are allowed to enter or leave.

Entry at night is not difficult. Haldon Pier displays a quick flashing green light and Princess Pier a quick flashing red, both of six miles visibility, although it is not always easy to pick them out against the blaze of lights from the town. Once inside, two vertical fixed green lights mark the end of the South Pier and the entrance to the Old (inner) Harbour.

The outer harbour and the marina have an average depth between 1.5m and 1.9m, except in the north-eastern corner, east of the fairway leading to the previously drying Old Harbour. This is now accessed three hours either side of HW over a sill at the entrance. Adorned with sculptural 'sails' at either end, the stylish footbridge above the sill opens on request – VHF Ch 14 – when the harbour is accessible, April – September 0700–2300. It is prohibited to pass under the footbridge when it is not open. The sill maintains a depth of between 1m and 2.8m in the Old Harbour, which is totally given over to local trot moorings. Anchoring is prohibited anywhere within the inner and outer harbours and there are heavy penalties for discharging marine toilets within the harbour.

THE MARINA AND BERTHING

The 500 berth marina occupies most of the western side of the outer harbour, and this includes a number of berths for visitors up to a maximum of 24m LOA on the long pontoons adjacent to the fairway. These are clearly indicated by a large notice giving berthing directions. A 24-hour watch is kept on VHF Ch 80, call sign *Torquay Marina*, so one can call ahead for instructions or berth in any empty space on the visitors' pontoons and report to the marina office once secure.

The visitor charge of £2.70 per metre per night is based on overall length – including bowsprits and davits. Although there is technically a 25 per cent surcharge for multihulls, this is rarely imposed

are simpler, which may or may not be deficiencies.'

Although the outer harbour provided infinitely better shelter than the open roadstead, it still suffered from an uncomfortable heavy surge in south-easterly weather. Amazingly, the short extension to Haldon Pier that eliminated this problem was not built until over a century later when a 2,500 ton caisson was towed into position and sunk here in 1984 to protect the new marina that had begun construction a year earlier!

The opening of Torquay Marina in 1985 greatly enhanced the facilities for yachts and since then the port has become an increasingly popular stopover for visitors. The harbour is particularly busy during Tor Bay Royal Regatta towards the end of August and also in the run up to and after the bi-annual Triangle Race to Brittany and Ireland which the Royal Tor Bay Yacht Club has organised since 1986.

APPROACHES

There are no immediate hazards in the approach to Torquay, and there is deep water to the harbour mouth, but as this is narrow it should be approached with care in strong south-easterly winds, which kick up an uncomfortable backwash. In these conditions Brixham is usually a far easier option for those seeking shelter in Tor Bay.

The entrance is only just under 50m wide and is well hidden at a distance because of the overlapping outer end of Haldon Pier. To direct vessels into the harbour mouth between May and September, a green conical buoy (QG) is situated

Torquay Marina visitors' berths are on its eastern flank and clearly indicated

unless the boat is of exceptional beam or takes up more than one berth. Facilities include luxury showers and toilets, fresh water, 240 volt shorepower, telephones, refuse disposal and a self-service launderette. There is a large adjoining car park and excellent 24-hour security.

The extravagant Art Deco Edwardian Pavilion dates from 1812 and overlooks the marina. It houses an elegant shopping mall, which includes a Torquay Chandlers (Tel: 211854) open seven days a week, the Pavilion Bar and Terrace Restaurant (Tel:211801), a delicatessen and off-licence.

The less expensive berthing options at £1.17 per metre per night are the Harbour Authority pontoons alongside the inner, eastern end of Haldon Pier, if space is available. It is best to make contact with the Harbour Authorities first on VHF Ch 14, call sign *Torquay Harbour*, otherwise berth and check at the harbour office on Beacon Quay once you are secure. The Harbour Authority has new visitors' showers and toilets on Beacon Quay.

FACILITIES AND THINGS TO DO

As might be expected in a popular holiday resort, facilities in Torquay encompass most large retail outlets and branches of all major banks in the town centre. However, the only supermarket within walking distance of the harbour is Iceland in Union Square Mall, otherwise a taxi will be required to get to Sainsburys, M&S, Co-op or Somerfield.There are a number of smaller convenience shops closer to hand including a Spar in Vaughan Parade.

It is a particularly convenient spot for fuelling, with diesel, petrol, LPG, Calor gas and water all available alongside the fuelling pontoon on the south side of South Pier from Torquay Fuels (Tel: 294509) which is open Mon – Sat 0830 – 1900, Sun 1000 – 1900 April – Sept and maintains a listening watch on VHF Ch M, call sign *Torquay Fuel*.

There is a large choice of hotels, pubs and restaurants, including excellent seafood at No 7 Fish Bistro (Tel: 295055), the Hole in the Wall, (Tel: 200755), Edwards' Brasserie (Tel: 290855), Cafe Sol (Tel:296090) or the Marina Restaurant (Tel: 292255). For a crazier evening out try a medieval style banquet at Camelot (Tel: 215399). Indian and Chinese cuisine abounds, of course, with Thai too at Annie's Thai Restaurant (Tel: 295746), or Persian at Le Peyala (Tel: 200397). The imposing but friendly London Inn opposite the inner harbour does good price bar meals.

Although it lacks the restful charm of the peaceful rivers, the bustling contrast can make an interesting change, with plenty of nightlife for the younger members of the crew. Older hands will probably prefer the more comfortable surroundings of the Royal Tor Bay Yacht Club (Tel: 292006) and visiting members of other yacht clubs are welcome to use the showers, bar and restaurant, open daily for lunch, with evening meals 1900 – 2230 Wednesdays and Fridays.

Agatha Christie was born in Torquay in 1890 and is undoubtedly one of the town's better known former residents. This is celebrated today by the walk known as the *Agatha Christie Mile* and a permanent exhibition in Torquay Museum in Torwood Street, which leads up from the Strand. Several of the locations for her mystery stories were located in and around Torquay, including the *ABC Murders*, which features the spacious Princess Gardens adjoining the marina.

The most recent tourist attraction to open is the Living Coasts Centre at the seaward end of Beacon Quay, a marine conservation exhibition with a large and ingenious aviary as its centrepiece. Here seabirds from all over the world including penguins and puffins can be viewed at close quarters from acrylic tunnels which lead under the artificial pools and lakes or the many viewing platforms, with the coastal effects created by wave making machines and large dump buckets which drop two tons of water at a time! Included in this attraction, with splendid views over Tor Bay is the Azure@living coasts (Tel: 202499) – a cafe by day, which becomes a smart *à la carte* restaurant in the evening

A fascinating excursion well worth the effort is to the remarkable model village at Babbacombe, which will amaze adults and children alike. This, and Kent's Cavern, can be reached on buses that depart from outside Debenhams on the Strand.

In contrast to the model village, Cockington, about two miles away, is the real thing – picturesque with its thatched cottages and carefully preserved vision of rural tranquility. This veritable time capsule can be reached by bus, on foot if you're in need of a good walk, or even by horse and carriage from the far western end of the Torquay seafront, where you can also enjoy the low water expanse of Torre Abbey Sands if you're looking for a traditional beach.

Torquay Port Guide
Area telephone code: 01803

Harbour Master: Captain Kevin Mowat, Harbour Office, Beacon Quay, Torquay, TQ1 2BG.
(Tel: 292429. Fax: 299257).
Office manned Mon – Fri 0900 – 1700 and weekends also, May – Sept.
E-mail:
marine.services@torbay.gov.uk
Web site: www.tor-bay-harbour.co.uk

VHF: Ch 14, call sign *Torquay Harbour*, office hours.

Mail drop: Harbour Office. Marina will hold mail and messages for customers. Royal Tor Bay Yacht Club will hold mail

Emergency services: Lifeboat at Brixham. Brixham Coastguard

Anchorages: In offshore winds, Torquay Roads, 3 cables south of harbour entrance. Anchoring prohibited within harbour

Mooring/berthing: Harbour Authority pontoon berthing for visitors alongside inner eastern end of Haldon Pier

Marina: Torquay Marina, Torquay, TQ2 5EQ. (Tel: 200210, Fax: 200225),
E-mail:
torquaymarina@mdlmarinas.co.uk.
Website:www.marinas.co.uk 500 berths including visitors. VHF Ch 80 (24 hours), call sign *Torquay Marina*

Charges: Harbour Authority, £1.17 per metre per day. Torquay Marina, £2.70 per metre per day. Short stay, up to 4 hours, £10

Phones: Beacon Quay. Torquay Marina

Doctor/dentist: ask at Marina or Harbour Office

Hospital: Torbay Hospital (Tel: 614567)

Churches: All denominations

Local Weather Forecast: At Harbour Office daily. Weatherfax at Marina and Harbour Office.

Fuel: Petrol, diesel and LPG alongside South Pier fuel pontoon from Torquay Fuels (Tel: 294509 or mobile 0385 226839) VHF Ch M, call sign *Torquay Fuel*, April – Sept, Mon – Sat 0830 – 1900, Sun 1000 – 1900

Water: Alongside South Pier. Torquay Marina. Beacon Quay. Haldon Pier

Gas: Calor from Torquay Fuels at fuel berth. Calor and Camping Gaz available from Torquay Chandlers who will deliver to Marina customers

Tourist Information Centre: Adjacent to inner harbour slipway (Tel:0906 680 1268)

Banks/cashpoints: All main banks in town have cashpoints

Post Office: Centre of town

Rubbish: Compactor, bottle and can bank in Marina car park. Skips and waste oil disposal on Beacon Quay

Showers/toilets: Harbour Authority showers and toilets, Beacon Quay. Showers and toilets in Marina for customers. Showers available at Royal Torbay YC.

Chemical toilet disposal: At Marina

Launderette: At Marina and in town

Provisions: Everything available, including most basics on Sundays

Chandler: Torquay Chandlers, The Pavilion. (Tel: 211854) Riviera Boats, Beacon Quay.

(Tel: 294509)

Repairs: Torbay Seaways & Stevedores (Tel: 296570)

Marine engineers: Ask at Marina or Harbour Office

Electronic engineers: Ask at Marina or Harbour Office

Sailmakers: Ask at Marina or Harbour Office

Transport: Regular branch line services from Torquay station (5 mins bus/taxi ride from Marina) to main rail network at Newton Abbot (Tel: 08457 484950). M5 motorway (20 mins). Exeter Airport (45 mins; Tel: 01392 367433) – UK, Ireland and continental connections

Car hire: Hertz (Tel: 294786)

Bike hire: Simply the Bike (Tel: 200024)

Taxi: (Tel: 213521 or 211611)

Car parking: Beacon Quay car park. Marina car park. Many public car parks

Yacht Club: Royal Torbay Yacht Club, Beacon Hill, Torquay TQ1 2BQ (Tel: 292006)

Eating out: Wide selection from fish and chips to bistros, restaurants and ethnic food

Things to do: Living Coasts Centre. Torre Abbey – art gallery. Kent's Cavern, underground prehistoric remains. Model Village Babbacombe. Preserved village, Cockington. Aqualand marine life centre. Zoo and Quaywest Waterpark at Paignton. Safe swimming from Torre Abbey sands, 400 yd walk from marina. Torbay Royal Regatta in August

Visitors are not able to berth in Brixham's colourful inner harbour, which dries completely at low water

BRIXHAM

Tides	HW Dover −0505
Range	MHWS 4.9m–MHWN 3.7m,MLWN 2.0m–MLWS 0.7m. Tidal streams weak
Charts	BA: 26, SC5602.5. Stanford: 12, CP22. Imray: WCP2400.3
Waypoints	Victoria Breakwater Head 50° 24'.33N / 03° 30'.77W
Hazards	Busy fishing and pleasure boat harbour. Inner harbour dries
Overnight charge	Marina £27. Harbour Authority pontoon £11.11

'Next day was the day of the trawler's race. It was still blowing extremely hard from the west but the rain had stopped. When we came on deck the smacks in the harbour already had their mainsails up, double reefed with big topsails over them. Those reefs were a good enough indication of the strength of the wind. One smack was lying right at the head of the harbour hemmed in by the dense crowd of yachts which always filled the harbour at regatta time. It was a lovely thing to watch her get under way. Just before she cast off her mooring she set a great balloon staysail, filled on the port tack, and with not an inch to spare began to forge ahead down the narrowest of lanes between the anchored craft. She was squeezed so close to the wind, and I could not but tremble to think what would happen if a puff came foul and she lost way; for there was no room to tack – indeed, there was no room to deviate a yard from her direct line. But such things do not happen to Brixham trawlers; their skippers I believe, possess a secret magic to circumvent them. She passed within a dozen yards of *Sybil*, going fast now, her deck lined with crew – there must have been fifteen of them. Then when she was clear of the harbour, her jib was blown to ribbons. In a couple of minutes she had set another, and was away for the starting line.'

Brixham and trawlers are synonymous. In the last century the port was renowned for the powerful gaff ketches that so entranced Aubrey de Selincourt, who was writing here of a pre-war Brixham when a few of these fine vessels still regularly fished as far afield as the North Sea. Today, the large fleet of sizeable steel vessels that continue the tradition are also graphic evidence of the remarkable reversal of the port's commercial fortunes; in the late 1960s the fishing fleet was struggling to survive. The creation of the Brixham and Torbay Fishermen's Cooperative resulted in this turn around and as new, much larger vessels were introduced the fish quays grew to accommodate them. Since then Brixham has flourished and now ranks as one of the main fishing ports in England, a success story that is impressive when compared to the recession that has dogged so many other places.

If you're here in early May – during Heritage Week – the Brixham Sailing Trawler race has been revived, and in contrast to the tanned sails you can also watch the modern trawlers racing – usually on the third Saturday in June. Brixham Regatta takes place during August.

Brixham Harbour and Marina are easily accessed in all weather

Much has changed since I first began to visit Brixham 30 years ago – there was far less commercial activity then and always plenty of room to anchor. We used frequently to nose our way in to find space to dry out alongside the wall in the inner harbour, but today this is all given over to grids and concrete hard standing for repair work. Today, first and foremost, Brixham is a busy fishing port, secondly it is an important pilotage station with large vessels regularly entering Torbay to take on or land Channel Pilots, and there is also a sizeable fleet of trip and angling boats. Brixham Marina opened in 1989, and its safe and easy access has made it an increasingly popular port of call for pleasure craft.

APPROACHES AND BERTHING

Brixham's half-mile long Victoria breakwater has a white lighthouse at the outer end (Oc R 15s) and is easy to locate about a mile west of Berry Head. Give the breakwater end a wide berth as large beam trawlers can often emerge from behind it at speed and you should then keep to the starboard side of the 75m wide fairway, which is clearly marked by port hand (Fl R) and starboard hand (Fl G) buoys right up to the fish quays and the marina. At night the fairway is covered by the white sector of a Dir Iso WRG 5s light located on

the southern side of the harbour, which has a quick flashing light immediately above it to help identify it against the background lights of the town. The eastern end of the marina wave screen breakwater is indicated by 2 Fl G 5s vert lights, the south-western end by 2 Fl R 5s vert.

Anchoring is prohibited in the fairway, and the only feasible place to lie to your own gear is to seaward of the moorings on the west side of the harbour, which is sheltered in all but north-westerly winds, but uncomfortable in north or north-easterly conditions when a ground swell runs in. The bottom is foul in places and a trip line is essential. Anchoring is also prohibited in the fairway along the inside of Victoria Breakwater, which is kept clear for the lifeboat.

An alternative anchorage, though less convenient for the town, is Fishcombe Cove just west of the harbour. It is sheltered and peaceful in southerly and westerly weather, and also free. On arrival in Brixham the harbour office is keen to encourage all vessels to make contact on VHF Ch 14 prior to entering the fairway.

Brixham Yacht Club (Tel: 853332), situated in the south-west corner of the outer harbour, has two 10m island pontoons immediately off the club which can be used by visitors at a daily rate of £0.85 a metre.

However, most visitors to Brixham usually opt for the convenience of MDL's 484-berth Brixham Marina, which now fills the greater part of the south-eastern corner of the harbour and is well protected by its wave screen breakwater. Visitors' berths are usually available: please call ahead on VHF Channel 80 call sign *Brixham Marina* for berthing instructions. Once secure, walk along to the marina control office for registration. Vessels over 18m LOA should make prior berthing arrangements with the dockmaster by VHF or (Tel: 882929). The overnight charge works out at £2.70 a metre.

The facilities are very

good, comprising diesel (outer end of 'C' pontoon, 0900 – 1800 May – Sept), water, electricity, showers, toilets, launderette, telephones, bar, restaurant, chandler, provisions, and excellent 24 hour security.

Facilities for visitors were further enhanced by Torbay Harbour Authority in 2000 with the creation of a large new town pontoon adjacent to the marina events pontoon in the approach to the inner harbour. This was partly funded by a European Regional Development Fund and is intended to provide a base for the increasing numbers of restored Brixham sailing trawlers that have been returning to their home port. It also affords berthing for visitors, with power and water available. The charge per day for a 10m boat works out at £11.11 for the first three days, after which the fourth day is free.

From the marina and town pontoon it is a short walk to the centre of town, past the Brixham Coastguard HQ on King's Quay, where interested visitors are welcome, providing they are not too busy.

The town retains much of its original fishing village atmosphere, climbing in a colourful

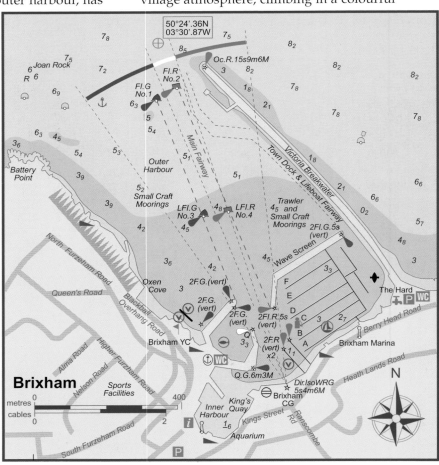

Brixham Harbour Authority's town pontoon is a popular visitor berthing option

profusion around the steep hills overlooking the drying inner harbour, which is given over to local moorings, repair work and trip boat activity. A popular but unsophisticated tourist spot, Brixham has a very distinctive character and is always bustling with waterside activity, from traditional artists painting on the quay to the holidaymakers swarming over the jaunty 'replica' of Drake's *Golden Hind* in the inner harbour.

Most other facilities can be found in pedestrianised Fore Street, the main shopping centre which follows the valley leading inland from the harbour. Here, there is a Somerfield supermarket, open 0800 – 1800 weekdays and 1000 – 1600 on Sundays, as well as branches of all

Brixham's secure and sheltered marina can usually provide visitor berths and is within easy walking distance of the town

the main banks, which all have cashpoints.

Several restaurants and bistros perhaps inevitably have seafood as a speciality, many of which will be found along the inner harbour quayside, including Beamers (Tel: 854777), Armada (Tel: 853418) and the Poopdeck (Tel: 858681). Yardarms (Tel: 858266) and the Oyster Catcher Bistro (Tel: 856738) are closer to the marina. There are, needless-to-say, plenty of pubs to choose from too, most of which serve food, including the Blue Anchor, the Rising Sun, and the Sprat & Mackerel. Fresh seafood stalls abound on the harbourside, and no visit to Brixham is really complete without a hefty helping of fish and chips, enjoyed in the cheerful bustle of the Brixham Fish Restaurant or *alfresco* on the Quay.

If you continue around the inner harbour and up the steep hill past the fishmarket you will reach Brixham Yacht Club (Tel: 853332) where you will be made very welcome. It has a bar and very good restaurant for evening meals, showers and fine views over the outer harbour.

The club was established in 1937 and its burgee includes a crown with an orange in the hoist. This is derived from the landing of Prince William of Orange in Brixham in 1688, when, supported by a Dutch invasion force of nearly 15,000, he set out to restore the throne of England to Protestantism and was in due course crowned as William III. A statue at the head of the inner harbour commemorates the event.

Brixham Port Guide

Area telephone code: 01803

Harbour Master: Captain Paul Labistour, The Harbour Office, New Fish Quay, Brixham, TQ5 8AJ. (Tel: 853321/851854. Fax: 852434). Office manned seven days a week in season 0900–1700

E-mail: brixham.harbour@torbay.gov.uk;

Website: www.tor-bay-harbour.co.uk

VHF: Ch 16, working Ch14, call sign *Brixham Harbour Radio* (office hours)

Mail drops: Brixham Marina. Brixham Yacht Club

Emergency services: Brixham Lifeboat. Brixham Coastguard

Anchorages: To seaward of moorings on west side of harbour, 4 to 5m LAT. Fishcombe Cove, west of harbour

Mooring/berthing: Brixham Marina, Harbour Authority Town Pontoon, Brixham Yacht Club pontoon

Dinghy landings: At Yacht Club, and public slipways/steps west and east side of outer harbour

Marina: Brixham Marina, Berry Head Road, Brixham, Devon TQ5 9BW (Tel: 882929. Fax:882737). 484 berths. E-mail: brixhammarina @mdlmarinas.co.uk. Website: www.marinas.co.uk VHF Ch 80 (24 hours), call sign *Brixham Marina*.

Charges: Brixham Marina: £2.70 per metre. Short stay, up to 4 hours, £10. Harbour Authority Town Pontoon, 10m boat £11.11. Brixham Yacht Club pontoon £0.85 per metre

Phones: Brixham Marina. At Yacht Club. Public phones by Harbour Office and at head of inner harbour

Doctor/dentist: ask at marina's dockmaster office

Hospital: Torbay Hospital, Torquay (Tel: 614567)

Churches: All denominations

Local Weather Forecast: At Marina and Harbour Office

Fuel: Diesel from fuel berth, Brixham Marina (0900–2000). Petrol in cans from garage or alongside in Torquay

Water: Brixham Marina. Town Pontoon. Tap at Yacht Club

Gas: Boat Shop Chandlery, Calor and Gaz

Ice: Ask at marina's dockmaster office

Tourist Information Centre: On Old Fish Quay, (Tel: 0906 6801268)

Banks/cashpoints: Branches of all main banks all with cashpoints

Post Office: Fore Street, centre of town

Rubbish: Marina has skips and can/bottle bank

Showers/Toilets: In Marina and Yacht Club. Public toilets on New Pier and Fishcombe car park

Chemical toilet disposal: In marina facilities block

Launderette: At marina and also Bolton Street, centre of town

Provisions: Everything available. Somerfield supermarket open 0800–1800 weekdays, 1000–1600 Sunday.

Chandlers: Boat Shop Chandlery, The Marina, Brixham (Tel: 882055/850582). Brixham Yacht Supplies, 72 Middle Street (Tel: 855254)

Repairs: Drying grid in inner harbour by arrangement with Harbour Office

Marine engineers: E G Hubbard & Co (Tel:853327) or ask at marina

Electronic engineers: Quay Electrics (Tel: 853030). BC Electrics (Tel: 858158). Marconi Marine (Tel: 851993) or ask at marina

Sailmakers: Nearest in Dartmouth

Transport: Buses to Paignton station to connect with branch line to main line at Newton Abbot (Tel: 08457 484950). Ferries to Torquay

Car hire: Ask at marina

Car parking: At marina multi-storey or car park in centre of town

Yacht club: Brixham Yacht Club, Overgang Road, Brixham TQ5 8AR, (Tel: 853332)

Eating out: Wide selection from fish and chips to restaurants and bistros

Things to do: Brixham Museum, including Coastguard Museum in centre of town. Aquarium. Walks to Berry Head Country Park

Brixham Yacht Club pontoons

RIVER DART

Tides	HW Dover −0510. Standard Port
Range	MHWS 4.7m–MHWN 3.5m, MLWN 2.1m–MLWS 0.6m. Can attain over three knots in entrance at springs
Charts	BA: 2253, 1634, SC5602. Stanford:CP 22, L15. Imray: WCP2400.4
Waypoints	Castle Ledge Buoy 50°20'.00N / 03°33'.11W
Hazards	Mewstone and rocks to SW of Mewstone (lit), Western Blackstone (unlit). Castle Ledge, Homestone, Checkstone, (all lit). Approaches rough in strong southerly weather/ebb tide. Fluky winds in entrance. Ferries between Kingswear and Dartmouth. Chain ferry just downstream of Dart Marina. Large part of upper reaches dry
Overnight charge	Harbour Authority from £10 to £15 alongside, £10 on mooring. At anchor £5 Marinas charge from £25 to £36.70. Baltic Wharf, Totnes £12.33

'A shipman was ther, woning fer by weste: For aught I woot, he was of Dertemouthe . . .'
Steeped in a seafaring tradition stretching back way beyond Chaucer's time,
when the Shipman's goodly barge *Maudelayne* plied her trade from
'Gootland to the Cape of Finistere, and every cryke in Britayne

and in Spayne', the deep, natural harbour of the River Dart is a must on any cruising itinerary. Often the first port of call after the long haul across Lyme Bay, its steep wooded shores and peaceful upper reaches provide a classic introduction to the area. Epitomising the essential character of West Country cruising, it is a tantalising foretaste of the further delights to come.

APPROACHES

Approaching the Dart from Berry Head and the east, it is not difficult to find the entrance to the river as the jagged triangular Mewstone, white with seabird droppings and gulls a-wheeling,

soon appears to seaward of the eastern side of the entrance, standing well clear of the land to provide a distinctive seamark. From further offshore though, to the south and the south-west, this island is lost against the shore and the entrance is completely hidden in the folds of the 170m high cliffs. It would still be a notoriously elusive haven if our predecessors had not bothered, in 1864, to build a 25 metre high column with a wide base high above Inner Froward Point to the east of the entrance, a fine daymark that is easy to spot. On the west side of the entrance, the row of white coastguard cottages about 100m above Blackstone Point are very conspicuous against the green hillside. However, once located, there are few other

The Dart's deep but narrow entrance is flanked by two castles

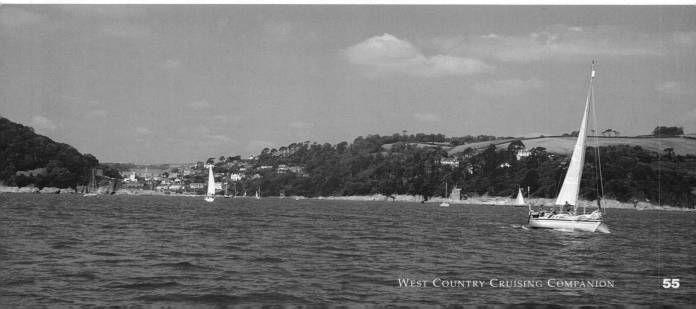

The River Dart is a classic West Country haven with a memorable approach

Dominated by the Royal Naval College, the River Dart has an abundance of facilties for visitors, including Darthaven Marina, off Kingswear in the foreground, Dart Marina in the far centre, and Noss-on-Dart Marina, just visible further upstream on the right

problems. Although the entrance is relatively narrow, it is extremely deep with the few hazards close to the shore.

Take care, though, in strong south-east to south-westerly winds and an ebb tide. This can run out at over three knots at springs, after heavy rain, or strong northerly winds. Confused seas will be found in the immediate approaches, and the high surrounding shore tends to create rapid and baffling shifts of wind, a factor that should be considered if entering under sail alone. Once inside, the shelter is excellent.

From the east, give the Eastern Blackstone and the Mewstone a wide berth as there are a number of drying rocks extending to the west. During 2003 this approach was much improved with the positioning of two YB south cardinal buoys, Mew Stone (VQ(6)+ LFl 10s), just to the south-east of the Mewstone and West Rock (Q(6) +LFl 15s), just to the south-west of West Rock. From here hold your course for the conical green Castle Ledge buoy (Fl G 5s) which should be left on your starboard hand. This buoy lies on the seaward limit of the harbour (an imaginary line joining Combe Point and Inner Froward Point) and from here on the 6 knot speed limit is strictly enforced throughout the river as far as the weir at Totnes.

Approaching at night, keep both Start Point (Fl (3)10s) and Berry Head (Fl (2)15s) visible until Castle Ledge buoy is located. This will bring you into the sectored light on the Kingswear shore (Iso RWG 3s) which covers the entrance to seaward, an area known as the Range, the red sector just clearing hazards to the west and the green sector hazards to the east. Keeping in the central white sector you have a safe and easy run in, leaving the red can Checkstone buoy (Fl(2)R 5s) on your port hand. Passing through the narrows, wait until the white sector of the inner light low down by Bayards Cove (Fl RWG 2s) is open before turning north-west into the harbour, keeping in midstream and taking care to avoid the large, normally unlit, mooring buoys in the centre of the channel just beyond Kingswear, although if a ship is anticipated during the night these buoys are lit (FlY).

Despite being straightforward at night, the whole approach should ideally be timed for daylight, as the imposing scenery, St Petrox

Church, and the two castles guarding the narrow entrance, are a sight not to be missed.

Kingswear Castle is privately owned, but Dartmouth Castle, to the west, dates from 1481, and at one time a 750 foot chain resting on six barges was stretched from here to the opposite shore to protect the port from raiders. It is now administered by English Heritage and open daily during the summer (1400 – 1830 Sundays) for a small charge. Walk out from the town or, easier still, take the small ferry from the Embankment to enjoy fine views of the entrance from the castle, where there is also a café. From here you can continue the walk through the woods and along the cliffs to Compass Cove, a shingly beach which is safe for bathing.

In daylight a closer approach can be made from the south-west, keeping near to the red can Homestone buoy (QR) marking a rocky ledge (least depth just under 1m LAT) to the north-west. A course can then be laid along the shore, keeping clear of the two Western Blackstone Rocks off Blackstone Point and the red Checkstone buoy just south of Dartmouth Castle and St Petrox Church, which is perched on the western shore. Once past the castle, keep to starboard and follow the eastern shore and the line of moorings below the Royal Dart Yacht Club, a gabled red brick building with a veranda, flagstaff and prominent dinghy pontoon. Immediately beyond the yacht club frequent passenger and car ferries ply between Kingswear and Dartmouth. They have priority at all times and care should be taken to keep clear even if under sail, and always pass astern.

Don't be taken aback if you hear a loud whistle and the sudden puffing of a steam train. Close by on the Kingswear shore the railway station is now the terminus for the Paignton and Dartmouth Steam Railway, a popular tourist attraction which is just guaranteed to send boys of all ages into nostalgic euphoria!

ANCHORAGE, BERTHING AND MOORINGS

Stretching before you, the large and virtually landlocked harbour is an impressive sight. Dartmouth and Kingswear overlook it from their respective steep hillsides in a colourful profusion of pastels, intermingled with the odd splash of black and white half-timber, and upriver, the imposing facade of the Britannia Royal Naval College, designed by Sir Aston Webb, which has dominated the view since 1905 when it replaced the old wooden walled ships HMS *Britannia* and *Hindustan*. Dartmouth has been the Royal Navy's primary officer training establishment since 1863, a proud association with the town which has, in its time, seen several Kings of England and the current heir to the throne among the cadets. Twice a week, from Easter to October, there are guided tours of the College (Tel: 677039 for details).

At first glance the harbour is one large mass of moorings and, though crowded in the season, you will always be able to find a berth somewhere in the Dart – even during the very popular Port of Dartmouth Royal Regatta which runs for three days at the end of August. If anything, you are spoilt for choice, but one thing is certain, wherever you go, it will cost you something, for the whole river as far as Totnes is administered by the Dart Harbour and Navigation Authority (DHNA) and dues are payable throughout the river at a rate of £0.50 per metre per day, which makes anchoring the cheapest but probably the least convenient option.

The anchorage is on the Kingswear side of the river between the line of large midstream mooring buoys and Darthaven Marina and the private pontoon moorings. Do not let go too close to the midstream buoys as their ground chains extend for quite a distance. The holding is good, but the ebb can run at up to two knots at springs, and it is a good dinghy ride across to Dartmouth. If the anchorage is crowded, wind against tide can also produce quite a few unpredictable antics, and a sudden glut of neighbours in embarrassingly close proximity. The other disadvantage with anchoring is that the Harbour Authority does not allow boats to be left unattended at anchor except for short periods (for shopping or meals) and neither must vessels be left unattended during the turn of the tide. Local fishing vessels work in and out of the adjacent moorings and an anchor light is essential.

Darthaven Marina has the unusual and added attraction of real steam trains passing close by!

Those seeking quieter surroundings can opt for the DHNA pontoon islands upstream of Kingswear

The DHNA is a totally independent and self-financing body which maintains all the facilities in the river, including lights, buoyage and waste disposal. Remarkably, its charges were actually reduced during 2000 and have increased only slightly since then while berthing facilities for small craft have continued to improve. Visitors' berths are clearly marked with blue flags and information signs with a blue background; all other information signs have a yellow background. Visitors' dinghy berths are marked by blue flags with a black St Andrew's cross. Further upriver, visitors' moorings are all blue and clearly marked with a black 'V'.

The daily rates vary according to location: a berth on the lower South Embankment pontoons off the Dartmouth Yacht Club (max. 9.5m LOA) or the North Embankment walk ashore pontoons works out at £0.75 per metre – very convenient for the town. Larger craft can lie inside the lower end of the Town Jetty for £1 per metre and between 1700 and 0845 (after the passenger boats close down) visitors can also use the outside berths for an overnight charge of £0.50 per metre. In all cases owners of multihulls will be charged double. There is also a half-day charge of half the full daily rate for vessels using the port between 0600 and 1800. In each circumstance you must add harbour dues to the prices quoted here.

Water and electricity are available free of charge on Harbour Authority facilities and close by on the Embankment, showers are incorporated in the public toilet block.

Both the Dartmouth Yacht Club (Tel: 01803 832305) and the Royal Dart Yacht Club (Tel:01803 752496) extend a friendly welcome to all visitors, with excellent showers and comfortable bars where meals and bar snacks are served at lunchtime and in the evening. The Royal Dart has a convenient dinghy pontoon with a handy fresh water tap.

The DHNA have a number of cheaper berthing options for visitors, with a pontoon island just north of the Town Jetty, another at the northern end of the Embankment for boats up to 4m LOA and 1.25m draught, and a long pontoon and visitors' moorings for larger craft just upstream of the private pontoon moorings above Kingswear. Both pontoons are free floating without access to the shore and cost £0.50 per metre. If you do not wish to use your own dinghy, the Harbour Authority runs a convenient water taxi service that can be hailed on VHF Ch 69 call sign *Yacht Taxi* (Tel: 07970 346571).The *Res-Nova* barge also runs water taxis that can be called on VHF Ch 08, call sign *Dartmouth Water Taxi*. Further upriver, below and off Dittisham, there are a number of visitors' moorings where you will also pay £0.50 per metre; another water taxi operates here, which can be hailed on VHF Ch 10, call sign *Greenway Ferry*.

Off Stoke Gabriel are three DHNA visitors moorings for boats up to 30ft LOA. Berths and moorings are normally allocated by the River Officers who are out on the water during the season from 0730 until dusk daily during the summer; VHF Ch 11 call sign *Dart Nav*. Volunteer staff also patrol outside of these hours for safety purposes, but do not collect fees or dues. If you arrive after hours take whatever seems to be the most convenient option. During the height of the season you will invariably have to raft up.

Temporary berthing is also possible alongside the north and south embankment in available space when the tide permits, which is handy for a quick shopping expedition. The North Embankment upstream of the ferry pontoon dries on most tides, while the South Embankment below the pontoon dries at springs. Daily Quay dues are applicable for anything more than a short stay at £0.50 per metre, multihulls £1 per metre. Note, too, that a very good scrubbing grid is situated on the embankment which can be booked through the DHNA. Both water and

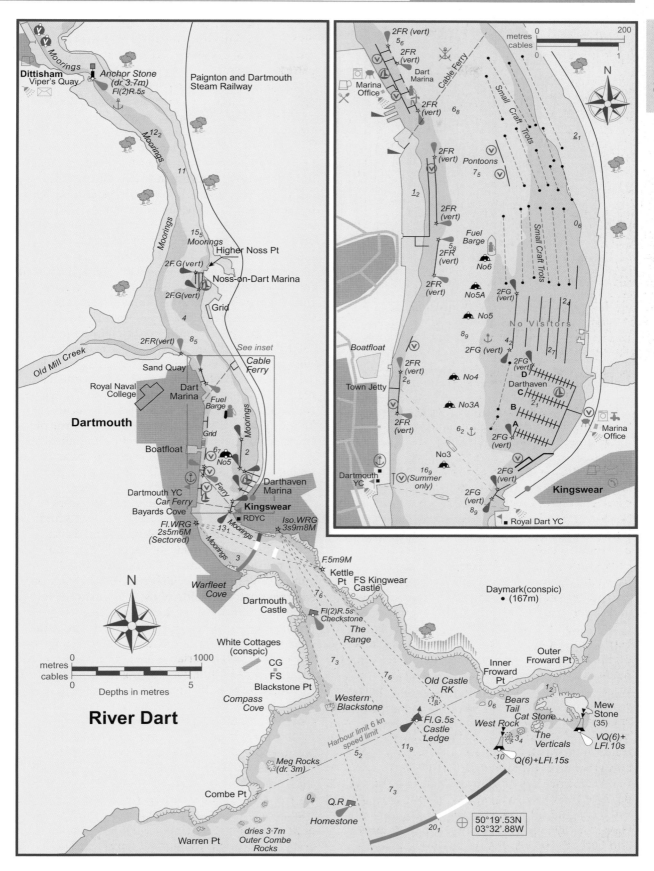

Dittisham
Viper's Quay

Anchor Stone
(dr 3.7m)
Fl(2)R.5s

Moorings

Paignton and Dartmouth
Steam Railway

12₂

11

Moorings

15₅
Moorings

Higher Noss Pt

2F.G(vert)

Noss-on-Dart Marina

2F.G(vert)

Grid

4

Old Mill Creek

2F.R(vert)   8₅

Sand Quay

See inset

Cable
Ferry

Royal Naval
College

Dartmouth

Dart
Marina

Fuel
Barge

Grid

Moorings

Boatfloat

No5

2

Dartmouth YC
Car Ferry
Bayards Cove

Ferry

Darthaven
Marina

Kingswear
RDYC

Fl.WRG
2s5m6M
(Sectored)

Moorings

13₁

Iso.WRG
3s9m8M

3

N

metres
cables

0   1000

0   5
Depths in metres

River Dart

Warfleet
Cove

Dartmouth
Castle

White Cottages
(conspic)

CG

FS

Blackstone Pt

Compass
Cove

Western
Blackstone

Meg Rocks
(dr. 3m)

Combe Pt

Warren Pt

dries 3·7m
Outer Combe
Rocks

F.5m9M
Kettle
Pt

7₆

Fl(2)R.5s
Checkstone

The
Range

FS Kingwear
Castle

Daymark(conspic)
(167m)

7₃

7₆

Old Castle
RK

Inner
Froward
Pt

Outer
Froward Pt

1₂

Bears
Tail

Cat Stone

Mew
Stone
(35)

Harbour limit 6 kn
speed limit

11₉

5₂

0₉

7₃

Q.R
Homestone

20₁

West Rock

The
Verticals

Fl.G.5s
Castle
Ledge

3₄

10   Q(6)+LFl.15s

VQ(6)+
LFl.10s

9₆

50°19'.53N
03°32'.88W

--- inset ---

metres
cables

0   200

0   1

N

2FR (vert)
5₆
2FR
(vert)

Dart
Marina

Cable Ferry

Small Craft Trots

2₁

0₆

Marina
Office

2FR
(vert)

6₈

2FR
(vert)
Pontoons

7₅

1₂

2FR
(vert)

Fuel
Barge
No6

5₈

Small Craft Trots

No visitors

2₄

2FR
(vert)

No5A

8₉

2FG
(vert)

2₇

4₂

No5

2FG (vert)

Boatfloat

2FR
(vert)
2₆

2FG
(vert)
D

Town Jetty

Darthaven

C

2FR
(vert)

No4

B

2₁

2FR
(vert)

No3A

A

6₂

2FG
(vert)

Dartmouth
YC

16₉
(Summer
only)

No3

2FG
(vert)

Kingswear

Marina
Office

2FG
(vert)
8₉

Royal Dart YC

An easy walk from the town centre, the Five Gold Anchor Dart Marina offers some of the most luxurious facilities in the West Country

electricity are available here and along the Quay.

Finally, there are the three private options – Darthaven Marina off Kingswear, Dart Marina just above the higher ferry and Noss-on-Dart Marina further upstream on the eastern side of the river.

On the southern side of its 270-berth marina, Darthaven has a clearly marked visitors' pontoon which can accommodate up to 25 boats. Adjacent to this, the inner pontoon has DHNA short stay berths (up to two hours) which are clearly indicated along with a visitors' dinghy berthing. This and the visitors' pontoon are both linked to the shore by the same bridge. Space for visitors within the rest of the marina is limited but you can usually be accommodated if berth holders are away. Advance booking is not possible so call *Darthaven Marina* on VHF Ch 80 or (Tel: 01803 752545) on arrival, or berth in any available space and check in at the berthing office. Latecomers will find vacant overnight berth numbers chalked up on the noticeboard by the office, and if your berth is not shown as vacant, move to one that is. Visitor charges are just under £2 per metre per night *plus* harbour dues of £0.50 metre. Facilities, including showers, toilets, launderette and a large chandler, are all located in the shoreside administration and amenity building on the other side of the railway line, and onshore services include a 35 ton boat hoist, shipwright, engineering and electronic repairs, including a seven-day 24-hour emergency call out service in season – engineer (Tel: 07973 280584), electronics (Tel: 07767 250787). The marina is also a Volvo Marine Centre with full breakdown facilities.

Opened in 1961, Dart Marina was the very first marina to be built in the West Country, and during 1997 it underwent a complete rebuild to a very high standard. As a result it gained the prestigious Five Gold Anchors award from the Yacht Harbour Association. It now has 110 fully serviced pontoon berths, each with water, electricity, phone, fax and TV terminals, with a PIN code accessed security gate. Visitors can usually be accommodated if permanent berthholders are away. Dart Marina monitors VHF Ch 80, call sign *Dart Marina*, 0800 – 2000 during the season, (1700 in winter). Call or telephone (01803 833351) ahead for berthing availability. The visitor charge during the season is £3.17 per metre per night *plus* harbour dues of £0.50 per metre, and facilities include showers, toilets, launderette and the ultimate cruising luxury – baths – in their quayside amenity building.

Diesel and a WC holding tank pump out facility are available at the fuel pontoon, which is open from 0800 seven days a week, and Calor gas is obtained through the office. The luxurious and totally refurbished Dart Marina Hotel is situated adjacent to the marina, with bar, outside terrace and Hauleys Restaurant (Tel: 832580) open to visitors.

Further upstream on the opposite shore, the 180 berth Noss-on-Dart Marina, run by the same parent company as Dart Marina, was originally restricted to permanent berth holders, but under new re-organisation about 15 berths are now reserved for visitors (more if permanent berth holders are away), providing a quieter alternative to Dart Marina. Here you will pay £2.23 per metre per night *plus* harbour dues; shore facilities include toilets/showers, launderette, a well-stocked chandlery and telephone. There is also a regular ferry service to Dart Marina and Dartmouth during the day. Noss on-Dart Marina monitors VHF Ch 80 from 0730 to 1800 daily, call sign *Noss Marina*. The final berthing option offered by Dart Marina is its fore and aft moorings upstream of Noss, which are available to visitors at £1.40 per metre per night *plus* harbour dues. This price includes use of the onshore facilities at Noss-on-Dart Marina.

DARTMOUTH

Ashore, Dartmouth has plenty to offer. Now a busy and popular holiday town, its growth as a major seaport like Plymouth or Falmouth was always restricted by the hilly hinterland which made transport to and from the port exceedingly difficult. Even in the 19th century it proved impossible to bring the Great Western Railway right into the town and they had to make do with it running down the opposite shore to Kingswear. But the advantages of Dartmouth as a secure deepwater anchorage and safe haven have always been utilised and it has enjoyed a rich maritime history. As early as 1147, 164 ships assembled here to begin the second crusade and 31 ships departed from here to assist with the seige of Calais in 1346.

In 1550 John Davis, the Elizabethan explorer, was born at Sandridge in the upper reaches of the Dart, and it was from Dartmouth that he set out on his three unsuccesssful voyages in search of the fabled north west passage. His contemporary Sir Humphrey Gilbert, half brother of Raleigh, lived at Greenway, opposite Dittisham and, although his expedition to find the north west passage was also unsuccessful, he did take possession of Newfoundland, the first English colony in north America in 1583. Not that he was able to reap the benefits. Homeward bound, his ship the *Squirrel* was overwhelmed by heavy seas off the Azores and all hands were lost.

In more recent times Dartmouth has celebrated other notable arrivals and departures. In 1923 George Muhlhauser ended his three year circumnavigation in the 36 ton, 40 year old yawl *Amaryllis*. It was a very significant milestone in the history of English cruising, for this was the first time a lightly crewed British yacht had achieved such a feat, although at the time it passed virtually unsung.

'We struck a fine day', he wrote to a friend, 'and Dartmouth, as we came in from the sea looked lovely'. Having encountered much bureaucracy and, far worse, much interest from the press in Australia, Muhlhauser was secretly dreading the arrival and was greatly relieved when the Customs Officer cleared them with the minimum of fuss. 'Here', he continued, 'not a soul has taken the slightest notice. It is delightful. I smile when I think of the ruses I planned to avoid reporters. Not a reporter has shown up. I am immensely relieved. This is a real homecoming to dear old casual England.'

Tragically, within weeks of his return. Muhlhauser was dead, his life shortened by the physical extremes of the voyage. He left *Amaryllis* to the Royal Naval College where she remained in use for cadet sail training until 1951 when she was towed to sea and scuttled on the 12th June.

In 1949 the intrepid brothers, Stanley and Colin Smith, arrived in Dartmouth in their diminutive home built 20 foot sloop, *Nova Espero*, after a 44 day voyage from Dartmouth, Nova Scotia. In 1951, rerigged as a yawl, she set sail again from Dartmouth crewed by Stanley Smith and a friend Charles Violet on another even more arduous east – west voyage across the Atlantic, making a landfall on Nova Scotia after 33 days and then proceeding on to New York to promote samples of British goods they had carried across from the Festival of Britain. In 1977, Dame Naomi James chose Dartmouth to begin and end her solo circumnavigation in the Gallant 53 *Express Crusader*.

Commercially, much of Dartmouth's wealth was founded around the export of cloth in the middle ages. The magnificent Butterwalk, a half-timbered row of former merchants' houses with their upper storeys perched on granite columns, dates from 1640 – its size and fine carvings are an indication of its former importance. The fascinating Dartmouth Borough Museum is now part of this fine building, and a foray into the steep winding back streets will reveal several other splendid examples of 17th century architecture. The attractive cobbled quayside of Bayard's Cove, just beyond the lower ferry, became familiar to many during the 1970s when the BBC used it as one of the locations for its *Onedin Line* series. More recently the Dartmouth waterfront and other south Devon locations such as Burgh Island have featured in the BBC's *Down to Earth* drama series.

A grumpy EE Middleton passed this way in 1869, early on in his *Cruise of the Kate*, an epic single-handed circumnavigation of Britain in a 21ft yawl. Weatherbound in a south-westerly gale, true to his gentlemanly form, he slept on board

The inside lower end of Dartmouth Town Jetty is always a popular berthing option for visitors

and 'went to the Castle Hotel for meals'. He could still do that today in surroundings that have probably not changed a lot! A good meal can be enjoyed at the Royal Castle Hotel (Tel: 833033), a popular haunt of the Britannia Cadets, either in the Adam Room restaurant or in the lively bar where themed buffets are a regular feature.

The Boatfloat, which is the focal point of the town's waterfront, lies right in front of the Hotel, an enclosed dinghy harbour entered under a bridge full of local boats. This is, however, not the place to leave your dinghy as it dries completely. There are ample landing steps along the embankment but remember to pull your dinghy clear so that others can get alongside or berth on the inside of the lower visitors' pontoon. In addition, just below the higher ferry, dinghies may be left on the outer end of the long, low tide pontoon off the embankment.

If you're feeling like a quiet walk take the higher ferry across to the Kingswear side of the river and, as you begin to climb up the road, look out for the marked footpath on the right which will take you up the steep wooded hillside to an elevated and easier path that eventually leads you through the woods to Kingswear, with some fine glimpses of the river along the way. From Kingswear, catch the lower ferry back to Dartmouth to complete this pleasant circuit. This is part of the much longer *Dart Valley Trail*, a circular route from Dartmouth to Dittisham, (where you can cross by ferry to Greenaway) and then back to Kingswear. The local Tourist Information Centre can provide full details.

FACILITIES

Facilities are excellent. Just a short walk from the Embankment, in Mayors Avenue, there is a Plymco supermarket (open daily 0800 – 2200, 1000 – 1700 on Sunday), which also houses the main post office. Two delectable delicatessens are Cundell's, next door to the Royal Castle Hotel, and the Smith Street Delicatessen, while you'll find the well stocked Dartmouth Vintners in the Butterwalk. An open-air Friday market takes place in the Market Square, and the Dartmouth Launderette is just opposite in Market Street. Lloyds TSB, HSBC and Natwest all have cashpoint facilities (there is no branch of Barclays Bank).

There are several chandlers and all repair facilities at hand, ranging from rigging to divers. Diesel and petrol are available from the convenient fuel barge moored in mid-river which is open daily 0900 – 1700 and can be contacted on VHF Ch 06, call sign *Dart Crusader* or (Tel: 07801

798861). Dart Marina can also provide diesel from 0800. Water is in plentiful supply from taps on the embankment, all marinas and the fuel barge.

Restaurants abound, from the acclaimed Carved Angel (Tel: 832465), at the top of the range, and Taylors Restaurant (Tel: 832748), overlooking the Boat Float, to bistros such as Jonathan's Fish Restaurant (Tel: 832999), Anzac Street Bistro (Tel: 835515), RB's Diner (Tel: 832882) and Johnny Chick's (Tel: 835272), or the popular Little Admiral Restaurant for a selection of tapas (Tel: 832572). Those seeking Indian food should try Chalimar (Tel: 835050) or The Spice Bazaar (Tel: 832224). There are plenty of pubs too: The Cherub Inn (Tel: 832571) dates from 1380 and has a comfortable upstairs restaurant and good bar meals, while the Dolphin (Tel: 833835) offers an impressive seafood menu. For beer, a pizza or a succulent Dartmouth crab sandwich perhaps, the Dartmouth Arms (Tel: 832903) remains the favourite with locals. Among the numerous cafes one definitely stands out – the bohemian Cafe Alf Resco is an absolute must for breakfast or lunch!

The large converted Dutch barge moored in the centre of the river just downstream of the fuel barge operates as the Res Nova Inn. This is open from 1000 until late and visiting yachts can berth alongside to use the facilities, which include morning coffee, lunch, an all-day bar and evening meals. Showers and overnight B&B accommodation are also available and there is a continuous water taxi service to the shore. *Res-Nova* monitors VHF Ch 08 (Tel: 0370 628967) if you want to go alongside.

KINGSWEAR AND FURTHER UPSTREAM

Kingswear, by way of a contrast, is a much quieter place, incorporating a general store, newsagent, post office, the Ship Inn and the Steam Packet (both offering food), a bistro, two chandlers, a launderette and, of course, the Royal Dart YC. The steam trains run regularly to Paignton and back – a great way to keep the kids and father occupied for an afternoon.

'I grudged the delay at Dartmouth', continued Middleton, 'but was recompensed in some measure by the natural beauty of the place, which gains its greatest charm, to my way of thinking, from the entrance to the harbour. I pulled some little distance up the river in the dinghy, but the scenery appeared much tamer, not nearly so beautiful as at the mouth.'

Sadly, the poor chap did not pull quite far enough! The name 'Dart' is derived from the Old English word for oak, of which there is plenty upstream where the real delights of the Dart emerge as the navigable river winds 10 wooded miles inland to Totnes. Until 1996 coasters of up to 1,000 tons and 4m draught regularly discharged timber just below the town, but this traffic has now ceased completely and the only commercial craft using the upper Dart are the many large trip boats. The channel is well-buoyed and well worth exploring on a rising tide if time permits, and a number of secluded and peaceful anchorages can be found in the upper reaches.

The first section of the river as far as Dittisham is quite straightforward, wide and deep with over 5m throughout the channel at LAT. The only real hazard is the upper car ferry, a sizeable vessel that runs across the river on wires and berths just downstream of the Dart Marina. Always pass astern and give it a wide berth, as the wires close to it are near the water surface.

Beyond Dart Marina, to port, the jetties and moorings all belong to the Britannia Royal Naval College, and a wary eye should be kept out for the numerous small naval craft running around with midshipmen under training. The wide mouth of Old Mill Creek dries completely, and the hulk on the northern shore is the remains of one of the last Irish three-masted trading schooners, *Invermore*, abandoned after an abortive attempt to sail her to Australia. Opposite, just upstream of Noss-on-Dart Marina, is the site of the famous Philip & Sons shipyard; established in 1858 it finally closed in 1999. Builders of many larger commercial vessels and lightships, it was also the birthplace of several famous yachts, notably Claud Worth's lovely *Tern IV* and Chay Blyth's original *British Steel*.

From here on, the shores are steep and wooded, the trees brushing the high tide mark along a wide reach lined with local moorings, which narrows considerably at the Anchor Stone, a 3.7m drying rock with a beacon and square red topmark (Fl (2) R 5s). This should be given a good berth and left well on your port hand. Here, according to local tradition, Sir Walter Raleigh reputedly smoked the first pipe of tobacco in England after being banned from trying it in his half brother's house at Greenaway! The tight passage between the rock and the western shore is definitely not recommended – this can be a spectacularly embarrassing spot to be stranded!

Anchoring is not allowed off Dittisham because of the extensive moorings and the anchorage just downstream of the Anchor Stone is the nearest, if not the most convenient for the village. Sound in just to the edge of Parsons Mud, upstream of the

One of the few remaining anchorages in the Dart is just downstream of the Anchor Stone

local moorings. The tide can run quite hard here and it can be uncomfortable with a fresh breeze against it; the mud drops away steeply and, as I have found out myself, it is not unknown for boats to drag into the deeper water. A brave row against the ebb, an outboard puts the Ferry Boat Inn within more tenable reach! However, if you are merely looking for a peaceful anchorage in sylvan surroundings and wish to go nowhere else you have found it – at least, once the trip boats wind up for the day.

DITTISHAM

There are a number of DNHA visitors' moorings available off Dittisham and during the season you will invariably have to raft up. Landing is easy at all states of the tide at the long dinghy pontoon, but do not obstruct or leave your dinghy on the very outer end as this is used by the passenger ferry to Greenway Quay, opposite, and also the Dartmouth to Dittisham ferry during the season.

Water is available from a public tap by the popular Ferry Boat Inn, which is conveniently situated almost on the foreshore and can provide a good selection of food and drink in convivial surroundings. From here Dittisham, pronounced locally as 'Ditsam', straggles up the steep hill, a mixture of pretty thatched stone and cob cottages leading to the village centre, which has a small but very well stocked grocery store/post office, 'phone box and another pub, the Red Lion, with fresh local salmon one of its specialities during the season. When the tide permits, walk along the foreshore from the Ferry Boat or along the lane that branches right just up the hill above the pub, to reach a grassy playing field known as the Ham, where the public toilet block also houses a free shower!

There are fine views upriver from higher Dittisham. Widening into a shallower tidal lake thick with moorings, the water stretches for a mile towards the distant buildings of the boatyards in Galmpton Creek, where the steep wooded shores fall away into gently rolling fields.

Above the moorings, the large area of Flat Owers Bank dries at LW and the main channel keeps close to the wooded south shore, swinging round across the entrance to Galmpton Creek where the Dartside Quay and Dolphin Shipyard are both situated at the head of the drying creek. Dartside Quay is a major repair facility with 53 ton and 16 ton hoists and a six ton mobile crane. On site services include repairs in wood, GRP and steel, chandlery, engineering, rigging, electronics and sailmaker. There is a vast area of hard standing. Normally the yard is accessible two hours either side of HW.

A number of moorings lie along the deep water, but care should be taken to avoid the Eel Rock (dries 1.5m), on the eastern edge of the channel south of the gabled boathouse on Waddeton Point. With sufficient water, there is a short cut to the west of Flat Owers Bank and from Greenway Quay steer straight for Waddeton boathouse, a course of about 020°T, until abeam of the port hand No 1 Flat Owers buoy, before altering slowly towards the second boathouse, Sandridge, and steering about 310°T. There are a few shallow patches, but with a couple of hours of flood you should get across.

From Sandridge boathouse, the channel deepens again and swings back close to Higher Gurrow Point. Steer for the port hand beacon ahead at the entrance to Dittisham Mill Creek, keeping close to Blackness Point, and then working back across the river to the delightfully named Pighole Point on the eastern shore. In the right conditions and providing you are clear of the main channel, it is possible to anchor just west of Higher Gurrow Point or just west of Blackness Point.

This wide reach of the river is known locally as the Lake of the Dart, as it is impossible to see a way out from the centre at High Water. It is not, however, a deep lake, for Middle Back, a large drying bank, extends right up its centre. Keep close to the line of moorings along the eastern shore and just south of the beacon with a green triangular topmark (Q Fl G) marking the entrance to the drying Stoke Gabriel creek. Here you will find the last three DHNA visitors' moorings, which can be used by vessels up to 30ft LOA. A channel marked by two port hand beacons with square orange topmarks leads to a dinghy pontoon and a tiny quay where it is possible to land, but beware, do NOT proceed any further than the quay – there is a tidal dam right across the creek, submerged at high tide.

Visitors will usually have to raft on the popular visitors' moorings off Dittisham for a foray to the Ferry Boat Inn

STOKE GABRIEL

A picturesque Devon village, with three pubs, a hotel and limited provisions, its claim to fame is the massive yew tree in the church yard, reputedly the oldest in England. A fleet of salmon seine boats lies here in the creek and during the season, (16 March – 16 August) the netsmen can be encountered anywhere in these upper reaches and should be given a wide berth if fishing.

BOW CREEK

The channel bears back to the western shore above Stoke Gabriel and, at the mouth of Bow Creek, passes between No 2 port hand and No 3 starboard hand buoys, turning sharply to the east and narrowing towards the tiny hamlet of Duncannon. Bow Creek is accessible for shallow draught boats a couple of hours either side of HW, so is probably best explored by dinghy.

A convenient anchorage is just under the northern shore by Langham Wood Point, or further into the creek, beyond the low promontory, where you will just ground on a muddy bottom at LW. The channel follows the north shore, where there is a starboard hand mark, then crosses to the south bank and is marked beyond the entrance by red port hand posts with square topmarks right up to the cluster of buildings at Tuckenhay. You are now as deep as you are likely to get by boat into the depths of rural Devon. The shoreline is of overhanging trees and rough pasture right to the water's edge where cattle graze and silently watch as you slip past over the brown, soupy water.

Tuckenhay is still a forgotten, sleepy place and today it seems amazing that in 1806 it was the ambition of Mr Abraham Tucker to develop it as a major port. His plan never came to much, but the gas house he built did put the village on the map as one of the first places in England to receive gas lighting, and for many years the nearby paper mill produced paper for banknotes. There was, when I first visited the creek, an ancient cider factory on the crumbling quayside, but developers of a different kind to Abraham Tucker have since moved in and converted the fine stone buildings into luxury homes. During the early 1990s the popular Maltsters Arms was owned by the ebullient TV gastronome Keith Floyd during which time, in his typically flamboyant style he changed the name to Floyd's Inn (sometimes)!

Two hours either side of HW, boats of moderate draught can moor alongside the quay adjacent to the pub, where it is possible to dry out with the owner's permission. As well as local ales, the Maltsters Arms specialises in fresh local produce, including salmon – reservations should be made for dinner (Tel: 732350) and it is advisable to phone ahead to book a berth if you intend to stay overnight. Basic provisions and water are available from the pub and its website: www.tuckenhay.com also contains detailed navigational information .

A pleasant half-mile walk along the tree lined lane leading towards the head of the creek will bring you to another friendly pub/restaurant, the Waterman's Arms (Tel: 732214).

Beyond Duncannon the river remains narrow and generally shallow on the inside of the bends. A large number of sizeable pleasure boats run regularly between Totnes and Dartmouth as the tide permits, and in these restricted waters passing can be tricky at times. They are plying their trade and you are there for fun, so pull in and let them pass – a courtesy they will greatly appreciate.

TOTNES

Leave No 4 buoy to port and keep close to the rocky east shore until the *Six Knot Speed Limit* sign is abeam. Then leave the beacon with red topmark to port to enter Ham Reach, where the shores are again steep and wooded. Keep can buoys Nos 5 and 7 to port and Nos 6 and 8 conical buoys to starboard, after which remain close to the west shore under Sharpham Woods, leaving the starboard hand beacon well to starboard as this is inshore of the edge of the bank.

Sharpham House, an impressive Georgian mansion standing high above the trees, was reputedly built with 365 panes of glass in its windows and has many other calendar inspired features. The 550 acre Sharpham Estate is now renowned for its vinyard, which extends over 11 acres and produces around 30,000 bottles of white wines from its *Madeleine Augevine* grape, which

has, to date, won the Best English Wine award five times. The vinyard also vinifies a red from Cabernet Sauvignon and Merlot grapes produced at the nearby Beenleigh Estate.

The Sharpham Creamery is another success story, producing a lucious Brie style cheese from the estate herd of Jersey cows. The vinyard is open to visitors throughout the season, Monday – Saturday 1030 – 1730 and tours, including a wine tasting session, are available at a moderate charge. Both the wine and cheese can be bought from the farm shop. It is possible to berth alongside Sharpham Quay for about two hours either side of HW. For further information call 732203.

Steer back to the eastern shore beyond Ham Point, leaving the next three can buoys Nos 9, 10 and 11 to port, and into Fleet Mill Reach, avoiding the saltings to port as the channel lies closer to the starboard bank past the remains of the old paddle steamer *Kingswear Castle* on the shore. Then edge back to the western side, passing near to the next port hand beacon before swinging back starboard, holding a course close to the rocky outcrop on your starboard hand. After this turn to port into Home Reach, where the buildings and distant tower of Totnes church will be in sight beyond the flat marshy fields and saltings.

The deeper water lies along the centre of the river for the next 200m, then closer to the stone wall to port, then back to the starboard bank until you reach Baltic Wharf, the 400m long former timber quay that is now the home of the Baltic Wharf Boatyard. It has an extensive area of hardstanding and undercover storage, can undertake all repairs and has a 16 ton hoist, a 10 ton crane and a large slipway. A chandler is also located on site. This quay can be used by visitors for overnight berthing by prior arrangement (Tel: 01803 867922) – here you will begin to dry out a couple of hours after HW in reasonably soft mud and it will cost £12.33 for a 10m boat. There are showers, toilets, water and electricity and very good 24 hour security in the boatyard.

Part of this long quayside is where Pete Goss and his *Goss Challenge* team built the massive but ill-fated *Team Phillips* catamaran. It was launched in March 2000 to worldwide media interest and named in London by the Queen. A catalogue of disasters dogged their attempt to enter *The Race* – the non-stop around the world challenge – culminating in December 2000 with abandonment in mid-Atlantic during sea trials due to steering failure during a severe storm.

Alternatively you can berth and dry out

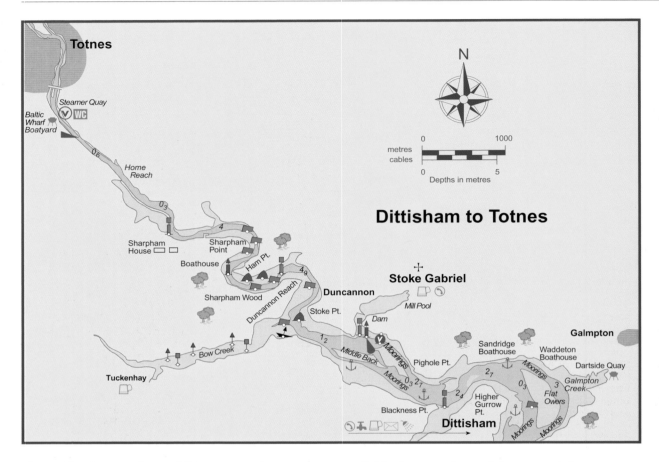

Totnes

Steamer Quay

Baltic
Wharf
Boatyard

0.6

Home
Reach

0.3

Sharpham
House

Sharpham
Point

Boathouse

Ham Pt.

4

Sharpham Wood

Duncannon Reach

4.9

Duncannon

Stoke Pt.

Bow Creek

Tuckenhay

Stoke Gabriel

Mill Pool

Dam

1.2

Middle Back

Moorings

Pighole Pt.

Moorings

0.3 2.7

2.7

2.4

Blackness Pt.

Higher
Gurrow
Pt.

Dittisham

Sandridge
Boathouse

Waddeton
Boathouse

Galmpton

Dartside Quay

Moorings

0.3

3

Galmpton
Creek

Flat
Owers

Moorings

Moorings

N

0   1000

metres
cables

0   5
Depths in metres

Dittisham to Totnes

alongside the wooden public quay on the opposite side of the river where South Hams council charges £0.50 per metre a night. Upstream, at Mill Tail, the river divides around Vire Island. The Steamer Quay to starboard is private and in constant use by pleasure boats, and beyond it the channel leading to the bridge is full of local moorings. The Totnes Boating Association has its clubhouse on the Steamer Quay and visitors are welcome when it is open at weekends. The port hand branch leads to the old Town Quay which is private and berthing is not allowed. The only other berths available for visitors are by the Steam Packet Inn (Tel: 863880) where there is about 20m of quayside by the pub garden with nearly 3m MHWS, and a clean, hard bottom to dry out on. Adjacent to the pub's children's play area there is a further 25m of quay with a muddier bottom.

On arrival, check with the pub that you are in a suitable spot. The Steam Packet has a restaurant as well as bar meals, and even provides breakfasts! No charge is made as long as you use its facilities. A slot metered electricity supply by the quay, a washing machine and dryer, as well as bathroom facilities and fresh water are all

available, but are charged for separately.

Totnes is a very attractive and unspoiled medieval town, rising up a steep main street to a hilltop surmounted by the remains of the Norman motte and bailey castle. It incorporates an Elizabethan museum, a 900 year old Guildhall and a Museum of Period costume – visit the Tourist Information Centre for full details. Interestingly, it has been the home to a number of famous writers over the years, including Mary Wesley, Desmond Bagley and Sean O'Casey.

Totnes has a bustling shopping centre, with all normal facilities available, including pubs, restaurants, bistros, banks, art galleries and it is renowned for secondhand bookshops. There are several supermarkets, including a large Safeway (open 0800 until late and from 1000 – 1600 on Sundays). Fuel is only available in containers from the local garage.

A busy outdoor market takes place on Fridays and Tuesday mornings throughout the summer. Be warned though – there is also a special charity market at which the locals dress in Elizabethan costumes, so don't be surprised when your shopkeeper emerges in ruff and pantaloons!

River Dart Port Guide
Area telephone code: 01803

Harbour Master: Captain Simon Dowden, Dart Harbour & Navigation Authority, 6 Oxford Street, Dartmouth TQ6 9AL (Tel: 832337 Fax: 833631). Mon–Fri 0900–1700, Sat&Sun 1000–1600
E-mail: hm@dartharbour.org.uk
Website: www.dartharbour.org.uk

VHF: Ch 16 and 11, call sign *Dart Nav*, office hours

Mail drop: Harbour office, Marinas, Royal Dart YC. Emergency services: Lifeboat at Brixham. Brixham Coastguard

Anchorages: Between large ship buoys and moorings on Kingswear side of river. Below Anchor Stone. Various possibilities upriver – call *Dart Nav*. Vessels must not be left unattended at anchor for any length of time

Moorings/berthing: Harbour Authority visitors' pontoons on Dartmouth waterfront, upstream of Kingswear and visitors' moorings off Dittisham and Stoke Gabriel. Check availability with River Officers. Berthing alongside the barge Res-Nova Inn.

Dinghy landings: At pontoons. Steps on embankment and low tide pontoon, all indicated by blue flags with black St Andrew's Cross

Water taxi: VHF Ch 69, call sign *Yacht Taxi* (Tel:07970 346571) 0800–23.00 daily during summer. VHF Ch 08 *Dartmouth Water Taxis* (Tel: 07770 628967). Dittisham, VHF Ch 10, *Greenway Ferry*

Marinas: Dart Marina, Sandquay, Dartmouth (Tel: 833351 website: www.dartmarina.com) Visitors' berths usually available.VHF Ch 80, call sign *Dart Marina*. Darthaven Marina, Kingswear (Tel: 752545, website: www.darthaven.co.uk), visitors' berths usually available. VHF Ch 80, call sign *Darthaven Marina*. Noss-on-Dart Marina, (Tel: 833351), visitors' berths, call sign *Noss Marina*

Charges: Harbour dues £0.50 per metre per day payable throughout river to Totnes. Charge for 10m boat alongside from £12.50 to £15 per day. £10 per day on pontoon island or visitor mooring; £5 per day at anchor. Dart Marina £3.17 per metre per night plus harbour dues. Darthaven Marina £1.99 per metre per night plus harbour dues. Noss-on-Dart Marina £2.23 per metre per night plus harbour dues. Dart Marina River mooring £1.40 per metre plus harbour dues. Baltic Wharf 10m boat drying alongside £12.33

Phones: By Boatfloat, opposite the Butterwalk. At Marinas, Yacht Clubs, Harbour Office

Doctor: Tel: 832212

Dentist: Tel: 835418

Hospital: Dartmouth (Tel: 832255) Casualties only

Churches: All denominations

Local Weather Forecast: At Harbour Office and marinas

Fuel: Diesel and petrol from *Dart Crusader* VHF Ch 06, 0900–1700. Diesel only from Dart Marina 0800–1800

Gas: Calor and Gaz, Darthaven Marina. Dart Marina, and Noss-on-Dart Marina.Gaz only, Battarbees Ltd, Lower Street (Tel: 832272)

Water: Taps on embankment, at all marinas. Tap at Dittisham, in front of Ferry Boat Inn. Public tap on slipway at Stoke Gabriel. At Steam Packet Inn, Totnes, charged by quantity

Tourist Information Centre: Adjoining Newcomen Engine House in park behind Embankment, (Tel: 834224)

Banks/cashpoints: HSBC, Lloyds TSB and Natwest have cashpoints. No Barclays

Post Office: In Plymco supermarket, Mayors Avenue

Rubbish: Dispose in bins marked *Yacht Waste* on DHNA facilities and at Marinas. Floating skip off Dittisham. Harbour Authority will dispose of pyrotechnics, and other toxic waste including batteries by arrangement – a charge will normally be made for this service

Showers/toilets: Available at Royal Dart YC. Dartmouth YC. Dart Marina, Darthaven Marina and Noss-on-Dart Marina. Res-nova Inn. Free showers in public toilets on Dartmouth Embankment and the 'Ham' Dittisham

Launderette: Dartmouth Launderette, Market Street. Launderettes at all marinas

Provisions: Everything available. Plymco supermarket in Mayors Avenue open 0800–2200 weekdays, 1000–1700 Sunday, Somerfield supermarket in centre of town, 0800–1800, 1000–1600 Sunday

Chandlers: Shipmates, Newcomen Road (Tel: 839292). Batarbees (Tel: 832272). Dartmouth Boating Centre, clothing, (Tel: 832093). Dartmouth Dock Services (Tel: 832776) Darthaven Chandlery, Kingswear (Tel: 752733). DMS Chandlers, Noss-on-Dart Marina (Tel: 833772). Baltic Wharf Chandlery (Tel: 867362). The Harbour Bookshop, Fairfax Place, Dartmouth has wide range of nautical books (Tel: 832448)

Repairs: Darthaven Marina, Kingswear (Tel: 752545). Philip & Son Ltd, Noss Works (Tel: 833351). Creekside Boatyard, Old Mill Creek (Tel: 832649). Dartside Quay, Galmpton, Churston (Tel:

845445). Dolphin Shipyard, Galmpton, Churston (Tel: 01803 842424). Baltic Wharf Boatyard, Totnes (Tel: 01803 867922)

Marine engineers: Darthaven Services 24 hour 7 day emergency call out (Tel: 07973 280584).Riverside Marine Engineering (Tel: 835166). Marine Engineering Looe (Tel: 844777) Tonto Marine Services (Tel: 844399). Ask at marinas, or contact boatyards – see above

Electronic engineers: AK Marine Electronics (Tel: 833300). Darthaven Services 24 hour 7 day emergency call out in season (Tel: 07767 250787) or ask at marinas

Sailmakers: Calibra Rigging & Sails (Tel: 833094). Dart Sails (Tel:832185)

Riggers: Calibra (Tel: 833094). Atlantic Spars (sparmakers) (Tel: 843322). Harris Rigging (Tel: 840160)

Divers: Millennium Marine (Tel: 856060)

Taxi: Kestrel (Tel: 0800 317858)

Car Hire: None

Bus/train connections: Main line rail station at Totnes (Tel: 08457 484950) with Western National No 89 bus connections (Tel: 01752 402060). Also regular River Link ferries (Tel: 834488) to Totnes Steamer Quay in season when tide permits but a good 10 minutes walk to station – best to pre-arrange taxi in Totnes (Tel: 866772). Paignton and Dartmouth Steam Railway, Kingswear, (Tel: 555872) connections from Paignton to main rail line at Newton Abbot

Car parking: Off Mayors Avenue behind embankment

Yacht clubs: Royal Dart Yacht Club, Kingswear TQ6 OAB (Tel: 752272, website: www.royaldart.co.uk). Dartmouth Yacht Club, South Embankment, Dartmouth TQ6 9BB (Tel: 832305, website: www.dartmouth-yacht-club.org.uk)

Eating out: Very good selection of restaurants and pubs

Things to do: Dartmouth Borough Museum, Butterwalk. Newcomen Engine House, Mayors Avenue. Dartmouth Castle/St Petrox Church. Friday Market. Steam Railway. Guided tours of Royal Naval College. Good walks on both sides of harbour entrance and river

Regatta/special events: The Port of Dartmouth Royal Regatta, three days at end of August. South Western Area Old Gaffers Race around end of July. Dartmouth Music Festival, May

PASSAGES
START POINT TO RAME HEAD

Favourable tidal streams

Start Point:
Bound West: One hour before HW Dover
Bound East: Five hours after HW Dover

Rame Head:
Bound West: Two hours before HW Dover
Bound East: Four hours after HW Dover

Passage charts for this sea area

BA: 1613 Eddystone Rocks to Berry Head
1634 Berry Head to Bolt Head
SC5602

Imray: C6 Start Point to Lizard Point.
WCP 2400.8 Start Point to Fowey

Stanford: 13 Start Point to Trevose Head

French: 4812 Du Cap Lizard à Start Point

Safety information and weather

Brixham Coastguard: Initial announcement on
VHF Channel 16, then switch to VHF Channel 10
(west of Start Point), Channel 84 (in Salcombe) at
0050, 0450, 0850, 1250, 1650, 2050 UT

Prawle Point NCI station (Tel: 01548 511259)

Rame Head NCI station (Tel: 01752 823706)

Waypoints

1   **Start Point** (2M SE of lighthouse)
    50°11'·92N / 03°36'·34W

2   **Prawle Point** (0.5M due south of headland)
    50°11'·61N / 03°43'·22W

3   **Salcombe approach**
    (4ca SE Bolt Head in W sector)
    50°12'·35N / 03°46'·67W

4   **Bolt Tail** (1M south of headland)
    50°13'·20N / 03°52'·22W

5   **Hillsea Point**
    (7ca due south of headland)
    50°16'·96N / 04°03'·05W

6   **Yealm approach**
    (6ca SE of Gt Mewstone SE shore)
    50°17'·97N / 04°05'·65W

7   **Great Mewstone**
    (6ca SW of island summit)
    50°18'·01N / 04°07'·08W

8   **Rame Head** (1M south of summit)
    50°17'·84N / 04°13'·39W

9   **Eddystone** (1M north of lighthouse)
    50°12'·35N / 04°15'·92W

Start Point from the south

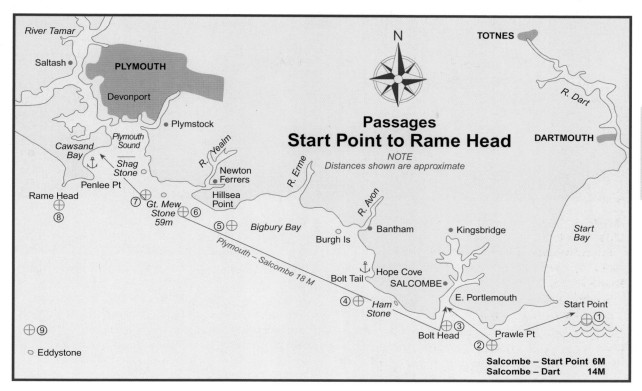

With some romanticism, Frank Carr summed it up very well. . .'West of the Start one begins to have the feeling that one is at last getting to deep seas and blue water; and although the mouth of the Channel is no more from Ushant to Scilly than thirty-nine leagues, it is quite wide enough and deep enough for small craft to be able to be caught out pretty badly . . .'

After the gentle, protected sweep of Start Bay, the rock fringed coast beyond Start Point can often feel exposed and almost inhospitable which, in poor weather, it most certainly is. Here, Devon projects its southernmost point far into the English Channel, prey to the weather and the full strength of the tidal streams. This combined assault on the coastline is clearly reflected as you move further west to the high cliffs between Bolt Head and Bolt Tail.

START POINT TO SALCOMBE

In the prevailing south-westerlies a long ground swell and much larger seas will be encountered once clear of Start Point. Carrying a fair tide westwards, the odds are certainly in favour of the wind being against it, and this can worsen wind and sea conditions.

Salcombe, six miles west of Start Point, is the most likely destination for cruising boats from Dartmouth. It is a particularly unspoiled estuary with excellent facilities for yachts, but does, however, have a bar which is extremely dangerous in strong southerly weather and certain combinations of ground swell and ebb tide. With a least depth of 1m LAT (1.3m on leading line), it is always best to cross after half flood.

Plymouth, the next real port of refuge, is accessible in all weather and lies almost 25 miles west of Start Point. These factors should be considered before setting out from the Dart or making a landfall on the South Devon coast.

However, in fair weather, Salcombe presents no problem. Ideally, leave Dartmouth towards local LW which will bring you to the Start with the main ebb running westwards. By the time you reach Salcombe the local inshore flood should ensure ample water over the bar.

Assuming that you pass over a mile to seaward of the Start to avoid the race, your course will take you well clear of any inshore dangers such as the isolated Blackstone and Cherrick rocks, and the Sleaden rocks, which extend about 400m south of Peartree Point. In calm weather, it is possible to pass much closer inshore, where the tidal streams turn approximately half an hour earlier, but attain considerably greater strength – up to four knots at springs. For this reason the

Heading west from the Start, Prawle Point with Bolt Head just showing in the distance

fisherman's passage inside the Blackstone is not recommended.

Beyond Start Point the coast is lined by low cliffs, ledges and small rocky bays backed with steep, higher land, a mixture of fields and heathland, with extensive gorse and ferns and just a few isolated houses. There are no dangers more than three cables offshore, but the large numbers of pot buoys can turn the passage into a slalom at times and a sharp lookout is essential.

Prawle Point, three miles west, is not particularly spectacular. There is a conspicuous terrace of old coastguard cottages immediately east of the Point which features a prominent NCI lookout on its flat, grassy top, with cliffs falling away to a rocky outcrop forming a natural arch when viewed from the west. As you pass the point, the rusting remains at the foot of the cliffs are of the Greek-registered *Demetrios*, wrecked here in December 1992 while on tow to the breakers. Just to the north, in offshore winds, Elender Cove is an attractive daytime anchorage,

The approach to Salcombe from the east is dominated by the distinctive bulk of Bolt Head

popular with local boats with a fine expanse of low tide sand.

In contrast to Prawle, Bolt Head is a dramatic sight as it emerges in the distance, over 100m high, and steep-to with distinctive jagged rocky ridges and pinnacles. The tide runs at up to two knots at springs and can kick up another small race off Prawle Point, which can be uncomfortable at times, so it is best to keep a good half mile offshore.

Salcombe lies at the head of the bay formed between Prawle Point and Bolt Head, and a course should be held towards the western side before turning north towards the entrance, which is not easy to spot from a distance. At night, Start Point light is obscured north of a line extending from the Start through Prawle Point; keep the light open across the bay until the leading light into Salcombe is located before turning north.

BOLT HEAD TO BOLT TAIL

Off Bolt Head are two isolated rocks, the Mewstone (19m) and the Little Mewstone (5m), close to the shore. Overfalls extend to seaward in their vicinity and this can often be an uncomfortable corner. For the next four miles the high, dramatic cliffs between Bolt Head and Bolt Tail have a particularly rugged and rather grim appearance – an uncompromising lee shore - which should ideally be given a good offing to avoid the dangers and the severe squalls that the high cliffs can generate: a phenomenon described with suitable drama by Hilaire Belloc in his *Cruise of the Nona*.

'As for the spill off Bolt Head, it fell after a clear midnight. . . and it was more than a spill; for it blew for the best part of an hour then ceased. But like its brother off Beachy, it was peculiar to the high land, for it came due northerly whereas the main wind had east in it. I was watching the morning star burning like a sacred furnace on the edges of the black hills when Satan sent that wind and tried to drown three men. But we reefed in time – there were three of us, one for the helm and two to reef; and when dawn broke, and the blessed colours of the east renewed the day, strange! – one end of the boom had three reefs down, and the other only two!'

The main hazards are the Gregory Rocks (least depth just under 2m) half a mile south-east of the Ham Stone, which is an isolated rock (11m) off Soar Mill Cove, where a grassy valley runs down to the only major break in the line of the high cliffs.

This rock is infamous for sinking one of the last great Finnish grain barques, *Herzogin Cecilie*, when she went ashore in thick fog on 25th April 1936. After seven weeks, the vessel was refloated and towed to Starehole Bay, at the entrance to Salcombe, as her rotting and fermenting cargo was unwelcome in the harbour. It proved to be her final resting place, for soon afterwards a summer gale from the south-east broke her back, and her remains can still be seen dimly today.

The *Herzogin Cecilie* was wrecked without loss of life; but in contrast the disaster of *HMS Ramillies* in 1760 was catastrophic. A 74-gun ship of the line, set to the east before a severe south-westerly, she mistook Bolt Tail for Rame Head, and realised her mistake too late when steep cliffs, rather than the entrance to Plymouth appeared through the murk. Unable to claw off the lee shore, she anchored, but eventually drove ashore. Only 26 survived from her complement of 734.

Tucked behind Bolt Tail, right, Hope Cove is a feasible anchorage in easterly winds

Few ships have held out once ashore on this particular stretch of coast; it has an uncomfortable feel about it and I, for one, invariably feel a certain relief once it is safely astern.

The cliffs remain steep right to Bolt Tail, and west of Soar Mill Cove there is a group of three tall radio masts (50m), and then two radio towers (25m) on the grassy plateau along the clifftop. The final hazard just east of Bolt Tail is Greystone Ledge (1.8m), extending a quarter of a mile to seawards. At Bolt Tail, a precipitous cliff with an isolated rock at its foot, the coast falls suddenly back into Bigbury Bay. The cliffs are steep-to and, if followed 200m offshore, the small village and harbour of Hope Cove will appear tucked snugly behind Bolt Tail where it is possible, in offshore winds in settled weather, to anchor in the centre of the bay.

Naval vessels regularly exercise in the area to the south and south-west of Bolt Tail, 5.4M south-west of which two yellow Naval Gunfire Support buoys are located – NGS East (FL Y 10s) at 50°11′·23N, 03°59′·06W, NGS West (Fl Y 5s) at 50°11′·13N, 04°00′·86W. Details of Naval Activity in the area – Subfacts and Gunfacts – are promulgated through the regular Coastguard MSI broadcasts or can be obtained from Naval Ops Plymouth (Tel: 01752 557550).

BIGBURY BAY

From Bolt Tail the Devon coastline bears away to the north-west, and the seven mile indentation of Bigbury Bay is usually passed by most cruising boats, as it lies inside the direct course for the Yealm or Plymouth. Although normally a lee shore, in easterly or northerly weather it can be

further explored by visiting the seldom frequented rivers of the Avon and Erme.

About a third of the way across the Bay, off the holiday resort of Bigbury-on-Sea, is the distinctive hump of Burgh Island which lies just to the west of the hidden entrance to the drying River Avon, bounded on the east by the beach and sand dunes, along with a line of low rock strewn cliffs below the golf course at Thurlestone Links. Further east, isolated Thurlestone rock (10m) is a conspicuous feature, rather like a large boat aground on the beach. Only accessible near HW in favourable conditions to boats of shallow draught, the Avon is a particularly beautiful small river where those able to dry out will find good shelter once inside. There is a temporary anchorage to the east of Burgh Island if waiting for the tide.

The River Erme, three miles to the north-west, although attractive, is very open and only really feasible as a daytime anchorage. Wells Rock and several other shoal patches extend a mile south of Erme Head, the eastern side of the river mouth. Within Bigbury Bay the tidal streams are considerably weaker, attaining a maximum of one knot at springs on the flood, which rotates in an easterly direction, beginning HW Dover +0415. The weaker ebb runs to the WNW, beginning HW Dover –0200.

Closing the western shore, Hillsea Point, rounded and grassy with low cliffs, has an old coastguard lookout and flagstaff just to the east. Hillsea Rocks and shallow patches lie up to mile offshore. Do not close the land if bound for the Yealm, but hold a course off the shore towards the Great Mewstone, an unmistakeably large pyramid shaped island, until the marks into Wembury Bay can be located, leading into the well-hidden delights of the River Yealm. One of the classic West Country havens, this is popular and inevitably crowded in season.

Plymouth approach − Great Mewstone and Rame Head far left

RIVER YEALM AND APPROACHES TO PLYMOUTH

Dominating Wembury Bay, the Great Mewstone (59m) is an impressive lump of rock, with sparse sea turf and ferns on the steep slopes that are now just the haunt of the sea birds that give it its name. At one time it was inhabited and the ruin on the eastern side, a single storey circular stone building with an unusual conical roof, was possibly built with the remains of a small medieval chapel that is recorded as being sited there. The last known inhabitants of the Mewstone were Sam Wakeham and his wife in the 1820s. It was their rent-free domicile in return for protecting the island's rabbits during the off-season for the Calmady family. Today, the island is owned by the Ministry of Defence, is a wildlife conservation area and being the subject of a special study it is closed to the public.

Shoals extend nearly a mile south-west and east from the Mewstone, and the passage between it and the mainland is rock strewn. Beyond it, the huge bay enclosing the naval and commercial port of Plymouth opens to the north. With the exception of the Shagstone, an isolated rock on the eastern shore marked with an unlit beacon, there are no hazards for small craft, and deep water is carried right into Plymouth Sound. The large outer harbour is enclosed by a central breakwater, with entrance to its east and west.

Tidal streams in the approaches to Plymouth are complicated by a clockwise rotation – at the eastern entrance the main flood commences half an hour after HW Dover, the ebb at HW Dover –0530. Streams in the entrances attain just over a knot at springs but they can be considerably greater in the Narrows within the harbour.

The approach to Plymouth is easy at night. It is well lit, with plenty of water, and the only real problem is likely to be distinguishing the navigation lights from the huge mass of the city lights. Care should be taken to keep a careful watch on other shipping, as the harbour and approaches are invariably busy.

Penlee Point on the western side of Plymouth Sound is a wooded and rocky headland with white buildings low down on the point. Shoals extend two cables to the south-east, and are marked by the Draystone red can (Fl (2) R 5s). A mile and a half to the west, Rame Head, the western extremity of Plymouth Sound, is a distinctive cone shape, its grassy slopes climbing to the conspicuous ruins of a chapel on the summit where there is also a NCI Lookout. The

The Eddystone lighthouse is surrounded by an impressive display of jagged rocks

shore is steep-to, and can be approached to within two cables, although rocks extend from the western side, and in conditions of wind against tide overfalls will be encountered for about half a mile south of the headland.

In good visibility, eight miles south of Rame Head, the thin pencil of the Eddystone lighthouse rises incongruously from the sea. A lurking nightmare for ships running into Plymouth, a light on this curious isolated reef was first established in 1698 by an aggrieved shipowner, Henry Winstanley, who had lost two vessels. His distinctly Heath Robinson structure, somewhat akin to a Chinese pagoda, survived a mere five years before it was washed away, taking by chance the luckless Winstanley and some workmen with it. In 1709 John Rudyerd erected a wooden lighthouse with considerably more success, but this was destroyed by fire, not water, after 47 years.

Four years later, John Smeaton's fine granite column began a vigil that was to last for 120 years, his design setting the pattern for many others, and were it not for the rocks crumbling beneath it, it would probably still stand there today. Instead, when the present lighthouse designed by Sir J N Douglass replaced it in 1882, Smeaton's dismantled tower was re-erected on Plymouth Hoe.

Just awash at HWS, the rocks extend in a radius of about three cables around the lighthouse which is a grey tower with a helicopter pad. The major light in this section of coast, it has a 17 mile range, (Fl(2) 10s 17M & Iso R 10s 8M)), the red sector (110.5° – 130.5°T) covers the paradoxically named

Hand Deeps – in reality a shoal with least depths of 7m – three miles north-west of the Eddystone. Hand Deeps, which breaks heavily in bad weather, and the Eddystone, are both very popular with sea anglers and in fine weather there are invariably a number of boats in the vicinity.

This passage area is not easy in fog. There are few aids and, although most of the dangers lie inshore of the 10m line, particular care should be taken to avoid being set into Bigbury Bay, the hazards approaching Yealm Head and the Great Mewstone and surrounding rocks. It is generally the best policy to maintain a good offing. The only sound signals are at Start Point (Horn 60s), the Eddystone (Horn (1) 30s) and Plymouth West Breakwater end (Bell (1) 15s). As an alternative to feeling your way into Plymouth, where the shipping movements continue in spite of fog, the anchorage in Cawsand Bay on the western side of the approaches is of easy access and well worth consideration in suitable weather.

Cawsand Bay is a popular anchorage in the western approach to Plymouth

SALCOMBE

Tides	HW Dover −0535
Range	MHWS 5.3m–MHWN 4.1m, MLWN 2.1m–MLWS 0.7m. Spring ebb attains up to three knots off town
Charts	BA: 28 and SC5602.10. Stanford: CP 22, L14. Imray: WCP2400.5
Waypoints	Wolf Rock Buoy 50°13'·53N / 03°46'·58W
Hazards	Bar dangerous in strong southerly weather and ebb tide. Bass Rock (lit) Wolf Rock (lit) Blackstone (lit) and Poundstone (unlit). Very crowded in season and cruising yachts are not permitted to sail within harbour during July and August. Large part of upper reaches dry
Overnight charge	Harbour Authority mooring £14.50. At anchor £7.25

Salcombe harbour looking towards Batson – the bulk of the visitors' moorings can be seen along the main channel and the Normandy short stay pontoon lies below the church tower

'Sunset and evening star, And one clear call for me! And may there be no moaning of the bar, When I put out to sea . . .'

So begins Tennyson's famous *Crossing of the Bar* inspired by the sound of the breaking sea upon Salcombe Bar during a stay in the harbour as a guest aboard Lord Brassey's yacht *Sunbeam* in 1889. Even then this was a popular if somewhat exclusive haunt of the wealthy, who were attracted by the romantic beauty and the mild almost Mediterranean climate.

That has changed little, and today Salcombe is one of the most popular cruising stopovers in the West Country, attracting over 10,000 visiting boats a year. Tucked away from the main tourist track through Devon, the small town has managed to resist most attempts to over-develop the area, relying totally on its natural attractions. There are several smart hotels, but a limited amount of accommodation ashore, and no amusement arcades or similar diversions to pull in the masses. Apart from the small fleet of 15 or so fishing boats, mostly crabbers, and the Kingsbridge ferry, there is no commercial traffic within the river and it is totally committed to pleasure boating in all its forms.

As harbours go, Salcombe is super-efficient, managing the ever increasingly large numbers of visitors with a polite but necessary authority. At times such as during the regatta weeks at the beginning of August – a tradition dating back to 1857 – the numbers have to be seen to be believed.

During the busiest months of July and August for safety reasons cruising yachts are not permitted to sail within the harbour and power boats will always find the speed limit of eight knots strictly enforced.

The estuary is a classic ria (a valley drowned as water levels rose after the ice ages) and is something of an anomaly as there is no Salcombe River flowing into it, merely a number of small streams that emerge from the eight large creeks that stretch inland into the attractive and rolling hinterland of Devon's South Hams.

This large area of inland saltwater is an important natural habitat and was made a Site of Special Scientific Interest (SSSI) in 1987. Navigable for four miles to Kingsbridge, a large area of the upper reaches dries, but within the lower half of the estuary there is plenty of deep water, some memorable scenery and a number of superb clean sandy beaches.

Salcombe never developed as a major port, partly because of it remote position right at southernmost tip of Devon, but also because of the shallow bar at the entrance. This becomes very dangerous with strong onshore winds or swell and an ebbing tide, when an approach should never be attempted.

Attractive and very popular, the Salcombe estuary stretches inland to distant Kingsbridge, top left. Limebury Point and Sunny Cove on right, South Sands, left

APPROACHES

The approach is memorable, the dramatic profile of Bolt Head forming a succession of jagged pinnacles and gullies rising 100m to a flat grassy top. If arriving from the east, keep a good half mile off the shore to avoid the Chapple Rocks, least depth 2.7m, and close the steep western shore to within a cable of the Eelstone, before turning northwards. However, be ready for very strong gusts and fluky winds beneath the cliffs. From the west, the Great Mewstone (19m) and Little Mewstone (5m) are large prominent rocks several cables to the south of Bolt Head. They can be passed within a cable and the harbour will then begin to open.

The Bar (least depth 1m) extends in a south-westerly direction from the rounded fern-covered Limebury Point, footed with low sloping cliffs on the eastern shore. A leading line, (000°T, least depth 1.3m) is formed by the beacon on the Poundstone (a red and white striped pole with red topmark) and another beacon elevated behind it on Sandhill Point (white with a horizontally striped red and white diamond topmark). The latter displays a directional flashing light (RWG 2s) and its white sector (357°–002°T) indicates the leading line. It is perhaps easier to enter at night, as in daytime the beacons are not easy to spot.

From a distance Sandhill Point appears as an evenly rounded hill, its wooded slopes dotted with detached houses. Prominent in the centre is a large red brick house with two white dormer windows in the roof and ivy covered gables at each end – the beacons lie exactly below the left hand gable.

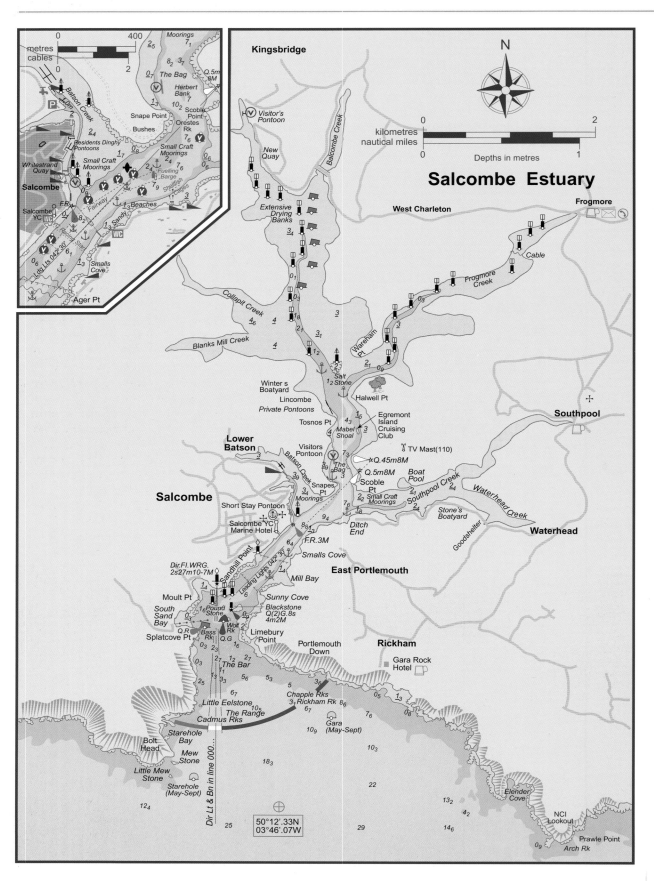

Salcombe Estuary

Kingsbridge

West Charleton

Frogmore

Southpool

Waterhead

Balcombe Creek

Frogmore Creek

Cable

New Quay

Visitor's Pontoon

Extensive Drying Banks

Collapit Creek

Blanks Mill Creek

Wareham Pt

Salt Stone

Halwell Pt

Winters Boatyard

Lincombe
Private Pontoons

Tosnos Pt

Mabel Shoal

Egremont Island Cruising Club

TV Mast(110)

Q.45m8M

Q.5m8M

Boat Pool

Lower Batson

Batson Creek

Visitors Pontoon

The Bag

Scoble Pt

Small Craft Moorings

Southpool Creek

Waterhead Creek

Stone's Boatyard

Goodshelter

Snapes Pt

Moorings

Salcombe

Short Stay Pontoon

Salcombe YC
Marine Hotel

Ditch End

F.R.3M

Sandhill Point

Leading Lights 042°30'

Smalls Cove

East Portlemouth

Dir.Fl.WRG.
2s27m10-7M

Mill Bay

Moult Pt

Sunny Cove

Blackstone Q(2)G.8s 4m2M

South Sand Bay

Pound Stone

Wolf Rk

Limebury Point

Rickham

Portlemouth Down

Gara Rock Hotel

Q.R

Bass Rk

Q.G

Splatcove Pt

The Bar

Chapple Rks

Rickham Rk

Little Eelstone

The Range

Cadmus Rks

Gara (May-Sept)

Bolt Head

Starehole Bay

Mew Stone

Dir Lt & Bn in line 000...

Little Mew Stone

Starehole (May-Sept)

Elender Cove

NCI Lookout

50°12'.33N
03°46'.07W

Prawle Point
Arch Rk

N

0   kilometres   2
nautical miles
0   Depths in metres   1

Inset (top left):

metres   0   400
cables
0   2

Moorings

The Bag

Q.5m 8M

Herbert Bank

Scoble Point
Orestes Rk

Snape Point
Bushes

Batson Creek

P

Residents Dinghy Pontoons

Small Craft Moorings

Small Craft Moorings

Fuelling Barge

Shellfish Cages

Whitestrand Quay

Salcombe

Salcombe YC
WC

F.R.

Fairway

Beaches

Sandy

WC

Ldg Lts 042°30'

Smalls Cove

Ager Pt

Salcombe approach – the leading marks

red and white beacons on the western shore off the remains of Fort Charles. At night, a pair of quick flashing (Q) leading lights situated just west of Scoble Point give a transit of 042°T that will take you up the centre of the harbour in clear water (least depth 5m) right to the town.

ANCHORAGES AND MOORINGS

In settled weather you will find a pleasant and popular daytime anchorage with a little under 2m at LW just north-east of the Blackstone off the sandy beach at Sunny Cove.

Because of underwater cables, anchoring is prohibited anywhere off the next inlet at Mill Bay.

The adjacent sandy cove on the starboard shore, Smalls Cove, is also a popular spot, along with Fisherman's Cove just upstream of the Portlemouth ferry. Sound in to the edge of the beach where there is about 2m at LW. All have clean sand with safe swimming.

On the opposite side of the channel, the first of the pink or yellow visitors' moorings, clearly marked *visitor*, lie off the prominent Marine Hotel. In season it is likely that one of the four harbour patrols will meet you in the vicinity and allocate a berth if you have not already contacted them on VHF Ch 14. Due to the popularity of Salcombe, during the height of the season you will invariably have to raft up. The overnight charge is £1.45 per metre or £0.75 per metre to anchor.

Just upstream of the Marine Hotel, Salcombe Yacht Club enjoys a commanding view of the estuary from Cliff House on the hillside, a large red brick building with a tower, veranda and

The depths are actually better just west of the leading line, with over 2m close to the rocky shore. Normally, in offshore winds, preferably after half flood with minimal ground swell, Salcombe Bar will present no problems, but if you have any misgivings, and particularly if you can see any breaking seas, call *Salcombe Harbour* (VHF Ch 14) for advice before you attempt to enter.

Once over the Bar, the red can Bass Rock buoy (QR) marks this 0.8m drying rock off Splat Point; steer up to leave the conical green Wolf Rock buoy (QG) close on your starboard hand. Wolf Rock dries 0.1m and only shows on the lowest of tides, but beyond it the Blackstone, which dries 5m, is nearly always visible. The extensive rocky shoal around its base is marked by a green and white beacon on its western extremity (Q(2) G 8s), and the channel lies between this and the line of

There is a popular anchorage off the enticingly named Sunny Cove

Approaching the short stay visitors' pontoon, with the floating rubbish skip on right

terrace. The Club was founded in 1894 and a warm welcome is extended to visiting yachts and their crews, with showers, bar and meals all available. Its starting line and dinghy landing with running mooring are on the waterfront below the club, where a line of small orange buoys run parallel to the shore, marking a fairway that must be used when races are starting as the centre of the river gets very congested.

The Ferry Inn, beside the ferry steps, has a beer garden and bars overlooking the harbour and is a popular spot for the pundits to gather and watch everyone else's mistakes from behind the safety of a pint!

Beyond the ferry, Batson Creek bears away to port, much of it drying but there is a clearly marked channel (G/W and R/W poles with topmarks) dredged to 1m. A floating rubbish skip is moored on the north side of the channel entrance. The channel leads to the *Normandy* short stay visitors' pontoon (least depth 1m), which is linked to the shore by a bridge onto Whitestrand Quay where the harbour office is located. Vessels over 12.2m (40ft) and 2m draught should first check access with the harbour patrol. This convenient daytime facility is for stays of up to half-an-hour only, for shopping or topping up water and must not be used overnight between 1900 and 0700. Tenders from visiting boats can be left on the inside of this pontoon providing they are marked with the parent craft's name. Beyond Whitestrand, the dredged channel continues along the creek to an all-tide small craft launching slip at Batson.

The main fairway, which must be kept clear, runs up the centre of the harbour. Most of the visitors' moorings are along both sides, and anchoring is not possible on the Salcombe side of the channel because of the large number of local moorings. By far the best spot is opposite, off **East Portlemouth**'s sandy beach, well upstream of the ferry towards Ditch End along the edge of the bank which drops off steeply. For this reason, and as the tide can run fast, don't skimp on the cable. Many a relaxed drink at the Ferry Inn has terminated prematurely with the sight of one's boat dragging resolutely to seaward!

SALCOMBE

Salcombe was not always the smart, respectable town that it is today. In 1607 the harbour was a much busier place and the justices reported that the town was 'full of dissolute seafaring men, who murdered each other and buried the corpses in the sands at night'.

The forlorn remains of Fort Charles at the harbour mouth date from the mid 1600s. The last garrison in England to hold out for Charles I, it endured six rather uncomfortable months while the Roundheads bombarded it from the Portlemouth shore.

As a commercial port, its heyday was in the mid-1880s when a large number of schooners were built to engage in the salt cod trade with Newfoundland and Labrador, many launched from the famous yard of William Date in Kingsbridge. After buying the fish, these small British vessels crossed the Atlantic to sell their cargoes in Spain, Portugal and the Mediterranean

Another popular anchorage can be found off East Portlemouth's sandy beach

A lone Salcombe yawl wends her way between the visitors' moorings – you will always have to raft during the height of the season!

and through this a new trade developed bringing citrus and soft fruit to England. Speed was of the essence for this financially precarious activity, and it produced a small but extremely fast type of schooner that was able to set large amounts of sail. They were typical of the ports of South Devon and of Salcombe in particular.

By the beginning of this century the port had lapsed into total decline and it was then that its new popularity as a select holiday resort was established. However, apart from the bombardment of Fort Charles, undoubtedly the most dramatic event to engulf the town was the arrival in 1943 of 137 officers and 1,793 men of the US Naval Construction Battalion in preparation for the D-Day landings. The old Salcombe Hotel and many other properties were

requisitioned, several rows of old cottages were bulldozed to make a loading ramp which has since become Whitestrand, and the large concrete slipway was built in Mill Bay. An impressive fleet of landing craft was assembled in the estuary and practice landings carried out on nearby Slapton Ley. On 4th June 1944, 66 vessels sailed from Salcombe. For the small town its invasion had ended, and in Europe, it was about to begin.

FACILITIES

Nowadays, the invasion is annual, and although not quite as swamped with visitors as some of the West Country's main holiday resorts, it is probably a good guess that in Salcombe's case 90 per cent of the people walking the narrow streets in mid-summer are doing something with some kind of boat. The town is compact and rather chic – really just one main shopping street where most normal requirements can be obtained. Cranch's Pantry in Fore Street has a good selection of groceries, and there is an excellent fishmonger. Coleman's Butchers can provide ice, as well as the obvious! Banks consist of Lloyd's TSB and HSBC, both with cashpoints, although the HSBC branch is only open 1030 – 1500 Mondays, Wednesdays and Fridays.

The varied choice of places to eat includes pizza at Captain Flint's – a great favourite with children, Dusters Bistro (Tel: 842634), which has live jazz on Sundays, or Regans (Tel: 844534) for seafood. Ever popular are the Galley (Tel: 842828) in Fore Street and Restaurant 42 (Tel: 843408), with great views of the harbour, while Boatswain's Brasserie (Tel: 842189) is tucked away in Russell Court. There are, predictably, a good number of pubs, all of which do meals and bar snacks.

During the season (end of May to mid-September), diesel and petrol are easily obtained from the fuel barge (open daily 0900 – 1800) moored off the entrance to Southpool Creek, opposite the town (VHF Ch 06, call sign *Fuel Barge* (Tel: 07801 798862 or 844261). Water taps can be found at the Normandy short stay visitors' pontoon.

Do not miss the fascinating Maritime and Local History Museum, located beneath the Tourist Information Centre, and the excellent Lifeboat House Museum on the waterfront. There is public internet access at the local library in Cliff House, should you wish to surf or check your e-mail, and no visit is complete without a taste of the local Salcombe Dairy ice cream. Such

Chapter 2

is its pedigree it is even sold at Sadlers Wells!

From a family point of view the attraction of Salcombe has to be the number of beaches. South Sands, at the entrance, is one of the safest and can be reached by a regular ferry. From here the signposted walk up through the woods brings you to the Overbecks Museum of natural history and curiosities and Sharpitor Gardens, boasting many exotic plants normally only grown under glass – such as banana, fig and lemon trees.

It is also worth walking on a little further to the spectacular viewpoint at Sharpitor and then on to Bolt Head.

If the tide is very, very low, you might just glimpse the ghostly outline of the ill-fated barque, *Herzogin Cecilie*, in her last resting place far below in Starehole Bay. This is all National Trust land and if you're feeling particularly energetic the fine elevated coastal path will take you all the way to Bolt Tail.

'For beauty and romantic walks', wrote Cowper 'especially along Sharpitor to Bolt Head, I think it beats every other place on the South Coast.'

As well as the beaches on the opposite side of the estuary, which are all easily reached by dinghy or the ferry, there are also good walks eastwards along the coast towards Start Point. A particularly pleasant round trip can be enjoyed by following the coastal footpath from Mill Bay out past Limebury Point and towards Prawle Point before turning inland to the Gara Rock Hotel, very conveniently situated for appropriate refreshment or even a cream tea, before following the quiet lanes back to East Portlemouth. Here there is a church (and telephone) as well as some lovely views of Salcombe and the upper harbour from its lofty heights. You then descend back to the harbour via the steep steps of Ferry Hill.

The harbour's large area of sheltered, clean water provides excellent sailing for dinghy sailors, not least the fleet of pretty Salcombe yawls. Clinker construction, broad transom and short bowsprit are the key to their ancestry, for they evolved from the traditional local fishing vessels of the early part of the 19th century. Three-quarter decked or open, between 14ft and 18ft overall, they were also used by local licensed watermen for hiring out to picnic parties and racing once a year during the local regatta.

The birth of the racing yawl is generally attributed to Jim Stone, a young local shipwright who built himself a 14ft yawl purely for the racing in 1917. Unable to afford the paint, he finished her off with creosote, decided to call her

Salcombe, looking upstream into the 'Bag' – fuel barge, bottom left, and visitors' pontoon just visible behind trees on Snapes Point, centre

Blackbird, and appropriately this dark horse won every race!

The design was further refined by Morgan Giles in 1937, when the overall length was standardised at 16ft with a heavy iron bulb keel and centreboard. They are still constructed locally, and open meetings often attract well over 50 boats for some very close racing.

Excellent sailing is also one of the main reasons that the famous Island Cruising Club has been based here since 1954, its members enjoying a varied fleet of vessels. It is an RYA recognised sailing school.

The club's name was derived from the Island, the area to the south of Shadycombe Creek where its original clubhouse (sold in 2000) backed onto the pleasantly salty backwater at the rear of the town. Today the clubship is the former Mersey ferry *Egremont*, moored further upriver in the Bag. Visitors are welcome to use the showers and bar, which also serves meals.

All manner of nautical activity lurks in Island Street – boatyards, engineers and various other boating businesses, including the only chandler in town, the Salcombe Boatstore. Even if you're not in need of anything, a pleasant hour can be spent nosing around the colourful old boatsheds, heavy with the tang of fresh sawdust and old hemp. You may chance on a new yawl being built, or an old clinker launch under repair.

If time further permits, it's a pleasant walk onwards around Shadycombe Creek to the sleepy backwater of Batson, with its picturesque hamlet at the head of the creek.

THE UPPER REACHES

However, nowhere is absolutely perfect. There are two things that can detract from a visit to Salcombe – the sheer number of boats at the height of the season, and the swell in a southerly blow. In spite of the apparently landlocked nature of the harbour, this swell will be experienced as far up as Scoble Point, rendering the anchorage and moorings surprisingly rough and uncomfortable, particularly on the ebb.

The solution to both these problems is to seek out one of the quieter, more sheltered spots further up the estuary. Southpool Creek dries almost to its mouth, but boats able to take the ground might find a spot just upstream of the moorings, grounding at LW. Ideally this is best explored by dinghy, slipping away from the bustle of Salcombe between the steep wooded shores and following the rising tide as it creeps along the muddy shores. At Gullet Point the creek divides, the starboard arm becoming Waterhead Creek where you will find the small, forgotten hamlet of Goodshelter; Southpool Creek is very shallow beyond Gullet but the quiet village of Southpool can be reached a couple of hours either side of HW. There are no facilities except a phone, although if you time it right a pint at the Millbrook Inn awaits.

Opposite the entrance to Southpool Creek

Middle Ground is a bank (least depth 1.5m) extending south and east from Snapes Point – deep water lies on the Scoble side of the channel. The ebb funnels through this gap at up to two knots at springs.

Opening before you is the traditional upper anchorage of 'the Bag', although now most of it is given over to permanent moorings. A handy corner can be found tucked in just north of wooded Snapes Point, close to the edge of the drying mud, where you will be sheltered from most weather. Alternatively, for the more convivial, there is a long visitors' pontoon a little distance upstream.

The oldest objection to the Bag used to be the long row to town. The outboard has dealt with the worst of that, although in a fresh southerly breeze it can still be a long, wet ride in an inflatable! Far more convenient is the taxi service run by the Harbour Authority which can be summoned on VHF Ch 12 (call sign *Salcombe Harbour Taxi*). Charges from Blackstone Rock to Scoble Point are £1 a head and from the Bag you'll pay £1.50.

Mabel Shoal (only 1.2m) lies inconveniently right in the middle of the Bag, and care should also be taken to avoid the rocks extending from Tosnos Point at the northern end of this stretch. The best course to avoid both hazards is to follow the line of moorings along the eastern shore past the wooded outcrop of Halwell Point, where an anchorage can be found close to the shore.

Just upstream of Tosnos, the remains on the foreshore are those of the 108ft yacht *Iverna* built by Fay in 1890 – she was winner of the Big Class in 1890-92. When I first visited the Bag in the 1960s, this and several other elegant large vessels were still afloat as houseboats along this reach.

Nestling in the small inlet at Lincombe you will see the buildings and slipways of Winter's Boatyard, which is approached by a narrow winding channel marked by small buoys. Ahead, the Saltstone Beacon, a striped pole with green triangular topmark, marks a large rock drying to 4.9m. This was once used by 17th century Non-Conformists for illegal religious meetings, as it belonged to none of the local parishes and was out of legal jurisdiction.

Between it and Halwell Point lies the entrance to Frogmore Creek. This, too, dries extensively, but a very peaceful anchorage can be found just inside the mouth, with 2m at LW, or you can anchor just west of the Saltstone in the same sort of depth. The latter berth is more likely to be affected by passing traffic, such as ferries, but with a bit of luck, you will find welcome solitude as evening descends.

After supper, dinghy over for a leg stretch on the lonely, pebbly, foreshore of Wareham Point, then drift back as dusk descends over the silent wooded shore, the ebb rippling quietly out of the

A quieter berth can usually be found on the visitors' pontoon in the Bag

creek and the peace broken only by the sudden startled cries of the birds settling for the night. With luck the morning will dawn warm and calm, the distant wooded shores indistinct in a gentle but rising mist as the early sun tries to burn through – it does sometimes happen!

If the tide permits, it's time for another trip in the dinghy, following the twisting creek further inland between the rolling fields and grazing cattle to the village of Frogmore. The channel is well marked along its port side by red and white striped poles with square topmarks, and shoal draught boats can get right up to Frogmore on a rising tide, although the final half mile is very shallow. Here a grocery, post office and the Globe Inn cater for most immediate needs.

After the grandeur of the entrance, above Frogmore Creek the character of the estuary changes completely, becoming wide and flat and meandering gently into peaceful South Hams – the name derives from the old English word *hamme*, meaning a sheltered place – and for an average draught boat it is a pleasant run up to Kingsbridge on a rising tide.

KINGSBRIDGE APPROACHES

Leave the Saltstone well to starboard, and off the wide entrance to Collapit and Blanks Mill Creeks pass the striped red and white poles with red topmarks, which clearly mark the western side of the channel, to port.

On the western bank, at the north side of Collapit Creek, is a conspicuous house with a mooring off it. Here the channel divides, the line of numbered red can buoys marking a subsidiary channel that leads away to the distant group of moorings by the bridge across Balcombe Creek. These buoys should all be left well on the starboard hand and, following the poles, the main channel takes you north towards High House Point, where the outskirts of Kingsbridge – a rather unsightly development of modern houses sprawling across a low rounded hill – can be seen. Beneath this point the channel turns sharply back to the western

shore, there are a number of local moorings along its edges, and upstream Kingsbridge begins to appear.

The bank on the eastern shore is large and shallow, so do not cut the corner. In contrast to the development opposite, trees and fields run down close to the channel on the western shore, which swings northwards again past a private pontoon with a number of local boats alongside. Just upstream is New Quay, formerly the site of Date's shipyard, and the boatyard and private pontoons all belong to the Kingsbridge ferry.

BERTHING

No public berthing is allowed anywhere along the length of this quay, but keep close and continue past the new buildings at its northern end before turning across the entrance of the inlet where there are a number of local boats moored on your port hand.

The channel now heads towards the slipway and quay on the western shore, which marks the beginning of the tree lined basin enclosing the head of the creek. The visitors' pontoon, with a bridge to the shore, will be found on the starboard hand; shoal draught boats should berth on the outside, and visitors with deeper draughts should use the berths which are clearly marked alongside the wall opposite. These berths are suitable for vessels of up to 12m, dry completely to soft mud and are only safely accessible two hours either side of HW. If intending to stay for a tide, it is advisable to confirm the berthing availability with the harbour office before proceeding upstream.

FACILITIES

Kingsbridge, an unspoilt country town with many fine Georgian buildings, forms the junction of four busy roads through South Devon. Although long dead as a seaport, it is an important shopping centre and bustles with activity, with a market on Tuesdays. All normal requirements except fuel can be found. Pubs, restaurants and cafes abound, and after the distinctly nautical atmosphere of Salcombe a taste of the country makes a pleasant contrast before returning downstream to the sea and yet another *Crossing of the Bar*:

'For though from out our bourne of Time and Place, The flood may bear me far, I hope to see my Pilot face to face, When I have crost the bar.'

Salcombe Estuary Port Guide
Area telephone code: 01548

Harbour Master: Captain Stephen Tooke, Harbour Office, Whitestrand, Salcombe TQ8 8BU (Tel: 843791, Fax 842033). Open 0900–1300, 1400–1645 daily during season, otherwise Mon–Fri only. E-mail: salcombe.harbour@south-hams-dc.gov.uk

VHF: Ch 14, call sign *Salcombe Harbour*, office hours. Harbour patrols, call sign *Salcombe Harbour* all monitor Ch 14 and 12 and operate 0600–2200 during the season

Mail drop: c/o Harbour Office or Salcombe Yacht Club

Emergency services: Lifeboat at Salcombe. Brixham Coastguard. Prawle Point NCI Lookout (Tel: 511259)

Anchorages: Sunny Cove, Smalls Cove, E Portlemouth beach, entrance to Frogmore Creek, W of Saltstone and shoal draught/drying anchorages in many other parts of estuary. Anchoring prohibited in area off Mill Bay

Moorings: Marked with a 'V' and details of maximum size, 21 visitors' swinging moorings off Salcombe for up to 15m, larger moorings available up to 17m, and three for up to 100 tons TM. Normandy short stay visitors' pontoon off town for up to half-an-hour only. Deep water visitors' pontoon in the Bag. Drying visitors' pontoon and berthing alongside wall at Kingsbridge

Dinghy landings: Whitestrand and Normandy pontoons. Salcombe Yacht Club steps. Ferry steps, E Portlemouth beach

Water taxi: Harbour launches double as taxi service. Call *Harbour Taxi* on VHF Ch 12, 0800–2345 during season, shorter hours at other times. Charges from £1 to £1.50 per person depending on location, landing/departing Whitestrand pontoon. Regular ferries from Salcombe to East Portlemouth, South Sands and Kingsbridge when tide permits

Marinas: None

Charges: Overnight charge on pontoons or moorings £1.45 per metre per night. At anchor £0.75 per metre per night

Phones: Whitestrand Quay

Doctor: (Tel: 842284)

Hospital: South Hams Hospital, Kingsbridge (Tel: 852349)

Churches: C of E and RC

Local Weather Forecast: At Harbour Office

Fuel: Diesel and petrol alongside fuel barge, end May to mid Sept only, daily 0900–1800. Monitors VHF Ch 06, call sign *Fuel barge*, or (Tel: 07801 798862 or 844261)

Water: Hoses on Normandy short stay visitors' pontoon. Tap on Whitestrand Quay

Gas: Calor and Camping Gaz from Salcombe Boatstore

Tourist Information Centre: Town Hall, Salcombe (Tel: 843927). The Quay, Kingsbridge (Tel: 853195)

Banks: LloydsTSB and HSBC (open 1030–1500 Mon, Weds & Fri), Fore Street, Salcombe, both have cashpoints. All main banks in Kingsbridge, but cashpoints only at Lloyds and HSBC

Post Office: Courtenay Street, Salcombe. Kingsbridge

Rubbish: Floating skip in entrance to Batson Creek

Showers/toilets: Salcombe Yacht Club. Public toilets at Whitestrand and Shadycombe car park

Launderette: Fore Street, Salcombe (7 days), also in Kingsbridge

Provisions: All normal requirements in Salcombe. All requirements at Kingsbridge

Chandlers: Salcombe Boatstore, Island Street (Tel: 843708)

Repairs: Yeoward & Stone, Island Street, (Tel: 844261). Winters Marine, Lincombe Boatyard, slipping to 30 tons (Tel: 843580). Drying out alongside by arrangement with Harbour Master

Marine Engineers: Sailing, Island Street (Tel: 842094). Quayside Marine Services (Tel: 844300). Winters Marine, Lincombe Boat Yard (Tel: 843580). SMS, Lincombe (Tel: 843655 VHF Ch 13 0830–1700, 24 hour breakdown service Tel 01548 843053). Reddish Marine (Tel: 844094). Wills Bros, The Embankment, Kingsbridge (Tel: 852424)

Electronic engineers: Andrew Jedynak (Tel: 843321). Richard Lewis (Tel: 843223)

Sailmakers: J Alsop, The Sail Loft, Croft Road (Tel: 843702). J McKillop, The Sail Loft, Ebrington Street, Kingsbridge (Tel: 852343)

Riggers: Salcombe Boatstore (Tel: 843708) Harris Rigging (Tel: 01803 840160). C Winzer (Tel: 07971 3227720)

Liferaft/inflatable repairs/ servicing: Danby Maritime (Tel: 842777)

Transport: Regular Tally Ho local buses (Tel: 853081) and ferries on tide to Kingsbridge, with Western National bus connections (Tel: 01752 402060) to main line trains at Plymouth (1 hour) or Totnes (40 mins): (Tel: 08457 484950)

Taxis: (Tel: 561577, 842914 or 842222)

Car hire: SMG Motors Kingsbridge (Tel: 853600)

Car parking: Large car park at Shadycombe, Salcombe. Large car park on Quay at Kingsbridge.

Yacht club: Salcombe Yacht Club, Cliff Road, Salcombe TQ8 8JQ (Tel: 842872)

Eating out: Varied choice of restaurants/bistros, pubs, cafes and fish and chips

Things to do: Salcombe Museum. Lifeboat Museum. Sharpitor Gardens and Overbecks Museum. Spectacular walks on both sides of estuary entrance. Good swimming from many sandy and protected beaches within the harbour. Public internet access at Salcombe Library, Cliff House

Regattas/special events: Salcombe Festival early June. Salcombe Town Regatta and Salcombe Yacht Club Regatta during first two weeks in August. Harbour is also popular for dinghy champion-ships throughout the season

BIGBURY BAY

Hope Cove is a pleasant anchorage in easterly winds. Hillsea Point is visible on the far side of Bigbury Bay

Tides	River Avon/River Erme: HW Dover −0523
Charts	BA:1613, SC5602.4. Stanford:13. Imray: C6, WCP2400.8
Hazards	River Avon: Tidal entrance with bar, dangerous in onshore wind. Strong currents within entrance. River mostly dries. Murray's Rocks in approach (unlit)
	River Erme: Wells Rock to SE, Edward's Rock, East and West Mary's Rocks in entrance (all unlit). Drying tidal river, dangerous in onshore winds

The seven mile stretch of Bigbury Bay is, in prevailing south-westerly winds, not a very attractive prospect and boats heading across it will usually remain a good two to three miles offshore. However, in calm, settled weather, there are several places within it which make an interesting detour from the normal cruising track.

Hope Cove is a small fishing village tucked away on the north side of Bolt Tail, which can sometimes provide a temporary anchorage in easterly winds. There are no off-lying dangers; sound into the centre of the cove between the small pier and the south shore, but beware the Basses Rock closer inshore which dries 1.3m.

THE RIVER AVON

The River Avon is, however, the real gem of Bigbury Bay, and for owners of shallow draught boats capable of drying out it can be a delightful spot for an overnight stop, providing there is no inkling of a change of weather to the south or west. Although perfectly sheltered within, in an onshore breeze and any ground swell, the river entrance is inaccessible. Once inside, if the weather does turn, you might not be able to get out for some time . . .

To find it, initially steer directly for the flattened pyramid of Burgh Island (pronounced *Burrr*), then hold more to the east and approach midway between the island and Longstone Point. The extensive sand dunes and beach of the Ham extend west from Longstone Point concealing the tortuous entrance to the Avon and, apart from a very narrow channel, the whole of the approach dries at LW. Ideally it is best to enter an hour before HW (HW Dover −0523) as the current runs strongly in the entrance.

I would personally recommend an earlier arrival when the drying Murray's Rocks, which stretch nearly 2½ cables to the south east of the island, will still be visible, However, beware the outermost, Blind Mare, which has just over 1m over it at MLWS. Murray's Rocks were previously marked by a useful beacon which has now been removed and I am informed by the harbour master that it is unlikely to be replaced. Sounding in with due care, a good anchorage in firm sand will be found just north-east of Murray's Rocks in about 2m. From here it is wisest to reconnoitre the channel by dinghy if you plan to enter the Avon, as it has become increasingly silted in recent years. Alternatively it's a handy daytime anchorage just for a visit to Burgh Island.

Burgh Island is tidal, linked by drying sands to the mainland and the trippery resort of Bigbury-on-Sea. At high tide, a remarkable 'sea tractor' with seats on an elevated platform maintains the link with the shore. In contrast to the mainland resort, privately owned Burgh Island sports an elegant Art Deco hotel, where Agatha Christie wrote several of her books. Today, it has become a popular location for films of similar style and period. On the foreshore, by the landing place, there is also a small pub, the atmospheric 14th century Pilchard Inn.

Returning to the Avon – the entrance to the river

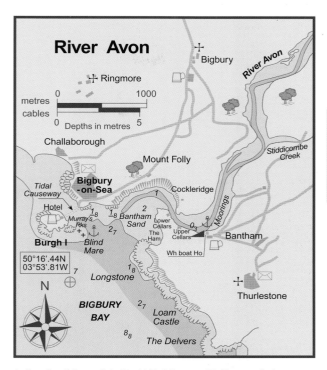

Burgh Island and the approach to the River Avon at half flood. Note how far Murray's Rocks extend to south east of the Island

is backed by a high cliff, Mount Folly, and the deepest water over the bar is found on a transit of the two conspicuous houses just east of the group of trees on the clifftop. Keep close to the beach on the western side, following the steep shoreline, until the white mark painted on the rock is abeam, before turning to starboard towards Lower Cellars Point, which is covered in turf and ferns

Looking upstream to Bantham, much of the inner Avon dries at low water

and above which protrudes the top of a solitary pine tree. Here the river narrows considerably, with a shingly bank along the northern shore. Steer close to the point, where the current can run up to five knots through the narrows on the ebb if the river is in flood.

Once through the gap, you have entered a real hideaway. The river widens, with the landing beach and houses ahead, and immediately to starboard, there is a sheltered pool off the quaint thatched boathouse and grassy quay, tucked beneath the dense foliage of the steep protective cliff. At first sight, with 2m at LW, this would seem to be the ideal anchorage, but holding is poor and the current runs strongly. Instead, follow the southern shore upstream towards the white building with a long thatch on the foreshore and anchor anywhere clear of the few local small boat moorings, where you will ground and probably dry out at LW.

Peaceful, totally unspoiled and far removed from the busier anchorages that you have visited so far, this delightful place is a rare find. Disappearing beyond cornfields sloping down to wooded shores, the river winds upstream between drying sandy banks and reedy saltings for another four miles to the village of Aveton (pronounced *Orton*) Gifford. It is a sleepy, almost forgotten waterway, but 50 years ago barges regularly worked their way inland with cargoes of lime, stone and coal for the South Hams farms, and the tiny quays at Bantham reeked of the pilchard catches as they were landed and cured. On a rising tide it is well worth further exploration in the dinghy, with the enticing prospect of a pint and a snack at the Fisherman's Rest pub at Aveton, perhaps?

Bantham itself is little more than a hamlet, a row of well cared-for cob and stone cottages, with deep overhanging thatches and tiny windows. The village is privately owned by the Evans Estates, which accounts for the admirable lack of development. Both Bantham and Aveton Gifford were until recently possessed of a post office and village stores and it is a sure sign of our times that these have now closed. Apart from a 'beach' type shop, the only other business in Bantham is the very popular Sloop Inn which does excellent bar food.

The large thatched building on the foreshore, in spite of its medieval appearance, was actually built in 1937 to celebrate the accession of King George VI, and is nothing more than an enormous boathouse with two fine figureheads at each end. Here you will find the helpful harbour master, Mr Neill Schroeter, (Tel: 01548 561196) Mon – Fri 0900 – 1600. There is a further surprise within, for you will probably also find Hugh Cater, a boatbuilder who produces magnificent traditional varnished clinker dinghies – the whole of the upper floor is full of them!

THE RIVER ERME

Nearly three miles further north-west, the other forgotten river of Bigbury Bay, the Erme, though very attractive and completely unspoiled, is only really feasible as a daytime anchorage in favourable conditions, and is not suitable for an overnight stop. Lacking a sheltering natural breakwater like the Ham, the river mouth is wide open to the south-west and dries completely beyond the entrance. As it is privately owned by the Flete Estate and designated as a wild life sanctuary, permission is needed to enter the inner reaches. However, in settled weather and an offshore breeze, a pleasant daytime anchorage can be found in the mouth off the fine sandy beaches at Mothecombe and Wonwell.

Although there are no offshore hazards, care must be taken in the approach to the Erme. There are several dangerous rocks, in particular Wells Rock (least depth 1.2m) just over half a mile south of Erme Head, the eastern flank of the river mouth. Within the entrance there are three more

The River Erme from south east. Fernycombe Point in foreground with East Mary's Rock covered and Mothecombe Beach on far side of river

rocks, West and East Mary's Rocks (dry 1.1m and 1.5m respectively) and further to seaward, three cables south of the low grassy Battisborough Island on the northern shore, Edward's Rock (least depth 1.1m). Shallow water extends south west from the Mary's Rocks, and the deep channel runs parallel to the sloping slab-like cliffs of the northern shore.

Keep to the west of all the hazards and steer for the southern end of Owen Hill, the prominent isolated cliff topped with a group of conspicuous pines. Mothecombe beach lies just to the west and, by sounding in towards it, a good sandy anchorage will be found inside the Mary's Rocks in about 3m, two cables due south of Owen Hill.

The River Erme is probably unique in that there are absolutely no facilities within a mile; the clean sandy beaches and clear water are perfect for swimming and, if time permits, a dinghy trip should certainly be made some of the way upstream, following the tide up the twisting channel between the sandy banks and steep wooded shores. There are few places on the South Coast that remain quite so unspoilt.

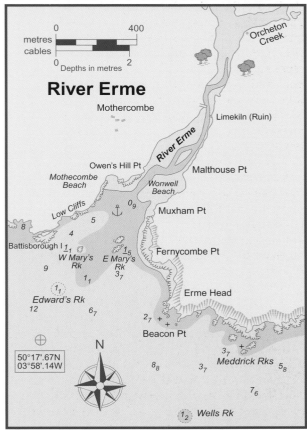

RIVER YEALM

Tides	HW Dover −0540
Range	MHWS 5.4m–MHWN 4.3m, MLWN 2.1m–MLWS 0.7m Attains up to three knots in entrance at spring ebb
Charts	BA: 30 and SC5602.8. Stanford:CP23. Imray: C14, WCP2400.6
Hazards	West and East Ebb Rocks, Mouthstone Ledge from east; Outer and Inner Slimer Rocks from west (all unlit). Bar across northern side of entrance (buoyed and lit).Under 2m within entrance at springs. Not recommended in strong S or SW wind and swell. Newton Arm and large area of upper reaches dry
Overnight charges	Harbour Authority mooring or pontoon: £12.50

Undoubtedly one of the classic havens of the entire South Coast, the small and beautiful River Yealm probably owes much of its unspoilt character to the fact that for many years the narrow and twisting entrance was a strong deterrent to visitors by sea, making it very

difficult to enter under sail alone. With no beaches or attractions for holidaymakers other than the natural beauty of its wooded shores, it was still very undeveloped well into the 1930s, and it is only since the war that the small cottages have become highly desirable as holiday and retirement homes. Ironically, as reliable auxiliaries overcame the problem of the entrance, they inevitably created another, for the river is now so popular in the height of summer that it is often a very tight squeeze to find a berth.

The Harbour is leased from the Crown Estate Commissioners and administered by the River Yealm Harbour Authority, a statutory non-profit-making organisation. In 1989 the Harbour Authority decided that, depending on the space

available, the number of visiting boats would have to be restricted at the busiest times of the year, usually during spells of settled weather and particularly on summer Bank Holidays. In general terms this usually means about 90 boats, but obviously the size and type of vessels has a significant bearing on the total. It is probably best to avoid the river altogether at these times, but YHA does stress that entry will never be refused to any boat seeking shelter in poor weather.

Don't be put off though. As long as you are not averse to rafting up, or are determined to have a secluded anchorage all to yourself, the Yealm is undoubtedly another essential on any West Country cruise. Ideally, visit it early or late in the season when it is altogether a different place.

Yealm Pool looking seaward. Landing pontoon, Newton Arm and visitors' pontoon, top left, Cellar Bay, top right and visitors' pontoon, bottom right

The inner reach, looking upstream towards the visitors' moorings which lie off the prominent house, centre

APPROACHES

In spite of the bar, the approach is not as difficult as it might at first seem, although the entrance to the river is totally hidden behind Misery Point. Care must be taken rounding Yealm Head from the east to avoid the Eastern and Western Ebb Rocks, which are just awash LAT three cables south-west of Garra Point. Normally they can be seen by the seas breaking, but are particularly insidious in calm weather. Keep a good half-mile off the shore and do not turn north into Wembury Bay until the conspicuous church tower at Wembury is bearing 010°T.

Approaching from the west, the sloping pyramid of the Great Mewstone provides a fine landmark to locate the river, but keep clear of the Mewstone Ledge (least depth 2m), which extends a cable south-westward, and the Outer and Inner Slimers (drying 1.5m and 0.3m respectively) two cables east of the island. Continue eastwards until you are on the same 010°T bearing on Wembury Church and these will safely be avoided.

The bottom of Wembury Bay is uneven and rises quickly to around 6m LAT. This can produce very rough seas in strong winds from the south and west, when no approach to the river should be attempted – the easy entrance to Plymouth is close by.

Holding 010°T, the first indication of the river mouth is usually other boats in the vicinity and, if the wind is off the land, vessels anchored in Cellar Bay. As Mouthstone Point draws abeam,

the leading marks will be seen above and to the left of Cellar Beach – two white triangular beacons with a black line down the centre, giving a transit of 088.5°T to clear rocky Mouthstone Ledge which stretches west for one cable from the point.

This line does not clear the sand bar which dries 0.6m LAT and extends from Season Point.

Its southern end is clearly marked by the red can Bar buoy (Fl R 5s, radar reflector), which should be left on your port hand. This is the only light in the river, so entry at night without local knowledge, except in ideal conditions and with a good moon, is not recommended, particularly on a first visit!

A green beacon with triangular topmark on a white backboard, perched almost opposite, marks the southern side of the 40m wide channel, and between the two there is a least depth of almost 3m LAT.

Once past the beacon, continue into Cellar Bay,

Yealm entrance

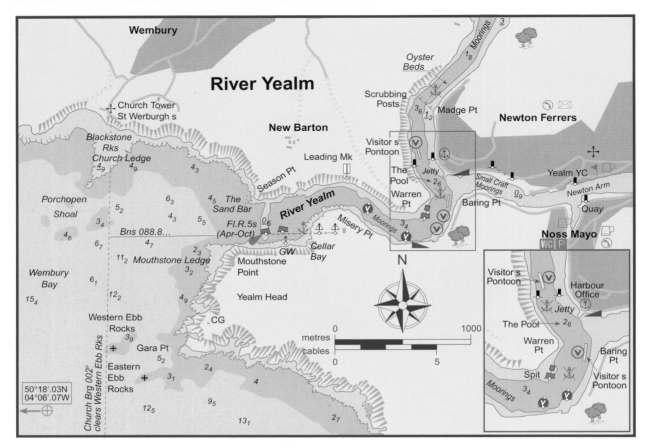

where you will leave the second red can buoy (unlit, summer months only), marking the eastern extremity of the bar, well to port before heading onto 047°T towards the square white leading mark with red vertical stripe, high in the gorse on the opposite cliff. If the weather is fair you can anchor off Cellar Beach where there is no charge; usually, though, it is crowded during the day.

Across this section of the river, on the lowest tides there will be no more than 1.2m of water until the sharp turn to starboard around Misery Point is completed and you are into the first inner reach. If in any doubt about the depth, do not attempt the entrance until a good hour after LW.

MOORINGS

Once inside Misery Point you enter a different world as the sea vanishes astern. The channel deepens to well over 2.5m and runs between steep wooded banks, with little indication that there is any kind of settlement, other than the sudden proliferation of moorings. **Due to the lack of swinging room, anchoring is not permitted anywhere in the river beyond Misery Point except for boats able to dry out in the Newton Arm.**

The first visitors' buoy just east of Misery Point

is for larger craft (up to 18m). Continuing inwards, the red can Spit buoy marks the drying sandy spit extending south from Warren Point. In spite of the buoy, this is a regular spot for unintentional grounding as there seems to be a compulsion for many to cut inside this port hand mark!

Opposite the Spit buoy, on the south side of the channel, are two 25 ton moorings which can accommodate up to three visitors at a time. A short distance further upstream on the starboard hand, the 150ft long visitors' pontoon can take up to about 26 rafted boats. The overnight charge for using any of the harbour mooring facilities is £1.25 per metre; the same charge also applies if you anchor and dry out in the Newton Arm.

You are now in the Pool, a fine landlocked natural haven surrounded by high hills, wooded right to the water's edge. However, though well protected from any seas, the river can be surprisingly violent in a bad blow, as the wind eddying round the high shores creates williwaws and very strong gusts. On several occasions I have seen, in this seemingly perfect shelter, small craft laid over almost on their beam ends and great columns of spume and spray whipped off the water!

The river divides at the Pool, which is overlooked by the prominent Yealm Hotel. Newton Arm leads off to the east, while the Yealm itself continues northwards beyond Warren Point. Here another visitors' pontoon along the western, Wembury shore is situated, with the capacity to raft up to about 20 boats. In addition to the Harbour Authority facilities, there is also an unwritten understanding in the Yealm – where space is at such a premium – that visitors can pick up any vacant mooring providing there is no tender or note attached to it. However, if you do so, you should not leave your boat unattended without the prior approval of the harbour staff.

The harbour master and his staff are invariably out on the water first thing in the morning and after 1600 in the afternoon to assist with settling people in. If you pick up a vacant mooring during the day, nip ashore to the new harbour office (due for completion in 2004) at Yealm Steps by the main landing pontoon. You can land and leave your dinghy here, but do not obstruct the outer end of the pontoon where there is a fresh water hose, as this all-tide berth (least depth 2m) is kept clear for temporary stays of up to half an hour to take on water. Alternatively, you can hail Bill Gregor's *Water Taxi* on VHF Ch 08 (Tel: 880079) which operates daily from 1000 to 2300 subject to demand.

The harbour office (Tel: 01752 872533) is normally manned from 0930 – 1200 daily during the season. There is no VHF watch, so if you wish to contact the HM at any other time you will either have to spot him on the water, leave a message on the answerphone or post a note through his letterbox. Here you'll also find

visitors' showers (£1 coin) and toilets, a holding tank pump-out facility, a public telephone, local weather and tidal information and rubbish disposal – bag it and place it in the bins by the steps.

The Newton Arm dries almost completely, but two hours either side of HW, the villages of Newton Ferrers, half a mile upstream on the northern shore, and the delightfully named Noss Mayo, opposite, can be reached by boats of average draught. At the head of the creek, another quarter of a mile or so, is a public quay at Bridgend and boats drawing up to 2m can get to it a couple of hours either side of HW springs. Here you will find berths alongside for scrubbing or repairs, with power and water available. This and the other drying berths at Pope's Quay, Noss Mayo, and the scrubbing posts at Clitters Beach, opposite Madge Point, can all be used on arrangement with the harbour master.

Bilge keelers can anchor and dry out comfortably on the foreshore off Newton or Noss on reasonably hard ground. The centre of the creek should be kept clear, and take care to avoid the Voss, a tidal footpath which links the two villages at low water, as well as the distinctly marked underwater power cables between Newton Ferrers and the eastern side of Noss Creek.

FACILITIES

From the Pool, Newton Ferrers is easily reached by dinghy if the tide permits or by a 10 minute walk along the pleasant path overlooking the steep sided creek. Alternatively, there are two landing places, Wide Slip and Parish/Kilpatrick Steps, opposite the visitors' pontoon on the south side of the entrance to Newton Arm. A delightful footpath leads through the National Trust woodlands to Noss Mayo.

Entering Yealm Pool. Note 'Spit 'buoy, left, and visitors' pontoon, centre right

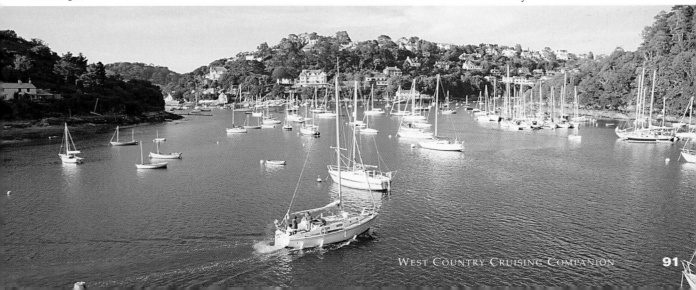

Newton was presented to Henri de Ferrieres by William the Conquerer as a reward for his assistance in the Norman invasion, which explains the strange name – Noss derives from the Old English for promontory. Both villages have been very well preserved, although in recent years there has been a regrettable spread of modern bungalows and houses around them. Looking out over the creek, the older cottages are immaculately kept, the whitewash emphasising doorways overhung with wisteria and roses. Their well-tended gardens are ablaze with flowers, and neat stone walls and lawns drop away to the water's edge.

Though small, Newton Ferrers has a useful selection of village shops, including a post office/newsagent/general store with limited cashpoint facility, a Coop off-licence and grocery (Mon – Sat 0800 – 2000, Sun 0900 – 1900 – cashback too) at the top of Newton Hill, an excellent bakery, grocery, butcher, chemist and even a hairdresser. There are no shops or post office in Noss Mayo. It should, however, be particularly noted that no fuel or gas is available anywhere in the river!

The Yealm remains a quiet, relaxing sort of place. The walks in the surrounding woods and beside the river are lovely, reflecting the origins of the river's name which is Celtic for 'kind'.

The walk over Warren Point out to Season Point, which overlooks the river mouth, is particularly fine, with good blackberrying in late summer. It is a memorable spot to watch the sunset over Wembury Bay and the Mewstone. Alternatively, land at Parish Steps, turn right and follow the lower path past Ferry Cottage, through Passage Wood and then onto the coastal path which will take you out past Cellars Bay to Mouthstone and Gara Points. Enjoy the fine views of the mouth of the river, before continuing to the NT car park. From here it is possible to return along the road via Hannaford to Noss Mayo and back to Parish Steps along the creek. In all, it is a 7km circuit of about two hours.

If you have worked up a thirst with all this exercise, there are three worthy pubs to choose from which also do good pub grub – the Swan and the Ship at Noss, and the Dolphin on the foreshore at Newton Ferrers.

Close by, the fourth option is the bar at the Yealm Yacht Club. The club was founded in 1933, visitors are very welcome and facilities include new changing rooms and showers (£1 coin). Bar meals and evening meals are available at the club in Blondie's Bistro (Tel: 872232) most days during the season.

THE UPPER REACHES

Beyond the Pool, the upper reaches are well worth a trip on the tide and in a small boat they are navigable for another two miles, although anchoring is prohibited throughout. Between Madge Point and the moorings further upstream at Thorn Pool the open area of water is reserved for recreational use, while along the shores there are extensive oyster beds marked by withies. The deepest water lies in the centre of the river and depths vary with as little as 0.3m LAT in places.

Beyond the oyster beds, upstream of the marked underwater power cable, the river is all privately owned by the Kitley Estate. Here, too, **anchoring and also landing anywhere on the foreshore are totally prohibited**, as the owner is attempting to maintain it as a nature reserve. At Steer Point the river divides, Cofflete Arm to port and the larger Yealmpton Arm to starboard. Both are muddy and dry at LW, but these wooded and peaceful backwaters, rich in bird life, can be explored by dinghy on a rising tide.

The Yealm steps landing pontoon by the harbour office can also be used for short stay berthing to take on water

The Yealm visitor's pontoon can boast a truly sylvan setting

River Yeam Port Guide

Area telephone code: 01752

Harbour Master: Mr Robin Page, The Harbour Office, Yealm Road, Newton Ferrers PL8 1BN (Tel: 872533). 0930 – 1200 daily in season. Afloat in launch early morning, and evenings

VHF: No radio watch

Mail drop: c/o Harbour Office

Emergency services: Lifeboat at Plymouth. Brixham Coastguard

Anchorages: Cellar Bay in offshore winds. Drying out in Newton Arm

Mooring/berthing: Harbour Authority has several swinging moorings to accommodate visitors from 18m – 7m LOA. Two visitors' pontoons. Local moorings available to visitors if unoccupied. Scrubbing/repair berths available alongside by arrangement with harbour master

Dinghy landings: By Harbour Office at Yealm Steps all-tide pontoon. Parish Steps, opposite visitors' pontoon. High water landing at Newton Ferrers slip, Noss Creek, Yealm Yacht Club, Bridgend Quay

Water taxi: *Yealm Water Taxi*, VHF Ch 8, (Tel: 880079), 1000-2300 during season subject to demand

Marina: None

Charges: £1.25 per metre per night. Cheaper rates for longer periods and boats can be left by arrangement with harbour master

Phones: Harbour Office,Yealm Steps. Outside Post Office, Newton Ferrers, and in Noss Mayo

Doctor: (Tel: 880392)

Hospital: Derriford, Plymouth (10 miles, Tel: 777111)

Churches: Newton Ferrers; Noss Mayo, both C of E

Local Weather Forecast: At Harbour Office

Fuel: None, nearest in Plymouth

Gas: None, nearest in Plymouth

Water: Hose at outer end of Yealm Steps pontoon at all states of tide

Tourist Information Centre: None

Banks/cashpoint: Post Office has limited cashpoint facility. Cashback at Coop

Post Office: Newton Ferrers

Rubbish: Bins by Harbour Office,Yealm Steps

Showers/toilets: At Harbour Office, Yealm Steps. Yealm Yacht Club. Both showers take £1 coin

Launderette: None

Provisions: All basics available in Newton Ferrers, including groceries and chemist

Chandler: None

Repairs: Ask harbour master

Marine Engineer: Ask harbour master

Electronic engineers: Tolley Marine, Plymouth (Tel: 222530).

Sailmakers: A Hooper (Tel: 830411)

Transport: Six buses a day (Tel:222666), weekdays, to Plymouth (time table available at Harbour Office). Main line train connections at Plymouth (Tel: 08457 484950). Airport at Plymouth (Tel: 204090)

Car hire: McMullin Motors, Plymstock (Tel: 401142)

Car parking: Very restricted

Yacht Club: Yealm Yacht Club, Riverside Road East, Newton Ferrers, Plymouth (Tel: 872291)

Eating out: Meals at pubs in Noss Mayo and Newton Ferrers. Evening meals at Yealm Yacht Club

Things to do: Many good local walks. Swimming at Cellar Beach. Tennis court in Noss Mayo

Mayflower International Marina
Millbay Docks and silo
The Hoe
Sutton Harbour and Queen Anne's Battery Marina
The Barbican
Drake's Island
Mount Batten Breakwater (Plymouth Yacht Haven)
The Bridge

PLYMOUTH

Plymouth in perspective

Tides	HW Dover –0540. Standard Port (Devonport)
Range	MHWS 5.5m–MHWN 4.4m, MLWN 2.2m–MLWS 0.8m. Ebb streams can attain in excess of three knots in Narrows, and five knots in upper reaches of Tamar
Charts	BA: 30, 1967, 1900, 1901, 1902, 871, SC5602.8&9. Stanford: 13, L13. Imray: C14
Waypoints	Knap buoy 50°19'·56N / 04°10'·01W. East Tinker Buoy 50°19'·21N / 04°08'·30W
Hazards	Shagstone (unlit). Much commercial and Naval shipping. Strong tidal streams in places. Much of upper reaches dry
Overnight charges	Marinas, Mayflower £22. QAB £27. Sutton £24. Yacht Haven £22. RWYC mooring £12.50. RPCYC mooring £10. Weir Quay mooring £10

'Plymouth is a Naval and commercial port and has one of the finest natural harbours in the country. It is not frequently used by yachts. . .' When my predecessor, D J Pooley, was writing the original West Country Rivers in 1957, this paradox held true, and remained so for many years afterwards.

Perfect for fleets of warships, the sheer physical scale of Plymouth had little to offer smaller craft, and apart from a few rather dirty commercial basins, there was never a really convenient place for visitors to lie. Most of the better anchorages are a long way from the town and are exposed in bad weather.

Today, however, there are five marinas – four of which have excellent facilities for visitors. Although still primarily a naval port with considerable commercial traffic, including regular ferries to Brittany and Spain and a busy fishing fleet, Plymouth has become internationally renowned as a premier yachting centre and the venue for a number of major events. These include the Single and Double Handed Transatlantic races as well as the Round Britain, and the city has been the finishing point for the Fastnet for over 70 years. It is also an increasingly popular location for club rallies and championship racing events.

OUTER APPROACHES

There are few natural hazards in the approaches to this vast harbour, which is bounded on the east by the Great Mewstone and Rame Head to the west. However, one danger to be aware of is the off-lying Shagstone on the eastern shore, which has an unlit beacon and is linked to the land by a partially submerged reef. Otherwise, the hazards are entirely man-made, with shipping and much naval activity the main considerations. The port is under the jurisdiction of the Queen's Harbour Master. All movements are controlled by the Longroom – the port's nerve centre - which is located in a tower just west of the entrance to Millbay Docks – VHF Ch 16 and 14, call sign *Longroom Port Control.*

Traffic light signals are displayed from the conspicuous tower on Drake's Island and from Flagstaff, Devonport, on the eastern shore of the River Tamar just downstream of Torpoint ferry. These signals, controlling shipping movements in Drake Channel, the Narrows and the Hamoaze, the wide stretch of water running inland west of the city where the Naval Dockyard is situated, are as follows:

a) Unlit = no restrictions to movement
b) Three vertically flashing red lights =

emergency, all traffic movements suspended unless directed otherwise by Port control

c) Occulting red light vertically over two occulting green lights = only outgoing traffic may proceed in recommended channels; crossing traffic to seek permission from Port Control

d) Two occulting green lights vertically over occulting red light = only ingoing traffic may proceed within recommended channel; crossing traffic to seek permission from Port Control

e) Two occulting green lights over occulting white light = vessels may proceed in either direction but to give wide berth to HM vessels.

If there are no traffic signals in force, from sunrise to sunset a wind strength warning light will be diplayed if necessary – (Oc)= wind force 5–7. (2 Oc vert) = wind greater than force 7.

Anywhere in the buoyed channels north of Plymouth breakwater Colregs Rule 9 applies: '....in narrow channels keep to starboard whether under power or sail. A yacht under 20m in length must not impede larger vessels confined to a channel.'

In practice there is no reason why small craft should get embroiled with big ship movements in Plymouth, as for the most part there is no need to follow any of the buoyed channels. Keep well clear and let common sense and good seamanship prevail.

The vast open roadstead of Plymouth Sound was transformed as a fleet anchorage by the completion of Sir John Rennie's central breakwater in 1841. Just under a mile long, Plymouth Breakwater consumed four million tons of materials, and took 29 years to build. The large round fort in the centre is its most conspicuous feature in daytime when the breakwater ends are not immediately easy to spot from well offshore. There is, however, a wide, safe passage around either end.

From the east: after passing the Great Mewstone, the Shagstone, a rock marked with an unlit white beacon, can be passed reasonably close, keeping you well east of the deep water channel, which is bounded on its western side by

Plymouth Sound is protected by a breakwater nearly a mile long

Chapter 2

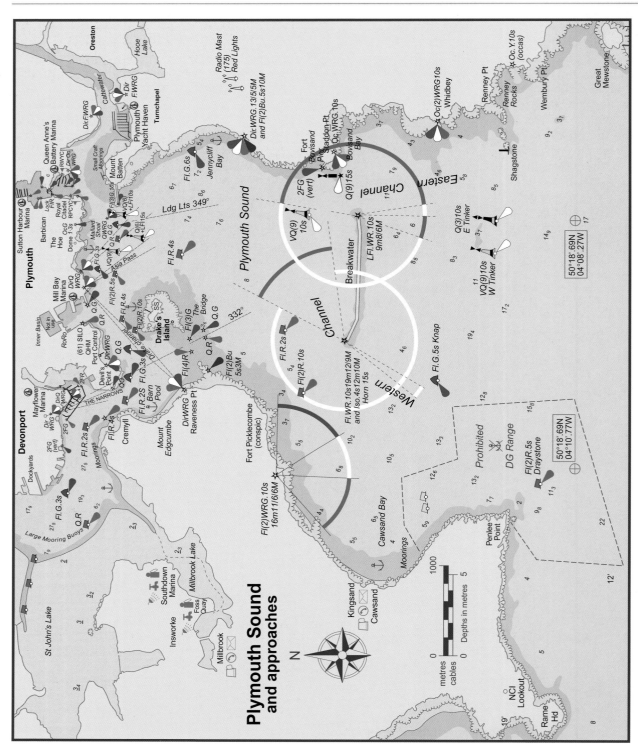

the Tinker shoal, least depth 3.5m.

This is marked on its eastern extremity by the East Tinker BYB east cardinal buoy (Q (3) 10s) to the west by the West Tinker YBY west cardinal buoy (VQ (9) 10s). Although normally not a problem, seas break heavily on this shoal in southerly weather, when the western entrance is

far better. Whidbey Light (Oc (2) WRG 10s 5M) on the eastern shore is the first of several complex sectored approach lights for the eastern deep water channel. The next, Staddon Point, east of the breakwater end, has a light beacon (Oc WRG 10s 8M) with R/W horizontal bands around its daymark base.

The attractive anchorage in Cawsand Bay is well sheltered from the west and always very popular with locals at weekends

The eastern breakwater end is marked by a conical daymark surmounted by a beacon with round ball topmark and a sectored light (L Fl WR 10s 9m 8/6M) showing: Red 001° – 018°, White 018° – 190°, Red 190° – 353°, White 353° – 001°.

The East Tinker buoy lies in the narrow white sector and you soon pass into the red. Large ships will then come onto the leading lights situated on and to seaward of the Hoe, the upper (Oc G 1.3s), the lower sector (Q WRG), with the white sector covering the leading line of 349°T.

Once past the breakwater end, a YBY beacon with west cardinal topmark (Q (9) 15s) marks the eastern side of the deep water channel; closer inshore (2FG vert) lights mark the outer end of Fort Bovisand pier. Several large Admiralty moorings are laid inside the breakwater, all of which are lit (Fl Y, 15s to 2s).

From the west: once past Rame Head keep to seaward of the Draystone red can south-east of Penlee Point (Fl (2) R 5s) and then steer straight for the lighthouse on the western end of the breakwater (Fl WR 10s 19m 12/9M, Iso 4s 12m 10M over sector 031° – 039°). There are several Admiralty buoys in this approach, of no navigational significance, which display lights (Fl Y).

CAWSAND ANCHORAGE

Cawsand Bay lies on your port hand providing an excellent anchorage in south-west and westerly weather, off the pleasant twin villages of Cawsand and Kingsand. This is a handy overnight stop on passage along the coast to avoid the detour into Plymouth and has the additional advantage of being free! Anchor anywhere clear of the local moorings in about 2.5m with good holding, keeping well into the head of the bay to avoid the degaussing range limits as shown on the Admiralty chart. This extends well along the north-eastern side of Penlee Point and anchoring is prohibited. At weekends Cawsand is a popular spot for local boats and is often very crowded.

Ashore the facilities are surprisingly good. The best selection of provisions will be found in Kingsand's Village Store which is open 0630 – 2100. The Shop in the Square in Cawsand has a very limited selection of food but a reasonable off-licence. Shipshape in Kingsand has a small amount of chandlery and also houses the local post office. A public telephone is situated up the road to the left of the prominent Kingsand clock tower. There is definitely no shortage of eating and drinking places though, with four pubs – the Cross Keys, Halfway House, Rising Sun and Devonport – as well as the Cawsand Bay Hotel, which is open to non-residents!

Summer ferries operate to and from the Barbican, which is within easy walking distance of Plymouth City centre. If you follow the delightful coastal footpath through the Mount Edgcumbe Country park, Cremyll ferry to Plymouth is just over three miles away – about an hour's walk. It is advisable to leave someone on board if such an expedition is planned, in case the wind hooks round to the east when you should get out fast and into the shelter of Plymouth before Cawsand becomes untenable.

PLYMOUTH SOUND

Approaching Plymouth from the breakwater, the most distinctive features are the large grain silo by Millbay Docks (which looks rather like a huge grey cathedral), Drake's Island to the west, the large square hotel building in the centre, and to the east the high ground of Staddon Heights, topped with radio masts.

Two prominent forts sit on either side of the Sound just inside the breakwater, Picklecombe on the western shore, now luxury flats, and Bovisand, opposite, which is the British Sub-Aqua Club diving training centre. Two of 'Palmerston's Follies', they were built in the 19th century as part of a defensive chain of forts along the south coast in anticipation of a French invasion that never materialised.

Decide early where you intend to berth, as Mayflower Marina is to the west of the town centre; Sutton Harbour Marina, Queen Anne's Battery Marina and Plymouth Yacht Haven are to the east. The other alternatives depend very much on the prevailing weather conditions – either anchoring or picking up a mooring, although here the choice is very limited.

The anchorages in the Sound are all free, but suffer from the disadvantage that they are remote from the centre of Plymouth. The southern end of Jennycliff Bay, protected by Staddon Heights, provides good shelter in easterly weather, although you will often be subjected to strong and squally downdraughts. Sound in to about 2m at LW, well clear of the conical green buoy (Fl G 6s) marking the wreck of the *MV Fylrix*, which dries LAT. The inshore area to the north of the buoy, across Batten Bay, is a water skiing area.

Both Drake's Island and Barn Pool afford shelter in west or south-westerly conditions and can be approached either by following the main deepwater channel round to the east of Drake's Island, or west of it by using the short cut across 'the Bridge', providing you have sufficient rise of tide.

Shallows, where the dangerous remains of wartime concrete obstructions and dolphins lurk, lie on both sides of this narrow passage. However, between them there is 1.7m, and the channel over the Bridge is clearly marked by four lighted beacons: the outermost No 1 green, with a green conical topmark (QG), which should be left on your starboard hand, No 2 a red port hand beacon with red can topmark (QR), No 3 green with green conical topmark (F l (3) G 10s) and the innermost, No 4 red with red can topmark (Fl (4) R 10s). Nos 1 and 4 have tide gauges, graduated in metres, indicating the height of tide above CD.

At springs, the stream can run through here at three knots, so use the passage with caution, ideally no earlier than an hour or so after LW, and do not wander from the channel. Unless you have a good following wind, proceed under power.

Once through, **Barn Pool** lies to port, under the

The 'Bridge' channel is well marked by these substantial beacons

wooded Mount Edgcumbe shore. Deep water carries close to the pebbly beach, so sound in and anchor in about 3 – 4m. A trip line is recommended as there are many underwater obstructions and the southern end of the bay is foul, supposedly with the remains of an old sunken barge. Although eddies extend into the pool at times, you will lie here comfortably out of the main tidal stream.

This is a delightfully peaceful spot surrounded by the magnificent woods and grasslands of the 800 acre Mount Edgcumbe Country Park, which is free and open to the public daily. In this former deer park Sir Richard Edgcumbe built Mount Edgcumbe House between 1547 and 1553. It survived a direct hit by bombs in 1941 and this fine red stone Tudor mansion was extensively restored between 1958 and 1964. It is open during the summer (Wed – Sun 1100 – 1700, entry charge), and a cafe in the old orangery normally operates during the summer. There is also a fine coastal footpath through the park which eventually takes you to Cawsand.

You can either stroll through the park or along the foreshore (except HW± 2hrs) to Cremyll for a pint at the Edgcumbe Arms, also serving good food. Close by you will find the Mashford Boatyard, an old family run business for many years. This traditional yard is where both Chichester and Rose fitted out for their circumnavigations. A regular passenger ferry runs from Cremyll to Stonehouse from where there are buses right into the centre of Plymouth.

The only other feasible anchorage lies north-east of Drake's Island, east of the pier, well clear of the local moorings and the underwater obstruction, (least depth 0.9m) 400m due north of the pier. Reasonable shelter will be found in winds between south and west, but the proximity to the busy main channel can make it rolly at times. Once known as St Nicholas's Island, this is

Barn Pool is a convenient anchorage off the Mount Edgcumbe Country Park

MAYFLOWER MARINA

With so few moorings or anchorages, and a choice of four marinas with visitors' berths normally available, most yachtsmen opt for the convenience of one of them.

Mayflower Marina (Tel: 01752 556633) was the first in the south-west to be awarded the prestigious Five Gold Anchors by the Yacht Harbours Association in 1986. It lies to the west of Plymouth and is approached either by the Bridge, if conditions permit, or along the deep and well-lit Drake's Channel, leaving the conical green W Vanguard (Fl G 3s) buoy to starboard before heading on through the narrows between Cremyll and the orange and white beacon on Devil's Point (QG).

From here the modern buildings of Ocean Court and the forest of masts in the marina are unmistakable – either call *Mayflower Marina* on VHF Ch 80 or M for a berth allocation, or tie up in the reception berth on the outer pontoon and report to the office. This is clearly marked between the striped flags. At night the marina has an approach light (Dir QWRG) and the south-eastern end of the outer pontoons is marked by 2 FR vert lights.

Much of the Mayflower's success is due to its

traditionally where Francis Drake lay with his battered *Golden Hind* on the return from his circumnavigation in 1580, cautiously waiting for news of the political climate that might greet him, before sailing on to be knighted at Deptford by Queen Elizabeth I.

Drake's Island is private and has been used in the past for a variety of purposes including adventure training, but is now uninhabited apart from a caretaker. Landing is not permitted.

The Five Gold Anchor Mayflower Marina is easily accessed through the narrows between Devil's Point and Cremyll. Barn Pool lies in the centre of the picture with Cawsand Bay in the distance

Always busy, the Mayflower Marina can usually find you a berth somewhere within its secure environs

ownership by a consortium of its berthholders. It has a particularly relaxed, quiet and friendly atmosphere and is a popular stop for long distance cruisers, giving it a genuinely international flavour. It is also a favoured venue for club rallies and cruises in company. Although its position away from the main centre of Plymouth would seem to be a disadvantage, it is in fact quite self-contained and the facilities are excellent, incorporating the Mayflower Chandlery & Store, the Brasserie café/bar and restaurant (Tel: 500008), luxury showers, toilets and a good self service launderette.

During the season (June – August inclusive) a courtesy bus runs daily into the centre of Plymouth and other services include the sale of diesel, petrol, LPG and Calor Gas (all available 24 hours) from the all-tide fuel berth, which is located on the eastern, inner side of the marina. To reach it, continue past the outer ends of the main pontoons and then bear round to port, where the fuel berth will be seen ahead next to the travelift dock. Leave the YBY west cardinal beacon (unlit), marking the outer end of the Cremyll ferry slipway, on your starboard hand.

Other facilities include electricity, latest weather information, marine and electronic engineers, riggers, divers, a 0.75 tonne crane and 25 ton travelift. Excellent 24-hour security makes it an ideal place to leave a boat for longer periods of time (special rates available).

There are 350 deep water berths for up to 34m LOA and 4m draught, with about 30 for visitors, although even at the height of the season they always manage to fit you in somehow. The overnight charge for a 10m boat is £22 (including electricity), while a multihull surcharge of LOA x 1.5 will only be made where the vessel takes up two berths. Mayflower Marina is also a member of Transmanche Marinas, a group of independent UK and European marina operators offering reciprocal berthing arrangements for their berth holders, who are entitled to a 50 per cent discount for the first five nights.

For a pleasant short evening stroll, leave the marina entrance and turn left along the footpath opposite, which leads to Mutton Cove and into the public gardens bordering Mount Wise. Here, on the restored site of the 17th century Redoubt, there is a spectacular 40m high landmark feature – a futuristic stainless steel mast and viewing platform – created in 1999 as part of the Mount Wise Park regeneration. This striking structure is loosely derived from the historical use of the Redoubt as a signalling station during the early 1800s. It was the westernmost end of the chain of shutter telegraph stations that once linked Devonport and other naval bases, like Sheerness and Portsmouth, directly with London.

This form of visual communication comprised six pivoted rectangular boards that could be read at a great distance, the message being relayed onwards along a chain of 28 telegraph stations. The Admiralty in London could receive a reply from Plymouth within 20 minutes! After the shutter telegraph was discontinued in 1814, a mechanical semaphore mast was erected here to communicate with ships in the Hamoaze, and the two uppermost features of the new mast hark back to these semaphore arms.

INNER APPROACHES

To Queen Anne's Battery Marina, Sutton Harbour and Marina, the Cattewater and Plymouth Yacht Haven:

As you approach from seawards and pass to the east of Drake's Island, Plymouth Hoe lies ahead. It runs east-west and on its high grassy slope the old Eddystone lighthouse, banded horizontally red and white, and the tall obelisk of the war memorial, are both prominent. At its eastern end the conspicuous fortress of the Royal Citadel and below it the Royal Plymouth Corinthian Yacht Club (RPCYC) overlook the entrance to the Cattewater and Sutton Harbour. The RPCYC extends a warm welcome to visitors and has two daytime moorings off the clubhouse for temporary use (although they can be very rolly) and two visitors' moorings in the Cattewater available at £10 a night. The impressive clubhouse, extensively refurbished during 1997 at a cost of over £400,000, partly funded by a Sports Council Lottery grant, is open daily 0900 – 1500,

1800 – 2300 (closed all day Monday and Sunday evenings). The club monitors VHF Ch M – superb showers, a bar and snacks are available.

Directly opposite, Mount Batten is a promontory with an isolated hill and old artillery tower which dates from the 1600s. Formerly the RAF's area maritime base, it is now home to the Mount Batten Centre, a major regional dinghy sailing and watersports centre. This is run by an amalgamation of all the watersports organisations in Plymouth following the allocation of £4 million of lottery sports funding and European finance at the end of 1997. It was opened by Prince Phillip in 1999.

The surrounding area, which had been closed to the public since it was requisitioned in 1916, has been newly landscaped with walks, viewpoints, picnic spots, a refurbished breakwater and the Mount Batten Bar and Shaw's Restaurant. If more clues as to who lived here are needed, look at the new street names hereabouts – Shaw Way and Lawrence Road – for this is where TE Lawrence arrived in 1929 to spend four years seeking anonimity as Aircraftsman Shaw after his First World War activities in Arabia.

Mount Batten was originally a seaplane base, and became home to two squadrons of flying boats during the 1920s, for which the large hangers were built. From 1952 onwards it was an air-sea rescue training centre, finally closing in 1992. The west hanger is now home to two boat

building companies, while the east hanger is part of the Plymouth Yacht Haven complex. Access is by a regular water taxi service from the **Barbican**.

The long Mount Batten breakwater extends towards a large dolphin on the Mallard Shoal (least depth 3.5m) and a somewhat confusing cluster of buoys marking the deep water channel. The dolphin has a triangular white topmark surmounted by a sectored light (QRWG) and is the lowest of the two leading marks for the main deep water channel. The upper, a beacon with white triangular topmark and (Oc G) light is on the eastern side of the Hoe giving a transit of 349°T. In practice there is no need for small craft to follow this line – instead pass between the South Mallard YB south cardinal buoy (VQ(6) + Fl 10s) and the end of Mount Batten breakwater (2FG vert) into the Cobbler Channel.

Ahead, Queen Anne's Battery Marina (known locally as QAB) has a breakwater fronted by vertical piling, with an orange/white horizontally striped daymark and orange spherical topmark on its southern side. Both QAB and Sutton Harbour are approached past Fisher's Nose, a granite quay on the western shore with *Speed Limit 8 knots to the east* painted on it and a flashing red light (Fl (3) R) at night. You must proceed under power in Sutton Channel (to the north of Fisher's Nose). This is always a busy corner as most of the large trip boats operate from here, besides which it is also the entrance to two marinas and the fishing harbour.

The River Plym continues eastwards, its mouth known as the Cattewater, which is commercial and administered separately by the Cattewater Harbour Commissioners. Due to the local

Sutton Harbour and Marina, left, with Queen Anne's Battery Marina, right. The imposing fortress of the Citadel is in the foreground with Fisher's Nose, and the Sutton Harbour access lock is in the centre, with the National Marine Aquarium prominent beside it

congestion, anchoring is prohibited here.

Plymouth Yacht Haven soon comes into view on your starboard hand, extending from Mount Batten across Clovelly Bay, the southern shore of the Cattewater. Beyond it, the houses and foreshore of Turnchapel are just under a mile upstream. Vessels proceeding to and from the marina pass through the approaches to Cattedown Wharves, so maintain a vigilant lookout and keep well clear of the deepwater channel and larger vessels at all times. A mile further on, the road bridge at Laira has a 5m clearance, which effectively closes the river to all but small craft.

QUEEN ANNE'S BATTERY MARINA

To enter, keep to the starboard side of the channel and follow the marina breakwater, watching out for and giving way to boats emerging, as they have priority. At night there is a sectored approach light (Oc 7.5s RWG) situated in the small clock tower on top of the marina building/RWYC clubhouse – the white sector indicates the approach through the Cobbler channel. The breakwater has an Oc G light on the south-western corner, and a QG light on the breakwater end.

Queen Anne's Battery Marina (Tel: 01752 671142), which is run by Marina Developments Ltd, can be contacted on VHF Ch 80 (call sign *QAB*) to request a berth. Around 60 are normally available for visitors alongside the continuous pontoon on the inside of the breakwater, although at the height of the season you will probably have to raft up. The finger piers are all reserved for permanent berth holders, but may be allocated to visitors if berth holders are away.

The marina opened in 1986 and took its name from the former use of the site as a gun emplacement built during the Napoleonic War. Today there are comprehensive onshore facilities, including two specialist warehouses, Yacht Parts Plymouth chandlers (Tel: 252489) and Dinghy & Rib (Tel:222265), as well as the Sea Chest (Tel: 222012), an excellent new and secondhand maritime bookshop and Admiralty Chart Agent. Other marine orientated businesses encompass a wide spectrum: from liferaft repairs to stainless steel fabrication, diving air to sailmakers and riggers. The popular Chandlers Bar and Bistro (Tel: 257772) is in the main building.

Water and electricity are installed on the pontoons, all of which have security gates, while diesel and petrol are available from the fuel barge (0830 – 1830) on the outer pontoon, adjacent to the marina entrance. Ashore you will find showers and toilets, a launderette, cafe and marina clubhouse/bar. There is also a large slipway and 20 ton travel hoist for repairs. The overnight charge is £2.70 per metre (up to 15m) and £3.40 per metre (over 15m).

The Royal Western Yacht Club (RWYC) of England was founded in 1827, is the fifth oldest yacht club in England. In early 1989 it moved to its smart premises within the marina after 25 years at the west end of the Hoe in the building that is now the Waterfront Restaurant. RWYC has four visitors' moorings in the Cattewater available on application (£12.50 a night), and visitors are welcome to the use the club (open 0900 – 2300), as well as its showers, bar and popular restaurant (Tel: 660077).

QAB is a major venue for international yachting events, most of which are organised by the RWYC, such as the Round Britain and Ireland Race, Fastnet finish, Twostar and, of course, the Singlehanded Transatlantic, now renamed the Transat. During these big race events space at QAB is inevitably at a premium and it is unlikely that you will find a berth without a prior booking.

The main nautical centre of Plymouth, the Barbican, and access to the rest of the city lie just across the water and can be reached by water taxi

Visitors berth on the long inner pontoon at QAB. The marina office and Royal Western Yacht Club are located in the long red-roofed building

(£1 a head). If you feel like a walk, turn left at the main marina entrance and follow the road and footpath past the National Marine Aquarium, which overlooks the marina. This large and fascinating complex demonstrates the circulation of water from a stream on Dartmoor to coastal reefs, deep oceans and coral reef, and includes a large shark tank. It is a favourite tourist attraction, so during the height of the season you will have to queue to get in! The swing bridge across the entrance lock into Sutton Harbour takes you right into the Barbican.

Barbican Leisure Park in Coxside is also within easy reach, providing a variety of diversions including a multiplex cinema, superbowl ten pin bowling, a health club and a variety of bars, restaurants and clubs.

SUTTON HARBOUR AND MARINA

Sutton Harbour is the home of the Plymouth fishing fleet, a large number of sea-angling boats and Sutton Marina, the first marina to be built in Plymouth (in 1973). Privately owned by the Sutton Harbour Company, the harbour is entered through a 44m long x 12m wide lock (opened in 1993 as part of the Barbican flood prevention scheme), which maintains an approximate depth of 3.5m above CD within Sutton Harbour. Entry and exit is available 24 hours daily and is free of charge. Towards HW the gates remain open to allow free flow, although the footbridge still has to be opened to accommodate craft with masts. Otherwise, the lock and footbridge are opened on request by the Harbour Control Office, which overlooks the lock on the eastern side (VHF Ch 12, *Sutton Harbour Radio*). If without VHF, stand by in the immediate vicinity, noting the traffic light signals displayed from the lock entrance: 3 vert red = STOP. 3 vert green = GO.

Sutton Harbour and Marina are accessed through a lock with convenient floating pontoons for temporary berthing – it is operational on request night and day

Sutton Marina is very convenient for the Barbican and within walking distance of Plymouth City Centre

3 flashing red = serious hazard, WAIT.

Transit is made easy with floating pontoons for temporary berthing inside the lock. At night, the lock is floodlit and the entrance is indicated by reflective chevrons, R/W to port, G/W to starboard.

Once inside Sutton Harbour, the old fishmarket and Barbican quays lie on your port hand, the large new fishmarket is to starboard and Sutton Marina is dead ahead, with the visitors' arrival berth clearly marked on the outer end, adjacent to the fuel pontoon. At night the eastern end of the outer pontoon displays a light (QR).

There are 280 berths and, subject to availability, Sutton Harbour can accommodate between 25 and 30 visitors (maximum 21m LOA). It is best to contact them in advance, especially during the season.

The marina office is located right at the end of Sutton Pier, overlooking the fuel pontoon, and a 24 hour VHF watch is maintained on VHF Ch 16 and 12, call sign *Sutton Harbour Radio*.

On-site facilities include showers, toilets, a small launderette and 24 hour security. A number of marine businesses, including electronic engineers and chandlery, are located on Sutton Pier beside the marina, with shops and the facilities of the Barbican just a short walk around the quayside. Water is available on the pontoons, and the diesel fuel berth is open daily (0830 – 1830 in summer, daylight hours in winter). Charges for a 10m boat work out at £2.40 per metre per night, with reduced rates for longer stays.

Close by on the eastern side ,Harbour Marine's comprehensive boatyard has a 25 ton slipway hoist, a crane and full repair facilities. Here, you will also find the Shipwrights Arms and the China House Restaurant which, in spite of its name, is not a Chinese restaurant!

PLYMOUTH YACHT HAVEN

The 450-berth Plymouth Yacht Haven (Tel: 01752 404231), which opened in April 1998, lies in the bay immediately to the east of Mount Batten and is easily approached through the entrance to the Cattewater. Visitor berthing is normally on pontoons P6, P7 and P8, which is the section of the outer marina breakwater immediately adjacent to the shore, the first you will see as you approach and clearly marked by signs. Here berths of up to 20m are available and larger vessels can be accommodated by arrangement by calling on VHF Ch 80 or M, *Plymouth Yacht Haven*.

Shoreside facilities include showers, toilets, laundry, electricity, telephones and 24-hour security. In the nearby eastern hanger Mount Batten Boathouse (Tel: 482666) has a large selection of chandlery and electronics and is open seven days a week. Calor and diesel are available

Looking across the Cattewater from the Plymouth Yacht Haven towards the Barbican, Mount Batten and its long breakwater are prominent with QAB and Sutton Marinas clearly visible in the distance. The Mount Batten Watersports Centre is just to the right of the two large hanger buildings

(24 hours) from the fuel berth. There is a hefty 65 ton travel hoist – the largest in the area – and a significant amount of laying up space, while general repairs can be undertaken on site. Other services include marine engineers, riggers and electronics specialists.

Overnight charges are £2.20 per metre, with reduced rates for longer stays. Although seemingly less conveniently situated for a visit to Plymouth, there is a water taxi service to the Barbican from the Mount Batten landing stage.

The lively Mount Batten Bar and Shaw's Restaurant (Tel: 405500) is the closest watering hole, while the foreshore walkway from the marina along with a footpath take you within a few minutes to Turnchapel village where the more traditional Boringdon Arms and New Inn both serve good value pub meals.

The Barbican

The bustling and historic area of the Barbican is the tourist centre of Plymouth, and is reputedly where the Pilgrim Fathers embarked aboard the *Mayflower* and sailed for the New World in 1620. This naval city was blitzed more heavily than

With regular ferries linking it to the Barbican, Plymouth Yacht Haven has become well established since it opened in 1998

anywhere else in Britain during the last war and, with large areas being completely destroyed, only the Barbican remains as an example of what this medieval city was like before 1941. It is a maze of intricate narrow streets, with fine examples of Tudor buildings, many of which are now shops – including a handy grocery mini-mart/off licence.

A cosmopolitan mix of bistros and restaurants ranges from seafood at Piermasters (Tel: 229345), Harbour Seafood and Pasta (Tel: 260717) or the Barbican Revival (Tel: 226353), steaks and fish at Platters (Tel: 227262), Italian at the Bella Napoli (Tel: 667772), Greek cuisine and fish at the Village Restaurant (Tel: 667688) to Indian food at the Jaipur Palace (Tel: 668711) or even selecting your own ingredients and watching them cooked by the chef at Cuisine Spontanee (Tel: 673757).

There are inevitably many pubs, usually all very lively at the weekend, and no visit to the Barbican is quite complete without a massive bacon sandwich and steaming mug of tea from Captain Jaspers right on the quayside!

The interesting and attractive area surrounding Sutton Pool has definitely come alive in the past few years with a dramatic proliferation of pavement cafés along the old quayside, together with art galleries and antique shops. There are several museums, including the Elizabethan House in New Street, and nearby the 16th century Merchant's House in St Andrew's Street, which houses the Museum of Plymouth History (weekdays 1000 – 1300, 1415 – 1730, 1700 on Saturdays).

Plymouth fishmarket was the focal point of the old quayside until 1995 when the business was transferred to the new buildings on the opposite side of Sutton Harbour. Since then the old fishmarket has been stylishly transformed into an intriguing tourist attraction – the Barbican Glass Works – where the public can watch skilled Dartington glassmakers producing the goods,

and hopefully buy them too!

In Southside Street, the former Dominican Priory where the Pilgrim Fathers reputedly spent their last night in England is now part of the premises of the famous Plymouth Gin Distillery. Established in 1793, it is famed as the basis for Royal Naval officers pink gins. Guided tours are available Mon – Sat throughout the season, and a Beefeater restaurant/pub (Tel: 224305) is located within the distillery.

The City of Plymouth

Plymouth has a population of over 250,000 and the city centre is 10 minutes' easy walk from the Barbican. The post-war redevelopment of the main shopping area surrounding Royal Parade is mostly redbrick and architecturally unimaginative, with wide boulevards and large shopping precincts; somehow one feels a great opportunity was lost in the rebuilding.

The wide selection of major shops can probably provide anything that might normally be required, and include a large Sainsbury's supermarket in the Armada Centre and a Tesco Metro in New George Street. Both are a taxi ride from the marinas, but useful if you're planning a major provisioning expedition.

Pubs and restaurants abound – everything from Burger King to expensive brasseries! If you're weatherbound with a restless family there are plenty of shoreside diversions – two multi-screen cinemas, the famous Theatre Royal, Plymouth Pavilions (swimming and ice skating) and ten pin bowling, as well as the City Museum and Art Gallery. It is also a convenient place to leave the boat for a day or two if you wish to hire a car and explore south Devon – Dartmoor is within easy reach. The main line railway station is to the north of the city centre, while the Bretonside bus and coach station, situated between the Barbican and the city centre, is nearer.

However, in contrast to the mid-20th century centre, the seafront is a grand spectacle. It is a short walk from the Barbican – follow Madeira Road up past the Citadel, and the elevated promenade winds beneath the grassy slopes of the Hoe, overlooking the rocky foreshore and cliffs below, which are dotted with bathing platforms, pathways and the large open-air swimming pool, currently awaiting restoration.

If you're feeling particularly energetic, seek out the full Plymouth Waterfront Walk, which was created in 1999 to celebrate Plymouth's history and its waterfront. It runs from Admiral's Hard, Stonehouse, opposite the Mayflower Marina, all

Chapter 2

the way to Mount Batten and Jennycliff. Points of interest along the way are highlighted with features and plaques, and full details and a map can be obtained from the Plymouth Tourist Information Centre in the Barbican.

Climbing higher onto the open space of the Hoe, the views across the Sound from this natural grandstand are magnificent, and even more so if you pay the extra 25p to climb to the top of Smeaton's former Eddystone lighthouse. It was built in 1759, dismantled in 1882, and rebuilt on the Hoe in 1884, and its continuing longevity was assured in 2000 when £400,000 was donated from the Heritage Lottery Fund towards its restoration.

Sir Francis Drake's remarkable display of *sang-froid* – contentedly playing on as the vast Spanish Armada sailed unchallenged into the Channel – means that the Hoe, bowls and Drake will forever remain synonymous. Far more a seaman than a bowls player, Drake knew only too well that his ungainly ships could not leave the Sound against the head wind until the ebb began . . .

THE HAMOAZE AND BEYOND

One of the real advantages of Plymouth if the weather turns against you is the great potential for exploring further inland along the Rivers Tamar and Lynher.

Heading west past the Hoe, Millbay Docks is commercial and of no interest to visitors. It is the terminal for the RoRo ferries to Roscoff and Santander, and care should be taken when these large vessels are entering and leaving.

On the starboard side of the docks entrance, the cluster of masts belongs to boats moored in Plymouth's fifth marina, Millbay Marina Village, owned by MDL. This is private and has no facilities for visitors, except for berthholders at other MDL owned marinas, but only by prior arrangement (phone ahead on Tel: 226785). Plymouth lifeboat is based within this marina.

Beyond the Narrows and the Mayflower Marina you enter the wide Hamoaze, its curious name derived from the thick mud that once oozed out of Ham Creek, long since buried beneath the extensive Royal Naval Dockyards that line the eastern Devonport shore. Established by King William III in 1691, these are now privately run by Devonport Management Ltd (DML), which is better known in the sailing world for the fleet of 16 identical 67ft racing yachts that were built here (1990 – 1992) for Chay Blyth's around-the-world British Steel Challenge. More recently 12 new 72 footers were launched

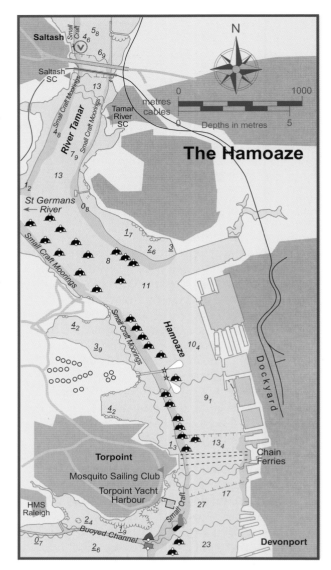

for the 2001 BT Global Challenge.

This is always a fascinating stretch of water, particularly for younger crew members, as there are invariably a variety of warships and submarines berthed along the quays. For the skipper, however, it is a more demanding exercise as it is usually busy and a careful eye should be kept on other ship movements. Remember, too, that civilian craft are not permitted to pass within 50 metres of military vessels or Crown Property or enter the dockyard basins.

The large figurehead of King William III at the southern end of the dockyards is known locally as *King Billy*. Behind him, the large covered slipway is the oldest in any of the former Royal dockyards and, as you pass upstream, the first group of three huge sheds is the undercover frigate repair facility, while the next complex with the large crane is where Britain's nuclear submarines are refitted.

Large chain ferries link Devonport with Torpoint on the Cornish shore and, until 1962 when the Tamar road bridge was opened at Saltash, a mile further upstream, these and the Saltash chain ferry were the only road links across the river. The ferries have right of way and display flashing orange lights at their forward end to indicate the direction in which they are moving. Give them a good berth.

In contrast the western shore is much less developed and, beyond the Mashford Bros Boatyard, the shallow inlet of Millbrook Lake stretches away to the west for over a mile to the village of Millbrook, making an interesting diversion for shallower draught boats on the flood, ideally three hours after LW.

Initially the channel heads directly for the buildings and slipways at Southdown Marina, a family run business on the northern side of the creek where there are moorings and pontoon berths that dry out in soft mud at LW. Visitors' berths are available at £0.50 per foot per day, but it is usually best to phone ahead (Tel: 01752 823084). Shore facilities include toilets, showers, telephone and washing machine and tumble drier. There is also a bar with pool table that opens 1100 – 2300, where Alf and Sheila Hopkins and their son Kevin will make you, your family and pets very welcome. For further details visit their website: www.southdownmarina.co.uk

The whole area taken up by the boatyard premises has an interesting history – the old quays first date from 1650 when a gunpowder factory was established here, while during the early 1700s the King's Brewhouse was also constructed on this site to provide ale for the Navy (it was used in preference to water as it tended to keep better!) In its heyday over 20,000 gallons a week were produced and shipped across the water to the fleet at Devonport!

A pleasant mile long walk from Southdown will lead you to the village of Millbrook.

Proceeding beyond Southdown, steer south-east towards the prominent house beneath the woods on the southern shore, which has the road running in front of it. As you pass this, bear west again, leaving both the black post with yellow 'X' topmark and the line of boats on green mooring buoys on your starboard hand, at which point you will see a long pontoon on your starboard bow extending from Foss Quay. This was once the site of a large brickworks and is now the home of the Multihull Centre Services Boatyard, run by Pip and Debbie Patterson, names well-known in the multihull world. If there is space on the pontoon, berth here and make contact with the office, otherwise berth alongside the quay. In both places you will dry at LW.

Visitors are welcome to stay for up to two nights free of charge, after which they will have to pay £5 a night or £25 a week. The yard can provide a shower and toilet, chandlery, repairs, diesel in cans, water and rigging, as well as a crane. Millbrook, which takes its name from the tide mill that once operated here, is within easy walking distance of a good Spar store with a cashpoint facility, a post office and three pubs, all of which serve food. The village hall is home to a computer centre where it is possible to receive and send e-mails.

Continuing northwards beyond the entrance to Southdown Lake there is little of interest along the western shore – the wide but mostly drying expanse of St John's Lake stretches away towards the modern buildings of *HMS Raleigh*, the Royal Navy training establishment.

Torpoint Yacht Harbour is on the western shore just south of the ferries and is located inside the old Ballast Pound, built in 1783 to shelter and load the barges once used to carry rock ballast out to ships that were sailing light of cargo. This impressive square compound has walls 20ft thick, is dredged to 2m inside, and has 80 pontoon berths with all tide access. The drying berths alongside the quay walls are accessible about three hours either side of HW. A few berths are usually available for short stays and it can make an interesting diversion – a 10m boat will cost £13.60 per night. Water, electricity, showers and toilets are available.

Torpoint's name derives from Tar Point – originally a careening beach where vessels could be caulked and tarred. Today most normal provisions can be obtained in the town centre, just a few minutes walk away from the yacht harbour where the friendly Torpoint Mosquito Sailing Club is situated right next door.

THE LYNHER/ST GERMAN'S RIVER

The Lynher or St German's River is the first opportunity to get away from the bustle of the Hamoaze. Its wide mouth opens to port, upstream of the dockyards, beyond the large warship moorings. The river dries extensively, but is navigable on the tide for four miles to the private quay at St German's where it is possible

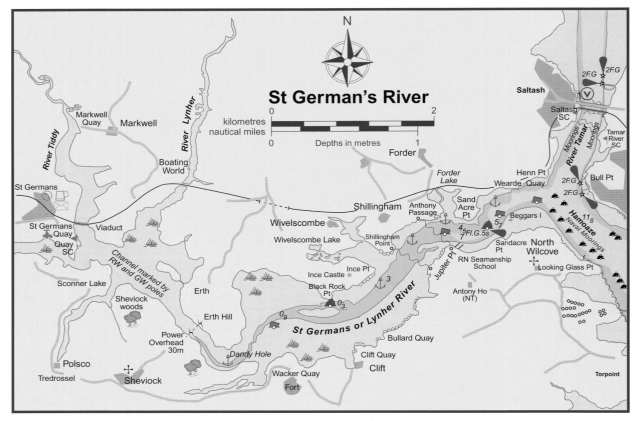

St German's River

for bilge keelers to dry out or larger boats to lie alongside by arrangement.

There are a few buoys in the lower part of the river; leave red cans to port and conical green buoys to starboard when navigating upriver. The channel enters along the northern side, past Wearde Quay, where there are local moorings, and the first port hand buoy 'Lynher Entrance'. This and a second red buoy clear Beggars Island, a gravelly shoal awash at HWS on the southern

St German's Quay is private, but it is sometimes possible to dry out alongside by arrangement with the Quay Sailing Club

side of the entrance. Just east of Sand Acre Point and the first green buoy, you will find a possible anchorage, but the proximity of the main line railway tends to disturb the peace.

Now the channel trends south to avoid the spit extending from the northern shore, marked by another green buoy, and you pass a number of moorings belonging to the RN School of Seamanship at Jupiter Point, a wooded promontory with a jetty and pontoons.

The next red buoy is close to the northern shore, off Anthony Passage, and it is possible to anchor off the mouth of Forder Lake. West of Forder Lake, as far as the next creek, Wivelscombe Lake, an underwater power cable and gas pipeline cross the river and anchoring is therefore not permitted.

Ince Point, on the western side of Wivelscombe Lake, is surmounted by Ince Castle, and south of it there is another anchorage in about 3m. At high tide this is a broad expanse of water, surrounded by lush fields and gently rolling hills, peaceful and unspoiled, with very little evidence of human intrusion. However, from here depths reduce

Chapter 2

An early morning run ashore – Dandy Hole at its very best!

considerably, with generally less than 1m, and drying banks are extensive on both shores. The various salty creeks are ideal for dinghy exploration.

The best is yet to come! Explore further on the flood, but with a wary eye on the sounder, and keep close to the next green buoy off Black Rock Point, where the channel narrows considerably. At the next red can the shores ahead close in, becoming steep and wooded along Warren Point, the river disappearing as it turns tightly behind the rounded slope of Erth Hill. Here, between Warren Point and the bend, there is a fine and isolated anchorage in Dandy Hole, a fortuitous pool with about 3m. Overlooked by high woods, this is as peaceful a spot as you are likely to find, well sheltered and totally away from it all.

From Dandy Hole to St German's the river dries completely and is easiest to scout by dinghy. The wooded shores open out again and the twisting channel is marked by red posts to port, green to starboard, swinging from the eastern shore above Erth Hill to the western off Sconner Lake, then north to a striped middle ground pole where the Rivers Lynher and Tiddy part company. The latter heads west towards St German's Quay, dwarfed beneath the

railway viaduct across the river.

The channel of the Lynher continues north, marked by occasional white posts, before passing under another railway viaduct (21m clearance) beyond which Boating World (Tel: 851679) is situated. Here you will find a large number of second hand craft, along with a sailmaker, chandler, marine engineer, 10 ton hoist and 35 ton crane. Normally this is accessible for boats of moderate draught from half flood onwards.

At St German's there are a number of drying moorings off this private quay, and other local boats berth alongside on the soft mud. Downstream of the old warehouse buildings where the Quay Sailing Club is based, no berthing is allowed, but upstream, space can sometimes be found for an overnight stay alongside by arrangement with the club. A noticeboard displays a phone number to contact when the club is closed – normally it is open on Wednesday evenings and at weekends. Services include a small dinghy landing pontoon alongside the quay and a water tap by the club.

This is a peaceful corner with just a few cottages and the old grassy quayside – disturbed only by the rumble of the trains overhead. The village is about a mile away where there are basic provisions, a post office and the Elliot Arms pub. If you walk up the road from the quay you will

Saltash looking downstream, Sailing Club and pontoon, centre right

pass a telephone box en route, or alternatively follow the pleasant footpath upstream beneath the viaduct, which will eventually bring you along old Quay Lane to the village, where there is a doctor's surgery. Occasional trains run to Plymouth from St German's station.

THE RIVER TAMAR

The Tamar, however, is altogether a far bigger proposition for it is 12 miles to Calstock, and ideally a whole flood tide is needed. In the narrow upper reaches the streams run strongly, particularly on the ebb, and attain in excess of five knots when the river is in spate. In these circumstances, due to the current and the amount of floating debris, trees and branches, such a trip is not recommended.

Today, the river is a tranquil place, a quiet rural waterway that belies its former importance as one of the busiest industrial areas in the West Country. Extensive granite quarries and rich tin,

Saltash Jubilee Green pontoon is free to visitors for stays of up to 12 hours

copper, silver and arsenic mines in the upper reaches were all serviced from the sea, with large sailing schooners, ketches and barges plying far inland. Apart from a few overgrown and derelict quays, it is now difficult to imagine such a hive of maritime activity, but fortunately the heritage has not been totally lost for at Cothele, far upstream, there is a restored Tamar barge and a museum, while Morwellham, almost at the head of navigation, is a former Victorian port that has been restored as a tourist attraction.

Above the entrance to the Lynher, the channel runs broad and deep past Saltash on the western shore towards the twin road and rail bridges. The latter, yet another of Isambard Kingdom Brunel's remarkable achievements, took seven years to build and was opened in 1859 to carry the Great Western Railway from London into Cornwall.

There are many local trot moorings off Saltash, and the enthusiastic and friendly members of the Saltash Sailing Club (Tel: 01752 845988) have their clubhouse on the first prominent quay, at the southern end of which you will find their short stay pontoon. There is ample water alongside it on all but springs, when you should approach it with care. Berth here temporarily and seek out the club administrator if you wish to stay longer – he will usually be able to sort out a club mooring if one is available.

The club is open most lunch times and evenings and visitors are very welcome to use its bar, limited restaurant facilities and showers. There are three pubs in the immediate vicinity of the waterfront, an area known as Waterside, where the large slipway remains as the only tangible evidence of the old Saltash Chain Ferry that ran across the river until the Tamar road bridge was opened in 1962.

A short but steep climb up the hill will bring you to the main shopping area, which can provide most normal provisioning requirements, including a Somerfield and Co-op supermarket as well as a Natwest, HSBC and Barclays bank.

Upstream, moorings continue beyond the bridges along the western shore where there is a convenient landing pontoon off Saltash's Jubilee Green. The inner fingers are private berthing

Chapter 2

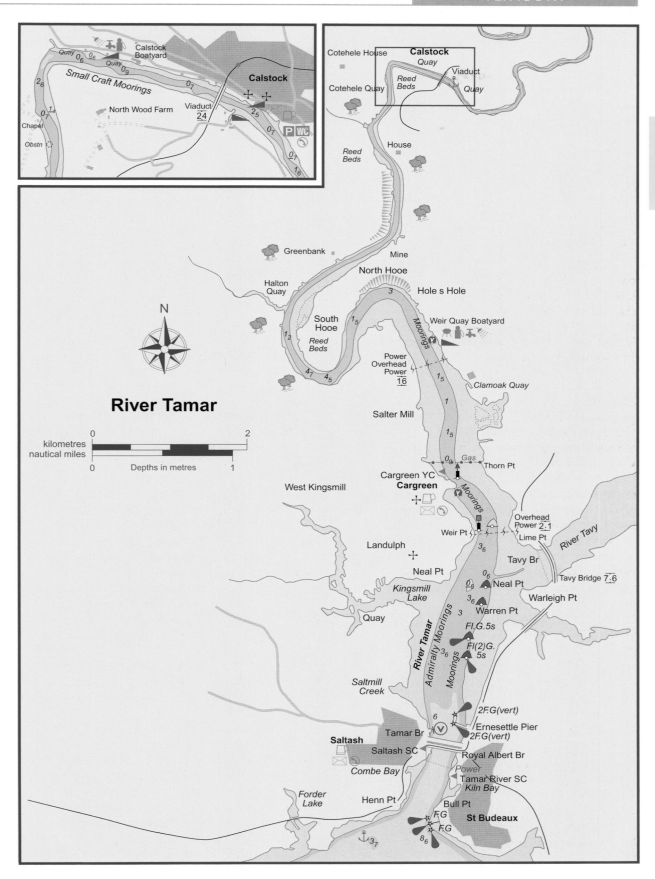

Calstock

Quay

Calstock Boatyard

Quay

Small Craft Moorings

0_6 0_6

0_9

2_6 0_7

1_4

0_7

Chapel

Obstn

North Wood Farm

Viaduct $\underline{24}$

2_5

0_7

P WC

0_7

1_6

Cotehele House

Calstock
Quay

Viaduct

Cotehele Quay

Reed Beds

Quay

Reed Beds

House

Greenbank

Mine

North Hooe

Hole s Hole

Halton Quay

3

1_5

Weir Quay Boatyard

South Hooe

Reed Beds

1_2

Moorings

4_7 4_5

Power Overhead Power $\underline{16}$

1_5

Clamoak Quay

1

Salter Mill

1_5

N

River Tamar

kilometres
nautical miles

0 ——— 2

Depths in metres

0 ——— 1

0_9 *Gas*

Thorn Pt

Cargreen YC
Cargreen

West Kingsmill

Moorings

Overhead Power $\underline{2.1}$

River Tavy

Weir Pt

Lime Pt

Landulph

3_6

Tavy Br

Neal Pt

0_6

0_6

Neal Pt

Tavy Bridge $\underline{7.6}$

Kingsmill Lake

3_6

Warleigh Pt

Quay

3

Warren Pt

3_6

Fl.G.5s

Fl(2)G. 5s

Saltmill Creek

River Tamar

Admiralty Moorings

Moorings

3_6

2F.G(vert)

6

Ernesettle Pier

Tamar Br

2F.G(vert)

Saltash

Saltash SC

Royal Albert Br

Combe Bay

Power

Tamar River SC
Kiln Bay

Forder Lake

Henn Pt

Bull Pt

F.G

St Budeaux

3_7

8_6

F.G

belonging to Saltash Sailing Club, but the outer end of the pontoon is available to visitors for stays of up to 12 hours, free of charge – very handy if you want to nip into Saltash to do some shopping!

On the eastern side of the river Ernesettle Pier is an MOD munitions depot, while two long trots of Admiralty barge moorings run upstream on either side of the main channel.

A line of four green conical buoys marks the eastern bank, and the northernmost lies off the entrance to the River Tavy. Sadly this attractive tributary has long been denied to sailing boats by the railway bridge across its mouth, with only a 7.6m clearance. The river dries almost completely at LW, but power boats or dinghies can explore it on the tide as far as Bere Ferrers, which boasts a pub and limited provisions.

Between the last green buoy and Neal Point, on the western shore, is a drying bank. Keep close to the starboard side of the channel before steering north to Weir Point, a wooded promontory where a large overhead power line crosses the river. Almost directly beneath it, the channel is marked by a post with square red topmark to port and a yellow conical buoy, marking the outer edge of a water ski area, to starboard. The latter sometimes dries at LWS, so hold close to the port hand mark.

The small village of Cargreen lies ahead, with three parallel trots of local moorings running north-south, indicating the deeper water. You should steer for the centre trot to avoid a shallow patch which lies just downstream of the end of the western trot.

The Upper Tamar, Cargreen in foreground with sailing club and slipway visible just upstream of village and Weir Quay Boatyard in far distance on opposite bank

CARGREEN AND WEIR QUAY

Before the first world war Cargreen was still a major crossing point of the Tamar, but the growth of motor traffic resulted in the enlargement of the Torpoint ferries and the decline of Cargreen. Today it is another peaceful village, not much more than a single street running down to the quay. There is a post office (open mornings only) and a general store which closes on Friday afternoons.

Anchor clear of the local moorings where there is about 2m, or pick up one of the visitors' moorings belonging to the Crooked Spaniards Inn (Tel: 842830), which is prominent on the foreshore, and see the landlord when you go ashore for a drink or one of their good value meals.

Cargreen Yacht Club, a little further upstream, made history in 1995 when it was the first in the West Country to be allocated lottery funds to build its fine new clubhouse – over £40,000 was given to the project. Visitors are welcome to use the bar and showers when it is open, usually on Friday evenings on weekends. A contact number is displayed on the door – somebody will usually be able to turn out and help if you have a problem, and you can often be found a mooring if members are away. A tap is located by the clubhouse and you can land at the club slip, which is particularly convenient for avoiding the extensive mud at low tide.

Beyond the moorings the channel is marked on the starboard side by a green beacon with triangular topmark, and it is a straight run northwards to Weir Quay Boatyard where 100 moorings lie along both sides of the deeper water. The moorings are operated at capacity, but visitors are always made very welcome at a flat rate of £10 a night. You should ideally contact the office (Tel: 01822 840474) or pick up the white 'visitor' mooring or the first empty mooring nearest to the slipway and await directions.

It is a peaceful spot for a stop-over and is ideal for walking and exploring this Area of Outstanding Natural Beauty. Information on walks and local attractions is available from the Yard office and visitors are welcome to use the facilities, incorporating shore power on the berthing pontoon, toilets, showers,

Chapter 2

Visitors are welcome at Weir Quay Boatyard in the tranquil upper Tamar

waste disposal, diesel in cans and gas. A chandlery is also available and its small provisions store provides most cruising essentials.

The yard has been in the ownership of Mike and Lisa Hooton since 1999, and facilities include a 12 ton crane, 15 ton boat transporter, with full time staff for repairs and engineering. Fine joinery is a speciality and Weir Quay takes a special interest in traditional and classic boats. Its website gives further details: www.weir-quay.com.

Continuing upstream, apart from a few deeper pools, there is less than 1.5m. The river narrows considerably and winds almost back on itself. The channel is not marked, but generally the deepest water lies along the outside of the bends.

Keep close to the wooded shore beyond Holes Hole, where there is an old quay and several hulks, following the low cliffs right round the outside of this bend as the bank extending from the south shore is very shallow, with a few moorings lying along its edge. From here onwards, between March and September, salmon netsmen will be encountered and care should be taken to pass slowly, keeping a lookout for their nets extending from the banks. As the expansive reed beds come abeam to starboard head across to the southern shore, again holding close to the steep woods.

Large trip boats run regular day cruises from Plymouth to Calstock and, if encountered in these upper reaches, there is not a great deal of water to spare. Their skippers appreciate it greatly if you can pull over to let them pass.

The channel continues to follow the western bank where Pentillie Castle is now mostly obscured by trees, and past Halton Quay with a curious

building rather like a railway signal box that is, in fact, one of the smallest chapels in England. Bear across the the eastern shore past extensive reedbeds, and upstream is a house with two gables just visible in the trees. Steer towards this with an eye on the sounder, then follow the deeper water as it first swings back to the western bank, then midstream as Cothele Quay appears.

COTHELE QUAY

With sufficient water it is possible to berth very temporarily (there is only 1.2m here at HW) alongside the quay, which has been preserved by the National Trust as part of the Cothele estate, although you are better off picking up the mooring in the river.

The quay is home to the restored Tamar barge *Shamrock*. A 57ft ketch, she was built in 1899 and is co-owned by the National Maritime Museum, and the only surviving example of the barges that were once an essential element in the life of the waterway. During the summer she is occasionally sailed by enthusiasts. There is a small museum on the quay devoted to the maritime history of the river, and about 10 minutes' walk from the quay, Cothele House, a splendid Tudor mansion and gardens, is open daily April – October, 1100 – 1800.

CALSTOCK

Beyond the moorings off Cothele Quay, the prominent building of the former Danescombe Hotel, now a private house with an elegant veranda, sits high on the hillside above the final sharp bend into the Calstock reach. As the reed beds open to starboard, the fine viaduct will come into view beyond them.

A line of moorings lies in the centre of the channel off the Calstock Boatyard on the port

Overlooked by its fine viaduct, Calstock is as far as most intrepid explorers of the upper Tamar are likely to reach

hand bank; some of these are usually available for visitors drawing up to 1m, but it is best enquire in advance (Tel: 01822 835986). Deeper draught boats may be able to dry out alongside their small quay, where diesel is also available. A charge of £10 a night includes the use of the showers and toilets ashore.

Anchoring is not recommended immediately above or below the viaduct because of the moorings, poor holding and the narrowness of the channel used by the pleasure boats, although it is possible a bit further upstream just beyond the last private mooring where the sounder will reveal a convenient pool.

In 1998 the Calstock Development Trust was created to rejuvenate the river frontage, since when a new landing slipway and jetty for the ferry operators have been built, but the proposed pontoon for visiting yachts has not yet materialised. The ferry operators have no objection to visitors using the jetty to drop off crew as long as the ferry is not impeded and boats are not left unmanned.

Calstock was once the busiest port in the upper Tamar, but looking at it today it all seems inconceivable. The quays where ships lay two or three abreast have mostly crumbled into disrepair, and the attractive cluster of cottages and small Georgian and Victorian houses, mostly dating from the 1850s, clinging to the steep roads up the hillside betray little evidence of their busy past.

On the opposite shore, now lost in the reeds and sedge, the famous shipyard of James Goss was building large wooden vessels as late as 1909. The ketch *Garlandstone* was the last of these, and today she is preserved as part of the former copper port of Morwellham just over two miles upstream, which has been restored by the Morwhellam Trust as a monument to the industrial past of the Tamar. Open daily during the season as a tourist attraction, it is even possible to take a train ride deep into one of the old copper mines. Beyond Calstock the river becomes much narrower, very shallow and tortuous, and is best explored only by dinghy or small shallow draught boats. Alternatively take the ferry from Calstock which runs if weather and tide permit.

If you need further proof of all this industrial heritage, or just an excuse for a pint, go and take a look at the photographs in the Tamar Inn (good bar meals). Other facilities include a newsagent and general food store, post office, two restaurants and another pub/restaurant, the Boot Inn, petrol at the garage and a branch of Lloyds TSB bank (open Mondays only 1000 – 1230). There are also trains to Plymouth.

Plymouth Port Guide
Area telephone code: 01752

Harbour Master: Commander I Hugo RN, Queen's Harbour Master, HM Naval Base, Plymouth. (Tel: 553740). Deputy QHM, Longroom, (Tel: 663225). Cattewater Harbour Master, Captain Tim Charlesworth, 2 The Barbican, Plymouth PL1 2LR, (Tel: 665934). Sutton Harbour Master, Mr Peter Bromley, North Quay House, Sutton Harbour, Plymouth. (Tel: 204186, Mobile: 07860 863150)

VHF: HM Naval Base Ch 16, working 14, call sign *Longroom Port Control* (24 hours)

Cattewater Harbour Office VHF Ch 12,14 and 80, (Mon – Fri 0900 – 1700)

Sutton Harbour *Sutton Harbour Radio* VHF Ch 16 and 12 (24 hours). See marinas below

Emergency Services: Lifeboat. Brixham Coastguard

Anchorages: Cawsand Bay. Off Jennycliff. Barn Pool. Drake's Island. St German's and Tamar Rivers

Moorings: RWYC, RPCYC. Weir Quay Boatyard (Tel: 01822 840474, E-mail info@weir-quay.com Website: www.weir-quay.com). Calstock Boatyard, (Tel: 01822 833331)

Dinghy landings: RPCYC. Mayflower SC

Water Taxis: QAB to Mayflower Steps. Mayflower Steps to Mount Batten

Mail Drop: Marinas. RWYC and RPCYC

Marinas: Mayflower Marina, Ocean Quay, Richmond Walk, Plymouth, PL1 4LS, (Tel: 556633. Fax: 606896. E-mail: mayflower@mayflowermarina.co.uk Website:www.mayflowermarina.co.uk). 350 berths, 30+ visitors, call sign *Mayflower Marina* VHF channels 80 and M (24 hours).

Queen Anne's Battery Marina, Plymouth PL4 0LP, (Tel: 671142. Fax: 266297 E-mail:qab@mdlmarinas.co.uk Website: www.marinas.co.uk) 240 berths including visitors, call sign *QAB* VHF Ch 80 (24 hours)

Sutton Harbour Marina, Sutton Harbour, Plymouth, PL4 0ES, (Tel: 204186. Fax: 223521. E-mail:admin@sutton-harbour.co.uk Website: sutton-harbour.co.uk). 310 berths, 30 visitors. Approached through free lock (access 24 hours), call sign *Sutton Harbour Radio* VHF Ch 16 and 12 (24 hours)

Plymouth Yacht Haven, Shore Way, Mount Batten, Plymouth PL9 9XH (Tel: 404231. Fax: 484177. E-mail: plymouth@yachthavens.com Website: www.yachthavens.com) 450 berths inc visitors, call sign

Plymouth Port Guide continued

Area telephone code: 01752

Plymouth Yacht Haven VHF Ch 80 and M (24 hours)

Charges: Mayflower Marina £2.20 per metre per night. Queen Anne's Battery Marina up to 15m £2.70 per metre per night, over 15m £3.40 per metre per night. Sutton Harbour Marina £2.40 per metre per night. Plymouth Yacht Haven £2.20 per metre per night

Moorings, per night :RWYC £12.50. RPCYC £10. Weir Quay £10

There is no charge for anchoring anywhere within the Plymouth area

Phones: At all marinas and yacht clubs. Cawsand, Cremyll, Southdown, Millbrook, St Germans, Torpoint, Saltash, Cargreen, Calstock

Doctor/dentist: Ask at marinas

Hospital: Derriford, (Tel: 777111)

Churches: All denominations

Local Weather Forecast: At marinas

Fuel: Mayflower Marina, diesel, petrol and LPG 24 hours. Queen Anne's Battery Marina, diesel and petrol, 0830 – 1830.Sutton Harbour Marina, diesel 0830 – 1830. Plymouth Yacht Haven, diesel 24 hours. Weir Quay and Calstock Boatyard, diesel only

Paraffin: At QAB and Mayflower marinas

Gas: Calor/Gaz at all marinas, 24 hours at Mayflower Marina

Water: At all marinas. In cans, Cawsand, Multihull Centre, Millbrook. St German's Quay, Cargreen, Weir Quay, Calstock

Tourist Information Centre: Barbican, opposite old Fishmarket

Banks/cashpoints: All main banks in Plymouth city centre, all with cashpoints

Post Offices: Barbican. Plymouth City centre. Cawsand. Millbrook. St German's. Cargreen. Calstock

Rubbish: Disposal facilities at all marinas

Showers/toilets: At all marinas. RWYC. RPCYC

Launderettes: At all marinas

Provisions: Everything obtainable. Many shops also open on Sundays.

Approach to Mayflower Marina

Chandlers: Yacht Parts Plymouth, (Tel: 252489). The Sea Chest, nautical bookshop/Admiralty Chart Agent. (Tel: 222012), both at Queen Anne's Battery. Marine & Leisure, Sutton Jetty (Tel: 268826). Marine Bazaar, Sutton Harbour, (Tel: 201023). Mayflower Chandlery & Store, Mayflower Marina (Tel: 500121). Mount Batten Boathouse (Tel:482666). Plymouth Yacht Haven. Saltash Boat & Mooring Services, Saltash, (Tel: 845482)

Repairs: Mashford Bros, Cremyll (Tel: 822232).Androdian Yacht Services, Mayflower Marina (Tel: 606707). Harbour Marine, Sutton Harbour (Tel:204690). A Blagdon, Richmond Walk (Tel: 561830). Embankment Road (Tel: 228155). Multihull Centre, Millbrook (Tel: 823900)

Marine engineers: Harbour Marine, Sutton Harbour (Tel: 204691). Marine Engineering Looe, QAB, (Tel: 226143) M&G Marine, Mayflower Marina (Tel: 862277). AS Blagdon & Sons (Tel: 228155) Ask at marinas or boatyards

Electronic engineers: Sutton Marine (Tel: 662129). Devtech Marine Electronics (Tel: 223388). Tolley Marine (Tel: 222530). Waypoint 1 (Tel: 661913) or ask at marinas

Sailmakers: Osen Sails (Tel: 563666). Westaway Sails, Ivybridge (Tel: 892560). Ask at marinas

Riggers: Yacht Rigging Services, Mayflower Marina and Plymouth Yacht Haven (Freephone 0800 915 8609 or Tel:226609). Sutton Rigging (Tel: 269756). Allspars (Tel: 266766) and Eurospars (Tel: 550550) both at QAB

Transport: Main line trains to London and the north (Tel: 08457 484950). Buses, Western National

(Tel: 402060). Good road connections to M5.

Plymouth airport, flights to London/Scotland/Eire (Tel: 204090). Ferries to Roscoff and Santander (Tel: 08705 360360)

Car Hire: Hertz (Tel: 207207). Avis (Tel: 221550) or ask at marinas

Taxi: (Tel: 606060, 222222 , 202020, 0800 175175 or 0800 123444)

Car Parking: All marinas have customer parking

Yacht Clubs: Royal Western Yacht Club of England, Queen Anne's Battery, Plymouth, PL4 0TW (Tel: 660077. E-mail:admin@rwyc.org Website: www.rwyc.org). Royal Plymouth Corinthian Yacht Club, Madeira Road, The Hoe, Plymouth PL1 2NY (Tel: 664327).Mayflower Sailing Club, Phoenix Wharf, Plymouth (Tel: 662526). Saltash Sailing Club, Waterside, Saltash (Tel: 845988)

Eating out: Vast choice from Indian to Greek, Spanish to Chinese. Restaurants, bistros, pub food, fish and chips

Things to do: Elizabethan House, Plymouth Museum in old merchant's house, Royal Citadel, Barbican, Barbican Glass Works. National Marine Aquarium. Smeaton's Tower, Plymouth Dome and Pavilions, audio/visual history of Plymouth, swimming and ice skating. The Hoe. Plymouth Waterfront Walk. Large shopping centre, two multi-screen cinemas, theatre

Regattas/special events: Port of Plymouth Regatta and Plymouth Classic Boat Rally end of July. Venue for many special events, including dinghy championships, and start/finish of major offshore races, including Fastnet, Transatlantics and Round Britain

PASSAGES
RAME HEAD TO THE MANACLES

Favourable tidal streams
Rame Head: *LEAVE PLYMOUTH*
  Bound West: Two hours before HW Dover
  Bound East: Four hours after HW Dover *LEAVE FOWEY*

Dodman Point:
  Bound West: Three hours before HW Dover
  Bound East: Three hours after HW Dover *SLACK*
  AT DODMAN

✕ AT DODMAN

Passage charts for this sea area:
BA: 1267 Falmouth to Plymouth.
          148 Dodman Point to Looe Bay
          (including harbour plan of Polperro).
          777 Land's End to Falmouth.
          3l Harbours on the south coast of
          Cornwall (Fowey, Charlestown, Par).
          147 Plans on the south coast of
          Cornwall (Helford River, Looe,
          Mevagissey)
          SC5602

Imray: C6 Start Point to Lizard Point.
          WCP 2400.8, 2400.9

Stanford: 13 Start Pt to Land's End and Padstow

French: 4812 Du Cap Lizard à Start Point

Rame Head from the south-west – a distinctive conical headland from every approach

Safety information and weather
In all cases initial announcement on VHF
Channel 16 then switch to:

Brixham Coastguard: VHF Channel 10 (west of
Start Point), Channel 86 (Fowey area and east of
Dodman Point) at 0050, 0450, 0850, 1250, 1650,
2050 UT

Falmouth Coastguard: VHF Channel 23 (west of
Dodman Point and Falmouth) at 0140, 0540, 0940,
1340, 1740, 2340 UT

Rame Head NCI station (Tel: 01752 823706)

Polruan NCI station (Tel: 01726 870291)

Charlestown NCI station (Tel: 01726 817068)

Portscatho NCI sation (Tel: 01872 580180)

Waypoints
1   **Rame Head** (1M south of summit)
       50°17'·84N / 04°13'·39W

2   **Looe Island** (1M south of summit)
       50°19'·23N / 04°27'·05W

3   **Udder Rock buoy**
       50°18'·93N / 04°33'·86W

4   **Fowey approach**
       (3 ca due S of Punch Cross)
       50°19'·33N / 04°38'·40W

5   **Gwineas Rock** (0.5 M SE of buoy)
       50°14'·16N / 04°44'·82W

6   **Dodman Point** (1.5M SE of Monument)
       50°12'·14N / 04°46'·52W

7   **Gull Rock** (0.75M SE of summit)
       50°11'·22N / 04°53'·47W

8   **Falmouth approach**
       (0.75 M due S of Zone Point)
       50°07'·60N / 05°00'·56W

9   **Manacles** (0.5 M due E of Manacle buoy)
       50°02'·82N / 05°01'·14W

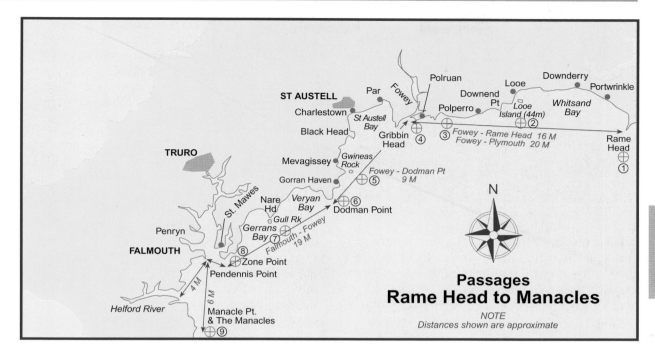

**Passages
Rame Head to Manacles**

*NOTE
Distances shown are approximate*

West of Plymouth and the Yealm, Fowey is the next probable destination on a coasthopping cruise and, over 20 miles away, it is one of the longest legs. Although no great distance in itself, yet again the odds are very much in favour of winds forward of the beam and once past Rame Head the tidal streams are weak inshore and of no great assistance. Three miles south of Looe the streams rotate in a clockwise direction, attaining a maximum at springs of about one knot, east by north at HW Dover –0520, but no more than a knot west by south at HW Dover +0035. Somehow, this passage always seems to take longer than anticipated.

The Dodman is 23 miles distant from Rame Head and, given reasonable visibility, its long, flat topped headland and distinctively rounded end will be on the horizon.

Whitesand Bay falls back immediately to the north-west of Rame Head – a succession of sandy beaches and rocky outcrops backed by a continuous line of steep and broken grassy cliffs between 30m and 76m high. *HMS Scylla* was scuttled here in March 2004 to form an artificial reef for divers. The direct course to Fowey keeps you a good couple of miles offshore, which is no great disadvantage as this is one of the less inspiring stretches of coast. Rocks extend a cable immediately to the west of Rame Head, and north-west of the point is a dangerous wreck awash at LWS and marked by a red can. Following the sweep of the bay inshore, there are rifle ranges by the old fort at Tregantle, where a

number of flagstaffs along the cliffs warn you to keep well clear if the red flags are flying.

Sounding like a perfect setting for an Enid Blyton children's adventure, Portwrinkle, almost two miles west of Tregantle, is a very tiny boat harbour, which dries completely and is fringed by extensive rocky ledges. A few houses are situated nearby, while the village of Crafthole can be seen on the skyline. From here onwards, the coast continues in a long, high sweep with further extensive rocky ledges and hazards stretching up to two cables offshore, including the Longstone, a prominent rock 18m high. At Downderry, which straggles along the cliffs, precipitous paths lead down to a beach, and to the south there are the Sherberterry Rocks, a large area of shallows extending just over two miles offshore, with least depths of 4.9m. These can produce an area of rough water, particularly in onshore winds when this whole stretch of coast should be avoided and a good offing maintained.

LOOE AND POLPERRO

Looe Island, a pleasantly rounded 44m high hump lies close to the shore, almost linked to the mainland at LW, and is a perfect natural daymark for the drying fishing port of **Looe** just to the east.

Looe from the south-east, with Looe Island clearly visible

Looe is mostly commercial with very limited facilities for yachts, and is dangerous to approach in fresh or strong south or south-easterly winds and ebb tide, as it has a long and very narrow entrance. In offshore winds, however, there is a good anchorage just off the harbour. Rounding Looe Island, **the Ranneys** is a group of drying rocks extending three cables south-east from the island, south of which shallower patches stretch for nearly a mile with least depths ranging between 9m and 11m – note that in fresh wind against tide this can create some unpleasant overfalls. The YB south cardinal buoy (Q(6)+LFl), which lies 1M SSE of the Ranneys, provides a useful distance mark – keep to seaward of this and you will avoid any problems. A 586m high TV mast can be seen 10 miles due north of Looe Island, displaying a number of fixed red lights at night.

Beyond Looe the coast becomes more interesting again. There is a measured mile (1,852.9m to be precise!) just west of the island, the transits formed by two white beacons with a vertical black stripe at each end, running as far as the approach to Talland Bay. This attractive sandy beach backed by trees and fields is popular with holidaymakers and stretches to the 100m high Downend Point, which

Polperro lies hidden in a narrow cleft in the high cliffs

has a large granite war memorial near the summit. Downend Shoals, a mile due south, have a least depth of 2.6m and should be passed well to seaward if there is any sea running.

If bound for Polperro, the small fishing village harbour just over mile to the west, it is best not to turn inshore until the white beacon on Spy Glass Point (Iso WR 6s 7M), just east of the harbour, is bearing north. Approaching from the west, a prominent TV mast will be seen high on the cliffs just before the village opens. Like Looe, Polperro is a place less frequented by yachts and space within the harbour is taken up by local boats so, weather permitting, you will either use one of the four visitors' moorings in the close approach to the harbour, or anchor just south of them. In bad weather a storm gate closes off the harbour completely.

From Polperro to Fowey, in good weather, the coast is very attractive with impressive cliffs up to 91m in height, occasionally broken by steep green and grassy coombes and gullies running down to small coves. The water is deep to within two cables of the shore and there are no hazards, except **Udder Rock** (dries $\underline{0}$.6m) two miles west of Polperro and half a mile offshore, which is marked by a YB south cardinal buoy (VQ(6) +LFl 10s). A white beacon on the cliffs along with a white mark on a rock on the shore also provide a transit (020°T) for this hazard, while a prominent white mark on the western side of Lantic Bay, just open of steep Pencarrow Head (135m high), gives a cross bearing of 283°T. At night, if you are in the red sector of Fowey light, you will pass Udder Rock to the south, although it is safer still to keep further to seaward in the white sector.

Generally, if making the passage from Plymouth to Fowey at night, the dominant feature is the Eddystone to the south-east, (Fl(2) 10s 17M), but you will be on the 13M limit of its fixed red sector (112° – 129°T). Rame Head is unlit, but a buoy 1M SSE of Looe island is lit (Q(6)+LFl), as is Looe harbour entrance (Oc WR 3s 8M). Also look out for a light just east of Polperro Harbour (Iso WR 3s 7M) and the Udder Rock buoy (VQ(6) +LFl 10s), two miles west of Polperro and Fowey (L Fl WR 5s, W 11M, R 9M).

FOWEY

In daylight, although completely hidden from the east, the entrance to Fowey harbour is not difficult to find thanks to the huge red and white horizontally striped daymark and a square pillar 104m high built by Trinity House in 1832 on

Approaching Fowey from the south, the entrance is easy to spot

Gribbin Head – a long promontory to the south-west of the river mouth.

A mile east of the entrance and immediately west of Pencarrow Head is Lantic Bay, backed by National Trust land, and its tidal beach is a beautiful stretch of clean sand with a good anchorage off it in northerly winds.

Beyond it is a conspicuous white house high on the cliffs, and a ruined tower. The Polruan NCI lookout (Tel: 01726 870291), in the Old Pilots' lookout building, is also located here. As the headland draws abeam, Punch's Cross, a white cross on a large rock, will come into view to starboard, with houses along the cliff above. The river mouth and town of Fowey will now start to appear, surrounded by high ground on either side.

Deep and free from hazards, Fowey can be approached in any weather, although strong southerly winds and ebb tide will produce very rough conditions and breaking seas in the

Udder Rock buoy looking west to Gribbin Head

entrance. As well as being a popular yacht harbour, this is also a very busy commercial port, exporting large quantities of china clay. Be ready for surprise encounters with sizeable ships in the entrance – which is only a cable wide at its narrowest point. These vessels have priority, so keep well clear!

ST AUSTELL BAY TO DODMAN POINT

The passage from Fowey to Falmouth is another 20 miles, and the tide is once again a definite factor to consider when rounding the Dodman. The Lizard and Start Point both instantly evoke an image of overfalls and races, but somehow the Dodman seems to elude such an association, which is strange, as there can often be quite an unpleasant amount of disturbance in its vicinity. Close to the point streams run at nearly two knots at springs and, with wind against tide, the uneven depths and shoals of the Bellows and Field can produce a small, but very unpleasant race extending a good mile offshore. If a westerly wind of any strength is prevailing, ideally try to round the point at slack water just before the main ebb begins to the south-west (about three

Gribbin Head

An unmistakeable and imposing headland, Dodman Point from the east

hours before HW Dover), which means leaving Fowey two hours after local HW (Dover –0600).

The whole promontory of the Dodman provides a considerable lee in westerly weather, and it should be remembered that a fresher wind and larger seas are likely to be encountered once past the point, particularly in a south-westerly when it can be a long 10-mile beat to windward along an exposed stretch of coast that provides no shelter until you reach Falmouth.

The only hazards between Fowey and the Dodman are both well marked. The first is Cannis Rock (dries 4.3m) marked by the Cannis Rock south cardinal buoy YB (Q6+LFl 15s) positioned a mile south-east of Gribbin Head in the western red sector of Fowey lighthouse. The second is the Gwineas Rocks, the largest of which dries to 8m. They are just over two miles north-east of Dodman Point, with Gwineas east cardinal buoy BYB (Q (3)10s) guarding them two cables to the south-east.

St Austell Bay opens to the north-west when clear of Gribbin Head, and the coast running away towards the Dodman, nine miles south-west of Fowey, provides a good sheltered area of water in westerly winds.

This is an attractive miniature cruising ground in its own right. The land rises beyond it, the distant sprawl of houses around St Austell. Sadly, the once spectacular and jagged skyline of the surrounding 'Cornish Alps' – the huge white spoil heaps from the extensive china clay workings – have now been re-profiled and planted with greenery and from offshore no longer appear as an enticing range of snow covered mountains when they catch the sun!

The china clay port of Par is commercial and of no interest to visitors, but does provide another very distinctive landmark on the northern shore of the bay – four large chimneys that are even more conspicuous when belching white smoke.

Further west the former clay port of Charlestown is now privately owned by the Square Sail Shipyard Ltd. Home to many classic and traditional craft, it is well worth a visit if time and weather permit. An NCI Lookout is located here (Tel: 01726 817068).

Your course will take you well away from the land, closing it east of the Gwineas Buoy, but the town and white lighthouse of Mevagissey are easy to spot on the western shore, a V-shaped gap in the cliffs, surmounted by houses on both sides. Gorran Haven, a drying small boat harbour, lies due west of Gwineas rocks. As always, particularly near the rocks, keep a good lookout for pot buoys.

This course will also lead you close to the Dodman Point Gunnery Range, which was established here after the closure of Portland Naval Base in 1996. There are three yellow spherical target buoys lying between 3M and 4.8M SSE of Dodman Point, the most southerly 'A' at 50°08'·53N, 04°46'·38W (Fl Y 10s), 'B' at 50°10'·03N, 04°45'·00W (Fl Y 5s), and 'C' at 50°10'·04N, 04°47'·04W (Fl Y 2s). Naval vessels usually fire on these from a position approximately seven miles to the north-east of the buoys, somewhere between 2.5M and 9M SSE of Gribbin Head.

Firing takes place in daylight only, roughly once or twice a week throughout the year, except during August and for two weeks over Christmas.

During exercises, which normally last for a maximum of two hours using flash/bang/smoke charges but no high explosives, a helicopter is stationed within 1M of the target buoys and a range safety boat, (23m LOA black hull/yellow superstructure) is normally on station and can be contacted on VHF Ch 16 & 10. The firing ship can be called on VHF Ch 16, 74 or 10, and it will also promulgate its intentions on VHF Ch 74 immediately prior to firing and at regular intervals throughout the exercise. Normally, the firing itself lasts little more than 15 minutes at a time.

No firing will take place if a vessel is within the safety trace area, which extends south-west and beyond the target buoys. There is no exclusion zone and vessels have a right of transit through the range area, but their co-operation is requested. Ideally try to transit the area on a NW/SE heading and remain two miles clear of the target buoys, and it is prudent to contact either the firing ship or the range safety vessel to discuss your intentions.

Details of firings – Gunfacts – are broadcast by the Coastguard on VHF Channels 10 & 73. Information is also displayed at Fowey Harbour Office and can also be obtained direct from Flag Officer, Sea Training Operations Room (FOST OPS) 24 hours a day either on VHF Channel 74 or Tel: 01752 557550.

Close to, the Dodman is an impressive 111m high rounded bluff. It is flat topped with steep cliffs along its eastern side, but with a more sloping western side comprising a lovely stretch of National Trust property covered in gorse, ferns and grass. High on the south-western tip is a large white cross erected in 1896 by a local vicar.

On a fine calm day it is quite feasible to pass within a cable of the foot of the cliffs, as the water is deep and unimpeded, but in any sort of sea or weather stand well out – up to two miles in fresh conditions. A once notorious headland for shipwrecks, particularly in fog, it is strange that no light or fog signal was ever established here, particularly as both St Anthony light (Iso WR 15s 16/14M, Red Sector 004° – 022°), and the Lizard light (Fl 3s 25M) are obscured from the Dodman. Apart from the lights of villages ashore, there are no aids to navigation at night until St Anthony light appears on a north-westerly bearing, although sometimes its loom will be seen sooner. There is also a noticeable set into the bays between the Dodman and Falmouth. In poor visibility or at night give this coast a wide berth.

DODMAN POINT TO FALMOUTH

Once past the Dodman, Veryan Bay opens to the north. It is an attractive but uncompromising cliff-lined stretch of coast, broken at intervals by small sandy coves. Nare Head, the western

St Anthony light emerges from behind Zone Point to reveal the wide entrance to the Fal. Pendennis Point on left

extremity of Veryan Bay, is five miles distant and looks similar to the Dodman, but has the distinctive triangle of Gull Rock, an island 38m high, a mile to the east. Although Veryan Bay is almost free from offshore dangers – with no rocks more than two cables from the shore – there is one notable exception. Lath Rock (least depth 2.1m) is almost midway across the bay, although fortunately just inside the direct line from the Dodman to Gull Rock.

Gull Rock is a jagged pyramid, with sparse grass around its whitened summit, clear evidence of the many seabirds that nest there and give it its name. In fair weather it is possible to pass between the rock and the steep 80m high cliffs at Nare Head, but the Whelps, a reef with a number of drying rocks, mostly 4.6m, extends a mile to the south-west of Gull Rock.

Gerrans Bay, much of which is surrounded by National Trust land, is of a similar aspect to Veryan, although the cliffs along its western side become less precipitous. Probably the best of all the anchorages along this section of coast is off Porthscatho, a little fishing village now popular with holidaymakers, which offers shelter from the west. There is a small pier on its southern side, affording protection to the drying foreshore, with a reasonable anchorage just to the north-east. Basic provisions, a post office and several pubs ashore make this a popular day sail from Falmouth. There is an NCI Lookout at Portscatho (Tel: 01872 580180).

Gerrans Bay has seen many shipwrecks in its time, with vessels mistaking it for the entrance to Falmouth, but the most spectacular in recent years was the capsize of pop star Simon Le Bon's maxi, *Drum*, after she lost her keel in gale force conditions during the 1985 Fastnet.

The Bizzies (least depth 4.2m) lie almost on the line from Gull Rock to Porthmellin Head and

should be avoided in fresh winds and ground swell, which can create quite an area of overfalls around them.

Beyond Gerrans Bay, the rounded profile of Zone Point continues to hide the elusive St Anthony light, (Iso WR 15s 16/14M, Red Sector 004° – 022°) and a certain nagging doubt can tend to creep in at this stage of the passage. There used to be a conspicuous row of coastguard cottages high on Zone Point, but these have since been demolished by the National Trust. It is surprising that no daymark was ever established here as the entrance is not easy to locate from the east until, at last, the white lantern peeps into view from behind the headland. Just over a mile south of the light, a rocky shoal called Old Wall (least depth 7m) rises steeply from the sea bed and can produce an area of rough water in strong southerly winds. In fine weather it is a popular fishing area and easy to spot by the number of angling boats in its vicinity.

The entrance to the River Fal is a mile wide and safe to enter in any condition. It is flanked on the east by St Anthony Head and Pendennis Point to the west, with the only hazard being Black Rock, right in the middle, marked by a conspicuous but unlit beacon which can be passed either side. In strong southerly winds, with an ebb tide out of the estuary, rough seas will be encountered in the approach and entrance. The ebb, up to two knots at springs if fresh water is running down the river, begins at HW Dover –0605.

HELFORD RIVER AND THE MANACLES

It is just over five miles from St Anthony Head to Manacle Point, away to the south-west, and between them Falmouth Bay is a fine natural roadstead, well sheltered from the north to south-west, but open to the east and south. It is much used by large vessels as an anchorage, and increasingly for offshore bunkering.

From Pendennis Point, neatly crowned with its castle, the hotels and beaches of the Falmouth seafront form a broad sweep to the west, and the large cream coloured Falmouth Hotel at the eastern end is particularly prominent. Depths reduce gradually towards the shore, which is fringed with rocky ledges, but there are no dangers further than a cable from it, except large numbers of poorly marked pot buoys. In offshore winds it is possible to anchor off Swanpool Beach, just north of the prominent and wooded Pennance Point. Maenporth is another popular

There is little to indicate the Helford from the east except the distant cluster of boats within

cove a mile to the south and, during the summer, a large inflatable racing mark is usually anchored to seaward.

From Falmouth, the entrance to the Helford River is not easy to distinguish; the various headlands of similar shape blending together. Low cliffs run between Maenporth and Rosemullion Head, which is flat topped, rounded and covered in gorse and thick bushes. Between it and Mawnan Shear there are steep grassy cliffs with a dense clump of woods and a conspicuous white house at its eastern edge.

The Gedges rocks (drying 1.4m) lie three cables ESE and are marked to seaward by the conical green August Rock buoy (summer months only). This is the only real hazard in the approach to the Helford River and, once past the buoy, the entrance opens clearly. It is exposed to the east, when the shallowing water produces particularly steep short seas and, being unlit, should not be attempted at night without local knowledge.

Gillan Creek is an opening in the southern approach to the Helford due south of the Gedges. This attractive, but mostly drying inlet lies between Dennis Head, which is grassy and 43m high, and Nare Point, a much lower promontory with an old square coastguard lookout on the end. Beware Car Croc, a rock just awash at LW in the entrance of Gillan Creek, marked with an east cardinal buoy (BYB) which should be left to starboard when entering. There are also rocky ledges extending a cable to seaward of Nare Point.

Proceeding south from Falmouth or the Helford, the extensive rocky nightmare of the Manacles involves a detour to the east. The yellow Helston buoy (Fl Y 2.5s), known locally as

the years. Their sinister name actually derives from the Cornish *maen eglos*, meaning Church stones, for the spire of St Keverne Church is prominent inland.

Close to the Manacles the tidal streams run at up to two knots at springs. If bound round the Lizard, aim to leave Falmouth or the Helford about three hours after local HW to gain the best advantage. There is an inshore passage through the Manacles regularly used by local fishing boats, but do not be tempted to follow them as it is very narrow in places with unpredictable eddies and currents exceeding three knots. Do not be too amazed if you see a sizeable coaster seeming to emerge from among the rocks. Incredibly, they regularly load stone at Dean Quarry alongside the cliffs just south of the Manacles.

At night, if approaching from the south, the Manacles lie within the red sector of St Anthony light, 004° – 022°T.

Before radar, a very large percentage of the wrecks along this section of coast occurred in calms and fog rather than extremes of weather. It is still difficult in poor visibility, as a number of the headlands and bays have a similar appearance and audible aids are few and far between. There are just eight in total: Eddystone Light (Horn(1) 30s), Nailzee Point (Siren (2) 30s if fishing fleet at sea), Udder Rock buoy (Bell), Cannis Rock buoy (Bell) – note there is no other fog signal at Fowey – Mevagissey (Dia 30s), Gwineas buoy (Bell), St Anthony Head (Horn (1) 30s), Manacles Buoy (Bell).

Remember that there is generally a northerly set into the bays and, although the 10m sounding line provides a good indication of relative position clearing most of the hazards close to the shore, such as the Dodman, this is for the most part little more than two cables off. If in doubt, err to seawards and do not follow local fishing boats, particularly close to the Manacles – there is no telling where they might be going!

the Three Mile Buoy, lies just over three miles south of St Anthony and almost the same distance east of the entrance to the Helford River. This part of the bay is much used for search and rescue exercises from RNAS *Culdrose*, and if you see Admiralty vessels and helicopters in the vicinity, keep well clear.

Manacle Point is a rather untidy looking headland, badly scarred by extensive old quarry workings. Just to the north, by the small cove of Porthoustock, are the unsightly remains of the huge stone loading chutes on either side of the bay. Jagged pinnacles of rock extend from the point, which continue to form the reefs offshore, marked by the Manacle east cardinal buoy (Q(3) 10s), a mile to the east. These tend to appear further out to sea than you anticipate, particularly when approaching from the south.

The Manacles are undoubtedly one of the most treacherous hazards along the Cornish coast. Lying right in the approach to a busy port, it was inevitable that this area of half-tide rocks and strong currents should claim so many ships over

A quiet morning at the Manacle buoy – note Black Head and houses of Coverack in the distance

LOOE AND POLPERRO

Tides	HW Dover −0545
Range	MHWS 5.4m–MHWN 4.2m, MLWN 2.0m–MLWS 0.6m. Strong streams within Looe harbour at springs
Charts	BA: 147 (Looe), 148 (Polperro). Stanford:13. Imray: C6
Waypoint	Looe: Banjo Pier Head 50°21'.06N / 04°27'.07W
	Polperro: West Pier Head 50°19'.87N / 04°30''.96W
Hazards	Looe: Looe Island and the Ranneys rocks to south (all unlit)
	Polperro: The Raney and Polca Rock in approaches (both unlit). Both harbours dry to entrance, and are dangerous to approach in onshore wind and sea. Polperro harbour mouth closed in bad weather. Busy fishing port keep clear of local boats. Beware pot and net buoys in approaches
Overnight charges	Looe: Harbour Authority alongside: £8
	Polperro: Harbour Authority mooring: £6

Midway between Plymouth and Fowey lie the small harbours of Looe and Polperro. Both are working fishing ports with restricted space and they dry almost completely at LW. Boats unable to take the ground comfortably or lie alongside can anchor off or, in the case of Polperro, use the moorings just outside the harbour. Neither harbour should be approached in onshore winds of any strength as they have narrow entrances.

LOOE

APPROACHES

From offshore, the entrance is easily located, lying to the east of the large rounded lump of Looe Island (44m) half a mile offshore. It is also known locally as St George's Island and, if approaching from the west, it is essential to keep a good half mile to the south to avoid **the Ranneys**, hazardous rocks drying to 4.5m. The tidal streams can at times be quite strong here and to seaward of the rocks a brisk area of overfalls will be created in certain combinations of wind and tide, extending nearly a mile to the south where a YB south cardinal buoy (Q(6)+LFl) provides a useful clearing mark.

Looe Island is privately owned and was bought in 1965 by two remarkable sisters, Evelyn and Babs Atkins, who abandoned a civilised existence in suburban Epsom for island life, a lifestyle change well described in their book *We Bought an Island*. Evelyn died in 1996, but Babs continues to live here.

Tales of contraband and smuggling inevitably abound, but the most bizarre episode in the island's history had to be during the last war when it was bombed by an over zealous German

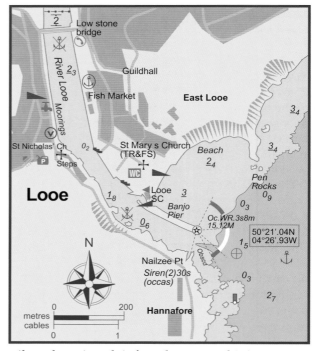

pilot who mistook it for a large warship!

Today it is a bird sanctuary and parts are open to the public. Trip boats run from Looe and a small landing fee is charged, the proceeds going towards its upkeep.

Do not attempt the passage between the Looe Island and the mainland, which is rock strewn and shallow. Ideally, approach Looe from the south-east, leaving the island a good two to three cables to port as you close the land, and head

Looe Harbour dries and its long narrow entrance is protected by the Banjo Pier. There is a good anchorage off the beach in settled offshore weather

directly for the end of the Banjo Pier – its shape gives it the name – which forms the eastern side of the harbour mouth. Midmain is an isolated rock south-west of the entrance identified by a lighted beacon with east cardinal topmark (Q(3) 10s), and on the rocks to the north are two red beacons closer to the harbour.

The entrance is long and little more than 50m wide at its narrowest point, drying right to the mouth at springs, and is accessible after half flood for boats of average draught. It is flanked by high cliffs along the western side, with rocky ledges at their foot. If you are early on the tide, anchor off east of the Banjo pier head in about 2–3m. At night a riding light is essential because of fishing boat movements.

Enter under power, keeping close to the Banjo Pier. The tide runs strongly, up to five knots on the ebb at springs, and careful allowance should be made for this when manoeuvring. Beware, too, of the numerous self drive motorboats (always an unpredictable hazard), the fishing boats entering and leaving and the small passenger ferry at the southern end of the harbour.

The pier head is lit, (sectored Oc WR 3s) – the white light covering the safe approach – and entry at night is much easier than it used to be as the entire harbour is lined with festoon lights from just inside the entrance to the bridge – they remain on all night during the season.

BERTHING

The only berth available for visitors is clearly marked *Visitors Berth* on the small white shower building adjacent to it at the southern end of the West Looe Quay, just upstream of the ferry steps. The quay is faced with wooden piles and a fender board will be very handy; you will ground here about four hours after HW, drying out on a firm sand and gravel bottom. The very reasonable charge per night ranges between £5 and £10, a 10m boat will pay just £8, which includes free showers. The quays on the east side of the harbour are reserved for the fishing fleet and, further upstream, the harbour office (open 0900 – 1700) is in the fishmarket. You should report to the harbour master, Mr ETR Webb, on arrival. An occasional VHF watch is maintained – call *Looe Harbour* on VHF Channel 14 or (Tel: 01503 262839). Below the bridge, a number of local boats lie on trot moorings, all of which dry, and anchoring is prohibited throughout the harbour because of the moorings and underwater pipes and power cables.

FACILITIES

Looe is a picturesquely situated little town, which clings to the steep hills overlooking the river. During the season it pays the inevitable price and is

Visitors to Looe berth by the small building on the quayside just ahead of the rafted motor boats

absolutely inundated with visitors, the crowds thronging through narrow streets that were never designed for such an influx. In East Looe gift shops abound, whereas West Looe retains more of the original feel of this old fishing community, with thick-walled pastel painted cottages clustered around a network of narrow alleyways and cobbled yards.

Shore facilities are good, with plenty of shops including a Spar in West Looe, close to the visitors' berth (Mon – Sat 0730 – 2200, Sun 0800 – 2200), and a Somerfield supermarket in East Looe (Mon – Sat 0800 – 2200, Sun 1000 – 1800). There is a launderette in both East and West Looe, fresh water taps on both quays and a convenient shower/toilet in the small Visitors' Berth building – the key is available from the ferryman.

Diesel can be obtained alongside from Looe Fish, but petrol has to be carried in cans from the local garage. There are branches of Lloyds TSB, HSBC and Barclays, all with cashpoints, in East Looe and post offices in both West and East Looe. Looe Chandlery (Tel: 01503 264355) will be found at the Millpool Boatyard upstream of the bridge. Marine Engineering Looe (Tel: 01503 263009) and Marconi Marine Electronics (Tel: 01503 265548) are based on the East Quay. Should you need medical attention, visit Looe Health Centre (Tel: 263196).

Clearly reflecting the number of hungry mouths that flock into the town, eating places abound and incorporate everything from the cheap and cheerful to the more up market, including plenty of good seafood at Tom Sawyers (Tel: 262782) in West Looe, while the Old Sail Loft (Tel: 262131), the Water Rail (Tel:262314), the Grapevine (Tel: 263913), Liasons Bistro (Tel: 265568) and Pepper's

Bistro (Tel: 263585) are all in East Looe. Seafood apart, you can eat American style at Dave's Diner (Tel: 262341), Italian at Papa Ninos (Tel: 264231) and Chinese at the Peking Gardens (Tel: 264500). Add to this plenty of cafés and nearly 10 pubs which all do food, including the perennial Ship Inn, the Fisherman's Arms and the Jolly Sailor – and if you're still famished there's always the grandly-named aPizza Palace and Kebab Shop. . .

Looe Sailing Club, in Buller Street, East Looe (Tel: 01503 262559) welcomes visitors to its licensed bar, with showers also available.

The South East Cornwall Discovery Centre is in West Looe, just upstream of the old tide mill, while East Looe has a *Living from the Sea* exhibition in the Guildhall museum, where the Tourist Information Centre is also located (Tel: 01503 262072). The scenic Looe Valley railway line connects with the main line at Liskeard. If the tide permits, try a dinghy excursion upstream of the bridge to explore the peaceful backwaters of the East and West Looe Rivers. Alternatively you might feel inclined to join the masses on East Looe's sandy beach where there is good safe swimming, or on West Looe's quieter but rockier Hannafore beach.

Like many other Cornish fishing ports, Looe has had its ups and downs, suffering very lean times after the collapse of the pilchard industry in the 1930s and the mackerel fishery in the 1970s. Since then the fleet of medium sized boats has been expanding, mostly potting, long-lining, trawling and scalloping. The holiday industry has in many ways helped to sustain the commercial fishermen through some of the harder times, as this has long been a popular sea angling port and is home of the Shark Fishing Club of Great Britain.

A surprising number of Porbeagle and Blue sharks are caught in the warm waters off

Cornwall during the summer although, nowhere in the league of *Jaws*, they are definitely not man-eaters and are rarely found close to the shore.

At the turn of the century a fleet of over 50 large luggers still worked from Looe. These decked boats were up to 50ft with transom sterns distinguishing them from the double ended luggers of the West Cornish ports. Pilchards, small fish similar to herring, were traditionally caught in long seine nets during the summer months by open boats working from coves and beaches, but as the shoals moved further offshore, the larger boats were built and long drift nets began to replace the seine.

Of all the Looe luggers, the best known and certainly the most travelled has to be the *Lily*, built by Ferris in 1896. Her fishing days were over sometime in the 1930s when a young, enthusiastic couple spotted her in nearby Polperro:

'Anne stood by the helm. "I think", she said, "we've found our ship". We scrambled aboard and went below. The fishwell took up the whole of the middle of the ship. We pulled up the floorboards and looked into the bilge. There were firebars, cannonballs, cogwheels and shingle. She was dry as a bone but smelt to heaven of fish and tar. In the fo'c'sle was a bogie stove eaten with rust, and a single locker on the starboard side. Aft was a single-cylinder Kelvin. Anne's face was flushed with excitement. "If she only costs us twenty-five pounds, we can afford to have her converted into just what we want. It'll be like buying a new boat." I hadn't the heart to tell her that a surveyor might find she was rotten.'

She turned out to be very sound indeed, and thus a humble Looe lugger was restored to become Peter and Anne Pye's famous gaff cutter *Moonraker of Fowey*. While her sister ships were towed to a final, rotting resting place up the Looe River, for it was considered unlucky to break them up, *Moonie* suffered no such ignominy. Ranging far and wide, her voyages from the Baltic to Tahiti and Alaska to Brazil were delightfully described by the Pyes in *Red Mains'l, The Sea is for Sailing* and *A Sail in a Forest*.

POLPERRO

There are no such bargains to be found in Polperro today, and the people who throng there are not searching for boats to buy, merely postcards, cream teas and souvenirs. It is not, however, a particularly recent phenomenon, as a guide book written in the 1920s reveals. . .

'. . . a human bees' nest stowed away in a cranny of rocks. Its industries are four: the catching of fish, the painting of pictures, handicrafts and – latterly – the entertainment of visitors, for it is probably the most charmingly unexpected village in all England. . .'

The pressure of visitors in recent years has resulted in the welcome banning of all cars from Polperro during the day, with a large car park on the outskirts. The 10 minute walk down the hill comes as a considerable shock to many of today's car-bound explorers unused to such inconvenience and exertion; with great relief, I suspect, they soon spot the horse drawn bus!

Polperro approach from the south. Spy House Point on right with west and east pier ends coming into transit to clear Polca Rock

Polperro's small drying harbour lies at the foot of a steep sided valley. Peak Rock, with the Raney extending underwater, is in the centre

APPROACH AND MOORINGS

This undeniably attractive harbour is set in a narrow cleft among the cliffs just under three miles west of Looe Island, and five miles east of Fowey. It is not, at first, the easiest place to find and no attempt should be made to approach it in any southerly wind and seas, particularly from south-east. Not only are the approaches dangerous in these conditions, it is quite likely that the protective steel gate across the entrance will be closed.

Once past Looe Island when approaching from the east, a pair of transit beacons will be seen on the mainland marking the beginning of a measured mile; the second set of beacons identifying its western end lie at Downend Point just east of Talland Bay.

From south of the point, a V-shaped cleft in the high cliffs will begin to open and houses of Polperro will come into view. Steer to within two cables of the inlet and Peak Rock, a pyramid-shaped spur topped with jagged boulders, will be seen on the western side. Spy House Point, where the harbour light (Iso WR 6s) is located, is on the eastern side. The main hazard is The Polca, a rock (least depth 1.2m) about 200m south-west of the point, while the Raney, two rocks drying 0.8m, will usually be spotted awash just off Peak Rock.

Proceed with caution and pass between these

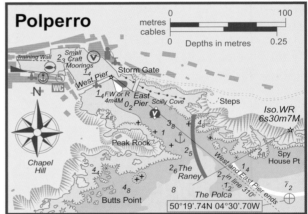

and the hidden Polca, before turning into the inlet and heading for the end of the East Pier. Alternatively, to pass east and north of The Polca, keep the outer ends of the West and East Piers just touching, giving a leading line of 310°T. There are four red visitors' moorings in the outer approach where there is about 1.8m LAT – depths begin to reduce quickly once you have passed them and the inner harbour dries as far as the outer pier at springs, but can normally be entered after half flood. If the tide is low or you do not wish to dry out inside the harbour, use the moorings, but if you intend to stay overnight it is best to moor fore and aft (NW/SE) between them to avoid swinging into the fairway to the harbour. Alternatively, anchor to seaward clear of them in 3m – 4m LAT showing a riding light.

BERTHING

Within the harbour, the East Quay wall immediately inside the entrance must be kept clear at all times, as this is the fuel berth for the local fishing boats, which also use most of the alongside berths on the West Pier, East Quay and the inner Fish Quay. The rest of the harbour has many drying fore and aft small boat moorings and berthing for visitors is therefore very limited. There is, however, usually space for up to two boats (maximum 10m LOA) to dry out alongside the wooden pile quay just beyond the Museum of Smuggling and Fishing where, conveniently, a large wooden ladder has been installed. At half tide there is usually about 1.5m here, but it is a berth best suited to bilge keelers or to those with fin keel boats who are used to drying out!

The overnight charge for the use of the outer fore and aft moorings works out at around £6. You usually pay a bit more if you dry out inside the harbour and Harbour Master, Chris Curtis, who is also is also a full-time fisherman, or his assistant will appear at some time to collect your dues. Their office is in the small fish market on the western side of the harbour (Tel: 01503 272809), and they can usually be contacted on VHF Ch 10 – call sign *Polperro Harbour Master* – should the need arise. They do their best to make you welcome, but as the fishing continues to decline, Polperro, in keeping with many other West Country ports, has realised that pleasure craft might ultimately be their only route to survival and plans are afoot to try and build a new inner pier to accommodate up to six visitors along with showers – that is, if the funding can be found.

FACILITIES

In spite of its popularity the village has fortunately not been over developed. It is carefully administered by the entirely voluntary Polperro Harbour Trustees with the declared intention of maintaining its unique character.

The tiny narrow streets and houses overhanging the harbour and the diminutive River Pol have probably outwardly changed little since 1762, when John Wesley was forced to change his lodgings because the room beneath him was 'filled with pilchards and conger eels, the perfume being too potent . . .'

Prior to the advent of the tourist industry, fishing and smuggling were the main activities, the rabbit warren of alleyways ideal for evading the Excise men. Special boats were built for the trade, and one, the *Unity*, was reputed to have made 500 successful trips, crossing to France in just over eight hours with a fair wind. Today this colourful past is well documented in the Polperro Museum of Smuggling and Fishing in the old pilchard factory on the east side of the harbour.

It is still an intriguing place to explore, particularly in the evening when the coaches and day trippers have gone on their way.

Considering the size of the village, the facilities are surprisingly good, with a grocer, butcher, baker, greengrocer, newsagents and a post office, which boasts a cash dispenser. The nearest petrol is by can from a garage about a mile distant, although the local fishermen will always help out with a gallon or two of diesel if you're desperate. Water taps are installed on both quays. There is a local Doctor's surgery here (Tel: 272768), and you'll also find a chemist up the hill in the area known as the Coombes.

Several restaurants include Neville's (Tel: 272459) for good seafood, Couch's Brasserie (Tel: 272554), the Buccaneer (Tel: 272394) and the House on the Props (Tel: 272310). In the Coombes you'll find the Cottage Restaurant (Tel:272217), the Kitchen (Tel: 272780), the Polmary Restaurant (Tel:2728280) and the Mermaid Hotel (Tel: 272502), which is open to non-residents.

And there's definitely no shortage of pubs offering bar meals, including several with suitably nautical names such as the Blue Peter, the Ship and the Three Pilchards.

In November 1824 three houses, the inner and outer piers, and 50 boats were destroyed in the worst south-easterly storm ever experienced, but on a balmy summer evening Polperro is a very different place. The cheerful red, green and yellow of the boats and the subtle backdrop of white, pink and slate hung cottages shimmer on the water at the height of the tide, while lingering holidaymakers bask on the warm, weathered stone of the harbour wall, eking out the very last of the sun's fading glow as the valley sinks into shadow.

The harbour can also be a surprisingly musical place at times, when the Polperro Fisherman's Choir performs on the quayside and especially during the Polperro Proms, the highlight of the summer season (usually the third weekend in August), when a temporary scaffolding stage is constructed in the middle of the harbour creating a spectacular setting for jazz on the Friday night, rock and pop on Saturday and the event's climax on Sunday night, a 50-piece classical orchestra!

FOWEY

'Fowey is the harbour of harbours. . .' The moorings are dense off Polruan; visitors' pontoon bottom left – note prominent daymark on distant Gribbin Head

Tides	HW Dover −0550
Range	MHWS 5.4m–MHWN 4.3m, MLWN 2.0m–MLWS 0.6m
Charts	BA: 31 and 148, SC 5602.7. Stanford:CP 23.13. Imray: WCP 2400.7
Waypoint	Cannis Rock buoy 50°18'.38N / 04°39'.95W
Hazards	Udder Rock 3M to east (lit), Punch's Cross (unlit). Cannis Rock (lit). Busy commercial port, beware shipping in narrow entrance. Upper reaches dry
Overnight charges	Harbour Authority mooring or pontoon £12. Mixtow pontoon £14

'Fowey is the harbour of harbours, the last port town left without any admixture of modern evil. It ought to be a kingdom all of its own. In Fowey all is courtesy and good reason for the chance sailing man . . . and I have never sailed into Fowey or out of Fowey without good luck attending me.'

Hilaire Belloc obviously rather liked Fowey, but he was not alone among literary men and women to succumb to the romantic charm of this delightful town and deep narrow river. Daphne du Maurier lived here for many years, Sir Arthur Quiller-Couch – Q – immortalised it in his famous sagas as *Troy Town*, and his friend, Kenneth Grahame, also used it in *The Wind in the Willows*.

APPROACHES

The entrance, although only a cable wide at its narrowest, is deep and easy except in strong onshore winds over an ebb tide. The only possible problems, day or night, are likely to be a large ship emerging and fluky winds.

Keep to the middle of the channel, leaving the white cross on Punch's Cross rock and the triangular white beacon on Lamp Rock to starboard, and high St Catherine's Point, with its small fortress, and the narrow inlet of Readymoney Cove to port.

At night, Fowey lighthouse (L Fl WR 5s) has red sectors covering the coast to the east and west. Make your approach in the white sector until the inner lighthouse on Whitehouse Point, midway up the western shore, provides a sectored light (Iso RWG 3s), the white sector of which leads straight in.

Once past St Catherine's Point (Fl R 2.5s) and Lamp Rock (Fl G 5s), the only other navigation lights are the fixed red lights at the end of the Polruan ferry landing and on Fowey Town Quay, and fixed green lights on Polruan Quay.

If departing at night, St Catherine's Point (Fl R 2.5s), visible 150° – 295°, and Lamp Rock (Fl G 5s), visible 010° – 205°, usefully indicate the dangers on either hand.

THE HARBOUR

Beyond Polruan fort, the river widens and the moorings, followed by the village of Polruan, will come into view along the eastern side of the harbour. Fowey stretches out along the western side – neat terraces climbing the steep hillside overlooking the harbour. Whitehouse Quay is a small pier on the Fowey shore where a small passenger ferry runs across to Polruan, along with a seasonal ferry to Mevagissey. A little further upstream, the low black and white twin gabled building with a veranda, awning and large flagstaff is the Royal Fowey Yacht Club.

There is an average of 7m at LWS dredged right through the centre of the harbour, and plenty of water to within half a cable of the shore as far as Town Quay. This is easily located by the tower of St Fimbarrus Church and the prominent King of Prussia Hotel behind it and, except for the slipway, dries at LW. It is used by local fishing and trip boats.

Albert Quay, a short distance beyond, has a sizeable short stay visitors' pontoon which is dredged and accessible at any state of the tide, although further inshore it dries at LW. You may berth alongside this pontoon free of charge for up to two hours – handy for shopping, landing crew or taking on fresh water. Small tenders can be left for up to 12 hours on the inside. Be warned

The approach to Fowey is straightforward and deep.
St Catherine's Point and the lighthouse on left, Polruan, right,
with Pont Pill and visitors' moorings beyond

though – boats abusing this excellent facility, by using it for an overnight stop for instance, will be charged five times the normal mooring rate in the harbour!

There may be a number of large ships moored fore and aft in the centre of the river, waiting to berth at the china clay wharves upriver, and although this narrow waterway seems on first appearance an improbable place for much commercial activity, you are now in the 11th largest exporting port in the United Kingdom, shipping over 1.5 million tons of china clay a year and handling nearly 850 ships. Most average between 7,000 and 8,000 tonnes, but the largest to date, the Finnish vessels *Astrea* and *Pollux*, were nearly 17,000 tons and 540ft in length.

It is fascinating to watch the apparent ease with which these vessels are manoeuvred to their berths, in particular the technique of 'drudging' them stern first up the river. This technique involves towing from aft with the anchor dragging on a short scope to hold the bows in position. Another spectacle during the summer months is the increasing number of cruise liners which are now making Fowey a regular port of call, the largest to date the 248m, 48,000 ton *Crystal Harmony*.

Considering that well over 7,000 yachts also visit the port annually, the commendable Harbour Authority manages to achieve a remarkable balance between intensive commercial activity and a large number of pleasure craft. Facilities have been

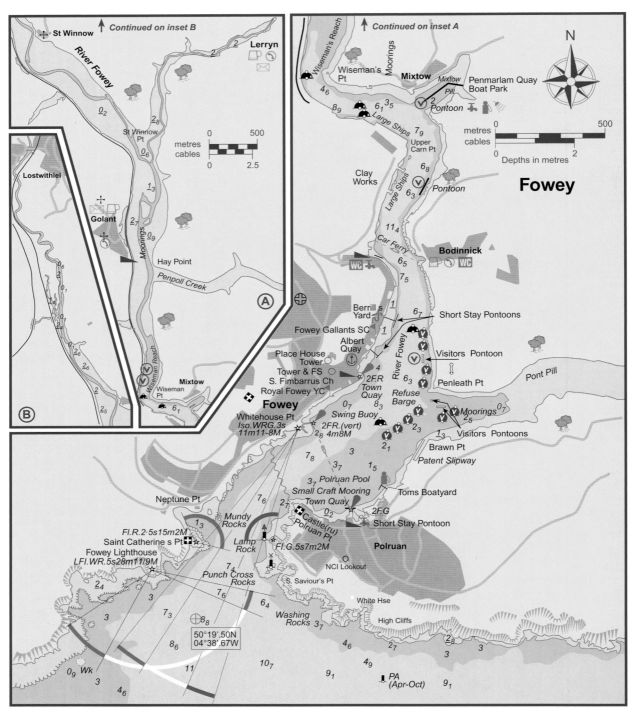

improved considerably in recent years and the main area for visitors to head for is the Swinging Ground just opposite the Royal Fowey YC.

During the season the Harbour launch, *Zebedee*, and the harbour master's dory, *Dougal*, (you can be forgiven for thinking you have arrived on the *Magic Roundabout*) are on the water seven days a week from 0830 until dark, and in the afternoon they keep a lookout to assist new arrivals.

Although the harbour office (Tel: 01726 832471) and launch monitor VHF Ch 16, they should be called on their working channel – Ch 12, call sign either *Fowey Harbour Radio* or *Fowey Harbour Patrol*. Note that the landlocked nature of the harbour tends to make reception poor from outside and you will probably not make contact until you are in the entrance, when you will have been spotted anyway. Because of this, the

The convenient short stay pontoon at Albert Quay can be used at any state of the tide for up to two hours, free of charge. Dinghies can be left on the inside

harbour office provides and maintains a direct land line VHF link to Brixham Coastguard.

BERTHING, MOORINGS AND ANCHORING

On the opposite side of the harbour the wide mouth of the creek, known as Pont Pill, branches away northeastwards.

There are a number of swinging moorings as well as a 36m pontoon for visitors up to 16m LOA along the east side of the river, just upstream of Pont Pill. Two identical pontoons lie just within the mouth of Pont Pill (dredged 2m for some distance). Fore and aft moorings are also available in Pont Pill – handy if you want a bit of peace away from the main stream and ideal for leaving a boat if stuck for time or weather. Additionally, a number of visitors' moorings are available in Polruan Pool, all with yellow or white buoys, clearly marked *FHC Visitor* and numbered.

The floating rubbish skip close by should be used in preference to taking it ashore, and the Harbour Authority runs a unique daily rubbish collection service free of charge during the peak season in its dory, *Dillon*. Free rubbish bags are also available and recycling facilities for cans and glass are provided afloat and ashore.

A short distance beyond Albert Quay pontoon is another short stay pontoon (max two hours) off Berrill's Yard, which is being developed by the Harbour Commissioners, and also a pontoon that is the home of Fowey lifeboat. Here you will find a rubbish skip, a marine toilet pump-out facility and oily waste disposal.

Further upstream there are several other

berthing options for visitors, see under *Upper Reaches* towards the end of this chapter.

Anchoring is not allowed anywhere in the fairway, near underwater cables or close to landing places. You may anchor off the entrance to Pont Pill to the east of the swinging ground, but only with the harbour master's permission, and this sometimes entails having to move when larger vessels are being manoeuvred.

As there is no difference in price between anchoring and using one of the Harbour Authority facilities, most visitors opt for the latter. The overnight charge for a 10m boat is £12, but there are reductions for longer stays. If you elect and pay in advance to stay for three days it would cost £28.80 for a 10m boat or £63 for a week during July and August. At other times of the year free nights are offered instead.

FACILITIES

Landing is easy at the Albert Quay pontoon where dinghies can be left on the inside. You can land also at the Royal Fowey Yacht Club (Tel: 01726 832245), but pull dinghies clear of the steps and remember that the foreshore here dries at LW.

The club was founded in 1905 and members of other clubs are welcome to use its facilities, including excellent showers (£1) and a very comfortable bar. Here, among the various burgees that adorn the walls, is one that, for me, a dyed

Visitor's pontoon, Pont Pill

in the wool romantic, always induces a certain nostalgic twinge – it belonged to *Moonraker of Fowey* and was presented to the club by Peter and Anne Pye.

The club serves good value lunches, teas and dinners as well as breakfast from 0800 – 1030 during the season. Racing takes place every Wednesday evening and Sunday afternoon and visitors are welcome to join in.

The Fowey Gallants Sailing Club (Tel: 01726 832335), just upstream from Albert Quay, was founded in 1950 and also extends a warm welcome to visiting yacht crews. Facilities include showers (£1), toilets and a bar that serves good food at weekends and exudes a pleasant family atmosphere.

The alternative to your own dinghy is the popular water taxi service which runs from Town Quay. This can be hailed on VHF Ch 06, call sign *Fowey Water Taxi* (Tel: 01726 870497 or mobile 07774 906730). It operates seven days a week in season from about 0800 until the pubs close, and for around £1.50 a head per trip it does away with the problem of worrying about the dinghy. Its sheltered cuddy is particularly enticing when it is pouring with rain and blowing. If you have a large crew or are planning to be around for a day or two, you'll save money by buying a book of tickets.

The town is essentially just one main shopping street, very narrow in places, with houses rising up from it – still very much as *Sea Rat* described it in *The Wind in the Willows*:

'. . . the little, grey sea town I know so well, that clings along one steep side of the harbour. There, through dark doorways you look down flights of stone steps, overhung by great pink tufts of valerian and ending in a patch of sparkling blue water. The little boats that lie tethered to the rings and stanchions of the old seawall are as gaily painted as those I clambered in and out of in my own childhood; the salmon leap on the flood tide, schools of mackerel flash and play past the quaysides and foreshores and by the windows the great vessels glide, night and day, up to their moorings or forth to the sea. There, sooner or later the ships of all seafaring nations arrive; and there, at its destined hour the ship of my choice will let go its anchor . . .'

Not quite as grey today, as most of the buildings are brightly painted and very well preserved. It is also busier than when Kenneth Grahame was writing, with cars and people squeezing through the narrow bottlenecks. Nevertheless, it is still a delightful place and spared the over-commercialism of so many other Cornish harbours – perhaps a

reflection on the fact that such a large proportion of its visitors come in by sea.

Belloc's eulogy continues, '. . . whatever you may need in gear is to be had at once' – which is certainly true except perhaps on Sundays, with everything that a cruising crew might require including Kittows, an excellent butcher renowned for its sausages; Fowey Fish; Jolly Jack's Delicatessen and Bakery; Fowey Mini Market (foodstore and off-licence, open 0800 – 2000 daily, 0900 – 2000 Sundays); a post office; newsagents; Bookends for secondhand nautical books; Lloyds TSB, HSBC and Barclays banks (the latter two have cashpoints); a sailmaker and several chandlers. The only facility still noticeably lacking is a launderette!

Diesel can be obtained from the pontoon off C Toms & Son boatyard in Polruan during the summer, weekdays 0815 –1615, weekends 1000 – 1200, call VHF Ch 08 or berth alongside. The only source of petrol is the Four Turnings Garage, a mostly uphill walk of over a mile and a half from the waterfront!

For its size, Fowey offers a wide choice of eating places. To get the day off to a good start, try the Lifebuoy Café's renowned all day breakfast, or the hearty alternative at the nearby Royal Fowey Yacht Club. And to end a perfect day try the Toll Bar (Tel: 833001), a perennial Fowey favourite, low ceilinged and atmospheric. Food for Thought (Tel: 832221) provides elegant dining, right on the Town Quay, while the

There are visitors' moorings off the entrance and within wooded Pont Pill, where you will also find the main visitors' pontoon

Waterfront, also situated on the quay, is a cheaper alternative, with good value family meals. The elegant Old Quay House Hotel (Tel: 833302) has a delightful waterside ambience or try the Commodore (Tel: 833594) for Italian. Sams (Tel: 832273) is a lively bistro with an excellent lunch menu; Sam's, The Other Place (Tel: 833636) is the venue for superb seafood and Taipan (Tel: 833899) the omnipresent Chinese!

Several local hotels, like the Fowey and the Marina, are open to non-residents for meals while the pubs – Safe Harbour, Ship Inn, King of Prussia, Galleon, Lugger Inn and Globe Posting House all have a good selection of bar meals. If you want a pleasant stroll before you eat, head towards the Bodinnick Ferry car park where Chuffers (Tel: 833832), resplendent in Great Western livery, harks back to the days when this was the site of Fowey's railway station.

POLRUAN

Polruan clings to an even steeper hillside than Fowey and can provide all the basics. It is an attractive, far quieter little village where visitors' cars are prohibited in season – they must be parked at the top of the hill.

During the summer there is a convenient short stay, all-tide landing pontoon provided by FHC and the Polruan Town Trust off the end of Polruan Quay.

The village incorporates a well-stocked mini-market/off licence (0830 – 1730, 1630 Sat; 0930 – 1200 Sun), post office, newsagent and a couple of good pubs – the Russell and the Lugger – and Crumpets cafe.

C Toms & Son boatyard is on the site of the former Slade boatyard, which built a number of well-known West Country schooners and was the inspiration for Coombes boatyard in Daphne du Maurier's *The Loving Spirit*. The yard is still very much involved with traditional boatbuilding, and a peep into its large shed often reveals a big wooden fishing boat under construction. Its slipway, one of the largest in the area, can take vessels of up to 28m and 160 tons, and there is also a 30 ton crane.

In addition, the Harbour Authority has a large slipway at Brazen Island in its own repair yard further along the Polruan shore, which is used to maintain its tugs, dredger and barges. Private vessels up to 450 tonnes and 30ft beam can be hauled out by arrangement. It is also possible for smaller craft to dry out alongside the wall here for scrubbing/repairs, with the harbour master's permission, at no extra charge.

TROYS AND GALLANTS

Fowey Classics, a gathering for traditional craft, takes place during the first week in August, culminating in a feeder race to Falmouth Classics.

Fowey Regatta Week, the major sailing event of the year, is during the third week in August, when the harbour is packed to absolute capacity. Feeder races from Plymouth and Falmouth include a large contingent of their gaff-rigged working boats, and racing takes place every day both outside and inside the harbour, including the very close competition among the local one design class, the *Troys*. These colourful 18ft three-quarter decked bermudian sloops, which sport a distinctive 4ft bowsprit, were first built in 1929. Eighteen survive today.

The spectacular finale of the week is the Harbour Race for the Falmouth Working Boats. However, if you are seeking peace and quiet, be warned – this is one week to avoid Fowey altogether!

Historically, Fowey has a wild and romantic past, which started when the port began to develop in the 12th century after the previous harbour at Lostwithiel, six miles inland, began to silt up. By 1346 it was able to supply 47 ships and nearly 800 men for the siege of Calais, more than any other port in England, and it seemed to give the Fowey men a particular taste for adventure. Little more than pirates, they continued to wage their own private war against the French long after hostilities had officially ceased, and daring raids and bloodthirsty skirmishes across the Channel not only earned them a lot of plunder, but also the nickname of *Fowey Gallants*.

Mixtow visitors' pontoon is linked to the shore at Penmarlam Quay where there are showers and toilets

The French hit back in 1457, raiding and setting fire to the town, forcing its inhabitants to take refuge in the seat of the Treffry family – Place House – the prominent large house with tall towers just behind the church. However, this attack only stimulated the activities of the *Gallants*, one of whom, John Wilcock, seized no less than 15 French ships in as many days, becoming a source of great embarrassment to King Edward IV, who sent a message to Fowey 'I am at peace with my brother of France'.

Not impressed, the *Gallants* proceeded to cut off the unfortunate messenger's ears and nose, an act of defiance that resulted in considerable punishment for the town. The ringleaders were hanged, goods seized, ships distributed to other ports and the huge protective chain slung from the forts as the harbour mouth was removed. Duly chastened, the wild men of Fowey returned to more peaceful pursuits, fishing, shipbuilding, trading and, of course, smuggling . . !

THE UPPER REACHES

Deeper draught boats normally remain in the lower part of the harbour except, perhaps, when it begins to blow from the south-west for, in spite of its landlocked nature, conditions can sometimes become very uncomfortable. Perfect in so many other ways, Fowey's one major drawback is the very annoying swell that sets

in off Polruan and, with strong winds against tide in the harbour, it can at times become surprisingly rough and very rolly.

Traditionally, boats used to run upriver and anchor in Wiseman's Pool, but it is now so full of moorings that this is no longer possible. Four visitors' moorings are available here, so it is worth contacting the harbour staff for advice, otherwise proceed upstream where the river narrows above the town past the pretty hamlet of Bodinnick, keeping a lookout for Ferryside, the prominent house by the waterside where the du Maurier family were brought up, and also, mounted on the corner of the building, the figurehead of the famous Polruan schooner *Jane Slade*. Watch out too for the Bodinnick ferry which carries cars and pedestrians across to Fowey, and pass well astern.

Beyond it, the extensive clay loading wharves appear along the west bank, a fascinating stretch of river with ships of many nationalities berthed alongside. Here everything, including the surrounding trees, is wreathed in fine white dust, like a gentle fall of snow. On the opposite side of the river, beneath the high wooded shore, you will find another 36m visitors' pontoon in this much more sheltered reach.

The other option is to continue even further to Mixtow Pill, which has excellent shelter in all weathers. Here you will find the Harbour Authority's 165m pontoon with visitors' berths along the south side. These berths are dredged to

2m LAT and fresh water taps are provided on the pontoon. An overnight berth works out at £14 for a 10m boat. The north side of the pontoon is reserved for local boats and must not be used, unless directed by the harbour staff. The pontoon is linked by a gangway to the Penmarlam Quay Boat Park, where you will find visitors' showers and toilets. Other facilities include a 7m wide slipway and a boat hoist capable of lifting vessels of up to 8.4 tons.

The foreshore on either side of the creek is private and landing is not allowed.

The deep channel turns sharply to port at Upper Carn Point, opposite the entrance to Mixtow Pill. Particular care should be taken to look out for large ships rounding this bend. At the end of this short reach, overlooked by high woods, the docks finish and the channel turns back to the north round Wiseman Point, a wooded rocky promontory, until Wiseman's Pool, thick with moorings, comes into view.

Although the river is still navigable for small craft on a good tide as far as the attractive small country town of Lostwithiel, beyond Wiseman's Reach it dries almost completely to a mixture of sand and mudbanks. Shoal draught boats and dinghies can explore on the flood, and bilge keelers are able to anchor and dry out off Golant, where there are a large number of drying moorings and a pleasant little village with a general store, post office and good pub grub at the Fisherman's Arms. Also, The Cormorant on the River hotel (Tel: 833426) has excellent seafood and a lovely view.

An FHC office is situated here, along with a freshwater tap, rubbish bins and a public telephone by the quay. Also a handy walkway along the embankment leads as far downriver as Wiseman's Pool.

Beyond Golant, Lerryn Creek, bearing away to the north-east, is steep-to and wooded. At Lerryn, there is a slipway and landing on the south side of the creek and the village can provide a Spar grocery/off-licence, the Ship Inn, public toilets and a phone by the head of the creek.

At St Winnow, on the way to Lostwithiel, a fine 15th century church is situated in a lovely setting close by the waters' edge, while the fascinating Barton Farm agricultural museum is nearby.

If the weather does turn and you are stuck in Fowey for a few days, take advantage of the fine walks in the area. A guided town walk is organised by the Tourist Information Centre every Tuesday (June to September), but for something longer my favourite is the Hall Walk, which skirts a large part of the harbour. Ideally leave the dinghy in Fowey and catch the ferry to Bodinnick where the walk is signposted on the right, halfway up the steep hill leading out of the village. Far from arduous, the grassy track gently follows the contour line right round Penleath Point to the large stone memorial to Sir Arthur Quiller-Couch, where magnificent views of the harbour might possibly have inspired this fine piece of doggerel from the one time Professor of English Literature at Cambridge:

'O the Harbour of Fowey Is a beautiful spot,
And it's there I enjowey To sail in a yot. . .'

From here, continue on through the woods and wild flowers above Pont Pill, and down to the hamlet of Pont with its old quay and water mill. The track then climbs another wooded hillside with more lovely views all the way back to Polruan, where a cream tea would seem to be an eminently sensible idea before catching the ferry back to Fowey where you will pass Quiller-Couch's former home, the Haven.

Another favourite is the walk to seaward of Fowey along the road to Readymoney Cove, where a track leads up on to St Catherine's Point. Pause to look at the old fortress built by Henry VIII in 1540 and the fine views into the harbour.

Above it is the curious structure that can just be seen when entering from sea. Two granite arches surmounted by a Maltese cross – looking like the top of a huge crown – is the tomb of William Rashleigh and his wife and daughter. They were descendants of Charles Rashleigh, who not only built the port of Charlestown, but also Menabilly on Gribbin Head. For many years this was the home of Daphne du Maurier and supposedly the house she immortalised as *Manderlay* in her novel *Rebecca*.

Following the coast path out towards Gribbin Head, you skirt the private grounds and woods surrounding Menabilly and, although you never actually see the elusive house, there are spectacular views of the harbour mouth, the coast, and some particularly lovely scenery around Polridmouth Cove – pronounced *Pridmouth*.

To visit this pleasant fair weather daytime anchorage, sound in towards the centre of the outer bay into about 2m. It is possible to proceed closer inshore with care, but there is a shallow sandbank in the centre of the inner part of the cove which has a tendency to shift! The beach has clean sand and is good for swimming, and from here the lovely coastal path continues onwards to Polkerris if you want to make a real day of it. Alternatively just walk as far as the splendid

Fowey Port Guide

Area telephone code: 01726

Harbour Master: Captain Mike Sutherland, Harbour Master's Office, Albert Quay, Fowey (Tel: 832471 or 832472. Fax: 833738). E-mail: FHC@foweyharbour.co.uk Website:www.foweyharbour.co.uk
VHF: Ch 16, working Ch 12, call signs *Fowey Harbour Radio* or *Fowey Harbour Patrol* 0830 – 2100 in season
Mail drop: Harbour Office or RFYC.
Emergency services: Lifeboat at Fowey. Brixham Coastguard
Anchorage: Only with Harbour Master's permission off entrance to Pont Pill, clear of moorings and coaster swinging ground
Moorings/berthing: Harbour Commission short stay pontoons (up to two hours) off Albert Quay, Berrill's yard and Polruan Quay. 22 deep water moorings, two visitors' pontoons near Pont Pill and two pontoons and fore and aft moorings within Pont Pill and in Polruan Pool. Visitors pontoon beyond Bodinnick opposite commercial wharves. Large visitors' pontoon in Mixtow Pill with access to shore for showers and toilets at Penmarlam Quay Boat Park
Charges: 10m boat overnight on FHC facility or at anchor £12. Mixtow pontoon £14
Dinghy landings: Inside Albert Quay pontoon, Berrills Yard pontoon, RFYC. Polruan Quay pontoon
Water taxi: From Town Quay, Easter – Sept, daily 0800 until pub closing time, VHF channel 06, call sign *Fowey Water Taxi* (Tel: 07774 906730) or hail
Marina: None
Phones: Near Town Quay, RFYC, Fowey Gallants, outside post office
Doctor: (Tel: 832541)

Hospital: (Tel: 832241)
Churches: C of E
Local Weather Forecast: Outside Harbour Office
Fuel: Diesel only from C Toms & Son boatyard pontoon, weekdays 0815 – 1615, weekends 1000 – 1200, call (Tel: 870232) or VHF Ch 08
Paraffin: Outriggers, Fowey.
Gas: Calor/Gaz, Outriggers, in Fowey
Water: Albert Quay and Berrill's yard and Mixtow pontoon
Tourist Information Centre: In post office (Tel:833616)
Banks/cashpoints: Barclays and HSBC have cashpoints. Lloyds TSB, no cashpoint
Post Office: In main street, turn right at Albert Quay
Rubbish: Floating skip off Pont Pill, bins ashore at Berrill's yard, Polruan Quay and Golant, all with recycling facility. Daily rubbish collection afloat mid-July to mid-September. Waste oil disposal at Berrills yard, Brazen Island and at Harbour Office
Showers/toilets: RFYC. Fowey Gallants SC. Penmarlam Quay boat park, adjoining Mixtow pontoon. Public toilets on Town Quay. Marine toilet disposal, Berrills yard
Launderette: None
Provisions: All requirements including delicatessen. Foodstore open late and Sunday, Fowey. Mini-mart/off licence open six days and Sunday mornings, Polruan
Chandler: Upper Deck Marine (Tel: 832287) and Outriggers (Tel: 833233), Admiralty Chart Agents, Albert Quay
Repairs/hauling: C Toms & Son boatyard (Tel: 870232), Polruan. Fowey Boatyard, Passage Street,

Fowey, (Tel: 832194). W C Hunkin & Sons, Millpool Boatyard (Tel: 832874). Fowey Harbour Commissioners (Tel: 832471). Peter Williams, Bodinnick Boatyard (Tel: 870987). FHC Penmarlam Quay and boat park (Tel: 832471)
Drying out: By arrangement with HM
Marine Engineers: C Toms & Son boatyard (Tel: 870232). Fowey Harbour Marine Engineers (Tel: 832806)
Electronic engineers: Marine Electronics Fowey, Station Road (Tel: 833101)
Sailmaker/repairs: Mitchell Sails, North Street, Fowey, (Tel: 833731)
Transport: Regular local buses (24 or 24A, Tel: 01208 79898) to main line railway station at Par (20 mins), but not all trains stop here. A 45 minute bus journey (24 or 24A) to St Austell connects with most main line trains (Tel:08457 484950)
Yacht Clubs: Royal Fowey Yacht Club (Tel: 832245), Whitford Yard, Fowey PL23 1BH Fowey Gallants Sailing Club (Tel: 832335), Amity Court, Fowey
Eating out: Very good selection for size of town. Fish and chips to bistros/restaurants
Things to do: Fowey Museum and Aquarium, both in middle of town. Guided town walks every Tuesday. Good walking, Fowey and Polruan. Headland garden, Polruan open every Thursday 1400 – 1800 during season
Special events: Daphne du Maurier Festival mid-May. Fowey Classics (traditional boat gathering) first week in August with feeder race to Falmouth Classics. Fowey Regatta/Carnival, third week in August

striped red and white daymark to enjoy the panoramic view from beneath this silent witness to so many departures and arrivals, such as *Moonraker*'s at the end of her Pacific voyage, 40 days out from Bermuda:

'The sun soaked up the haze, and the town of Fowey was just out of sight. In an hour or two, or three or four, a breeze would come and we should sail in through the Heads into the harbour from which we had set out three years ago. What changes should we find, I wondered, and how should we take to living on the land? Would

Christopher pad about the city in barefeet and bowler hat, and should we be content with creeks?

My thoughts were disturbed by the sound of a vessel's engine and a boat came up that was familiar. She stopped, her sails casting their shadows upon the water. Her people welcomed us.

"Come aboard", I said, "and have some coffee" and I hurried down to start the Primus.

Presently Anne looked out. "Hullo", she said, "where have they gone to?"

"They wanted to get in", said Christopher. "They've already been two nights at sea."'

MEVAGISSEY AND ST AUSTELL BAY

Tides	HW Dover −0600 (Mevagissey and St Austell Bay)
Range	MHWS 5.5m–MHWN 4.4m, MLWN 2.2m–MLWS 0.8m
Charts	BA:147, 148, SC5602.2 (Mevagissey only). Stanford:13. Imray: C6
Hazards Mevagissey	Inner harbour dries. Black rock off North Quay (unlit). Busy fishing harbour Dangerous to approach in onshore wind, and outer harbour very exposed in easterly gales
Overnight charges	Harbour Authority alongside or on mooring £10
Hazards Charlestown	Inner floating basin entered by narrow drying entrance and tidal lock. Dangerous in onshore winds. Drying rocks to south and east
Hazards Gorran Haven	Shallows extend well to seaward. Cadycrowse rock east of pier (unlit). Fine weather anchorage only and dangerous in onshore wind

Mevagissey and St Austell Bay are well sheltered from the west, tidal streams are weak and depths reduce gradually. Polkerris is a small fishing cove on the eastern side of Tywardreath Bay and has a good anchorage off it in easterly winds. On passage from Fowey around Gribbin Head, the only hazard more than two cables from the shore is Cannis Rock and, once the south cardinal buoy (lit) guarding it is astern, there are no hazards more than two cables from the shore.

You can safely follow the coast this distance off around the western side of the Gribbin for a couple of miles, until the houses and small harbour wall of Polkerris come into sight.

To stay afloat, anchor about three cables to the south-west of the pier in about 1.5m at LW. The

Polkerris is a pleasant daytime anchorage with a popular pub!

little bay dries out completely, but boats able to take the ground can anchor inside the harbour or lie alongside the pier. It is an unspoilt little hamlet tucked snugly beneath the cliffs and trees, with a high wall along the sandy foreshore protecting it from the seas which roll in unchecked in southerly gales.

At one time this was such an important fishing harbour that the whole bay, now known as St Austell Bay, was called Polkerris Bay. The pier was built in 1735 and it became a thriving centre for the catching and salting of pilchards. The old curing cellars, the largest concentration in Cornwall, can still be seen backing onto the beach – but today it is a much quieter place, little more than a cluster of houses. The Rashleigh Inn is a good pub/restaurant, and there is a café in the old lifeboat house, which was closed in 1922 when the station was transferred to Fowey.

Par, with its four conspicuous chimneys further to the north-west, is tidal. This privately owned harbour is a busy china clay port, swathed in white dust, and of no interest to leisure sailors. Entry is only permitted in an absolute emergency, when it is approached over a large area of drying sands. Midway across the bay, on the outer edge of Par Sands, Killyvarder Rock (dries 2.4m LAT)

is marked by a red beacon. There is often a cluster of coasters at anchor in the clay-tinged turquoise water to its south, all waiting to berth at Par.

Charlestown is a former china clay port two miles south-west of Par, and is of much more interest. It has been privately owned by Square Sail Shipyard Ltd since 1993, and the inner floating basin is the home port of its fleet of square rigged sailing ships, including the *Kaskelot*, *Earl of Pembroke* and *Phoenix*. It is entered through a very narrow entrance and tidal lock, yet another masterful bit of engineering by John Smeaton, who built the third Eddystone lighthouse.

Charlestown has become a popular port of call for other traditional and classic sailing vessels, and the sight of them forces an evocative step back into the past. This unspoiled 19th century harbour has been used by the BBC for episodes of the *Onedin Line*, and by several other companies for location filming.

A few pleasure craft are based here and, with wind in the west, it is possible to lock into the basin two hours either side of HW by prior arrangement with the harbour master (Tel: 01726 70241/67526) or VHF Ch14. There are two waiting buoys two cables south of the harbour; alternatively, in offshore winds anchor just east of the piers and dinghy ashore for a visit. The harbour mouth dries completely, well beyond the outer breakwaters at springs, but when there is

There is always plenty to see at Charlestown, the home of Squaresail Shipyard. The lovely Tern IV, *built for Claud Worth, is in foreground*

Visitors to Mevagissey normally lie alongside the South Pier, which was extensively rebuilt in 1998

sufficient water, land inside at the slip to the left of the lock gate. For further information visit the website:www.square-sail.com.

Apart from the harbour interest, the village of Charlestown has a large Shipwreck and Heritage Centre. This boasts one of the most impressive collections of shipwreck artifacts in the country, an audio visual display and life size animated scenes guaranteed to keep the children amused. There is a café in the centre, and the post office and store, pubs and restaurants are all close by.

St Austell Bay has many fine sandy coves and beaches and, with no dangers extending more than a cable from the shore, in favourable weather it is possible to sound in and anchor off most of them. Robin's Rock, just south of Porthpean dries, and there is an isolated rock drying 0.1m cable off Ropehaven beach.

Black Head, a bold rocky point with a grassy summit 46m high, forms the division between St Austell and Mevagissey Bays, and the fishing port of Mevagissey is two miles further to the south-west. Midway between them is the lost harbour of Pentewan, at the northern end of the long stretch of Pentewan sands, another tidal basin once approached by an artificial channel that has now completely silted up. It was built in 1826 to export clay, and was at times as busy as Charlestown. The

channel was always prey to the shifting sands and, in 1862, 16 ships were trapped in the harbour for five weeks because of silting. Eventually it was the closure of the railway in 1916 that finished this port, with the last clay shipped in 1929. Ships were still able to use the harbour as late as 1940, but today the inner basins and old locks are still quite intact but completely landlocked.

MEVAGISSEY, or *Mevva* as it is known locally, is the best known harbour in the bay. This classic Cornish fishing town offers good shelter in the prevailing winds, but is exposed in easterlies, when it can be dangerous to enter and very uncomfortable inside. It comprises an outer

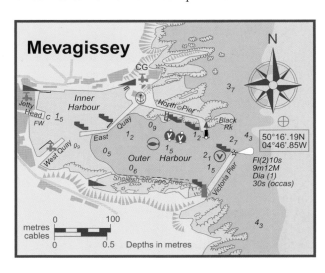

harbour, where fishing boat moorings take up most of the available space, and an inner harbour which dries completely and is restricted to local boats only.

It is predictably popular with holidaymakers and becomes very busy in season, but in spite of a certain amount of commercialism it retains much of its character; slate hung pastel cottages, with cement washed roofs creep up narrow alleyways to overlook the harbour, rather like a small version of Brixham. It is well worth a visit providing there is no inkling of the wind turning to the east. However, fishing is still a very important part of the town's life, with quite a large trawling and potting fleet as well as a number of trip and angling boats, so commercial activity takes precedence at all times. That said, visiting boats are very welcome as long as they are prepared to work around the port activity, and do not impede fish landing and other boat movements.

The approach is easy, with no off-lying dangers except the Gwineas rocks south of Chapel Point. Steer for the white lighthouse (Fl (2)10s 12M) on the South Pier, keeping close to it, as a shallow sandy bank (drying 0.3m LAT) extends east from the end of the North Pier which has a 6ft wide concrete apron around its base. This covers at half tide and is marked on its southern corner by a pole with conical green topmark.

The outer harbour is available even at LWS, with depths over 2m alongside the inside of the outer end of the South Pier. Visitors normally berth here between the steps, rafting alongside the fishing boats, but do not leave your boat unattended in case you have to move. Alternatively there are two visitors' buoys in the outer harbour. Before picking them up contact the Harbour Office who will explain the local mooring system. Captain Hugh Bowles, the Harbour Master, listens on VHF Ch 16 and works on Ch 14, 0900 – 2100 (April – Oct). His office (Tel: 01726 843305) is a clearly marked white building on the North Pier; further information will be found on its website: www.mevagissey harbour.co.uk

Strengthening works on the pier completed in 1998 extended it by 4.5 metres and widened it by three metres. Bollards and ladders were also installed on the seaward side of the pier to provide berths in fine weather – however it should be noted that here the new piled base of the pier projects nearly a metre from the main wall MLWS level, so good sized fenders are necessary. The harbour office will also provide

Well sheltered except in easterlies, Mevagissey is a classic Cornish fishing port with a drying inner harbour

fender boards if required. Boats able to dry out can sometimes lie on Sandy Beach on the seaward side of the inner West Pier, with the harbour master's permission. Because of the restricted space, anchoring is not permitted and visiting boats are not allowed in the inner harbour.

Regardless of LOA, all visiting boats will pay £10 for an overnight stay, either alongside or on the buoys.

Mevagissey was a rough, unruly place in its heyday, renowned for smuggling activity. It was also one of the largest centres for the 18th and 19th century pilchard fishery on the south coast of Cornwall, when it would have reeked of fish as the huge landings, sometimes in excess of 30 to 40,000 fish per boat, were counted by hand.

Today you can revisit this interesting past in the excellent small museum close to the harbour office, which is housed in a fine old wooden building dating from 1745 – once part of a boatyard. Right next to it, another real boatyard remains, where John Moore still builds beautiful traditional wooden fishing boats. There is also a fascinating aquarium run by the Harbour Trustees.

Although busy in summer, a wander around the town is pleasant, but the facilities are limited

to a small convenience store, a chemist and off-licence, a Lloyds TSB bank (Mon, Wed, Fri 0930 – 1230), and numerous gift shops. There are plenty of cafés, fish and chips, some excellent Cornish pasty shops, several restaurants and good pubs. A small amount of chandlery, Calor and Camping Gaz are available, and diesel can be had from the fuel berth at the inner end of the South Pier if you contact the harbour master. Water can only be obtained in cans from a tap by the harbour office or the jetty in the inner harbour. Also a marine engineer is on hand if needed. The nearest place for petrol (again in cans) is at Pentewan, a mile away, and garden lovers should note that the famous Lost Gardens of Heligan are within a similar distance and can be reached on foot.

Just south of Mevagissey, Porthmellon is a small cove of passing interest only, but of some significance in the history of yachting for this is where Percy Mitchell's famous boatyard was based between 1925 and 1981. Initially a builder

of fishing boats, he gained a reputation for yachts during the 1930s, and was described as 'an artist in wood' by Claud Worth.

Building the boats was only half the battle, for they then had to be manoeuvered 550 yards along the road to the beach and several were even launched over the sea wall. One of these was the 28 ton *TM Windstar*, which was later owned by the Sir Phillip Hunloke, King George V's sailing master and Commodore of the Royal Squadron, aboard which the Royal Family, including the young Princesses Elizabeth and Margaret, regularly cruised before and after the war.

Many other fine yachts to the design of Mylne, Harrison Butler and Laurent Giles emerged from this yard, and its fascinating history was related in *A Boatbuilder's Story*, Percy Mitchell's autobiography, which was published in 1970 shortly before he died. The yard was sold in the late 1980s and has since vanished beneath a new housing development.

Gorran Haven is an attractive fine weather anchorage, sheltered in westerly winds, with a drying small boat harbour and a gently shelving clean sandy beach. Approaching from the north, keep midway between Gwineas Rocks and the low promontory of Chapel Point, sound in and anchor two cables east of the sea wall. In settled weather bilge keelers can dry out comfortably closer inshore.

This narrow street of old fishermen's cottages has a post office, general store (open Sundays), several cafés and a pub. It is the starting point of a lovely coast path up to Dodman Point.

In offshore winds you can anchor off or dry out in the small harbour of Gorran Haven in the lee of Dodman Point

FALMOUTH

Tides	HW Dover +0600
Range	MHWS 5.3m–MHWN 4.2m, MLWN 1.9m–MLWS 0.6m. HW Truro approx 8 mins after HW Falmouth Streams attain over two knots in upper reaches at springs
Charts	BA: 32, 154, 18. SC5602.6. Stanford: 13, CP23. Imray: C6, Y58
Waypoint	Eastern dock breakwater end 50°09'·34N / 05°02'·96W Black Rock E Cardinal buoy 50°08'·68N / 05°01'·74W
Hazards	Black Rock (unlit, but outside lit buoyed channel). St Mawes Buoy/Lugo Rock (unlit). Busy commercial port, beware shipping movements in vicinity of docks and upper reaches of Fal. Large areas of upper reaches dry. Beware pot and net buoys
Overnight charges	Harbour Authority Yacht Haven £17 swinging mooring £11.10, at anchor £5.70 Port Pendennis Marina £20. Falmouth Marina £20. St Mawes mooring £15, at anchor £9. Mylor Yacht Harbour marina £25, mooring £15. Truro Harbour Authority pontoon, mooring or alongside Town Quay £8, at anchor £2.50

'Falmouth for orders' – these few words evoke so much. Although lofty spars, square yards and billowing spreads of canvas no longer grace the Western Approaches and deep laden rust streaked hulls waiting on the whims of commerce have long ceased to swing at anchor in Carrick Roads,

Falmouth, by virtue of its far westerly position, is still a major port of landfall and departure for many smaller sailing vessels that now cross the lonely oceans of the world. The ensigns of many nations are a familiar and romantic sight around

Looking west from St Mawes, the mile wide entrance to the River Fal presents few problems except Black Rock; note beacon, centre left. Pendennis Point lies beyond, with the docks and Falmouth Inner Harbour upper right

the harbour during the summer months.

For the majority with less exotic cruising ambitions, the River Fal and its tributaries offer everything that a yachtsman might require. I must admit to a degree of bias, as this was for many years my home port, but most visitors would probably agree that it is one of the finest sailing areas in England and certainly deserves its reputation as one of the great natural harbours of the world.

APPROACHES

Flanked by St Anthony Head to the east, which is grass topped with low cliffs and a white lighthouse (Iso WR 15s 16/14M, Red Sector 004° – 022°) built in 1835, and Pendennis Point and castle nearly a mile to the west, the entrance is easy and can be safely negotiated in any weather, even a southerly gale. If combined with an ebb tide, however, this will not be a gentle ride!

There is, however, no such thing as total perfection and, despite being deep, the entrance does have one notable hazard sited perversely right in the middle. Black Rock uncovers at half tide and is marked by a distinctive but unlit black conical beacon with an isolated danger mark (pole and two spheres) on top. You can enter either side of Black Rock, either by the buoyed deep water channel for commercial shipping to the east, or the western channel which is quite safe for small craft, having a least depth of 6m. Do not be tempted to pass close to Black Rock, as shallows extend nearly 200m to the north and south.

Strangers arriving at night should keep to the deep water channel, which is well lit, with Black Rock BYB east cardinal buoy (Q (3) 10s) to port and Castle conical green (Fl G 2.5s) to starboard. From here, steer up towards West Narrows red can (Fl (2) R 10s), but midway between them you can bear away towards the distant eastern breakwater end (Fl R 2s), leaving the Governor BYB east cardinal buoy (VQ (3) 5s) on your port hand.

Pendennis Castle, initially completed in 1543, was part of Henry VIII's massive chain of coastal defences from Milford Haven to Hull, built in response to fears of religious inspired invasion

Safely in before the squall! St Anthony lighthouse is always a welcoming sight

from Europe. His daughter Elizabeth then instigated the building of the large outer walls during the war with Spain, following the raiding and burning of Penzance, Newlyn and Mousehole in 1595. The awaited attack never came and Pendennis never fired its guns in anger.

The castle is preserved by English Heritage and has audio visual displays covering its history, including recently restored artillery from WWII sea defence fortifications, notably the impressive big guns in the Half Moon Battery. Pendennis Castle and its counterpart at St Mawes are open daily during the summer, and the walk up to the headland along Castle Drive, with a grandstand view of the docks, estuary and Falmouth Bay is definitely recommended.

Just below the castle ramparts, the squat modern building on the hillside is the Falmouth Coastguard Maritime Rescue Co-ordination Centre, now regularly involved in rescues on the other side of the world thanks to satellite technology. Monitoring VHF Ch 16, the local working channels are 67, 10, 23, 73, 86 call sign *Falmouth Coastguard*.

BERTHING AND MOORINGS

With anchorages, moorings, berths alongside and several marinas, the Fal has a bewildering variety of options for visiting boats, but Falmouth itself does tend to be the first stop, and with ample deep water well into the inner harbour. Follow the line of the northern arm of the docks, keeping a watchful eye on shipping movements in and around them, particularly when rounding the western end. This should be given a wide berth as tugs, ferries, fishing boats and sizeable ships have a nasty habit of emerging, often at speed.

Falmouth Docks, which date from around 1860, can dry dock ships up to 100,000 tons for repairs and has an important bunkering facility. Various

Looking seaward from the Penryn River, Falmouth Marina in foreground, Flushing on left with the inner harbour and docks beyond. St Anthony Head and Carrick Roads in far distance

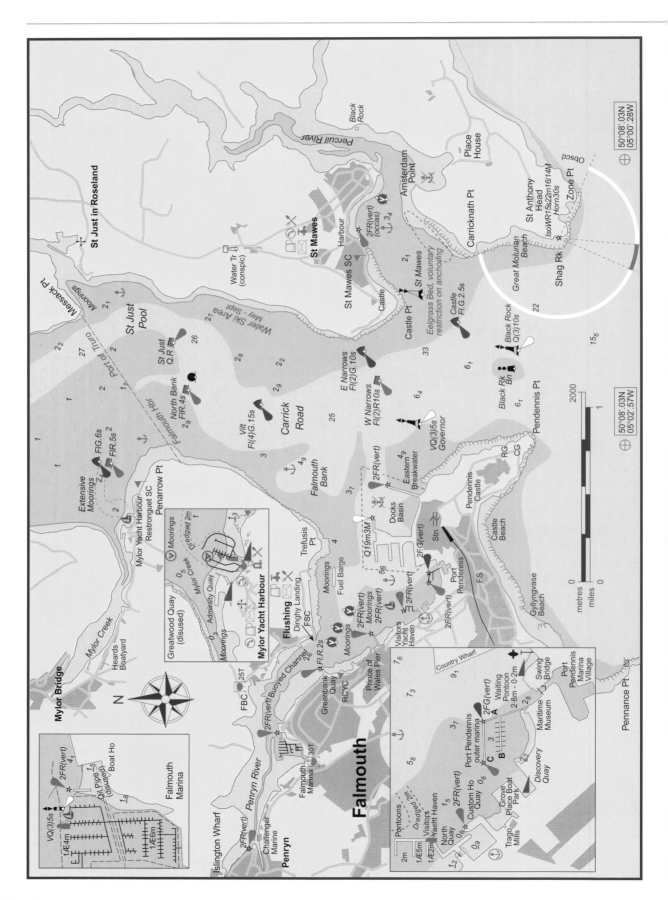

Falmouth inner harbour and docks. Custom House Quay and the Visitors' Yacht Haven is on bottom left, with Port Pendennis outer and inner marina on bottom right. The visitors' anchorage is in the centre

plans to enlarge it over the years have been mooted, perhaps the most ominous, in the late 1980s, was the proposal of the unsuccessful Falmouth Container Port Company to build a major container transhipment port to the east of the docks stretching a third of the way across the entrance to the Fal!

Within the docks complex, Pendennis Shipyard specialises in the building and refit of large luxury yachts, which can often be seen lying in the wet basin at the eastern side of the docks. It has a 500 ton slip and 80 ton hoist, and is internationally renowned for its high quality work. The yard was devastated by a major fire in 1994, but re-emerged phoenix-like from the ashes within months, a triumph epitomised by the

magnificent 43m schooner *Adela*, which was launched here in 1995 and won the 1997 Atlantic Challenge race for classic yachts from New York to Falmouth.

VISITORS' YACHT HAVEN

The picturesque town of Falmouth climbs in all its colourful and intriguing profusion along the hillside overlooking the mass of moorings in the inner harbour. Bear round past the western side of the docks and steer for Custom House Quay dead ahead, where you will find the main anchorage and the Falmouth Harbour Commissioners' (FHC) 100 berth Visitors' Yacht Haven.

The approach channel is dredged to 2m and indicated by two leading marks – posts with large orange triangle topmarks, one on the end of North Quay and the other on the pontoon by the fuel barge. The northernmost corner of the Yacht Haven is lit (2FR vert), and the pontoon walkways are also illuminated.

The berths along the eastern breakwater spine are all dredged to 2.5m, the two outer western

Falmouth Harbour Commissioners Visitors' Yacht Haven is one of the most popular berthing options – the entrance to the inner pontoons is to the left of picture. Fuel berth and yacht anchorage on right

pontoon arms have 2m and the innermost 1.5m, and these are entered along the northern side of the Visitor's Yacht Haven. Keep close to the pontoons – outside the dredged area the water to the north and west of the Yacht Haven is very shallow at MLWS.

Charges for a 10m boat are £17 per night – but it is worth noting that advantageous weekly rates are available on all the FHC berthing facilities. A week on the Yacht Haven, for example, works out at £102 for a 10m boat. The harbour office (Tel: 01326 312285 or 314379), call sign *Falmouth Harbour Radio*, monitors VHF Ch 16 and works on 12, as does its patrol launch *Killigrew*, which is usually on hand to assist during working hours when there is also a Supervisor on the Yacht Haven.

Facilities includer water hoses and electric points on the pontoons, as well as the FHC fuel barge which has diesel, petrol and water, (open daily 0900 – 1800). An alternative source for diesel, particularly for larger vessels, is the *Falmouth Industry*, a long blue motor barge moored just south of Trefusis Point on the far side of the harbour. This is open Mon – Fri 0800 – 1630, Sat 0800 – 1200, call sign *Falmouth Industry*, VHF channel 16, otherwise berth alongside.

Yacht Haven security is good as the pontoons are accessed with a PIN number through a shoreside gate by the Yacht Haven Supervisor's office. There are rubbish bins on North Quay and, just around the corner, the Yacht Haven Amenity Centre has excellent showers, toilets and laundry facilities. Access is by a swipe card that can be obtained from the Yacht Haven Supervisor or the harbour office.

PORT PENDENNIS AND THE MARITIME MUSEUM

Port Pendennis Marina Village lies opposite the Visitors Yacht Haven in the south-eastern corner of the inner harbour. It is the base for Falmouth Maritime, which has been the prime mover in revitalising this part of the waterfront, notably with the £10 million awarded by the Heritage Lottery Fund in 1997 to establish a Maritime Museum and events centre on the waterfront site, now known as Discovery Quay.

A joint venture between the National Maritime Museum, Greenwich, and Falmouth Maritime Museum, the National Maritime Museum of Cornwall was officially opened in March 2003 by Prince Andrew and has rapidly achieved international acclaim and many awards for its imaginative displays and architecture. The distinctive landmark building, with its prominent 'lighthouse' tower, provides a permanent home for the National Maritime Museum's Small Boat Collection and is definitely a 'must visit' attraction! With a wealth of historical information, it also encompasses hands-on displays, interactive

Port Pendennis Marina is overlooked by the National Maritime Museum's landmark building

entertainment and the diverse collection of 140 boats, including many famous names such as the Dragon *Bluebottle*, raced for many years by the Duke of Edinburgh and Uffa Fox, The Dye's much travelled Wayfarer dinghy, *Wanderer*, the very first Mirror dinghy, and the converted Quay Punt *Curlew*, in which Tim and Pauline Carr circumnavigated and completed many voyages to high latitudes under sail alone. And back in the waters where she began and ended her epic non-stop circumnavigation in 1969, Sir Robin Knox-Johnston's *Suhaili* is also based here as part of the floating display.

A public piazza with shops and cafés lies adjacent to the 70 berth all-tide marina (minimum depth 3.5m, up to 4.2m on main walkway of outer marina). This includes approximately 40 berths for visitors alongside the outer pontoons, with a few finger berths usually available inside.

Access is around the SW corner of the breakwater pontoons, which extend from the southern side of the entrance to Port Pendennis Inner Marina. There are lights (2FG vert) on the eastern end of the outer pontoon and equivalent red lights on the western end. Power and water is available at all berths, including 100amp 3 phase for larger yachts.

Port Pendennis Marina is well-established as a venue for national and international sailing events, hosting the Atlantic Alone feeder race for the 1998 Around Alone, La Solitaire du Figaro 2000 and the International Dragon Gold Cup in 2004.

Port Pendennis inner marina is also accessible to visitors if space permits, and is a particularly safe spot if you have to leave your boat for a while. Entry is through an automatic dock gate approximately three hours either side of HW. Call *Port Pendennis* on VHF Ch 80 or M for berthing availability in either marina, or berth on the north side of the breakwater pontoon in the approach to the gate and check in with reception (Tel: 01326 211211 or 311113), which is open during normal office hours.

Onshore facilities include showers, toilets, a laundry room, car parking and even a tennis court. The marina office has a lounge for yacht crews with telephone, fax and internet access. There is also a 40 ton slipway hoist. Ideally placed for crew changes, the Falmouth Town railway station is within three minutes walk, and hire cars are available on site. There is total security throughout Port Pendennis and the only access is through PIN control gates, making it by far the safest berthing in town. The overnight berthing charge of £2 per metre is the same in both marinas. Short stay, up to four hours, is £6.80. The local lifeboat and RNLI base are situated adjacent to Port Pendennis.

Port Pendennis and the Visitors' Yacht Haven together provide the most convenient alongside berthing in Falmouth, with pubs, restaurants, bistros and shops all within easy walking distance. Close by, Custom House Quay, which surrounds the drying inner basin, is over 300 years old and forms an attractive focal point on the Falmouth waterfront. Here, yhe Chain Locker and the Quayside Inn both offer good pub food and have outdoor tables and seats on the quay overlooked by some fine old buildings, including the harbour office and the 1815 Custom House with its

One of the best views of the Falmouth waterfront is from the Maritime Museum tower. Port Pendennis in foreground, Custom House Quay and Yacht Haven beyond

adjoining 'Kings Pipe', a brick chimney still used for burning contraband!

A summer ferry to St Mawes runs from Custom House Quay. To the east of the quay, beyond the large Trago Mills discount store (well worth investigating), the Harbour Commissioners have an extensive boat park and large launching slip in Grove Place, adjacent to the Falmouth Watersports Association clubhouse where visitors are welcome to use the facilities.

In Quay Hill, which leads up from North Quay, you'll find the Seafood Bar (Tel: 315129) and The Hut (Tel: 318229). Turn left into Arwenack Street for the Hunkeydory Restaurant and Bar (Tel: 212997), tapas and live music at Blue South (Tel: 212122), north African cuisine at Bodenes (Tel: 210759) and Indian dishes at Balti Curries (Tel: 317905), or right to the Seafarers (Tel: 319851) and Bistro de la Mer (Tel: 316509). If you head towards the opposite end of town for a fun family meal, you can choose from a selection of ingredients and have them cooked by the chef at Steppes (Tel:210353), or try Café No 33 (Tel: 211944), Powells Cellars (Tel: 311212), Chinese at Ming's Garden (Tel: 314413) and more Indian, Asha (Tel: 211688) or Gurkha (Tel: 311483). There are a number of fast food outlets, cafes, fish and chips and a veritable surfeit of Cornish pasty shops – for my money Rowes still produces the best. . .

The major shops are strung out along the town's main street or in the area known as the Moor, which is close to Prince of Wales Pier. Here, there is a medium sized Tesco supermarket, open Mon – Sat 0700 – 2000, Sun

Chapter 3

1000 – 1600, and also the main post office.

Conspicuous right on the waterfront, the Bosun's Locker chandler (Tel: 312212), and Marine Instruments (Tel:312414) Admiralty chart agents and compass adjusters are just minutes away from the Yacht Haven. There are also three secondhand bookshops with a good nautical selection: Bookmark, at the top of Quay Hill, Browsers in St George's Arcade or the Archway Bookshop opposite Prince of Wales Pier.

THE ANCHORAGE AND VISITORS' MOORINGS

If you decide to anchor (more privacy, and less to pay – £5.70 for a 10m boat), let go just east of the Yacht Haven, clear of the quay and local moorings, but also well away from the docks, as anchoring is prohibited within a cable of the jetties. This area of water is regularly used for swinging large vessels into their berths, when the anchorage often has to be cleared. Details of impending ship movements are displayed at the Yacht Haven Office and the harbour staff will give you good warning.

Depths vary between 1.5m and 2.5m, and the holding ground and shelter is good in anything except northerlies, although the wash from the ferries and pleasure boats can make it fairly lively at times and in the season it gets pretty crowded. The best place to land is on the innermost Yacht Haven pontoon, by the linking bridge to the Quay, where dinghies can be left afloat.

Finally, between Custom House Quay and Prince of Wales Pier there are seven FHC visitors' swinging moorings, R101 – R107, and between Prince of Wales Pier and Greenbank Quay there are a further 11 FHC visitors' moorings, K1 – K6, L1 – L4 and T5, all with green support buoys (marked FHC) and costing £11.10 a night for a 10m boat.

Shelter is normally good throughout the rest of the inner harbour except in strong east, north-easterly or south-easterly winds when it becomes surprisingly rough as seas build across the open fetch from the St Mawes shore. Fortunately, easterly gales are rare, particularly in summer. Keep well clear of the Prince of Wales Pier as it is constantly busy with large trip boats and ferries to Flushing and St Mawes. There is a good dinghy landing in the boat harbour on the inner end of the pier, which is particularly handy for the Tesco supermarket.

The Royal Cornwall Yacht Club also has two moorings available at reasonable cost, marked RCYC Visitor, off its fine clubhouse. This stands on its own quay below the elegant row of tall Regency houses along Greenbank, just upriver of the extensive Packet Quays waterfront development. These moorings can be reserved in advance through the Club Office (Tel: 01326 312126) and visiting yacht crews are always made very welcome.

The club was established in 1871 and was originally located in the Greenbank Hotel. In 1883 it leased its present waterside premises in Greenbank House, which was eventually purchased by a syndicate of members in 1911. It is open every day except Monday during the summer months and, among its many activities, organises the popular Azores And Back Race every four years.

Facilities include showers, bar and dining room; there is a good dinghy landing and a club launch, which operates daily between 1015 and 1845 (later on racing evenings – Tues and Fri) except for a 1300 – 1400 lunch break. RCYC mooring rental includes use of this free taxi service, call sign *Club Launch* on VHF Ch M. Fresh water and scrubbing alongside the club quay is also possible by arrangement.

A fast, 35-knot water taxi service, Aqua Cab (Tel: 07971 242258), also operates on request throughout the Fal and Helford area.

PACKETS, QUAY PUNTS AND WORKING BOATS

Sir Walter Raleigh, on his way home from El Dorado in 1596, put into the Fal and found little more than a small fishing village known as Smithick, and the nearby manor house at Arwenack, home of the Killigrew family. His advice that it might make a good harbour was not then taken up, but by 1670 the Killigrews had got round to building Custom House Quay. This turned out to be a stroke of luck rather than foresight, which ultimately transformed Falmouth into a thriving seaport of major importance.

Impressed by the new quays, the post office decided to establish its Packet Service here in 1688. This fleet of fast, armed sailing ships, generally brigantines of around 200 tons, with appropriate names like *Speedy* and *Express*, were all privately owned and chartered to the Crown to carry mail, bullion and passengers, not only to Europe, but as far afield as the West Indies and the Americas, averaging a round trip of between 15 to 18 weeks. It was a tough, dangerous business, the valuable cargoes resulting in frequent attacks by privateers and pirates, but many owners and captains made fortunes. Around Falmouth, particularly along Greenbank and opposite, in the small village of Flushing, large elegant houses rose along the waterfront, graphic evidence of the new-found wealth, for by 1800 over 40 packet ships were based in the port.

As the first port of call for most inbound shipping, before the days of wireless, Falmouth often received the first news of dramatic events abroad – such as the death of Nelson. Ship's masters were not only anxious to notify owners of their safe arrival, but also to find the final destination – orders – for their cargoes, which resulted in much trade for Falmouth and led to the development of the famous Quay Punts' to service the deep water visitors.

These deep, sturdy and mostly open boats were between 25 and 32ft long and ranged the approaches to the Lizard, seeking ships before they arrived off the port. The particular rigours of the job produced a remarkably seaworthy craft, yawl rigged with a stumpy mainmast to enable them to sail in under the lower yards of the big sailing ships. Only one, named *Fat Boat*, was ever lost whilst performing her job. She specialised in collecting the accumulated used cooking fat from the incoming ships to sell ashore, but when swamped off Black Head in 1904, she sank in seconds.

Many of her more fortunate contemporaries – some still sailing – were eventually decked and converted to yachts, notably *Curlew* which can be seen at the Maritime Museum, and a number of yachts were built along their lines. The quay punting still continues in Falmouth, but today it is by a small fleet of sturdy motor launches operated by the Falmouth Licensed Watermen.

The other traditional craft that originated in the estuary of the Fal are the Working Boats, the sailing oyster boats that are now unique in Europe, their freak survival resulting from the local bye-laws prohibiting the dredging with anything other than sail or oar. These are gaff cutters ranging between 20 and 32ft in length, although mostly around 28ft, and a number of these three-quarter decked boats still work the natural oyster fishery during the winter season from 1st October until 31st March, drifting down tide across the banks in the upper part of Carrick Roads and hauling their dredges by hand.

During the summer they race, a tradition continued by the Falmouth Working Boat Association, formed in 1979 to preserve the unique character of the class.

Some of the wooden boats are over 100 years old, and the most famous has to be the late Toby West's *Victory*, launched in 1884. With her distinctive bright yellow hull, she was always campaigned hard by her equally colourful owner until his death in 2001. Fisherman, yachtsman and lifeboat coxwain, he was undoubtedly one of the last of Falmouth's real waterfront characters; if you want an entertaining read, try and find a secondhand copy of his autobiography *A Sailing West*. Today, in common with several of her sisters, *Victory* is owned and keenly raced by a local syndicate.

In the 1970s Terry Heard produced the first GRP working boat hulls and many more have followed. There have, however, been a few modern boats built in wood and even one in ferrocement. The impressive fleet numbers 20 boats at times and, with huge gaff rigs, lofty coloured topsails and long, lethal bowsprits, this is one of the most spectacular sights in Falmouth.

If you are around at the weekend, the boats, with their large open cockpits, have plenty of room for crew, and if you feel like trying it, just ask – someone will invariably take you along.

In marked contrast, the other distinctive Falmouth racing fleet, the Sunbeams, epitomises the elegance of the 20s and 30s, and the halcyon days when the mighty J-class raced in Falmouth Bay. They are classic three-quarter decked bermudian sloops with long overhangs, just under 27 ft overall and immaculately maintained. This colourful fleet, established in Falmouth in 1924, is one of two in the country, the other is based at Itchenor. Originally designed in 1922 by Alfred Westmacott as a one design class for the Hamble, most of the Sunbeams were built in the Solent.

However, look out for *Milly* (V45). Crafted by Mylor Yacht Harbour's master shipwright, Brian Crockford, and launched in 1999, she was the first new Sunbeam to be built for over 20 years and the first ever to be built in Falmouth; since then two more have been built at Mylor, *Kitty* for the local fleet and *Spray* for Itchenor, maintaining the tradition that their names all end in 'y.'

Racing of every description in Falmouth is very active all year round, but Falmouth Regatta Week, during the second week of August, organised by The Port of Falmouth Sailing Association (POFSA), is the major event, beginning with the spectacular 'Falmouth Classics' weekend for traditional craft. For further details, telephone 01326 211555 or visit its website: www.pofsa.org.

The advent of the steam ships finally removed

the good fortune that Falmouth had enjoyed for over 150 years, and in 1852 the post office transferred the mail service to Southampton. Wireless did away with the need to call for orders, but the decline in the port was brief. The new docks were commenced in 1858; building ships, repairing them and cashing in on the new needs of the steamers for bunkers.

With the arrival of the railway in 1863, another new industry – tourism – began to emerge. In 1865 the Falmouth Hotel was the first to rise from the fields along the seafront as the holidaymakers began to arrive. Today, more than ever, they are the mainstay of the town's prosperity.

FLUSHING

Opposite Falmouth, Flushing is an attractive little village with a post office and limited provisions, two pubs which both serve good food – The Standard and Seven Stars – and also the Sticky Prawn Restaurant (Tel: 373734) on the quay, where the small fleet of local fishing boats land their catches.

The building on the lower New Quay is Flushing Sailing Club, which is generally only open at weekends or when evening racing is taking place. It has a bar, but no other facilities. The walk from Flushing out to Trefusis Point (and all the way round to Mylor if you are feeling energetic!) provides some fine views of the Fal. There is a pleasant sandy beach at Kiln Quay, popular with locals, and a regular spot for barbeques.

FALMOUTH MARINA

The biggest boating facility in the estuary, Falmouth Marina is about a mile further upstream, on the Penryn River beyond Greenbank Quay, which is not difficult to find as it has Greenbank Hotel in huge letters along it and a prominent sign pointing the way to Falmouth Marina.

From here on the river becomes shallower, but the main channel has over 2m and is buoyed, with red cans to port and conical green buoys to starboard, the first red can being the only one that is lit (QR). The southern shore is particularly shallow; drying banks extend well out and are covered with oyster beds where anchoring is prohibited and you run aground at your peril.

Falmouth Marina is hidden beyond a jetty with warehouses on the port hand at Boyers Cellars, or Coastlines as it is known locally, called after the coastal shipping line of the same name which acquired the jetty in 1936. It was a regular port of

call for their 10 day runs between Liverpool and London. Coastal petrol tankers continued to discharge here until 1996, but now it is only used by fishing boats. Opposite, at Little Falmouth, are the slipways and large sheds of Falmouth Boat Construction Ltd (FBC), where there has been a boatyard since the early 1880s and which was the site of the first dry-dock in Falmouth.

The proposal to dredge out and build a marina in the muddy creek at Ponsharden was greeted with great local scepticism when it was first proposed in 1979, but the success of the 350-berth Falmouth Marina (Tel: 01326 316620) has long since proved all the pundits wrong, and usually there are up to 60 visitors' berths available. It has been owned by Premier Marina Group since 1997, and the company has undertaken a major refurbishment programme, including the acquisition of the former Port Falmouth Boat Yard adjacent to the marina in 2000. This has enabled the marina to infil the old slipway and enlarge the winter storage space ashore, providing more car parking space during the summer. It is anticipated that the outer basin will be dredged during 2004 to enable 'F' pontoon to be extended southwards and create an extra 30 berths.

The dredged approach channel provides access for boats drawing up to 1.8m at LW, although a certain amount of care is recommended at LWS. The isolated pontoon just beyond Boyers Cellars is private berthing for local boats with lights (2FR vert) on its northern end. Beyond, visitors must keep to port of the BY pole with east cardinal topmark (Fl (3) 5s) and proceed to the arrivals and fuel berth ('J' pontoon), which is clearly marked.

Here, the berthing master will allocate a berth. It is advisable to call ahead (*Falmouth Marina* –

The final approach to the marina is well marked – keep the east cardinal beacon on your starboard hand

Falmouth Marina is well sheltered and usually has up to 60 berths for visitors

VHF Ch 80 or M), particularly if you are over 13m LOA. Berthing masters are on duty from 0700 – 2100 during the season, and there is also a night watchman providing 24 hour security who can also allocate berths. Charges are £2 per metre per night, with a minimum charge of £17.60.

The BY pole with yellow 'X' topmark (Fl 2s) beyond the fuel berth marks the northern and western edges of the dredged channel. At night this light should be kept open to port of the east cardinal light in the final approach.

The marina has a very friendly atmosphere and excellent facilities, comprising toilets and showers, a 24 hour launderette, Calor and Camping Gaz, fresh water at the berths, and electricity if required. Diesel is available 24 hours – either call ahead on VHF or berth on the fuel pontoon and if no one is in attendance contact the marina office with the phone provided. Petrol can be obtained in cans from a nearby garage.

Without a doubt the focal point is the large Marine Bar and Restaurant (Tel: 313481) which overlooks the marina. Other on site businesses include Fal Chandlers (Tel:212411) and Skywave Marine (Tel: 318314) chandlery and marine electronics. Global Marine Electronics (Tel: 316740) is also based here, along with two charter operators, car hire, hairdressers and brokerage. In addition there is a 30 ton mobile hoist, 25 ton mobile crane and full onshore repair facilities.

Five minutes' walk away, the Co-op Pioneer supermarket is particularly convenient for replenishing the stores and is open on Sundays too. The centre of Falmouth is a gentle 20 minutes walk away, with fine views of the inner harbour. Alternatively there are regular buses and plenty of taxis.

PENRYN

Between the marina and Penryn, a mile further upstream, the river dries almost completely. During the Middle Ages Penryn was a port of considerable importance until its trade was wrested away by the development of Falmouth and the gradual silting of the river. It is possible to reach Penryn quay after half flood, but it is much used by local fishing boats and the mud is sticky and deep at LW. Scenically the river does not really have a lot to recommend it, although the town is architecturally very interesting. However, if you have any problems, Penryn is where you're likely to end up as most of the main marine businesses are located in the area; if you wish to avoid going upriver by boat, regular buses run from the centre of Falmouth.

Falmouth Yacht Brokers Boatyard and Challenger Marine, which has some drying pontoon berthing available for visitors (access HW±3 hrs), are further upstream. Right at the head of the creek, a number of nautical companies, are situated at Islington Wharf where it is possible to dry out alongside on mud. On Commercial Road, which runs parallel to the creek, you will find the Boathouse chandlery (Tel: 374177), SKB Sails and Robin Curnow, the outboard specialist.

ST MAWES

The real beauty of the Fal is that it can provide within its limits most of the ingredients of any enjoyable cruise – magnificent scenery, safe water for sailing and some delightful anchorages where you can find some welcome peace and quiet and escape from the crowds ashore.

Extending nearly three miles inland and almost a mile wide, Carrick Roads is a broad stretch of water surrounded by rounded hills, fields and low rocky shores. At the south-eastern end, opposite Falmouth, is the entrance to the Percuil River and St Mawes, which has only one hazard in the approach, Lugo rock, two cables south of the prominent castle (least depth 0.8m). It is marked by the unlit YB south cardinal, St Mawes buoy, which should be left on your port hand when entering. The houses of the small village of St Mawes run along the northern shore, off which there are a number of local moorings, while beyond is the small boat harbour.

The St Mawes Pier & Harbour Company has 10 visitors' moorings, green buoys marked St Mawes, off the Quay. These are available through Harbour Master Captain Roy Maddern, whose office is on the Town Quay (Tel: 01326 270553). He maintains a VHF watch on Ch 16, working Ch 12, call sign *St Mawes Harbour Radio* and is often afloat in a RIB marked *Harbour Master St Mawes*. For a 10m boat, a 24 hour stay on a mooring works out at £15. Alternatively you can anchor well clear of the

St Mawes from the Percuil River. Amsterdam Point on the left

moorings, but do not obstruct the fairway up to the jetty end, which is used constantly by the ferries and pleasure boats. Twenty four hours at anchor will cost £9 for a 10m boat.

Land on the large slipway or beach and keep clear of the pier. Alternatively, call the St Mawes to Place ferry on VHF Ch 71, which operates a water taxi service on request.

The Falmouth Bay & Estuaries Initiative is requesting yachtsmen to refrain from anchoring close to the shore in the traditionally popular area along the south side of the entrance to St Mawes between Carricknath and Amsterdam Points. This is a voluntary anchoring restriction aimed to protect an eelgrass bed extending out to seaward of the low tide mark to a depth of 3m. It is still possible to land on the beach by dinghy just to the west of Amsterdam Point and from here, if you're in need of a pleasant walk with good views, you can follow the coastal footpath out to St Anthony lighthouse – as seen in the children's TV series *Fraggle Rock*. This passes Carricknath and Great Molunan beaches, which can provide plenty of sand and swimming at LW and are popular anchorages with locals in easterly winds – sound in to a suitable depth.

St Mawes is a former fishing village with a particularly mild climate. Being off the main holiday track has probably resulted in its popularity for retirement and, more recently, holiday homes, which may be why it has escaped over-development and commercialism.

Built at the same time as Pendennis, St Mawes

Castle is a particularly well preserved example of its type, a clover leaf formation of three immense bastions, now open to the public and surrounded by gardens with fine views across to Falmouth.

The village provides all the necessary basics, including a Spar foodstore, Barclays and Lloyds TSB banks (no cashpoints), a post office, a delicatessen, cafés, and even a small chandlery. You will also find restaurants open to non-residents at The Idle Rocks Hotel (Tel: 270771), Rising Sun Hotel (Tel: 270233), Ship & Castle Hotel (Tel:270401), St Mawes Hotel (Tel: 270266) and the Tresanton Hotel (Tel: 270055), while there is good pub fare at the popular Victory Inn.

Fresh water is available alongside at the quay and also in cans from a tap on the quay near Lloyd's Bank, but diesel can only be had (in cans) from the Freshwater and Percuil boatyards further upriver. Camping Gaz refills can be obtained from the Emporium, whilst Calor Gas and some chandlery can be bought from Percuil Boatyard.

St Mawes Sailing Club overlooks the quay and visitors are welcome to use the bar and showers.

The anchorage off St Mawes is perfect in easterly winds, but exposed to the south-west, when shelter can be found up the Percuil River, around the bend past Amsterdam Point, although anchoring is difficult because of the large number of local moorings. You might just find space to anchor clear of the moorings in the bight off Place House, a peaceful spot overlooked by silent woods, but the foreshore to MLWS is owned by Place and the owner does not allow boats to dry out here overnight.

The Percuil River winds away inland, drying to a large extent, but shallow draught boats can follow it – the deeper water indicated by the line of moorings – with a rising tide as far as Percuil. Here it is possible to anchor clear of the moorings in mid-stream, just grounding at LWS, but do not wander anywhere close inshore above Polvarth Point as oyster beds, marked by withies, lie on both sides of the river.

This is one of those places ideal for exploration by dinghy, its quiet creeks alive with herons and other wildlife. There is excellent blackberrying late in the summer.

MYLOR YACHT HARBOUR

Leaving the narrow Percuil, do not be lulled into a false sense of security by the broad waters of Carrick Roads, for large areas are shallow at LW, as many have discovered to their surprise. However, the main channel is very deep,

averaging 25m, and trends towards Penarrow Point, a low promontory with a prominent pillar on the western shore, then over to the eastern bank towards St Just Creek, where there are a number of moorings. At half flood there is ample water everywhere, but upstream of St Mawes Castle, St Mawes Bank extends from the shore, least depth 1.2m in places.

Mylor Creek, west of Penarrow Point, is a popular base for a large number of boats which lie on extensive moorings in Mylor Pool off Mylor Yacht Harbour, but the surrounding shallows in the approaches have as little as 1.2m in places and, with springs or a draught over 1.5m, it is always best to wait until a couple of hours after LW, passing close to the North Bank red can buoy off Penarrow Point. Next steer for and pass between the two smaller red can and conical green approach buoys to Mylor Pool, which mark the beginning of the dredged (2m below CD) approach channel to Mylor Yacht Harbour Marina.

Restronguet Sailing Club, a very active dinghy racing centre, is a modern building on the foreshore, and beyond it are the houses, quays and pontoons of Mylor Yacht Harbour.

Formerly the Royal Navy's smallest dockyard and base for the old wooden waller *HMS Ganges*, this picturesque corner began to develop into a busy boatyard from the late 1960s. Since 1997 the considerable upgrading of facilities under new ownership has culminated in the creation of a new marina and all tide approach channel, which has made Mylor Yacht Harbour much more accessible than it once was.

There are extensive moorings on both sides of this channel, which follows the clear fairway between the moorings towards the line of heavy concrete pontoons forming the eastern breakwater arm of the marina. The entrance to the marina is around the northern end of the eastern breakwater pontoons and visitors normally berth on the inside of the western breakwater pontoons.

The marina (Tel: 01326 372121) has visitors' berths for vessels up to 22m which can be booked in advance or on arrival. A 24-hour listening watch is maintained, call *Mylor Yacht Harbour* on VHF channel 80 or M for berthing instructions. Swinging moorings are also available and these include a complimentary water taxi service operating from 0800 till late seven days a week during the summer. The overnight charge for a 10m boat for most of the summer season, including free showers, is £20 alongside in the marina or £10 for a swinging mooring, rising during August to £25 and £15

A major boating facility, Mylor Yacht Harbour can provide marina berths or swinging moorings for visitors

respectively. If you stay a week you will get the seventh night free, and there is a 10 per cent reduction for stays of over four weeks.

No public transport goes to Mylor Yacht Harbour, but it is very self-contained, incorporating water, showers, toilets, a launderette, diesel, petrol and electricity. The comprehensive yard facilities include a 35 ton travelift and repairs, while Marine Trak Engineers (Tel: 376588) and Simrad Marine Electronics (Tel: 374411) are also based on site.

Right on the the quayside you'll find the ever popular Ganges licensed restaurant (Tel: 374320) or try Castaways restaurant and wine bar (Tel: 377710), just next door, for tapas, seafood and lighter meals. Both Mylor Harbour Cafe and foodstore and Mylor Chandlery and Rigging (Tel: 375482) are open seven days a week. Last but not least, the very friendly Mylor Yacht Club is on the quay and visitors are very welcome to use the clubhouse and bar.

The old quays of the dockyard form a sheltered and attractive setting overlooked by the lovely church of St Mylor, where some of the gravestones are a fascinating reflection of the local maritime heritage, the peaceful resting place of packet commanders, sailors, oyster dredgermen and a luckless shipwright who died in 1770 and whose epitaph reads:

'His foot it slip and he did fall
Help Help he cries and that was all.'

The narrow entrance into Mylor Creek is overhung with trees and very congested with moorings, but widens further in, continuing for nearly a mile to the village of Mylor Bridge, where there is a post office, shops and occasional buses to Falmouth. All of the upper part of the creek dries, and at Tregatreath is Gaffers and Luggers Boatyard, where traditional shipwright work blends harmoniously with modern technology as gaff-rigged fibreglass working boats and pilot cutter replicas are built here by Martin Heard.

ST JUST

From Mylor Pool, it is tempting to head directly for Restronguet Creek just upstream – certain disaster if the tide is near LW, as beyond the outer moorings the extensive banks almost dry at LW. Instead, return to the main channel, heading for the moorings off St Just. This is a pleasant spot in an east wind, when Mylor inevitably suffers!

There are many local moorings, but a good anchorage, popular with locals in easterlies, can be found to the south of the entrance to the creek off the shingly beaches along the rocky shore. Be warned though – the holding can be patchy so allow plenty of scope.

The coastal footpath provides a fine walk south towards St Mawes, or north to St Just where it

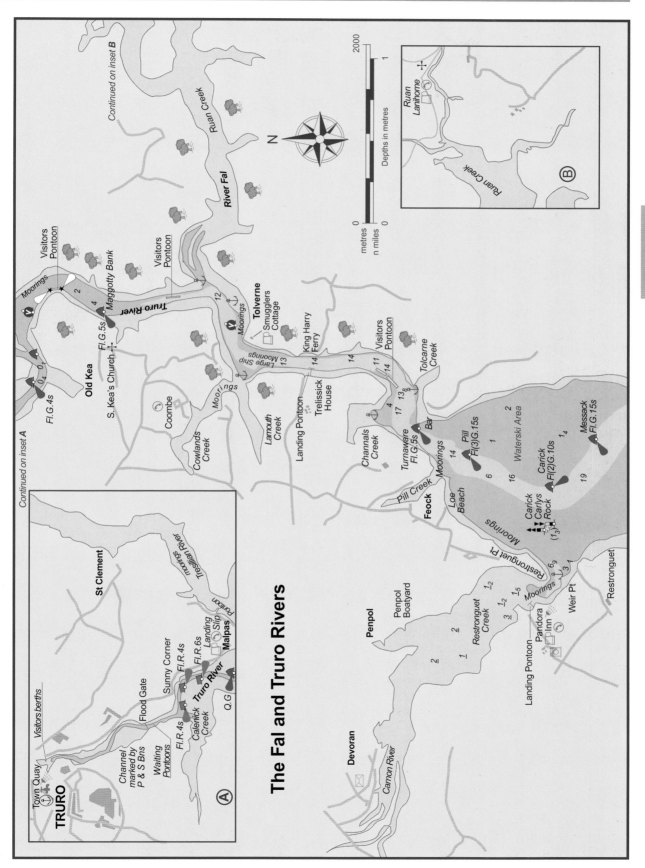

The Fal and Truro Rivers

A peaceful anchorage in the entrance to Ruan Creek

past the conical green Messack buoy (Fl G 15s), and towards Restronguet. As you leave the main channel it becomes shallow when passing to the south of Carick Carlys Rock (N and S cardinal beacons), with little more than 0.5m, but with a couple of hours of flood you should be able to get up to the Pandora Inn, the most likely reason for a visit to the creek!

There are concentrated moorings in the deep pool at the narrow mouth of the creek off Restronguet Point, which is a low promontory with some very expensive looking properties along it. Here the stream runs fast through the narrows. Deep draught boats can anchor short of the moorings, east of the entrance off Weir Point. Either land on the beach and walk along the path to the pub, or take the dinghy, an easy row with the tide, and make sure you return on the ebb. Boats able to dry out, however, can go right up to the large pontoon off the pub.

With its huge thatch and attractive waterside location, 'The Pan' is a very popular local watering hole which takes its name from *HMS Pandora*, the ship that captured the Bounty mutineers. On his return in 1790, her commander bought this 13th century inn and today it is notably yacht friendly, for not only can you find food and drink, but there is also a handy shower and toilet block, a small launderette and a fresh water supply.

Restronguet Creek widens considerably above the Pandora and is fringed down to the water's edge by woods and fields. Restronguet Yacht Basin (drying) lies just upstream on the south shore, while the Penpol Boatyard is situated on the northern shore at the entrance to Penpol Creek. All of Restronguet Creek is very shallow and dries extensively, but can be explored by dinghy for over a mile as far as Devoran, a small village on the northern shore where there is a post office and general store. It was a busy port in the 1880s, exporting copper and tin, for ships were once able to berth as far inland as the Perran

leads to the undoubted pride of the creek, the 13th century church. Lavishly described by Sir John Betjeman as 'to many people the most beautiful churchyard on earth', it certainly has one of the finest settings in England, nestling against the wooded hillside overlooking the peaceful creek and surrounded in spring by a breathtaking blaze of camelias and rhododendrons. Shoal draught boats can work their way right into the creek and dry out if space permits. Land on the shingle beach at the head of the inlet that encloses a drying tidal pool, where you will find Pascoe's Boatyard nearby. Small quantities of diesel are available here, in cans, and also Calor refills.

RESTRONGUET

Near low water keep within the main channel, which bears north-west from St Just buoy (QR),

Wharf on the main Falmouth to Truro road. Eventually the alluvial deposits from the Carnon valley mining caused its demise, silting the river to such an extent that it is now only accessible a couple of hours either side of HW.

THE UPPER REACHES

Beyond Restronguet, leave Carick Carlys Rock to port, and if on a falling tide keep to the deep water channel, which is marked by two more conical green starboard hand buoys, Carick (Fl(2) G 10s) and Pill (Fl (3) G 15s). The bank to the east is particularly shallow, as little as 0.2m in places at LW, and this is the main area of the oyster fishery in winter. Opposite, there are many moorings off Loe Beach which, comprising shingle and sand, is popular for swimming. A few visitors' moorings are sometimes available through the cafe, otherwise anchor off. Just above the beach, Pill Creek is a narrow wooded inlet, completely taken up by moorings.

The real upper reaches of the Fal and Truro Rivers begin at wooded Turnaware Point and its low shingle foreshore on the eastern bank. The change is dramatic as the wide expanse of Carrick Roads narrows into a deep waterway and the most attractive part of the river begins.

Keep close to the western shore, which is covered in trees and fringed with cliffs, where the notorious grounding spot, Turnaware Bar, extends north-west from the Point. It is clearly marked by a green conical buoy (Fl G 5s) which must be left to starboard. Here the streams begin to run strongly, 2 – 3 knots at springs. A small amount of commercial traffic still uses the upper reaches, notably the *Diction* which dredges maerl (calcified seaweed) from the estuary and discharges her cargo at Truro to be used as a fertiliser, or the occasional coaster carrying building materials. The river is much used by trip boats too.

Immediately north of the buoy is Channals Creek, a popular anchorage that is well sheltered in anything except southerlies and out of the main tidal stream. All the upper reaches are under the jurisdiction of the Truro Harbour Master and visitors will be charged £2.50 a night for anchoring anywhere north of Turnaware Bar. Sound in off the edge of the deep channel to about 2m at LW. Shoal draught boats can get much closer inshore where they will ground.

A fine sweep of grassland leads up from the water's edge to the impressive facade of Trelissick House, built in 1750 and now owned by the National Trust. The House is not open to the

There are several convenient visitors' pontoons in the upper Fal. Note distant ships moored in King Harry Reach

public, but the spectacular gardens featuring rhododendrons, camellias, azaleas and magnolias are open daily, 1030 – 1730, from February to October. Land at the rocky point on the east side of the bay and follow the scenic footpath along the shore through the woods.

The anchorage inside of Turnaware Point is another popular spot at weekends, particularly for picnics and barbeques. Another good anchorage can be found nearby off diminutive Tolcarne Creek, which is overlooked by steep woods, just clear of the deep water. The only thing that can detract from this delightful spot is its increasing use by water skiers, but it is usually peaceful mid-week.

Rounding the corner you reach the first Truro Harbour Authority visitors' pontoon, which has a rubbish bin. Charges here, and on the other visitors' pontoons further upstream, are at a flat rate of £8 a night, and dues are collected by the harbour master's launch. This monitors VHF Ch 16 and 12, call sign *Carrick Three*. Truro Harbour Office uses the same channels, call sign *Carrick One*.

The biggest surprise of the Fal now comes into sight! Here, in this land-locked and narrow river, surrounded by high wooded shores, you will often find large merchant ships lying on fore and aft moorings. The numbers vary depending on the fortunes of the international shipping trade, but at times there are over 20 vessels laid up in the river, as this is one of the cheapest places in the world, with deep water, between 13m and 15m, and excellent shelter. Although somewhat incongruous, these silent, waiting leviathans have a certain mournful fascination, but do not be too distracted by them; the tide runs strongly and the high shores and ships make the breeze very fluky, resulting in it being easy to get set on to the large moorings. In addition, midway along this reach is the King

Harry Ferry, which runs on chains, providing a short cut for cars between Falmouth and St Mawes. Identical at both ends, ascertain which way it is running and always pass astern, and not too close!

Just downstream of the ferry, the new Truro Harbour Authority landing pontoon is for local trip boats bringing visitors to Trelissick. There will, however, be space provided for dinghies, a freshwater tap and it is anticipated that visiting boats will be able to berth here overnight once the commercial boats have finished for the day.

Next, Lamouth and Cowlands Creeks open to port, both attractive and wooded, and both drying almost as far as the moorings at their mouth, where an anchorage can be found between these and the deep water. Small craft are able to explore further on the tide, as far as the peaceful hamlets of Coombe and Cowlands, renowned for their plum orchards, where bilge keelers can dry out on the foreshore. A public telephone is installed at Cowlands. Owned by the National Trust, Roundwood Quay, where the creeks meet, is a finely preserved granite quay once used for shipping minerals. There are several pleasant walks leading away from it.

The river turns sharply to the east off Tolverne Point, with more large ships sometimes in midstream, and on the shore you will see the thatched Smugglers Cottage, a popular spot with a landing pontoon and a number of mooring buoys at £8 per night or free if you are eating at Smugglers Cottage.

This corner has an interesting history as, during the last war, it was used as an assembly point for part of the American fleet of D-Day landing craft and was visited by General Eisenhower. For nearly 100 years, trip boats have run here from Falmouth for cream teas, and it has a licensed restaurant (it is not a pub) where lunches, suppers and barbeques are a regular feature in good weather. The fascinating collection of photos and mementoes in the cottage are well worth seeing, in particular the *Uganda* room, devoted to the famous cruise ship and Falklands veteran that was laid up in the Fal between 1985 and 1986.

At the next junction, just above Tolverne, the rivers divide, the Fal fading away rather insignificantly into Ruan Creek, which continues to the east, and the Truro River, heading northwards.

There is a peaceful anchorage just within the entrance to Ruan Creek, off the old ruined boathouse on the north side where there is about 2m at LW. However, watch out for three very large abandoned mooring blocks close to the

shore, marked with a yellow pole and 'X' topmark, which only begin to uncover after half tide. The south shore dries extensively, so shoal draught boats can push a bit further into the creek and dry out at LW beneath the dense woods along the edge of Lord Falmouth's estate.

Beyond the first bend, the creek dries completely and there is a voluntary restriction on anchoring within this Site of Special Scientific Interest, although small craft and dinghies can explore it on the tide, penetrating deep into the rural depths of Cornwall to Ruan Lanihorne, three miles away. Here there is an old quay for landing and the Kings Head pub within five minutes' walk.

Just upstream of Ruan Creek is a second Truro Harbour Authority visitors' pontoon, sections of which are constructed from recycled plastic. It is also possible to anchor anywhere along this reach out of the main fairway, although it is busy with trip boats during the day and an anchor light is advisable at night. Beyond tiny Church Creek on the west bank, where the ruined spire of Old Kea Church rises above the trees, the Truro River becomes much shallower and the Maggotty Bank extends across the river from the eastern shore (least depth 0.7m). The channel is very narrow between the west shore and the conical green buoy (Fl G 5s) at the outer edge of the bank.

Follow the bend round to starboard past Woodbury Point, where there is an isolated white house, to a deeper pool where the next Truro Harbour Authority visitors' pontoon is located and just beyond it there is another longer visitors' pontoon. Finally, further upstream in Malpas Reach, three smaller visitors' moorings are suitable for up to about 7.5m LOA. There are many other moorings here, and at LWS there is as little as 0.3m in places. The tide runs strongly, reaching a good two knots at springs.

At Malpas, pronounced *Mope-us*, the elevated houses overlook the river, and below them is the yard of Malpas Marine and a private landing pontoon. It can often provide visitors' moorings at around £8 a day; to enquire either phone ahead (Tel: 01872 271260) or berth on the end of its pontoon, but do not leave your boat unattended as it is used by ferries to Falmouth.

For a charge of £2 visitors can leave their dinghies on the pontoon, and a shower/toilet, water and diesel in cans are also available. Close by, overlooking the river, the popular Heron Inn (Tel: 01872 272773) does good food, while other amenities include a very small shop-cum-post office, a public telephone, and occasional buses to

The line of darker water clearly shows the final approach to Truro. Sunny Corner is on the bottom right, with Calenick Creek leading off to the left. Lighterage Quay and the flood gate are in centre from where the channel meanders on towards Town Quay

Truro, which is now within walking distance, albeit not close.

Tresillian River branches to starboard and mostly dries. Truro River continues past Malpas and is well worth exploring as far at Truro. The channel, which is used by coasters, is well-marked, but do not leave Malpas any earlier than three hours before HW Truro and keep in midstream, leaving the conical green buoy and private landing pontoon off the housing development at Victoria Quay to starboard.

A large bank extends west of the next long bend, so keep well towards the western shore before turning north past the first of two more conical green buoys. Beyond the second, the channel swings back to the eastern bank, high and wooded, past three port hand red cans, and then north-west again off Sunny Corner where there are always a number of boats laid-up on the beach. At the final red can, steer for the end of the Lighterage Quay, where the river narrows to about 100m wide.

Coasters occasionally berth here, and at the northern end of the quay there is a flood prevention barrage with a flood gate that normally remains open except when higher than average tides are anticipated. The gate is 12m wide and normally poses no problems, but make allowance for the fact that the tidal flow increases through this restriction. There is a waiting pontoon just downstream if the gate is closed or if you arrive too early on the tide to make Town Quay.

Beyond it is a launching slipway on the eastern, Boscawen Park, shore. Here, the river widens into a broad shallow reach, the Cathedral and houses of Truro now clearly in sight but the channel, marked by red posts with square red topmarks to port and green posts with triangular green topmarks to starboard, winds back to starboard past the playing fields, then close to the eastern bank before it swings back towards the long quay on the western bank. Following the line of this shore it narrows, with a large Tesco superstore to port, and the deepest water closest to the old warehouses to starboard. Around the bend at Town Quay the river divides into three cul-de-sacs – berth in the port hand one, adjacent to the harbour office.

There is water here for about two hours either side of HW; if you wish to remain longer you will dry out in soft mud and it will cost £8 a night. Amenities include a toilet and shower on the quay, fresh water, electricity points, rubbish bins and a chemical toilet disposal facility. It is perhaps not the most scenic berth in the West Country, but a comfortable one, and the attractive Cathedral City of Truro, within five minutes' walk, more than makes up for this. This major shopping centre is able to provide all normal requirements, including Penrose's chandlery right on the quay, and another, Reg Langdon's, in New Bridge Street. You will find many good pubs and restaurants, as well as a main line railway station should you need to land or pick up crew.

Falmouth Port Guide

Area telephone code: 01326

Harbour Masters: Falmouth: Captain Mark Sansom, Harbour Office, 44 Arwenack Street, Falmouth TR11 3JQ (Tel: 312285 or 314379. Fax: 211352).E-mail: harbourmaster@falmouthport.co.uk Website:www.falmouthport.co.uk Truro/Penryn: Captain Andy Brigden, Harbour Office, Town Quay, Truro (Tel: 01872 224231 or 272130, Fax: 01872 225346). E-mail: harbouroffice@carrick.gov.uk Website:www.portoftruro.co.uk St Mawes, Captain Roy Maddern, The Quay, St Mawes (Tel: 270553)
VHF: Falmouth, VHF Ch 16, working 12. 0800 – 1700 daily, call sign *Falmouth Harbour Radio*. St Mawes, Ch 16; 12, call sign *St Mawes Harbour Radio*. Truro, Ch 16; 12, call sign *Carrick One*
Mail drop: Harbour Office will hold mail, also RCYC, Falmouth Marina and Mylor Yacht Harbour. Truro Harbour Office
Emergency services: Lifeboat and inshore lifeboat at Falmouth. Falmouth Coastguard
Anchorages: Off Custom House Quay, in harbour clear of moorings. Off St Mawes, St Just, off Restronguet, Loe Beach and in upper reaches of river. Charges apply throughout Falmouth harbour, St Mawes and upper Fal
Moorings/berthing: FHC Visitors' Yacht Haven, North Quay, Falmouth 100 boats, max 15m LOA, up to 2.5m draught, and 18 deep water visitors' moorings. RCYC 2 visitors' moorings off Club. Mylor Yacht Harbour Ltd, Mylor, Nr Falmouth (Tel: 372121). Malpas Marine, Malpas, Nr Truro (Tel: 01872 71260). Truro Harbour Authority, visitors' pontoons above Turnaware, off Ruan Creek and Malpas, visitors' buoys at Malpas, drying berths alongside at Truro Town Quay.
Marinas: Falmouth Marina, North Parade, Falmouth (Tel: 316620. Fax: 313939. E-mail: falmouth@premiermarinas.com Website: www.premiermarinas.com). 350 berths, up to 60 visitors. VHF Ch 80 /M, call sign *Falmouth Marina*. Port Pendennis Marina, (Tel: 211211. Fax: 311116.

E-mail:marina@portpendennis.com Website: www.portpendennis.com) 70 berths, 40 visitors, VHF Ch 80 /M, call sign *Port Pendennis*. Mylor Marina, Mylor Yacht Harbour (Tel: 372121. Fax: 372120. E-mail: enquiries@mylor.com Website: www.mylor.com). VHF Ch 80 /M, call sign *Mylor Yacht Harbour*
Charges: FHC: Yacht Haven, up to 8m £14.50, 8m up to10m £17, 10m up to 12m £19. Short stay, (all boats, up to 2 hours) £5. Swinging moorings from £7.40 to £18.10, depending on LOA; at anchor from £4 to £9.20 depending on LOA. Special rates for over a week. Port Pendennis Marina, £2 per metre per night.
RCYC moorings, price on application depending on LOA. Falmouth Marina £2 per metre per night.
St Mawes, from £10 to £18 for 24 hours on visitors mooring depending on LOA. At anchor £8 to £12 for 24 hours depending on LOA.
Mylor Yacht Harbour, alongside in marina £2 per metre per night (summer season), but £2.50 per metre per night during August. On mooring £1 per metre per night (summer season) but £1.50 per metre per night in August. Malpas Boats £8. Truro Harbour Authority pontoons/alongside £8, at anchor £2.50
Dinghy landings: Visitors' Yacht Haven, North Quay. Fish Strand Steps, inner end of Prince of Wales Pier, RCYC. Mylor yacht harbour pontoon. St Mawes, slipway and free steps
Water taxi: If using RCYC moorings, boatman and launch, 1015 – 1845 daily in season VHF Ch M call sign *Club Launch* (lunch 1300 – 1400). St Mawes to Place ferry operates water taxi service, call on VHF Ch 71. *Mylor water taxi* VHF Ch M , for Mylor Yacht Harbour customers. Aqua Cab fast water taxi (Tel: 07970 242258)
Phones: Nearest to Yacht Haven in Chain Locker pub or Grove Place. Port Pendennis. RCYC. Falmouth Marina. St Mawes harbour. By church at Mylor. Malpas

Doctor: (Tel: 434802)
Dentist: (Tel: 314702)
Hospital: Falmouth Minor injuries Unit (Tel:434739) Nearest casualty Treliske, Truro (Tel: 01872 250000)
Churches: All denominations. Local Weather Forecast: Visitors' Yacht Haven Supervisor's Office. Falmouth Yacht Marina office
Fuel: Fuel berth on Visitors' Yacht Haven, open all year, petrol and diesel, 0900 – 1800. *Falmouth Industry* fuel barge in harbour, diesel only Mon – Fri 0800 – 1630, Sat, 0800 – 1200. Falmouth Marina, diesel only, 24 hours. Mylor Yacht Harbour diesel alongside, petrol in cans during season 0830 – 1730, 1700 Sat
Paraffin: Cox's Home Hardware, The Moor, Falmouth
Gas: Calor/Gaz. The Bosun's Locker. Falmouth Marina. Mylor Chandlery, Mylor Yacht Harbour
Water: Visitors' Yacht Haven, Port Pendennis Marina, Falmouth Marina, Mylor Yacht Harbour, St Mawes, Malpas, Town Quay, Truro
Tourist Information Centre: The Moor, Falmouth (Tel: 312300). St Mawes Car Park. City Hall, Truro
Banks/cashpoints: All main banks in Falmouth and Truro, with cashpoints. Barclays and Lloyds TSB St Mawes, no cashpoints
Post Office: The Moor. Sub post office in newsagents close to Custom House Quay
Rubbish: Bins on North Quay. Bins at Falmouth Marina and Mylor Yacht Harbour, St Mawes harbour, Turnaware visitors' pontoon, Malpas, Town Quay, Truro
Showers/toilets: Yacht Haven Amenity building. Port Pendennis Marina. RCYC. Falmouth Marina. Mylor Yacht Harbour. Pandora Inn. St Mawes SC. Malpas Boats. Town Quay, Truro. Chemical toilet disposal facility at North Quay, Mylor, Truro Town Quay, Penryn Quay
Launderettes: Yacht Haven Amenity building. Port Pendennis Marina. Falmouth Marina. Mylor Yacht Harbour. Pandora Inn
Provisions: All requirements in Falmouth. Number of shops open on Sundays – Tesco centre of town,

Falmouth Port Guide continued

Area telephone code: 01326

Spar at Albany Road, 10 minutes walk from harbour, and Co-op Pioneer supermarket, 5 minutes walk from Falmouth Marina. Most provisions also at St Mawes, good selection of basics at Mylor Yacht Harbour Cafe, seven days a week in season. All shops, Truro

Chandlers: Bosun's Locker, Upton Slip, Falmouth (Tel: 312212). Fal Chandlers (Tel: 212411), Skywave Marine (318314) both at Falmouth Yacht Marina. Challenger Marine, Falmouth Road, Penryn (Tel:377222). The Boathouse, Commercial Road, Penryn (Tel: 374177). Monsons, (bonded stores) West End Ind Estate, Penryn (Tel: 373581). Mylor Chandlery and Rigging, Mylor Yacht Harbour (Tel: 375482) seven days in season. Reg Langdon, New Bridge Street Truro (Tel: 01872 272668). Penrose Outdoors, Town Quay, Truro (Tel: 01872 270213)

Admiralty Chart Agents/compass adjusters: Marine Instruments at Bosun's Locker, Falmouth (Tel: 312414)

Liferaft service/repair: Inflatable Boat Services, North Parade (Tel: 313800)

Repairs/hauling: Falmouth Boat Construction Ltd, Little Falmouth Yacht Yard, Flushing, Nr Falmouth (Tel: 374309) 100 ton slipway/25 ton hoist. Port Pendennis (Tel: 211211) 40 ton hoist. Pendennis Shipyard, Falmouth Docks, 80 ton hoist (Tel: 211344). Falmouth Marina Services, 30 ton hoist (Tel: 316620). Falmouth Yacht Brokers, Freemans Wharf, Penryn, 50 ton slip (Tel: 370060). Jubilee Wharf Boatyard, Penryn (Tel: 378742). Islington Boat Yard, Penryn, (Tel: 378700). Mylor Yacht Harbour (Tel: 372121) 35 ton hoist. Heard's Boatyard, Tregatreath, Nr Mylor, Falmouth (Tel: 374441). Freshwater Boatyard, St Mawes (Tel: 270443). Percuil Boatyard (Tel: 01872 580564). Pascoe's Boatyard, St Just in Roseland (Tel: 270269).

Malpas Marine, Malpas (Tel: 01872 71260) **Marine engineers**: Marine-Trak (Tel: 314610, or Mylor Yacht Harbour Tel: 376588). Challenger Marine, Penryn (Tel: 376202). Falmouth Boat Construction (Tel: 374309 – 24 hour emergency call out 0468 178746). Mylor Yacht Harbour (Tel: 372121). Robin Curnow, outboards/Seagull agents, Penryn (Tel: 373438). S.Caddy, Penryn (Tel: 372682). S.Francis, (Tel: 377122) St Mawes – David Llewellen (Tel: 07973 523320) or Andrew Cox (Tel: 07974 250533)

Electronic engineers: Skywave Marine Electronics (Tel: 318314), Global Marine electronics (Tel: 316740), both at Falmouth Marina. Simrad Marine Electronics (Tel: 374411) at Mylor Yacht harbour

Sailmakers/repairs: Penrose, Upton Slip, Falmouth (Tel: 312705). SKB Sails, The Sail Loft, Commercial Road, Penryn (Tel: 372107).

Riggers: www.riggers-uk.com, the Boathouse, Commercial Road, Penryn (Tel: 374177). Challenger Marine (Tel; 377222). Falmouth Boat Construction, Flushing (Tel: 374309). Mylor Chandlery and Rigging (Tel: 375482).

Divers: Sea-Wide Services, (Tel: 375095). Falmouth Divers, (Tel: 374736)

Transport: Branch line to main line rail connections to London and North at Truro. (Tel: 08457 484950). Daily bus and coach connections with rest of country, Western National (Tel: 01209 719988). Road connections to M5 via Plymouth. Newquay Airport, 45 mins (Tel: 01345 222111)

Car hire: Europcar at Falmouth Marina (Tel:315204). Eurodrive (Tel: 377456). Falmouth Garages (Tel:377246)

Car parking: Several large car parks in Falmouth. Mylor Yacht Harbour. St Mawes Quay and harbour car park

Yacht Clubs: Royal Cornwall Yacht Club, Greenbank,

Falmouth (Office Tel: 312126, Bar, 311105. E-mail: admin@royalcornwallyachtclub.org Website: www.royalcornwallyachtclub.org). Falmouth Watersports Association, Grove Place (Tel: 211223). Flushing Sailing Club, New Quay, Flushing, Nr Falmouth (Tel: 374043). Mylor Yacht Club, Mylor Yacht Harbour, Nr Falmouth (Tel: 374391). Restronguet Sailing Club, Mylor Yacht Harbour, Nr Falmouth (Tel: 374536). St Mawes Sailing Club, The Quay, St Mawes (Tel: 270686)

Eating out: No shortage of options! Seafood to curries, tapas to pasties and the rest in between

Things to do: National Maritime Museum Cornwall. Pendennis and St Mawes Castles. Good safe beaches/walks. Ships & Castles leisure pool, Pendennis Head

Special events: Falmouth Regatta Week/Falmouth Classics, second week in August. Gig and Working Boat racing throughout summer.

The famous Victory, *a classic example of a Falmouth Working boat in full racing rig*

Chapter 3

HELFORD RIVER

A peaceful evening. The moorings in Helford Pool looking to seaward with Bosahan Point on right

Tides	HW Dover +0600
Range	MHWS 5.3m–MHWN 4.2m, MLWN 1.9m–MLWS 0.6m. Streams attain up to two knots in river at springs
Charts	BA:147, SC 5603.6. Stanford: 13. Imray: Y57
Waypoint	Voose N Cardinal buoy 50°05'.81N / 05°06'.96W
Hazards	Gedges/August Rock, Car Croc Rock, Voose Rock (all unlit). Bar/shallows within river on north shore. Rough approach in strong east wind/ebb tide. Beware pot and net buoys. Large areas of upper reaches dry
Overnight charges	Mooring Authority mooring £12

'When the east wind blows up Helford river the shining waters become troubled and disturbed, and the little waves beat angrily on the sandy shores. The short seas break above the bar at ebbtide, and the waders fly inland to the mudflats, their wings skimming the surface, and calling to one another as they go.

Only the gulls remain, wheeling and crying above the foam, diving in search of food, their grey feathers glistening with the salt spray. The long rollers of the Channel, travelling from beyond Lizard Point, follow hard upon the steep seas at the river mouth and mingling with surge and wash of deep sea water comes the brown tide, swollen with the last rains and brackish from the mud, bearing on its face dead twigs and straws, and strange forgotten things, leaves too early fallen, young birds and the buds of flowers.

The open roadstead is deserted, for an east wind makes an uneasy anchorage, and but for the few houses scattered here and there above Helford Passage, and the group of bungalows about Port Navas, the river would be the same as it was in a century now forgotten, in a time that has left few memories . . .;

So begins *Frenchman's Creek*, Daphne du Maurier's bestseller that made the name of the Helford familiar to all – the haunt of the heroine Dona and hideaway for the Frenchman and his ship, *La Mouette*.

Although the numbers of yachts have certainly increased in the roadstead, her words are very true, and large areas in this gem of a river still remain untouched. Overshadowed by the busy harbour at Falmouth, commercially there was never any reason for the Helford to develop – it merely served the needs of the surrounding farms and communities, with a few small granite quays dotted along its banks. Apart from the scattered fishing hamlets, it remained '. . . unvisited, the woods and hills untrodden, and all the drowsy beauty of midsummer that gives Helford river a strange enchantment, was never seen and never known.'

The few people that did pass along this unpopulated, silent waterway into the depths of rural Cornwall, bounded by high shores and deep mysterious woods, were mostly heading for

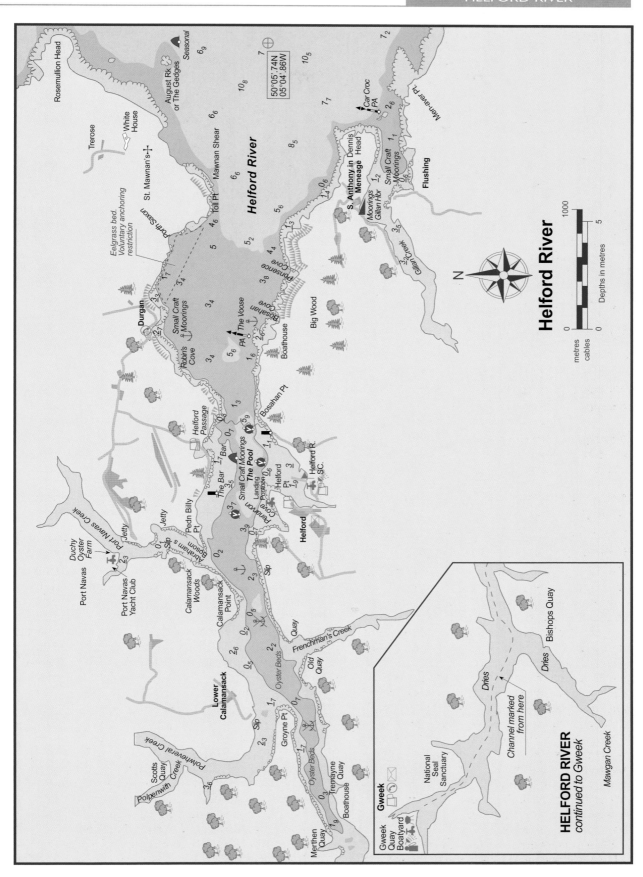

Chapter 3

Rosemullion Head

August Rk or The Gedges

Seasonal

6₉

Trerose

White House

St. Mawnan's

50°05'·74N
05°04'·86W

7

Helford River

Eelgrass bed. Voluntary anchoring restriction

Porth Saxon

Toll Pt

Mawnan Shear

6₆

6₆

6₆

5₆

5₂

4₆

5

3₄

1₇

3₄

10₈

10₅

7₂

Car Croc PA
2₆

7₇

8₅

Men-aver Pt.

S. Anthony in Meneage
Moorings Gillan Hbr

Dennis Head

Small Craft Moorings

1₁

Flushing

1·4

0·6

1₃

4·4

3·8

Ponsence Cove

Bosahan Cove

Gillan Creek

3₅

Durgan

3₇

Small Craft Moorings

Robin's Cove

3₄

5₆

PA
The Voose

1·6

2₆

Boathouse

Big Wood

N

Helford River

1000

5

Depths in metres

metres
cables

0

0

Bosahan Pt

1₃

Helford Passage

0·8

0·9

The Bar

1·7

3₅

The Pool

Small Craft Moorings

0·1

Landing Pontoon

0·6

1·9

Helford Pt

3

Helford R. SC.

Jetty

Port Navas Creek

Duchy Oyster Farm

2·3

Jetty

Slip

Pedn Billy Pt

Bosahan's

Penarvon Cove

Helford

3₁

3·9

Port Navas

Port Navas Yacht Club

Calamansack Woods

Calamansack Point

0·2

0·5

Slip

2·3

Quay

Frenchman's Creek

Old Quay

2₂

Lower Calamansack

0·2

0·5

2₆

2·5

Polwheveral Creek

Scotts Quay

Slip

2·3

Groyne Pt

1₇

0·1

1·7

Oyster Beds

Merthen Quay

1·9

3₆

Tremayne Quay

Boathouse

0·3

Polpenwith Creek

Gweek

Gweek Quay Boatyard

HELFORD RIVER
continued to Gweek

National Seal Sanctuary

Dries

Channel marked from here

Dries

Bishops Quay

Mawgan Creek

Gweek, right at the head of navigation. As the nearest access to the inland town of Helston, this was the focal point of waterborne activity, with sailing coasters and barges slowly working their way up on the tide, bringing cargoes of coal, timber and lime and taking away granite, tin and farm produce. However, the advent of rail and motor transport and gradual silting resulted in its decline at the turn of the century, when the river slipped back into obscurity.

The other reason for the remarkable natural preservation of the inner reaches is the Duchy of Cornwall oyster fisheries. Reputedly dating back to Roman times, these extensive beds have always inhibited the spread of moorings and other commercial development. This and very limited facilities mean that today the Helford River, except in high season, can still have an almost deserted quality, a solitude that is increasingly rare and, fortunately, cherished by those who come here to seek it.

APPROACHES

At just under four miles from Pendennis Point, the Helford is a regular jaunt across the bay for many Falmouth boats, perhaps pausing to anchor off a beach or for a quick run ashore to the pub, but as the afternoon draws in, most return home. Although the entrance is well hidden away to the south-west, other boats entering and leaving will give a good indication of its position. As you close Rosemullion Head, the green conical buoy, August Rock (seasonal), to seaward of the Gedges rocks (drying 1.4m), should be left on

The entrance to the unspoiled Helford River presents no undue problems. Toll Point is on the right, with Durgan and Helford Passage beyond. The cluster of moorings lie in the Pool with Helford Village on left

your starboard hand before bearing round into the river mouth as it opens ahead, running due west.

There are no further hazards except very close to the shore, and depths average between 3m and 4m in the entrance. There can be a noticeable funnelling effect within the mouth when beating in, but the shelter inside is excellent in anything, except of course, easterly winds, when this is a place to avoid. Not only does Falmouth Bay and the approaches kick up a very short steep sea, but also the swell within the moorings and anchorage, particularly with wind against tide, makes for a lot of discomfort. Unless you can tuck yourself away in one of the creeks, you are much better off in the Fal.

On the southern shore, in the approach to the Helford, the hidden entrance to Gillan Creek is easily located by the distinctive hump of Dennis Head across its mouth. This can be a delightful spot in the right conditions, but is really only of interest to shallow draught boats, as it dries for the most part and the only deep water within its mouth is almost totally taken up with moorings. Car Croc, a particularly nasty rock (dries 1m), sits almost in the middle of the entrance, marked by an east cardinal buoy, BYB, but be warned, it extends further to the south-east than might be imagined so give it a good berth, passing midway between it and the south shore when entering. Also beware of the rocks extending to seawards from Men-aver Point.

Ideally, for a first visit, arrive just after LW when all the hazards are easy to see, and feel your way in on the tide, anchoring clear of the local moorings off the houses at Flushing if you can, or go further into the creek to the picturesque hamlet and church at St Anthony, where you will dry out, well tucked away in this hidden corner. Here, on the shingly foreshore is the small yard of Sailaway St Anthony

(Tel: 01326 231357) – it might be able to provide a mooring. The densely-wooded creek beyond the sandy spit is particularly attractive when the tide is in, perfect for a dinghy trip or just a walk along the road that follows it inland.

Back in the main river, with wind between north and west, there are some good sheltered anchorages just within the entrance, tucked up in the bight along the northern side between Toll Point and the small boathouse at Porth Saxon, as well as off shingly Grebe beach further to the west. However, under the new Falmouth Bay & Estuaries conservation initiatives, as off St Mawes, a further voluntary restriction on anchoring in this area is now in operation to protect another eelgrass bed. This one extends outwards from the low water mark for approximately 200 metres.

No doubt the seahorses and other small creatures that inhabit the eelgrass are delighted, but I have to confess to being saddened to see yet another anchorage now effectively denied to yachtsmen. As it's the anchors and cable that do the damage, perhaps some visitors buoys could provide a compromise?

You will therefore either have to anchor much further out than previously, or further west, off the hamlet of Durgan, clear of the local moorings towards Polgwidden Cove.

Durgan is a picturesque cluster of old fishermen's cottages, partly owned by the National Trust, as is the valley running down to the village in which the 25 exotic acres of Glendurgan Gardens are situated. Renowned for its trees and shrubs, it was created from 1820 onwards by the well-known Fox family, Quakers who still live here. Donated by them to the National Trust in 1962 the gardens are open to the public from March – October 1030 –1630. There are no facilities at Durgan except a phone.

From here, Grebe or Porth Saxon, you can follow the attractive coastal footpath back up over the headland to Mawnan Church, which is set among the trees on the cliff-top overlooking the entrance to the river. This is a particularly lovely spot, and it is not difficult to see why. Among the gravestones you can find those of two eminent yachtsmen, Claud Worth, the grandfather of modern cruising, and his son Tom, who circumnavigated the world in 1953 aboard the Giles-designed cutter, *Beyond*. His epitaph is particularly succinct – 'Tom Worth, Who Sailed *Beyond*'.

The southern side of the entrance is less hospitable, fringed with rocks and a couple of small coves. Locals claim that the large house here was the Manderley of Daphne du Maurier's *Rebecca*, rather than Menabilly on Gribbin Head. Certainly, Ponsence Cove and the tiny boathouse

August Rock buoy (now unlit), with the Gedges uncovered on a big spring tide

seem to fit the bill. One thing is certain, there is no doubt where the inspiration for *Frenchman's Creek* came from – just over a mile upstream you can explore it for yourself.

Continuing west from Ponsence, the Voose is a drying rocky ledge that has snared a surprising number of boats, in spite of its north cardinal BY buoy. As an alternative to Durgan, it is possible to anchor just east of the Voose Rocks, off Bosahan Cove. As you approach the narrows, if the tide is low, keep just over a cable off the steep wooded shore leading up to Bosahan Point, taking care to avoid the line of fishermen's store pots. Continue towards the large concentration of moorings ahead, but beware the northern, starboard side – here, shallows extend up to a cable from the shore with not much more than 0.5m in places. Head on past the small boat moorings, the beach, the modern houses and the pub at Helford Passage, as far as the green conical Bar buoy (seasonal). This can be difficult to spot amongst the surrounding boats and inshore it dries extensively into a sand and mud bank at LWS; popular with locals for digging cockles. It stretches as far as the entrance to Port Navas Creek.

Being easy to reach by road from Falmouth, Helford Passage is the most commercialised part of the Helford River, centred around the Ferry Boat Inn, which has a restaurant as well as bar food and often live music. There is also a telephone, a passenger ferry across to Helford Point and another pleasant coastal footpath leading to Durgan via Polgwidden Cove. Garden lovers can follow the road up the hill for just over half a mile to find the entrance to the sub-tropical Trebah Gardens, which are open daily from 1000 to 1700.

MOORINGS, ANCHORAGE, AND LANDING

The bulk of the Helford moorings are located in the Pool, which is nearly 15m deep in places, averages about 6m and extends up the centre of the river. To port is the entrance to Helford Creek (note that at LWS this dries extensively), on a line from Bosahan Point to Helford Point, where there is a ferry slipway and landing pontoon.

In November 1884 the *West Briton* newspaper revealed that '. . . the beautiful Helford River has been visited this summer by an unusual number of yachts – as many as five having been at anchor there at any one time.;

Plus ça change! Today nearly all the available space in the Pool is taken up with moorings and anchoring should not be attempted. However, there are plenty of visitors' moorings available – dark green support buoys (or any support buoy), all with dark green pick-up buoys, some of which are marked *Visitor*. Either grab one or contact the Moorings Officer, Simon Walker or his staff, who might be listening on VHF Channel M in the ferry kiosk on the north shore of the beach in front of the Ferry Boat Inn at Helford Passage, call sign *Moorings Officer*. More often than not he will be out on the water in an 18ft open white launch or on board the red ferry, and is ever ready to assist (Tel: 01326 250770).

Remarkably there is still no charge for anchoring, and the overnight rate for a mooring remains a reasonable £10 for boats up to 10m (32ft 5ins), £12 up to 11m (36ft), £14 up to 12m (39ft) and £17 for boats 12m and over. Vessels over 20m (65ft) should, however, seek advice and assistance from Simon or the duty officer. If you are tempted to stay for a while, the seventh consecutive night is free!

You may drop people ashore at the ferry slipway, but do not leave dinghies here – use the pontoon just upstream. This is private, but the owner does not mind it being used as long as you leave a small donation towards its upkeep in the honesty box provided. The alternative, an hour or so after LW, is the landing pontoon off the Helford River Sailing Club, the impressive Scandinavian style wooden building among the trees on the eastern side of Helford Creek.

The ferry and Mooring Officer run a water taxi service; call VHF Ch M or phone Tel: 01326 250770. This service is available to and from anywhere in the river and the cost is based on the distance travelled – although the norm is £1.20 per person each way, with a maximum charge of £8 per boat. Both ferries are licensed for up to 12 persons and, subject to weather, they operate from 0900 to 1700 April, June, September and October, and to 2100 during July and August.

Continuing on the subject of voluntary donations, all the navigational buoys in the Helford, including the August Rock buoy, are privately maintained and, although marked on the charts, there is no legal requirement for them to be in place, so beware in case they have been removed. The Helford River Navigational Aids Committee is a very worthy cause run by local yachtsmen, raising the funds to cover the cost of servicing these vital aids which amounts to several thousand pounds a year. All river users are invited to contribute towards the cost of their upkeep and Simon and his staff will be only too happy to accept your donation!

There are three recommended places for anchoring, all of which will require an anchor light and a dinghy with outboard. As already mentioned, you can let go west of Durgan, off Polgwidden Cove, or east of the Voose Rocks off Bosahan Coves, and larger vessels should anchor anywhere between these two areas. Anchoring is not permitted west of the Voose on the south shore because of the fishermen's store pots, or in the narrows east of the Pool because of the exposed underwater power cable. The third alternative is upriver, clear of the last moorings, but no further west than the three oyster buoys marking the beginning of the oyster beds. This will provide refuge in easterly winds, although it can still be uncomfortable with wind against tide.

Particular care must be taken not to anchor in the new fairway channel. This runs from just west of Bosahan Point, flanked on the south side by the fishing fleet moorings and on the north side by a line of visitors moorings, then through the Pool with visitors moorings on both sides, on towards the south bank as far as the oyster buoys and finally close under Penarvon Woods. This channel is frequently used at night by local

In settled weather there are several pleasant anchorages within the mouth of the Helford, but you should try to avoid the clearly marked eelgrass beds inshore

fishing boats and also by Seacore Limited, the core sampling and drilling specialist, which often moves its rigs on high tides at night.

FACILITIES

The small village of **Helford** is not really evident from the river – one sees just a few houses along the shore which disappears into the narrow creek. Normally it is best to pay the fee and land at the Helford Point pontoon to avoid the worry of the dinghy drying out. A short walk along the point brings you to the Shipwright's Arms, a classic thatched waterside pub which holds a strange attraction for thirsty crews! It has a small restaurant, an outside terrace and a reputation for its summer barbecue menu.

Winding on above the creekside quays and boathouses, the narrow lane squeezes past thick-walled stone cottages, whitewashed and covered in climbing roses; their tiny gardens, where you can sit and enjoy a cream tea, overflowing with flowers. Helford Post Office & Stores is the only shop on the lower part of the river – beyond it you will find a public telephone.

At the head of the creek, a bridge and shallow ford lead to another row of equally picturesque cottages that make up the rest of Helford village, and fortunately for its residents, cars are banished to a car park on the outskirts during the summer. To reach it, continue up the hill out of the village. A track leads down from the car park to the Helford River Sailing Club (Tel: 01326 231460), which is open daily during July and August and every day except Mondays throughout the rest of the year. Facilities include a good bar serving food, showers and a launderette. When the bar is open, the club monitors VHF channels M and 80.

PORT NAVAS

Continuing upstream, just before you reach Pedn Billy Point and the entrance to Port Navas Creek, the large house with a small quay close to the water's edge is *Bar*. Built by Claud Worth in 1928 for his retirement from medical practice as an eminent eye surgeon, he lived here until his death in 1936.

Port Navas is another attractive wooded creek, although the eastern bank did not escape development and has a number of large expensive houses overlooking it. Just within the entrance, tucked away behind the point, the small quiet pool at Abraham's Bosom is now full of moorings and there is no longer space to anchor. Most of the creek beyond the pool is shallow with extensive oyster beds that are clearly marked by buoys, and a number of moorings all of which dry at LWS. However, after half flood, it is possible to get up to Port Navas Yacht Club (Tel: 01326 340065), which lies in a smaller creek on the port hand side. Keep in the centre and berth alongside the quay, which is equipped with a water tap. This friendly yacht club welcomes visitors and boasts showers as well as a bar serving meals during normal licensing hours – it is advisable to pre-book. One can, by arrangement, dry out alongside for a night for a small charge.

Port Navas is a peaceful little backwater, overhung with dense woods, with just a few stone cottages overlooking the narrow creek. The nearest provisions are at Constantine, a good half hour's walk away. It is also the home of the Duchy Oyster Farm, where nearly a million oysters are processed every year. You will find their buildings beside the main creek by following the road back towards its mouth from the Yacht Club.

Should a sudden extravagance overcome you, it is possible to buy some of these oysters, while reflecting, as they slither down as rapidly as your bank balance, that these were once the staple diet of the poor. Mussels, too, are produced by the farm, and *moules marinieres à la Port Navas* are probably a good bet for tonight!

THE UPPER REACHES

By far the most unspoilt area of the river lies beyond the great rounded woods at Calamansack, a clear stretch of water where there are no moorings because of the extensive mussel buoys and oyster beds along both sides of the river. These are clearly marked by buoys and stakes, and anchoring is prohibited throughout the upper reaches. The deeper water lies along the south

Helford Pool. Helford Passage is on bottom right, with the landing at Helford Point opposite, centre, and Helford Village beyond. The Helford River Sailing Club and landing pontoon is on the left

shore, which is also heavily wooded with low, steep cliffs, but just before Frenchman's Creek depths reduce considerably to little more than 1m at LWS, and half a mile further on, the river dries extensively. Yet again, this and the other creeks are ideal for the dinghy, although on a reasonable flood moderate draught boats can make it all the way to Gweek, which is accessible a couple of hours either side of HW for up to a 2.9m (9ft 6ins) draught at springs. It is possible to dry out alongside at Gweek Quay Boatyard should you wish to stay overnight. To calculate the depth alongside the quay wall at Gweek, deduct 3m (10ft) from the predicted height of HW at Helford.

It is impossible not be drawn into the romance of Frenchman's Creek, where '. . . the trees still crowd thick and darkly to the water's edge, and the moss is succulent and green upon the little quay where Dona built her fire and looked across the flames at her lover.'

The reality is very much as it is described in the book, with glistening mud at low tide, where herons and oyster catchers roam. As the thin trickle of the flood creeps inland again, like the yachtsman in the book, 'the sound of the blades upon the water seeming overloud' you, too, can follow its winding course in your dinghy, past blackened tree stumps emerging like creatures from the mud, to where the dense trees close in like a tunnel, brushing the incoming tide, and the silence becomes profound. The atmosphere of Frenchman's Creek is undeniable.

At Groyne Point, just a short distance upstream, Polwheveral Creek branches off to starboard and, although just as attractive, somehow it has none of the mystery. If you are seeking some real solitude, shoal draught boats can find plenty of space to dry out round the bend beyond the moorings.

Following the flood up to Gweek, the river passes between high wooded banks with mud-fringed rocky shores most of the way. The deeper water lies in midstream. It is possible to land at Tremayne Quay, which is owned by the National Trust, from where you can follow a lovely woodland walk. Just downstream of Mawgan Creek, the orange mooring buoy in the centre of the channel belongs to a local fishing boat, beyond which point the river dries completely at LW. Bishop's Quay on the south shore is private, and opposite the entrance to the creek, a large bank fills the centre of the river, the channel swinging to port around it.

Fortunately from here on it is dredged and marked with port and starboard hand buoys as it meanders from one side of the river to the other, until you reach the very narrow bottleneck with steep woods on either side just below Gweek. Once through the gap, the head of the river widens, the old coal quay lies to port, with more private quays to starboard. Once almost in the saltings, Gweek Quay Boatyard (Tel: 01326 221657) is straight ahead. It is usually possible to lie alongside and dry out overnight for a small charge.

This old quay will always be a nostalgic place for me, for here, back in 1973, I found my own boat, Temptress, laid up and neglected, and spent many long happy weekends putting her to rights and dreaming of where we would eventually sail. The atmosphere of Gweek has changed little – it is still a relaxed and peaceful place, although the yard has grown considerably, with storage ashore for over 300 boats. Visitors are welcome and services include good toilets and showers, 240 volt power at the quayside, diesel and water. Among the yard facilities are a 25 ton slipway hoist, a 40 ton crane, a chandlery, an engineer and wood and GRP repairs.

In the small village close by is a well-stocked grocery store (open Sundays), a post office and a garage, where petrol is available in cans. The Gweek Inn serves pub meals, while there are also a couple of café/restaurants and occasional buses to Falmouth and Helston. The most unlikely thing that Gweek can provide, and one that children particularly adore, is the Seal Sanctuary, where injured and sick seals are looked after before being returned to the sea. It is on the north side of the creek, just downstream from the village, and opens daily during the summer.

PASSAGES
THE MANACLES TO LAND'S END

Favourable tidal streams
Lizard Point:
  Bound West: Two hours before HW Dover
  Bound East: Four hours after HW Dover

Passage charts for this sea area:
BA: 2565 Trevose Head to Dodman Point.
         777 Land's End to Falmouth.
         154 Approaches to Falmouth.
         1148 Isles of Scilly to Land's End.
         2345 Plans in South-West Cornwall –
         this is particularly useful as it has
         a large scale section covering
         the Lizard
         SC5603 covers the area in considerable
         detail

Imray: C6 Start Point to Lizard.
         C7 Lizard Point to Trevose Head,
         including Isles of Scilly
         WCP2400.9, 2400.10

Stanford: 13 Start Point to Land's End and
         Padstow

French: 2218 Du Cap Lizard à Trevose Head.
         4812 Du Cap Lizard à Start Point

Safety information and weather
In all cases initial broadcast on VHF Channel 16
then switch to:

Falmouth Coastguard: VHF Channel 23 (east of
Lizard and Isles of Scilly), Channel 86 (Lizard to
Trevose) at 0140, 0540, 0940, 1340, 1740, 2340 UT

Bass Point NCI station (Tel: 01326 290212)

Penzance NCI station (Tel: 01736 367063)

Gwennap Head NCI station (Tel:01736 871351)

Waypoints
1   **Manacles** (0.5M due E of buoy)
     50°02'·82N / 05°01'·14W

2   **Black Head** (1.5M SE of headland)
     49°59'·19N / 05°04'·45W

3   **Lizard** (3M due S of light)
     49°54'·62N / 05°12'·14W

4   **Mountamopus** (0.5M SW of buoy)
     50°04'·32N / 05°26'·85W

5   **Low Lee** (0.25M due E of buoy)
     50°05'·56N / 05°30'·99W

6   **Runnelstone** (0.5M SW of buoy)
     50°00'·89N / 05°40'·94W

7   **Longships** (0.75M due W of lighthouse)
     50°04'·04N / 05°45'·95W

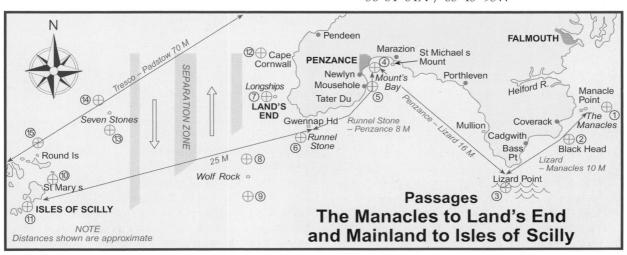

**Passages
The Manacles to Land's End
and Mainland to Isles of Scilly**

NOTE
Distances shown are approximate

The Lizard is the most southerly point of the British Isles, a major headland and tidal gate. This point and the coast to the west of it into Mount's Bay and around Land's End has a justifiably notorious reputation and should always be treated with due respect and caution.

Composed for the greater part of precipitous granite cliffs – a firm favourite with the rock-climbing fraternity – this inhospitable and rugged coast is open to the prevailing winds. It is an area of strong tides, and invariably suffers from the long Atlantic ground swell, not to mention concentrated shipping and no absolute harbours of refuge. But don't despair – in reasonably settled weather with an experienced crew in a well-found boat it can be explored safely, but here, more so than ever, a wary eye should be kept on the weather, with options for shelter always kept in mind.

Jack Pender, an old Mousehole fisherman, told me many years ago as I languished there in early September that 'west of the Lizard's no place for a small boat, come the end of August'. I confess to a certain youthful panic and I sailed that very night, scurrying back to Falmouth.

His words were born of a lifetime navigating these difficult waters and I, when working as a commercial fisherman for several years, often recalled them as we turned to run for home before the grey sea and sky piling to the west, white crests blowing before it, and the high, dim shore to leeward suddenly vanishing in the gathering gloom. Conditions can deteriorate in a matter of hours, and a contrary tide sometimes produces large, steep and tumbling seas. It is not difficult to see how this particular coast has claimed so many ships and men over the years.

TIDES

Bound west, take full advantage of the ebb tide out of Falmouth Bay, which starts to run to the south three hours before HW Dover (three hours after HW Falmouth) and, once past the east cardinal BYB Manacle buoy, a course of 220°T will pass all offshore dangers in the approaches to the Lizard. To clear the race, this course should be held until a position three miles to the south of the headland is reached. Adequate allowance should also be made for the tidal stream setting to the west, which begins about one hour before HW Dover. If bound round Land's End, because of the division of the streams into the Irish Sea and English Channel, a favourable tide can now be carried for nearly eight hours.

Bound east, unfortunately, the passage is not so obliging; a vessel carrying a fair tide down the North Cornish coast and round Land's End will invariably run into a foul tide off the Lizard – from the turn of the tide at the Longships (five hours before HW Dover) only three hours of favourable tide can be carried across Mount's Bay. Once round the Lizard the ebb, starting from Falmouth Bay, will be gathering in strength against you. Bound east from Mount's Bay to Falmouth, it is therefore, advisable to arrive at the Lizard at slack water just over three and a half hours after HW Dover. Hopefully you will be sailing this spectacular section of coast in daylight and good visibility when it can be appreciated to the full. In favourable weather and settled conditions, the coastline can for the most part be followed much closer inshore.

LOWLAND POINT TO THE LIZARD

From Lowland Point, the land rises to a distinctively flat topped profile, steep-to and rocky with cliffs between 30 and 50 metres in height, and few off-lying dangers. It is interspersed with many attractive coves and bays, so if time permits, or if waiting for the tide, some of the smaller havens of the Lizard peninsula can provide good temporary anchorages and an interesting diversion.

Coverack, the first of these, is easily located by the conspicuous large hotel just south of the clustered houses of the village. Black Head, a mile to the south, is the next prominent feature and can easily be mistaken as Bass Point on the Lizard when approaching from the east in poor visibility. Tidal streams run up to three knots at springs, and in strong southerly winds steep breaking seas will be encountered when wind is against tide in the vicinity. If running for Falmouth in such conditions, lay a course several miles to seaward of both Black Head and the

Manacle buoy. Black Head in distance

Manacle buoy, where similar poor conditions can also be encountered.

Beyond Black Head, the coast falls back to form a wide bay, well sheltered from the west and a one time favourite haunt of the Falmouth Pilot vessels and quay punts waiting for business, and also of a Falmouth tailor's cutter, standing by to put a man aboard homeward-bound ships so that the crews could walk ashore in brand new suits. In the centre of this bay, Cadgwith nestles in a rocky cove, the houses wedged tightly at the mouth of a narrow valley. Parn Voose Cove and Church Cove, with a small landing slip, lie about a mile to the south. The present Lizard/Cadgwith lifeboat station is spectacularly sited close by in a narrow crevice in the high cliffs at Kilcobben Cove.

Special care is needed sailing inshore along this section of the coast and the large scale Admiralty Chart No 2345 or SC5603.2 is a must.

The Craggan Rocks, with less than 2m over them, lie just over half a mile SSE of Cadgwith, and the Voge Rock, covered by only 1.6m, lies two cables east of Church Cove. The yellow buoy further offshore marks the end of a sewer outfall. Bass Point is steep and topped by an NCI lookout (Tel: 01326 290212) with the distinctive white building of the former Lloyds signal station close by – the Spernan Shoals lie almost a mile to the east.

The notorious Vrogue Rock, only covered by 1.8m, lies four cables ESE of Bass Point, its position indicated by transit beacons ashore, and the passage between this rock and the shore should only be used in settled conditions. Normally, approaching from Black Head without any diversions inshore, your course should be laid well to seaward of Bass Point. With rocks extending over half a mile to the south of the Lizard, and overfalls that are severe with wind against tide, it is advisable to give the whole area a good berth in anything but settled conditions, standing off between two and three miles. In rough weather, five miles is not unrealistic for the seas inshore can be very confused.

Tidal streams are strong – the west-going ebb can run at over three knots at springs, the flood slightly less, and it goes without saying that a fair tide is essential for a sailing vessel with limited power. In westerly winds its full force will not be felt until clear of the Lizard, and after spells of weather from that quarter, a considerable ground swell will be encountered.

This is a headland to approach with extreme caution in poor weather or bad visibility; the vast list of vessels lost in the vicinity over the years are

The Lizard from the south. Bass Point, centre, Black Head, right

an adequate testimony to its natural dangers. Care should also be taken to note shipping movements as they concentrate towards Land's End, as well as the activities of fishing boats, and, yet again, beware of poorly marked pot and net buoys, often without flags and half-submerged in the tide. One unusual hazard that certainly added a few grey hairs on one occasion was the sudden appearance of a totally unmarked rock nearly three miles south of the point, black, awash with breaking waves, and right ahead. The chart indicated no such horror; and several minutes of dry-mouthed panic elapsed before it dawned on me that it was an enormous basking shark, a harmless plankton-eating summer visitor to Cornish waters!

The Lizard lighthouse is a prominent and distinctive long white building with two octagonal towers, the easternmost topped by its its five million candlepower light (Fl 3s 26M). The first warning light on the headland, notable as the first such navigational aid in Cornwall, was established in 1619 by Sir John Killigrew amidst much local protest at the adverse effects on the profits from the wrecking; significantly Killigrew himself eventually abandoned his light in favour of the more lucrative spoils from the sea!

Several other attempts to provide a lighthouse on the headland ensued during the 1700s, notably Fonnereau's twin towers with a fire in each and a cottage in between, in which an overlooker lay on a couch watching for any relaxation of the firemen's efforts; a blast on a cowhorn 'awakening them, and recalling them to their duty!' The introduction of oil lighting in 1813 put an end to such navigational uncertainty and by the end of the century both an electric light and a foghorn had been established, with a correspondingly dramatic decline in the loss of shipping.

The Boa, a rocky shoal two miles west of Lizard point, is the last offshore hazard in the vicinity and, although well covered (over 20m), it creates a lot of overfalls and even breaking seas in south-westerly gales. If the Lizard has been given a berth of three miles, as recommended, heading into Mount's Bay you should pass clear to the south of the Boa. Its location is usually easy to spot from the concentration of pot and net buoys.

LIZARD POINT TO MOUNTS BAY

The western side of the Lizard, exposed to the full force of the Atlantic gales is high, rugged and spectacular for the next five miles as the coast bears north-west into Mount's Bay. The tall jagged pyramid of Gull Rock and Asparagus Island, enclosing the beauty spot of Kynance Cove are a distinctive feature, and both Rill Point and Predannack Head should be given a reasonable berth. Mullion Island will begin to open as Predannack Head is passed, and in favourable easterly conditions, an anchorage can be found off the small harbour of Porth Mellin (Mullion). Although a passage exists between the island and the mainland, it is not recommended, and the approach is best made to the north of the island.

The character of the coast begins to change considerably as Mount's Bay is entered further. Beyond Pedngwinian Point, the high cliffs recede, and the long sand and shingle beach of Gunwalloe and Loe Bar stretches away northwards. Particularly vulnerable to southerly gales, many vessels struggling to escape round the Lizard from Mount's Bay have come to grief on Loe Bar, including the frigate *HMS Anson* in 1807 when 100 men were lost in the surf trying to reach the shore. Witnessing the catastrophe, Henry Trengrouse was inspired to invent the rocket propelled line throwing apparatus, which is still used by the coastguards today.

Porthleven lies at the northern end of Loe Bar, has a conspicuous clock tower by the harbour mouth and should only be approached in offshore winds and settled conditions. From here the northern shore of Mount's Bay begins to trend more to the west, with Welloe Rock (dries 0.8m) lying three miles due west of Porthleven, and the Mountamopus shoal (1.8m LAT) a mile south-west of Cudden Point.

Tater Du lighthouse, Gwennap Head in distance

Passing to the south of the Mountamopus YB south cardinal buoy (Q(6) +Lfl 15s) marking this hazard, the distinctive pyramid of St Michael's Mount, topped by a spire and turrets, is unmistakeable, and keeping it on the starboard bow, Penzance, two miles to the west, is easy to locate, with no further hazards except the Gear rock (dries 1.8m) marked by a black and red isolated danger beacon (Fl (2) 10s) just under half a mile due south of the harbour entrance. Pass to seaward of the Gear if bound across the bay to Newlyn.

MOUNTS BAY TO LAND'S END

Heading for Land's End or the Isles of Scilly from Penzance, you will pass to the east of the Low Lee BYB east cardinal buoy (Q(3) 10s). Departing from Newlyn, a course can be laid just over a cable from the shore inside Carn Base and Low Lee shoals past Penlee Point, with its old lifeboat house and slipway. This, and the memorial garden beside it, remain as a sad reminder of the tragic loss of the lifeboat *Solomon Browne* with its entire crew of eight on the 19th December 1981 while attending the wreck of the coaster *Union Star* near Lamorna Cove. It was the last launch from the slipway, and the replacement Penlee lifeboat is now kept afloat in Newlyn harbour.

Once past St Clement's Isle and Mousehole, the impressive grass-topped granite cliffs form a continuous line, broken only by a few tiny coves and sandy beaches such as Penberth and Porthcurno, and finally the section between Gwennap Head and Land's End is particularly precipitous.

Stay half a mile offshore until abeam of Tater Du light (Fl (3)15s 20M), when a course is best laid directly to pass just south of the Runnel Stone YB south cardinal buoy (Q(6) + LFl 15s), marking the outer end of a rocky ledge extending nearly a mile southwards from Gwennap Head, with the drying Runnel Stone at its extremity. It is not unknown for the Runnel Stone buoy to break adrift in the heavy seas that often run along this most exposed corner, and this hazardous place has been the scene of many wrecks.

There are two conical beacons inshore on Hella Point, the outer red and the inner black with a lower white band, providing a transit of 352°T over the position of the rocks. To assist you in judging distance off – when the white base of the inner beacon is also visible above the cliff top you will pass safely to the south of the hazard. This is, in any circumstance, an area to be navigated with extreme caution. Three and a half miles west of the Runnelstone buoy, Carn Base shoals have a least depth of 9.9m which can create heavy seas in

Runnelstone buoy and Land's End, centre. Longships, left and Gwennap Head, right

strong winds; they are marked on their south-western corner by the Carn Base YBY west cardinal buoy (Q (9) 15s).

Although the tides in Mount's Bay are weak, they rapidly gather in strength towards the Runnel Stone, probably attaining five knots at springs, becoming increasingly unpredictable as the main tidal stream divides into the Irish Sea and English Channel.

Bound round Land's End from Mount's Bay, if you leave about one hour before HW Dover you will have a favourable tide for the next seven hours and, hopefully, soon be well on your way. As mentioned earlier, this is a very unfair tidal gate – the north-west stream begins three hours before HW Dover and runs for nearly nine hours; the east-going stream six hours before HW Dover lasting for a mere three.

The Atlantic ground swell is rarely absent for a passage 'around the Land' to the north Cornish coast. This, and the coast beyond, is an area to take very seriously. **A favourable forecast is essential to attempt Land's End or the passage to the Isles of Scilly, which is covered in detail on page 201.**

THE MANACLES TO LAND'S END AT NIGHT

This passage area is well lit although, once south of the Manacle buoy (Q (3) 10s) steering 220°T, the Lizard light (Fl 3s 25M) will be obscured for the next five miles until you are a couple of miles

Land's End comprises a rugged stretch of granite cliffs topped with a prominent hotel complex

south-east of Black Head. Inshore, Coverack and Cadgwith show only small clusters of lights. Once clear to the south of the Lizard, Tater Du lighthouse (Fl (3) 15s 20M) will be seen away to the north-west on the far side of Mount's Bay, and in the far distance to the west, Wolf Rock lighthouse (Fl 15s 23M).

This is a busy stretch of water: shipping bound to and from Land's End converges on the Lizard and fishing boats are likely to be encountered trawling at night. Their movements should be carefully observed and avoided, as should the regular Naval exercises in the area.

When entering Mount's Bay, the whole of the northern shore appears as a continuous mass of lights from Marazion to Newlyn, and it is worth noting that both the Lizard and Tater Du lights become obscured in the approach to Penzance, although by then the lighthouse on the south pier (Fl WR 5s 17/12M) should easily be visible, along with the harbour light at Newlyn (Fl 5s 9M). Other lights in the approaches to Mount's Bay are the Mountamopus buoy (Q(6)+LFl 15s) on the northern side and Low Lee buoy (Q (3) 10s) on the southern side, while Gear Rock beacon (Fl (2) 10s) is in the closer approach to Penzance.

Heading west to Land's End beyond Tater Du, the Runnel Stone buoy (Q(6) + LFl 15s) lies within the red sector of the Longships lighthouse (Iso WR 10s 16/13M) and is also covered by a (FR) light showing 060°T to 074°T from Tater Du, so it is wisest to stand on past the buoy to westwards towards the Carn Base buoy (Q (9) 15s) until the white sector of the Longships is fully open before altering to the north-west. Pass well to seawards of the Longships, the tide in its vicinity runs hard and is unpredictable. You are now in the Land's End inshore traffic zone and a lot more shipping is likely to be encountered.

In poor visibility, additional aids to navigation are the fog signals at the Lizard (Horn 30s), Wolf Rock (Horn 30s, Racon T 10M) and Longships (Horn 10s). In addition, the Manacle buoy has a bell and the Runnel Stone buoy a whistle.

Coverack harbour

COVERACK AND CADGWITH

Tides	HW Dover +0600
Charts	BA 777, SC 5603.6. Stanford 13. Imray C6, C7
Hazards	**Coverack**: Small boat harbour dries completely. The Manacles. Isolated rocks off Dolor Point (unlit) and to NW of harbour. Fine weather anchorage only and dangerous in onshore wind
	Cadgwith: Bow Rock (unlit) in entrance to cove. Fine weather anchorage, but dangerous in onshore wind

Lying between the Manacles and Black Head, Coverack is a small, picturesque drying harbour popular with tourists and still the base for a small fleet of fishing boats, open craft used for potting and handlining and known locally as cove boats or toshers. In settled weather with offshore wind and an absence of ground swell, the bay makes a tenable anchorage, although with any indication of a shift of wind to the south-east it is no place to linger.

APROACHES

The conspicuous large hotel to the south of the village is the easiest landmark to spot, and with the Guthen Rocks off Chynalls Point to the south and the Dava Rocks extending nearly half a mile from Lowland Point to the north end of the bay, do not attempt to cut corners. Enter on a westerly course, sounding your way in to the best anchorage in about 3m, a cable or so NNE of the pierhead. There is no charge for anchoring, but care should be taken to avoid the fishermens' keep pots which fringe the bay.

The harbour, enclosed by a small, sturdy granite wall, dries to beyond the entrance with a clean, sandy bottom, but the shore immediately

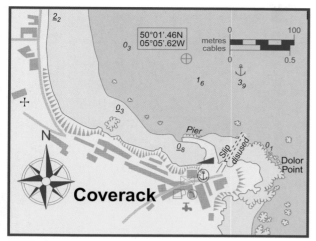

Coverack has a small drying harbour. In settled offshore weather visitors normally anchor off

to the west is rocky and very foul. Although there is a minimum depth of 2.4m alongside the pier end at MHWN, due to the crowding of the local boats which lie on heavy rope fore and aft moorings, drying out is not really a viable proposition. Far better to anchor off and dinghy in, where you are welcome to land at the ladders on the pier or the large slipway across the head of the harbour as long as you do not hog the access.

Coverack, like so many other Cornish harbours, grew with the extensive pilchard fishery. The former salt store overlooking the harbour is now a gift shop and the Old Lifeboat House is a restaurant and fish and chip takeaway. All the basic facilities are available; provisions, post office (EC Tues), several cafés, pub/hotels, including the curiously named Paris Inn, which is nothing to do with the EU or *entente cordiale*, but named after the *City of Paris*, an American liner stranded nearby in 1899. Her 700 passengers were brought safely to shore by local boats before she was eventually refloated. Water is available from the harbour master, Mr PW Barker (Tel: 01326 280679), but there is no fuel.

CADGWITH

'There is a bench from which the whole of the bay can be seen where the fishermen sit in patience, and scarcely turn their eyes from the sea. It really is very exciting to hear the 'pilchard' cry for the first time; visitors rise up and leave their dinner and amusements, and every man who dwells in the village, whatever he may be doing, is called by a strange and terrible cry to come and help in the take. The boats are always ready in the bay, but the real time to see the pilchard take is by moonlight, when the fishes look like living silver . . .'

Cadgwith, it would seem, was popular even as far back as 1885 when this was written and, although the huge shoals of pilchards vanished in the 1930s, the holidaymakers still descend in their droves. Nevertheless, it is still very much a working fishing community, and the traditional atmosphere of the village lingers in the tight cluster of cottages nestling snugly in a steep green valley at the head of a tiny cove. Almost too photogenic, white painted walls and heavy encrusted thatches contrast sharply with the more familiar granite cottages and the curious dark green serpentine rock that is local to the Lizard.

There is no harbour, and the fleet of small fishing boats is hauled up the shingle on wooden rollers, a daily spectacle much enjoyed by the visitors. Thumping softly, an ancient and magnificent single cylinder Hornsby donkey engine powers the winch, and in the cool, dark cellar where it lurks, the walls are covered with faded paintings, curling sepia photographs, all pervaded by the sweet aroma of warm oil.

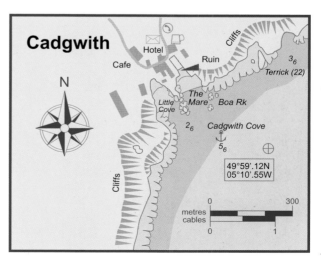

Chapter 4

Cadgwith village lies at the head of a small cove split in half by the Todden, a rocky outcrop from which the covering Mare Rocks extend to seaward

APPROACHES

Well sheltered from the west, the cove should only be approached in settled weather and offshore winds, and is not recommended for an overnight stop. The houses will be spotted from offshore, forming a break in the flat line of the cliffs, and closing them you will find what is effectively two coves, split in the middle by a low rocky outcrop called the Todden. The extension of this, a group of rocks called the Mare, runs to seaward, and it is advisable to sound in and anchor off them in about 2 – 3m. Do not proceed

Cadgwith is an attractive and interesting stop in settled westerly weather

any further into the cove as the Bow is a dangerous rock right in the centre which covers at quarter tide, and the entrance is also in frequent use by the local boats. Landing is easy anywhere on the shingle beach, but make sure you keep your dinghy well clear to avoid obstructing the winching operations.

There are limited provisions, a post office, the Cadgwith Cove Inn , a hotel, a café and a pleasant walk up on to the cliffs overlooking the cove, past some lovely cottages to a small black hut high on the headland. It was here that those fishermen used to sit waiting and watching, and once the cry of 'Hevva! Hevva!' sent them to sea, with the 'huers' directing the boats from this high vantage point towards the shoals by a series of special hand signals and wild shouts through a large tin megaphone.

Huers' huts can still be seen in many places along the Cornish coast, abandoned after the strange demise of the pilchard and the herring. The huge shoals that were once the livelihood of so many small villages like Cadgwith began to dwindle mysteriously in the mid 1930s, and after the war they were never found again, a phenomenon that has never really been explained.

Today, the fleet of cove boats works nets, pots and handlines, rock hopping along this beautiful, but at times very wild, stretch of coast.

MULLION AND PORTHLEVEN

Tides	HW Dover +0555
Charts	BA: 2345, 777, SC5603.2. Stanford: 13. Imray: C7, WCP 2400.10
Hazards	**Mullion**: Mullion Island, many rocks close inshore. Fine weather anchorage only and dangerous in onshore wind
	Porthleven: Harbour dries. Deazle rocks, Little and Great Trigg rocks (all unlit) to west and east of entrance. Dangerous to approach in onshore winds
Overnight charge	Porthleven, Harbour authority drying alongside: £12

Athough this small drying harbour three miles north-west of the Lizard is closed to fin keel boats, and no overnight stays are permitted in any craft, Mullion's spectacular location in a magnificent stretch of coast can provide a memorable overnight anchorage in offshore winds and settled weather;

it can also prove useful if waiting for a fair tide eastwards round the Lizard.

APPROACHES

The approach is straightforward: both Mullion Island and the conspicuous Mullion Cove Hotel high on the cliffs above are easy to see. Although local boats use a narrow channel between the island and the mainland, it is not recommended and the northern end of the island should be

Mullion Cove and Island with Porth Mellin's small drying harbour, inset

given a good berth, entering the anchorage midway between it and the small Porth Mellin harbour wall. This was built in 1895, a somewhat lethargic response to the disastrous loss of the cove's entire fishing fleet 50 years earlier during a freak storm. Today only a few small boats are based here, for the years have done nothing to change its exposure to the prevailing wind and sea. The harbour is now owned by the National Trust and from May to September there is a resident harbour master (Tel: 01326 240222).

Although there is a temporary berth alongside

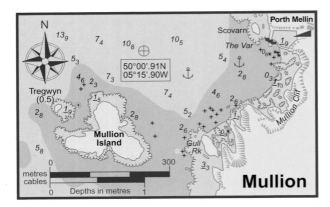

the western wall (as long as it is not being used by the fishing boats), it cannot be recommended as there is frequently much surge in the harbour. The anchorage between the harbour and Mullion Island is, therefore, the only option. It is well sheltered to the north and east, with good holding on a sandy bottom in 7m midway between the harbour entrance and the northern end of the island, which is a nature reserve on which landing is not allowed.

This seems like an unusually remote anchorage, well off the normal track, but it has not always been so. RT McMullen anchored here in a north-easterly gale aboard his *Orion*, counted 64 vessels sheltering, and wrote in September 1868: '. . I was surprised to see how regularly they were arranged according to their ability to work offshore if the wind were to fly in. The *Orion* was first in line with three pilot cutters, then came the sloops and yawls, and a brig-rigged steamship. Next schooners and ketches, then brigs and barks; those in the first division were almost still on the water, the second were rolling perceptibly, the third decidedly uneasy, and the last, having no protection at all from Mullion Island, were rolling miserably.'

FACILITIES

Dinghy ashore when the tide allows and land on the slipway at the head of the harbour, where there are just a few houses, a café, gift shop, telephone and public WC. Off the main tourist track, it is a particularly unspoilt little corner with some magnificent views and excellent walks along the cliffs in both directions.

Most normal provisions are available at Mullion village, an uphill walk of just over a mile, and the Mullion Cove Hotel is open to non-residents with meals available in the bar. Owing to the potentially exposed nature of the anchorage, I would not, however, recommend leaving your boat unattended for any length of time,

and up anchor at the slightest hint of a wind shift to the south.

PORTHLEVEN

I always feel rather sorry for Porthleven, for it is certainly a magnificent example of the harbour builder's art, a long protective entrance leading to a fine basin enclosed by massive granite walls.

However, its history reveals little commercial success. Its chapter of disasters began when a group of speculators obtained an Act of Parliament in 1811, ostensibly to build a harbour of refuge. Disagreement and squabbling dogged the venture and the harbour was not completed until six years later, surviving for another six before it was devastated by a storm, a fact that did little to encourage shipowners to use it.

Although it was rebuilt and greatly improved in the mid-1800s, its fundamental failings were that it dries completely, and the narrow entrance faces right into the prevailing south-westerlies, frequently rendering it unapproachable and forcing its closure with large baulks of timber in heavy weather. Few winters seems to pass without spectacular photographs of huge seas breaking over the seafront appearing on the front pages of the national press!

Today, Porthleven is mostly used by pleasure craft and a small and diminishing fleet of fishing boats. However, as with all the other small harbours of the Lizard, with offshore winds and settled conditions, it makes another interesting place off the regular cruising track to visit, and a feasible overnight stop, providing you don't mind drying out.

APPROACHES

The harbour mouth lies at the northern end of Loe Bar, the long shingle beach that begins just over two miles north of Mullion Island. The houses on the hillside are easily visible on the cliffs, and the south pier, with its prominent clock tower at the landward end, should be closed on a bearing of 045°T.

The harbour dries right to the entrance at MLWS, but is accessible from half-tide onwards. If waiting for water, anchor in the outer entrance to the harbour or pick up one of the six moorings, where average draught boats will lie afloat except at low springs. Care must be taken to avoid the submerged **Little Trigg rocks** off the pier end, though there are no further hazards once past the old lifeboat house on the north shore.

Pass through the outer entrance and into the

Porthleven entrance should be approached with care – the darker water in the foreground indicates the extent of Great Trigg Rocks, left, and Little Trigg Rocks off the pier

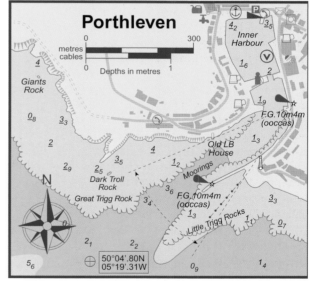

inner basin where the local boats mostly lie on fore and aft moorings on heavy ground chains running north-south up the harbour. Visitors should berth inside the entrance on the East Quay and seek out the harbour master, Phil Ward, if he has not already spotted you. His office is at the head of the harbour and he will advise on the most suitable berth. Overnight charge for a 10m boat is £12.

There is a VHF watch Ch 16, 08 during normal working hours, but all vessels should call ahead to arrange a berth (Tel: 01326 574270 or Mobile 079666 30944). The South Quay has a crane at its end for lowering the storm timber baulks – it is used by the local fishing boats and should be avoided.

FACILITIES

A popular place with holidaymakers, Porthleven provides a curious contrast of old fishermen's cottages and converted net stores, and a long row of typically bold Victorian semi-detached houses that completely dominate the entrance. All normal facilities are available: post office, the well-stocked Porthleven Supermarket (open daily 0800 – 2200), banks and a launderette. Water and fuel can be obtained locally; ask at the harbour office.

Eating places consist of cafés, pubs and restaurants, including the inevitable Ship Inn, overlooking the harbour entrance, and the Harbour Inn on the east side of the inner harbour.

To stretch the legs, head east along the great shingle sweep of Loe Bar as far as Loe Pool, a large freshwater lake formed when the bar sealed off the estuary of the Cober, a river once navigable as far inland as Helston. It is part of the large Penrose Estate, now owned by the National Trust, and there are some delightful walks through the woods along its banks.

PENZANCE

Tides	HW Dover +0550
Range	MHWS 5.6m–MHWN 4.4m, MLWN 2.0m–MLWS 0.7m. Tidal dock gate manned every tide from two hours before to one hour after HW
Charts	BA: 2345, SC5603.7. Stanford: 13. Imray: C7
Waypoint	South Pier Head 50°07'.06N. 05°31'.68W
Hazards	Gear Rock (lit). Outer harbour dries, tidal wet dock. Harbour approach very dangerous in strong southerly weather. Pot and net buoys in Mount's Bay. Keep clear if *RMS Scillonian*, or other commercial shipping, is entering or leaving
Overnight charge	Harbour Authority, alongside, £13.40

When McMullen put into Penzance in 1868, it was still in its busy commercial heyday and he moaned bitterly about the state of the quays, '. . .which are allowed by the Corporation to be in so offensive a state, encumbered with coal dust that nothing short of real distress will drive me into the nasty harbour again.'

The coal has long vanished from the quays of Penzance but so, too, has most of the waterborne trade. Now a busy centre for tourism, the town grew around the export of tin, reaching its peak in the mid 1800s when nearly half of the minerals mined in Cornwall passed through the port, stacked in 300lb ingots on the quayside for shipment to places as far afield as Russia and Italy. A major centre for the export of salt herring and mackerel, there are records of a thriving trading and fishing village here as early as 1300, but the major extensions to form the present day harbour were made in 1745-72 when the Albert Pier was built, with further improvements during the 19th century. The dry dock was built in 1814 and is still operational today.

Penzance was also home to the first lifeboat in Cornwall in 1803, but this was discontinued in 1917 and the lifeboat is now based in Newlyn. Until the late 1980s this was the westernmost Trinity House buoy depot and today it is a museum, the Trinity House National Lighthouse Centre, which is open daily during the summer.

The outer harbour dries almost completely at LAT and is given over to a large number of local moorings on fore and aft trots. Visitors normally use the tidal wet dock, entered through a hydraulic gate, **and is only accessible for two hours before HW until one hour after HW**. Here there is

ample berthing for up to 50 yachts, afloat at all times in total protection.

A small amount of commercial traffic still uses the basin, and it has become popular for refits and repair work. By arrangement, boats can be left unattended without worry for a few days or longer, making it an ideal base to explore west

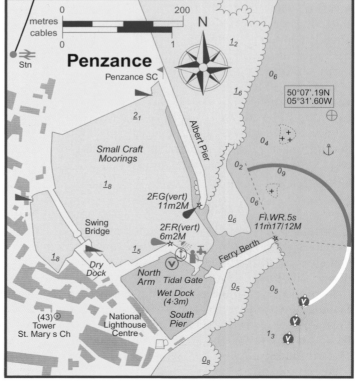

Penzance has a large drying outer harbour, but visitors can lie afloat and secure in the wet dock, bottom left, which is accessed through a tidal gate, or on visitors' buoys off the South Pier in settled weather

Cornwall and the rugged Land's End peninsula, with good bus services and cars for hire.

APPROACHES

Approaching from the east, pass to the south of the south cardinal YB Mountamopus buoy (Q(6)+LFl 15s) marking a 1.8m shoal, holding the unmistakeable bulk of St Michael's Mount on your starboard bow. The conspicuous tower of St Mary's Church provides a good landmark to locate Penzance. In the approach from the south-west, Gear Rock (dries 1.8m) lies just over 800m, almost due south of the harbour entrance, and is marked by an isolated danger beacon (Fl (2) 10s). Penzance Harbour lighthouse, a white tower, displays a red and white sectored light (Fl WR 5s, white 268 – 345°T 17M; red 159 – 268°T 12M). The white sector safely clears Gear Rock and, if approaching from the east cardinal BYB Low Lee buoy (Q (3) 10s), steer a north-easterly course until the white sector opens. There are vertical lights displayed from the harbour master's office by the north side of the dock gate to indicate whether it is open or closed: three vertical red = closed; three vertical green = open.

Penzance should not be considered as a harbour of refuge in bad weather. Although it is safely accessible in winds from the south-west to north, heavy breaking seas can build up in the shallowing approaches, often breaking over the south pier and making the whole entrance highly dangerous in winds from the east through to the south.

In these conditions Newlyn is the only place to consider. Approach with extreme caution and as near to HW as possible.

During the season there are 12 orange visitors buoys about 150m due south of Penzance lighthouse in about 2m LAT, which can either be used to await entry into the tidal basin or for an overnight stop in settled weather and offshore winds. A temporary small craft anchorage can be found just over 350m NNE of the end of the Albert Pier, in about 1.2m LAT, or further offshore, depending on your draught, ensuring that you are clear of the fairway into the harbour entrance. Alternatively anchor 350m due south of the south pier head.

The harbour office monitors VHF Ch 16 during office hours, and works on Ch 12, call sign *Penzance Harbour Radio*. It is also manned HW–2 to HW+1 when the tidal dock is open. Although the outer harbour is full of moorings, with the harbour master's permission it is possible to dry out alongside the Albert Pier where Penzance Sailing Club is based.

A fascinating variety of craft can often be found in Penzance wet dock – a safe place to leave your boat if you wish to explore West Cornwall inland

If waiting for the tide, the alternative to mooring or anchoring off is lying on the inside of the South Pier in the berth used by the Isles of Scilly ferry, *RMS Scillonian III*, which is normally empty Monday to Friday from 0930 to 1830, and Saturdays (summer) from 1400 to 1830. At low water, keep close to the south pier as the water shoals rapidly on the northern side of the entrance, but between the convenient ladder half way along the wall and the lighthouse, a depth of 1.8m will be found, even at LAT. You can lie alongside the large floating fenders – be warned, though, if you clamber onto them they roll instantly, and you'll end up swimming. Check in with the harbour master once berthed and do not leave the boat totally unattended or obstruct the stone steps by the entrance to the wet basin as this is in constant use by local fishing trip boats.

The dock gate is manned two hours before HW every tide, day and night, and opens soon afterwards. Once in the basin, the berthing master will allocate a berth, charges are £1.34 per metre per day, with every third day free, providing someone remains aboard the vessel. There are special weekly rates available for unattended vessels should you have need to leave your boat.

You will be given an access code to the newly refurbished toilets and showers (£1 charge), situated beneath the harbour office in the end of the large white building nearest to the lock gate. The berthing master can also arrange for water and small quantities of diesel. Calor and Gaz refills can be obtained from nearby Penzance Marine Services, but petrol is only available in cans from the garage near the railway station.

FACILITIES

Penzance is a popular tourist centre, as well as a busy and interesting old market town with many fine buildings. This is the largest town in the far west and just about all normal requirements will be found. The main shopping centre, the curiously named Market Jew Street, derived its name from the Cornish *Marghas de Yow* meaning 'Thursday Market' and climbs up the hillside past the main post office towards the impressive granite Market House, with its ionic columns and domed roof, which also houses the Lloyds TSB Bank. In front of it is a statue of Penzance's famous son, Sir Humphrey Davy, best known for his invention of the miner's safety lamp. Close to the station, on the road out of town, there is a good launderette open seven days a week, 0900 – 1930.

The wide choice of options for eating ashore include several good pubs close to hand, notably the Turks Head, Dolphin and the Admiral Benbow, all of which serve food. Restaurants within easy reach include the Beachcomber (Tel:794844), the Bosun's Locker (Tel: 366746) and, heading towards the centre of town you'll

Penzance Port Guide
Area telephone code: 01736

Harbour Master: Mr Neil Clark, Harbour Office, North Arm, Penzance Harbour, Penzance, TR18 4AH, (Tel: 366113. Fax: 366114) Mon-Fri 0900 – 1300, 1400 – 1800.

VHF: Ch 16, working Ch 12, call sign *Penzance Harbour Radio* (office hours and HW−2 to HW+1)

Mail Drop: Harbour Office

Emergency Services: Lifeboat at Newlyn. Falmouth Coastguard

Anchorages: In fair weather 350m ENE of Albert Pier, clear of fairway or similar distance due south of South Pier

Mooring/berthing: 12 visitors' buoys off South Pier. Tidal wet dock (maintained depth 4.3m) entry 2 hours before to 1 hour after local HW. Pick up mooring, anchor off or berth inside South Pier if Isles of Scilly ferry berth available when waiting to enter

Dinghy landings: Steps on inside of Albert Pier

Marinas: None

Charges: £1.34 per metre per day. Every third day free providing boat is attended

Phones: Nearest public phone on promenade

Doctor: (Tel: 363340 or 363866)

Hospital: West Cornwall Hospital (Tel: 362382)

Churches: All denominations

Local Weather Forecast: Harbour office

Fuel: Diesel by arrangement with berthing master. Petrol in cans from garage

Gas: Calor/Gaz from Penzance Marine Services, Wharf Road, (Tel:361081)

Water: See berthing master

Tourist Information Centre: At railway station, (Tel: 362207)

Banks/cashpoints: All main banks, all with cashpoints

Post Office: Market Jew Street

Rubbish: Bins on quay

Showers/toilets: Under Harbour Office, coded entry lock. £1 charge for shower

Launderette: Near railway station

Provisions: All normal shops. Tesco in Market Jew Street. Large Safeway supermarket at Long Rock, bus/taxi ride away, open Sunday in season

Chandler: Ocean Blue, Coinagehall Street (Tel:364004)

Repairs: Drying out by arrangement with harbour master

Marine engineers: Albert Pier Engineering (Tel: 363566). R&D Engineering (Tel: 360253). Mounts Bay Engineering,

(Tel: 363095). Penzance Marine Services (Tel: 361081)

Electronic engineers: Marconi Marine, Newlyn, (Tel: 361320)

Sailmakers: Ocean Blue (Tel: 364004)

Riggers: Ocean Blue (Tel: 364004)

Transport: Main line rail terminus (Tel: 08457 484950) Buses (Tel: 01209 719988) Ferry service to Scilly (Tel: 0845 710 5555) Helicopter service to Scilly (Tel: 363871)

Car Hire: Europcar (Tel: 360356) at railway station. Economy Hire (Tel: 366636). Tucker (Tel: 362980)

Bike Hire: Pedals (Tel: 36060)

Taxi: (Tel: 330864, 350666 or 366166)

Car Parking: Large car park adjoining inner harbour

Yacht Clubs: Penzance Sailing Club, Albert Pier (Tel: 364989)

Eating out: Excellent choice of pubs and restaurants

Things to do: Trinity House Lighthouse Centre. Penzance Town Museum. Trips to Land's End/St Michaels Mount. Golowan Festival last week in June

find a host of others, including Harris's (Tel: 364408) for seafood, tapas at Bar Coco (Tel: 350222) and fine views of Mounts Bay from the Abbey (Tel: 330680). Most other tastes are amply catered for, with Italian, Indian, Chinese and very good fish and chips from Captain's Fish Bar!

Chapel Street, leading back down from the top of Market Jew Street towards St Mary's church and the harbour, has a number of fine listed buildings, many of them gift shops, and also the bizarre Egyptian House, restored by the Landmark Trust. During the last week in June the town bursts into colourful activity with the Golowan Festival, celebrating ancient Celtic traditions with music, dance, street theatre and fireworks.

If time permits, a trip inland to the north coast or Land's End is well worth the effort, and there are regular bus services to St Michael's Mount if you decide against a visit by sea. Should the

weather scupper your plans to sail to the Isles of Scilly, you could always console yourself with a day trip to the islands, (Tel: 0845 710 5555, website: www.ios-travel.co.uk). As well as the *Scillonian*'s daily sailings there are also frequent helicopter flights from nearby Penzance Heliport (Tel: 363871, website: www.scillyhelicopter.co.uk).

The small town Museum is located centrally in the Penlee Memorial Park. Apart from historical accounts and old photographs of the harbour, it is also the home of the town's permanent collection of the Newlyn Painting School. This provides a romanticised glimpse of the town's final years as a simple working port, before Brunel's Great Western Railway wiped out the isolation of the far west and the first large hotels began to rise along the new promenade at the shingly head of the bay. There's nothing like a bit of nostalgia; we conveniently tend to forget all that coal dust!

Yachts must lie alongside the locals in the busy fishing port of Newlyn

NEWLYN

Tides	HW Dover +0550
Range	MHWS 5.6m–MHWN 4.4m, MLWN 2.0m–MLWS 0.7m. Main harbour dredged to 2.4m LAT
Charts	BA: 2345, SC5603.7. Stanford:13 SC23. Imray: C, WCP2400.10
Waypoint	South Pier Head 50°06'·18N / 05°32'·57W
Hazards	Low Lee Rock (lit). Gear Rock (lit). Busy fishing harbour, beware vessels in narrow entrance. Approach dangerous in strong southerly weather, heavy swell sets across entrance. Many pot and net buoys in Mount's Bay
Overnight charge	Harbour Authority alongside: £6

If we are to believe a plaque on a house overlooking the harbour, Newlyn, not Plymouth, was the last port of call in England for the *Mayflower* and her intrepid crew before setting out on her voyage to the New World. Recent research asserts that she berthed on the Old Quay on the 16th August 1620 to take on water, as Plymouth's supply was tainted with fever and cholera. Whatever the truth, Newlyn's abiding claim to fame has always been as a busy fishing port, alive with colour, boats and activity, and you walk the streets at your peril as large articulated refrigerated lorries, fork lift trucks and spraying hoses create an assault on all sides!

In contrast with its declining neighbour Penzance, Newlyn saw considerable commercial expansion during the 1980s after the opening of the Mary Williams pier, and is now the largest fish landing port in England and Wales, with around 9,500 tons of fish landed annually representing a value of approximately £20m.

The port is dredged to an average depth of 2.4m LAT and is accessible at all states of the tide, providing the only real harbour of refuge in Mount's Bay and where yachts are made very welcome. However, in strong south or south-easterly winds, a heavy sea builds up in the shoaling water at the head of the bay, particularly at LW causing a

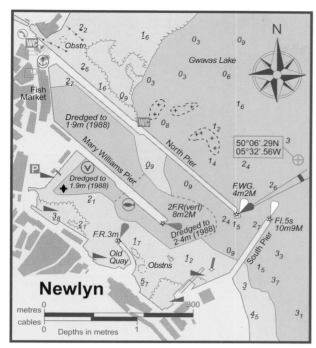

quarters of a mile to the north-east of the harbour entrance, which dries 1.8m and is marked by an isolated danger beacon. From the west, Low Lee shoal, least depth 1.5m LAT, is marked by the Low Lee BY east cardinal buoy (Q(3) 10s), but Carn Base shoal, three cables to the north-west is unmarked, has a least depth of 1.8m and breaks in heavy weather.

However, once St Clement's Island, off Mousehole, is abeam, a course should be held just over a cable from the shore. This will lead inside all the shoals, past Penlee Point with its former lifeboat house, from where the white lighthouse on the end of the south pier (Fl 5s vis: 253° – 336°T) is easy to spot against the town, which rises up the hillside overlooking the harbour. The entrance is 47m wide and the northern side has a (FWG) sectored light (green 238° – 248°T). The only other hazard to consider, particularly at night, is the significant amount of pots along this stretch of coast and also the large numbers of small craft that will be found working them. As always, fishing craft restricted by gear should be given a generous berth and your intentions made obvious at an early stage.

considerable run across the harbour entrance.

This should be carefully considered if heading for shelter, and entry is best attempted as close to HW as possible.

APPROACHES

Approaching from the east, the run across Mount's Bay is straightforward, passing to the south of the Mountamopus YB south cardinal buoy (Q(6)+LFl 15s) and well clear of Gear Rock (Fl (2) 10s), three-

ANCHORAGE AND BERTHING

In offshore winds, it is possible to anchor 200m SSE of the harbour entrance, sounding in to about

Newlyn, one of the busiest fishing ports in England, has all-tide access, but should be approached with extreme caution in strong winds from the south or east. Visitors normally berth on the west side of the central Mary Williams Pier

The Mayflower's *last berth before the Pilgrims departed for America? The Old Quay, Newlyn, where huge granite blocks are weathered and mottled with orange lichens*

3m, or alternatively, a similar distance to the north-east in Gwavas Lake. Owing to the frequency of fishing boat movements and the intensity of the background lights on the shore, a very good riding light is essential.

Newlyn is a busy commercial harbour with no specific facilities for yachts, but they are nevertheless made welcome and the inherent disadvantages are offset by the all-tide access, which is particularly useful if you are on passage and wanting to make the most of the tides or intent on an early start. Visitors will usually find space alongside the fishing boats on the west side of the central Mary Williams pier, which tends to be occupied by local vessels that are laid up for refits or repair. There is less movement here in contrast to the continual comings and goings elsewhere in the harbour, where the fleet lands daily.

As in all busy fishing harbours, remember that commercial activity takes absolute precedence over pleasure. Sailing and anchoring is prohibited anywhere in the harbour except in an emergency.

As well as breast lines to your neighbour, bow and stern lines should be taken ashore if intending to stay overnight and, with the boats often five or six deep, this will involve quite a scramble. The best bet is to moor temporarily and check with Harbour Master Mr Andrew Munson, whose office is at the head of the harbour by the north pier above the fish-merchants' offices. He is very helpful and will endeavour to find you a quiet berth. The wet dock in Penzance is the nearest place where a yacht can be left unattended for any length of time.

FACILITIES

Newlyn is a bustling working town, its fishmarket central to its life. Early risers, providing they keep out of the way of the very serious business in hand, can spend a fascinating hour or two watching the landings and daily auction which starts at around seven in the morning, Monday to Saturday.

The old town, a pleasant meandering sort of place, climbs up the hillside in tight rows of sturdy granite cottages, sheltered courtyards and narrow alleyways. It has been a fishing harbour since medieval times and the magnificent remains of the original pier, a gently curving wall of huge granite blocks, weathered and mottled with orange lichens, can still be seen forming part of the small inner basin beneath the cliff on the west side of the harbour.

The present harbour, built between 1866 and 1888, was the centre of the huge mackerel and pilchard fishery and, in 1896, was the scene of the infamous riots when the devout local fishermen ran amok, angered by visiting east coast boats landing fish on Sundays. Hurling

Newlyn Port Guide

Area telephone code: 01736

Harbour Master: Mr Andrew Munson, Harbour Office, Newlyn (Tel: 362523) Mon – Fri 0800 – 1700

VHF: Ch 16, working Chs 12 and 9, call sign *Newlyn Harbour*, office hours only

Mail Drop: c/o harbour office

Emergency Services: Lifeboat at Newlyn. Falmouth Coastguard

Anchorages: In fair weather to NE or SE of harbour entrance clear of approaches. No anchoring within harbour

Mooring/berthing: Alongside fishing boats on west side of central Mary Willams pier.

Charges: Per night, up to 8m £4, 8m – 12m £6. Over 12m £9. Every third night free. 50 per cent surcharge for multihulls

Phones: By harbour office

Doctor: (Tel: 363340)

Hospital: (Tel: 362382)

Churches: All denominations

Local Weather Forecast: At harbour office

Fuel: Ask at harbour office for diesel. Petrol in cans from garage

Gas: Ask at harbour office

Water: Available on quays

Banks/cashpoints: Barclays Mon – Fri 1000 – 1230. No cashpoints. All banks in nearby Penzance have cashpoints

Post Office: By harbour office

Rubbish: Bins on quays

Showers/toilets: Royal National Mission to Deep Sea Fishermen, North Pier. Shower near fishmarket. Public toilets on quay

Launderette: Nearest in Penzance

Provisions: Co-op Supermarket (open Sundays), butcher, newsagent

Chandler: Cosalt, Harbour Road (Tel: 363094). South West Nets, Harbour Road (Tel: 360254)

Repairs: Large slip for commercial craft. Drying out by arrangement with harbour master

Marine engineers: Mount's Bay Engineering, North pier (Tel: 363095/363014). See also Penzance port guide

Electronic engineers: Marconi Marine (Tel:361320)

Sailmakers: Lodey Sails (Tel: 331557)

Transport: Buses to Penzance. Mainline rail terminus at Penzance

Car Hire/taxi: See harbour master

Car Parking: Near Fishmarket

Eating out: Pub food, bistros, fish and chips and excellent pasties

Things to do: Pilchard works and museum. Newlyn Fish Festival, late August bank Holiday. Newlyn Art gallery. Pleasant walk along bike trail to Mousehole

Chapter 4

their catches back into the sea, the bloody disturbance that ensued was only eventually put down by military intervention.

Renowned for their speed and sea-keeping ability, the magnificent 30-50ft luggers that once filled these west Cornish ports have mostly vanished, but the restored Mount's Bay mackerel driver *Children's Friend*, PZ101 is now based in the port, while the *Barnabas*, a fine example of a St Ives lugger owned by the Maritime Trust, is based in Falmouth where she can often be seen sailing during the summer months.

The present fishing fleet has grown considerably in recent years and ranges from large beam trawlers and scallopers that venture as far afield as the North Sea and Irish Sea, to the smaller pot, net and mackerel boats that work the tricky inshore waters round Land's End.

The town, although small, provides most necessary provisions, catering as it does for the fishing fleet. There is a Co-op supermarket close to the harbour, which opens on Sundays. Anything unobtainable in Newlyn can usually be found in Penzance, a pleasant walk along the promenade, or by bus every 15 minutes. Hot showers, for both men and women, can be

obtained at the Royal National Mission to Deep Sea Fishermen or, alternatively, use the shower near the fishmarket – the key is available from the Security Office which is in the tower on the Mary Williams Pier.

This part of Cornwall has a long tradition of popularity with artists, in particular the famous Newlyn School of the 1890s, whose realistic paintings have enjoyed a great resurgence of interest – fishing and fisherfolk its central themes. Today's cultural diversion is provided by the Newlyn Art Gallery on the seafront, with regular local and visiting exhibitions. There is a fascinating Pilchard Works which continues this Cornish tradition, with an adjoining and informative museum, and the lively Newlyn Fish Festival takes place at the end of August.

Gastronomic diversion is well catered for, with several fishermen's cafés, very fresh fish and chips, a Chinese takeaway and Aunty May's Pasty Co for a superlative lunchtime pasty. There are several good pubs with food, the Tolcarne, Red Lion and Fisherman's Arms. The Smuggler's (Tel: 331501) has an adjoining restaurant with predictably a good choice of seafood. For something different, try the Meadery (Tel: 365375).

ST MICHAEL'S MOUNT AND MOUSEHOLE

Tides   HW Dover +0550

Charts   BA: 2345, SC5603.7 Stanford: 13, 23. Imray: C7, WCP2400.10

Hazards   **St Michael's Mount**: Hogus rocks, Outer Penzeath Rocks and Maltman Rock (all unlit). Harbour dries

              Mousehole: St Clement's Island (unlit). Harbour dries

Overnight **St Michaels Mount**: drying alongside: £10

charge   **Mousehole**: drying alongside:£10 (multihulls £12)

Providing an interesting alternative to the larger Mount's Bay ports of Penzance and Newlyn, St Michael's Mount and the old fishing harbour of Mousehole are well worth a visit if conditions permit. Both have small harbours which dry completely at LAT, but are normally accessible after half flood.

ST MICHAEL'S MOUNT

There is no problem identifying St Michael's Mount, Cornwall's own mini version of the famous Mont St Michel in Normandy, for this dramatic tidal island rises into a distinctive 90m pyramid in the north-east of Mount's Bay, topped by a fairy tale castle at its summit, in which the St Aubyn family have lived since the mid-1600s. They continue to do so, but the island was presented to the National Trust in 1954 by the present Lord St Levan. During the summer months, the Mount and parts of the castle buildings are open to the public on weekdays, 1000 – 1700; there is a charge for admission.

Historically, the tiny harbour on the northern side of the Mount was once the most important in Mount's Bay. This major centre for the export of tin was chronicled by the Romans in the first century BC, when the ore was brought overland from the mines on the north coast to avoid the treacherous journey around Land's End. A Benedictine monastery was established here in 1135, making it an important place of pilgrimage, but this was dissolved by Henry VIII during the Reformation, and during the Civil War the Royalists held the Mount for four years, a vital siege as the fortress was an ideal place for the import and stockpiling of arms and ammunition brought in from France.

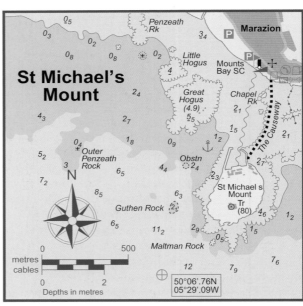

In 1727 the modest harbour was rebuilt and extended, and by the early 1800s it had prospered considerably, with over 50 houses on the island and a population of about 300. As you will see from the many pictures and prints if you visit the castle, large numbers of vessels regularly lay here, anchored in the bay or crammed into the tiny harbour, discharging timber from Scandinavia, coal and salt, before loading the return cargoes of copper, tin and cured fish that was exported in considerable quantities all over Europe. It was, however, the new harbour at Penzance that

St Michael's Mount is an island at high water and, although covered, the causeway to Marazion is clearly visible here. The darker patch, top left, indicates the position of Great Hogus Reef – visitors can anchor between this and the western harbour wall

eventually sealed the fate of the Mount and by the turn of the century it had lost all the trade to its larger rival.

APPROACHES AND ANCHORAGE

The best anchorage for a visit to the Mount is just to the north-west of the harbour entrance, or it is possible to lie alongside in the harbour where you will dry out on hard sand. The approaches have a number of rocks and shoals and should only be considered in fine weather, offshore winds and on a rising tide. Do not attempt it at night, and under no circumstances should an approach ever be made to the east and north of the Mount where there are extensive rocky shoals.

From Penzance keep offshore to avoid the reefs across the head of the bay; Western Cressar Rocks and Ryeman Rocks are both marked by a YB south cardinal beacon and a course towards the southern extremity of the Mount will clear both these and the Outer Penzeath Rock, awash LAT and unmarked.

Closing the Mount, approach on a north-easterly course keeping a good 300m from its steep western side to avoid Guthen Rocks, a shoal patch with just over 2m LAT, due west of the castle. Sound in towards the anchorage where about 2m will be found at LW, over a firm sandy bottom between the Great Hogus reef,

which dries 4.9m and the western pier end.

After half-tide, the harbour is accessible to average draught boats – stay a reasonable distance from the pier heads and beware of the constant stream of ferry boats. Known locally as the hobblers, they operate from the steps on both sides of the entrance continuously as soon as the tide covers the causeway and should not be obstructed in any way. Berth between the ladders on the western wall and report to Keith Murch, the harbour master, whose office is the opposite side of the harbour; if you can't find him immediately don't worry – he is also the island's postman and is probably dealing with the mail! A charge of about £10 will be made for a night's stay, well worth it for the eventual peace and quiet.

FACILITIES

Today, the Mount is the focal point of a very different kind of industry – tourism – and at times is almost overrun by the hordes of holidaymakers streaming, with a wary eye on the tide, like the Israelites along the causeway from Marazion, or packing the continuous fleet of small ferries that run during the summer months when the tide is in. In spite of it, the small harbour, with its simple row of neatly restored cottages, is well worth a visit.

Despite the dire warning that the climb to the castle 'should not be attempted by those suffering from any kind of heart condition', it is not as steep as it looks and provides spectacular panoramic views across Mount's Bay. In the evening, when the crowds have gone, this is once again, for a few

Spectacularly overlooked by the fairy tale castle, visitors to St Michael's Mount can dry out in the small harbour or anchor in the lee of the island

brief hours, a peaceful and tranquil place.

There is a restaurant, cafe and gift shop by the harbour when the Mount is open, and the Harbour Master can fill a container of water if you're desperate. Most normal provisions, telephone, post office and several pubs can be found at Marazion.

MOUSEHOLE

Mousehole is in many ways similar to St Michael's Mount, for this is another picturesque honey pot around which the tourists swarm. Available from half tide, this small, oval harbour with massive granite boulder walls is the epitome of a Cornish fishing village, though long past its heyday during the mackerel and pilchard fishery. The residue of the fishing fleet once based here is now kept in Newlyn, but a few local pot, net and angling boats can be seen lying on fore and aft trots along with a number of small pleasure craft.

From early November until the end of March, the harbour is closed completely with heavy wood baulks across the mouth, and few winters pass without some damage to the seemingly impregnable walls as the south-easterly gales roll into Mount's Bay. Privately administered by its own Harbour Commissioners, the unfortunate dominance of car parking beside the harbour and on the quays does pay for its upkeep, and the small charge for visiting yachts contributes to it too. In suitable conditions, the harbour provides a worthwhile diversion for an overnight stay or just a daytime visit.

APPROACHES AND ANCHORAGE

Approaching across Mount's Bay the houses of Mousehole climbing the hillside are easy to spot to the south of Newlyn, although St Clement's Isle, a low rocky outcrop with a small obelisk on its highest point just east of the harbour mouth, will be lost against the land until much closer.

Approaching from the south, from Penzer Point the island is much easier to see as it lies clear of the land. You can anchor south of a line between the obelisk on St Clement's Island and the harbour entrance, taking care to avoid the submarine power cable running between the north-west side of the island and the mainland shore which is used to light the tableau that is erected on the island at Christmas. If you are merely waiting on the tide, let go to the south-west of Shag rock.

Although local fishing boats regularly use the inshore passage to the north of the island, there are rocks on both sides and a very narrow channel at LW. Strangers should always use the approach from the south of the island, which is far wider and safer, and enter mid-way between the island and the shore. Beware Tom Kneebone ledge (least depth 0.9m LAT) 100m south of the obelisk – do not cut the corner, but enter on a north-westerly course, midway between the island and the south pier head before turning in towards the harbour entrance as it begins to open.

Closer inshore, about 100m south and slightly east of the entrance, isolated Chimney Rock dries 2.3m, but the biggest hazard is probably the many pot buoys around the island and along the shore – be particularly wary in the approach and, if remaining at anchor overnight, a riding light is essential.

BERTHING

After half-tide there is plenty of water inside the harbour. As a guide, there are a number of horizontal concrete ledges on the outer corner of the northern wall, and **if only the top three are showing** there will be a good eight feet inside the outer ends of the harbour walls.

Visitors should berth on the South Pier where you can dry out alongside on a firm sandy bottom, but keep clear of the stone steps as these are used by the local boats for landing fish and crews. Bilge-keelers intending to dry out should not attempt to anchor among the fore and aft moorings for local boats which fill the centre of the harbour without the harbour master's permission. As there is no harbour office, the harbour master, Mr Frank Wallis (Tel: 01736 731511), will probably wander down in the evening to collect the dues – a flat rate of £10 a night, (£12 for multihulls). He can also point you in the direction of the water tap at the inner end of the quay, while a public toilet is located in the car park.

Mousehole is a bustling, colourful place where

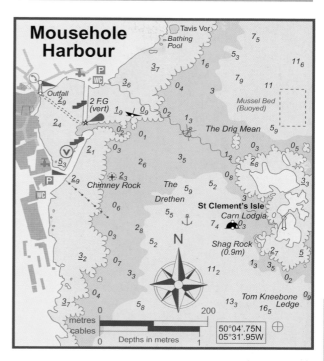

Mousehole is another attractive drying harbour. Visitors normally berth on the South Pier, right. Note St Michael's Mount in distance

visitors bravely compete with the traffic trying to squeeze through the narrow streets. Its unique charm has not only survived the onslaught of recent years, but also considerable mayhem in the Middle Ages when the village, then the most important port in Cornwall, was raided and burnt to the ground by marauding Spaniards in 1595, and Keigwin House, with its splendid granite pillared porch, now tucked away in the back streets, was one of the few buildings to survive. Mousehole also enjoys a certain fame today as the home of Dolly Pentreath who died in 1777, reputedly the last person to speak Cornish as her native tongue, and a commemorative plaque can be found on the wall of her cottage

close by the harbour. Perhaps she would have been able to provide the answer (although presumably few of us would have been able to understand it . . .) to the village's curious name, for which there seems to be no definitive explanation. Remember, though, that it is always pronounced as *Mowzull* and never, never as *Mouse Hole*!

After Dolly Pentreath, Tom Bawcock is probably the other most celebrated former inhabitant, and Tom Bawcock's Eve on 23rd December recalls the time when this fabled local fisherman put to sea in desperation after weeks of gales, returning with a fine catch of seven different kinds of fish to provide Christmas feast for the starving village. Hopefully you will not be visiting by sea at this time of year – not only will you find the storm baulks in place, but you will also be confronted by the infamous Starry Gazy Pie, a hideous creation with the heads of the seven varieties of fish poking through its crust.

FACILITIES

Starry Gazy apart, most other basic provisions are available in the village: groceries, off-licence, post office, butcher and newsagent. Eating places comprise several cafés, a good fish and chip shop and the Ship Inn which, in spite of the tourism, has managed to retain a distinctively village pub

atmosphere. There is also a small, reasonably priced restaurant adjoining the Ship (Tel: 01736 731234). On the outskirts of the village on the Newlyn road, the Old Coastguard Hotel (Tel: 01736 731222) does meals for non-residents and has fine views of Mount's Bay.

Just about everything else is obtainable in Penzance, to which there is a regular bus service. The more energetic can hire bikes just outside the village on the Newlyn Road and follow the new bike trail running along the coast through the remains of the old Penlee Quarry workings. Whether you need to work up an appetite or not, the fine walk along the cliffs to the south of the village towards Penzer Point and the beautifully named Lamorna Cove should not be missed. The Wink pub can provide refreshment en route. Children will also be fascinated by the Wild Bird Hospital on Raginnis Hill, on the south side of the village.

Mousehole, like many of its counterparts in Cornwall, has a famous male voice choir. If you are lucky you may hear soft Cornish voices drifting in a strangely haunting harmony across the natural arena of the harbour into the gathering twilight around the bay, for sometimes they assemble on the quayside on balmy summer's evenings. It will be one of those evocative moments that you, like me, will never forget!

Mousehole – the epitome of a Cornish fishing village

INTRODUCTION TO THE ISLES OF SCILLY

'White gleaming beaches, rocky hills covered with heath and gorse . . .', the spectacular south east side of Tresco looks positively Caribbean on a fine day like this!

Tides	HW Dover +0607
Range	St Mary's MHWS 6.0m–MHWN 4.3m, MLWN 2.0m–MLWS 0.7m. See special note (6) on tides at end of this section
Charts	BA: 34, 883, 1148, 2565. SC5603. Stanford: 2 . Imray: C7
Waypoints	See Passages, Mainland to Scilly
Hazards	Many unmarked rocks and shallow ledges, large areas between islands dry. No harbour offering all weather security
Overnight charge	St Mary's Harbour Authority mooring or anchoring £13. Tresco Estate mooring £13, at anchor £5. Tean Sound Hotel mooring £10

'A straggling collection of barren rocks, wonderfully broken up, narrow strips of land bordered with marvellously white gleaming beaches, rocky hills covered with heath and gorse, intersected by ravines running down to the loveliest little bays, piles and piles of strangely weird grey, lichen covered rocks,

little dales where bask a few isolated cottages festooned with mesembryantheums and giant geraniums sheltered by a few tangled tamarisks . . .'

Frank Cowper, on his first visit to the Isles of Scilly in 1892, was clearly impressed by what he had found; over a century on, his appraisal still holds good.

Set in water of breathtaking clarity, this tantalising archipelago of 48 islands, some little more than glorified rocks, extends over an area of approximately 45 square miles between 21 and 31 miles WSW of Land's End. Only six islands are

inhabited, St Mary's, St Martin's, Tresco, Bryher, St Agnes and Gugh. Of the rest, 18 are described by the Admiralty Channel Pilot as 'being capable of bearing grass, the remainder are barren'.

Their warm oceanic climate prompted the Romans to name the area *Sillinae Insulae*, meaning Sun Isles, from which Scilly now derives its name. This is something of a moot point, for although many loosely refer to the islands as the Scillies – and I have been guilty of this – the locals let it be known that they prefer their archipelago to be called the Isles of Scilly or just

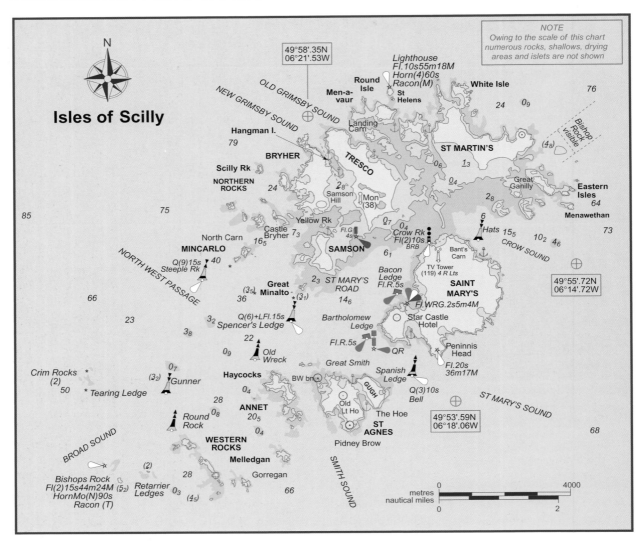

The map/chart labels (reading as placed on the chart):

Isles of Scilly

N

NOTE
Owing to the scale of this chart numerous rocks, shallows, drying areas and islets are not shown

49°58'.35N
06°21'.53W

Lighthouse
Fl.10s55m18M
Horn(4)60s
Racon(M)

Round Isle
Men-a-vaur
St Helens

White Isle

76

24   0₉

OLD GRIMSBY SOUND

NEW GRIMSBY SOUND

Landing Carn

Bishop Rock visible

(4₈)

Hangman I.
79

BRYHER

TRESCO

ST MARTIN'S

0₆   1₃

Scilly Rk

NORTHERN ROCKS

24

0₄

Great Ganilly

Eastern Isles
64

75

28°
Samson Hill

Mon (38)

2₈

Menawethan

85

Castle Bryher
16₅

Yellow Rk

Fl.G 4s

Crow Rk
Fl(2)10s
BRB

6
Hats 15₅   10₂ 4₆   73

CROW SOUND

North Carn

MINCARLO

Q(9)15s
Steeple Rk   40

7₃

SAMSON

6₁

0₇ 0₄

Bant's Carn

NORTH WEST PASSAGE

Great Minalto
36

(35₄)

2₃ ST MARY'S ROAD
14₆

Bacon Ledge
Fl.R.5s

TV Tower
(119) 4 R Lts

SAINT MARY'S

49°55'.72N
06°14'.72W

*(3₁)

Q(6)+LFl.15s
Spencer's Ledge 3₂

Bartholomew Ledge

Fl.WRG.2s5m4M

66

23

3₈

22

Old Wreck

Fl.R.5s

Star Castle Hotel

0₉

QR

Fl.20s
36m17M

Peninnis Head

Crim Rocks (2)
50

(3₂) Gunner

Haycocks

BW bn

Great Smith

Spanish Ledge

Q(3)10s
Bell

ST MARY'S SOUND

0₇

* Tearing Ledge

0₄

GUGH

28

ANNET
20₅

Old Lt Ho

The Hoe

ST AGNES

49°53'.59N
06°18'.06W

68

Round Rock
0₈

0₄

Pidney Brow

BROAD SOUND

WESTERN ROCKS

Melledgan

Gorregan

SMITH SOUND

(2)

28

66

Bishops Rock
Fl(2)15s44m24M
HornMo(N)90s
Racon (T)

(5₂)

Retarrier Ledges

0₃ (4₅)

metres
nautical miles

0   4000

0   2

---

plain Scilly. Nor do they take kindly to being described as Cornish – they are Scillonians, most definitely, and proud of it!

In fine and settled weather it is hard to believe that you are still so close to mainland Britain. It is easy to imagine, if momentarily, that you are in a far more exotic location, given a few more palm trees in addition to those that already flourish here. However, such delights are, alas, not always so lightly enjoyed! As a cruising ground the Isles of Scilly can have a definite downside. It is not an area to be trifled with, and a clear understanding of the potential problems will go a long way to ensuring a successful visit.

The first consideration is getting there. It will involve an offshore passage of over 20 miles, admittedly not a great distance, but one that takes you out into the Atlantic and a particularly exposed sea area renowned for sudden changes of weather and poor visibility. With strong tides,

shipping, including the Land's End Traffic Separation Scheme (TSS), and the rarely absent Atlantic ground swell, this is no place for the inexperienced. Even for the experienced, it can be a very unpleasant stretch of water to get caught out in.

The second consideration is Scilly itself. Apart from the obvious dangers of any group of islands strewn with rocks, most unmarked, large areas of shallow water and strong and often unpredictable localised tidal streams and races, it also lacks a harbour or anchorage that can be considered secure in all weather. As each anchorage is only safe in certain combinations of wind and sea, any amount of time spent in the islands will inevitably involve shifting as the weather changes, often in deteriorating conditions.

Once among the islands, distances are not great, usually only a matter of a few miles, but the problems of riding out bad weather have

The Isles of Scilly, a tantalising archipelago ... Hell Bay, Bryher, looking east over Tresco Flats to distant St Mary's. The Eastern Isles and Crow Sound, top left

Chapter 5

been greatly exacerbated by the demands made on the available anchorages by the ever increasing numbers of visiting yachts, particularly during August when large numbers of French boats arrive.

The third consideration is the relative lack of facilities for visiting yachts compared with the mainland. Although the past few years have seen a dramatic increase in the number of visitors' moorings in St Mary's Pool, New Grimsby Sound, Old Grimsby Sound and Tean Sound, overnight berthing alongside and afloat is not available anywhere in the islands, and **in most other places you will have to anchor**. Simple enough, one might think, but the holding ground in most places is of fairly indifferent quality, either fine loose sand, sand covered with weed or weed covered rocks.

Finally, owners of deeper draught boats should be aware of one other little mentioned factor which can at times seriously detract from full enjoyment of Scilly – the all-pervading Atlantic ground swell. This was particularly evident during July 1994 when much of this research was carried out and it plagued us in most anchorages, usually at its worst towards HW and when the wind was at its lightest – calm weather does not

necessarily mean a calm sea in Scilly.

As one restless night succeeded another, I became convinced that the ideal craft for exploration of these waters is a boat of moderate draught, able to edge close inshore or, even better, a bilge keeler able to dry out completely, for then the options for a more relaxing stay increase considerably.

However, the object of all this is not to deter, although this is often the reaction on first perusal of the large scale chart. The hazards seem myriad and the pilotage overly complicated, not least the abundance of transits which are traditionally associated with Scilly as leading and clearing lines for passages and hazards. For many, these can prove confusing, particularly on first arrival when the topography is itself bewildering enough. The 307°T leading line to clear the Spanish and Bartholomew Ledges in St Mary's sound, 'North Carn on Mincarlo in line with south side of Great Minalto', is a typical example, as Great Minalto, in spite of its name, is a actually a much smaller rock than Mincarlo!

The leading lines are not critical to navigation. They are an aid as long as you can identify them, but often the visibility is such that the more distant marks are indistinguishable.

Transits are also useful to gauge any tidal set across your course, but if you do decide to try using them, leave nothing to chance. Many rocks have a tendency to look similar – once you believe you have identified your leading marks, check that they tally with the heading on the compass – remembering that all bearings are True From Seaward and will need to be corrected for magnetic variation. If in any doubt, don't panic, concentrate instead on making your approach in the normal fashion using any other visible criteria you have at your disposal.

The choice of anchorages I have described is limited to those most likely to be used during a first visit, and I am also assuming that most readers will be approaching from the mainland. The western side of the islands has by far the greater number of isolated offshore hazards and in my opinion it should be avoided, certainly by newcomers to the area. For this reason the western approaches through **Broad Sound**, **Smith Sound** and the **North West Passage** are deliberately not covered in any great detail, although the latter, formerly known as the **North Channel**, has been much improved with two significant buoys – see Passage, Scilly from North Cornish Coast. If you are keen to see the Western Rocks at close quarters there is much to recommend a trip in one of the local pleasure boats . . .

There are, of course, numerous other possible anchorages and more intricate passages requiring suitable weather and local knowledge that might appeal to the more adventurous or those who have already explored the more familiar places. However, my only intention here is to try and ensure a safe and pleasant stay in these waters. To this end, my own pointers for a first and, hopefully, trouble free visit to the islands would be summarised as follows:

1. Have a well found boat with a reliable engine, a crew of adequate strength and experience, and, absolutely essential, up to date editions of Admiralty charts 883 (Isles of Scilly, St Mary's and the principle off-islands) and 34 (Isles of Scilly), which includes tidal charts for the islands, or their excellent Small Craft Folio 5603 (Falmouth to Padstow including the Isles of Scilly).

   The chartlets accompanying this text are simplified and much detail has been omitted to assist clarity. They must therefore not be used for navigation.

   Familiarise yourself with the layout of the area in advance. Although the pilotage seems complicated it is, for the most part, more straightforward after you have got your initial bearings. Once you have arrived make every

A Scilly pilot gig, with very appropriate name. . .

effort to identify and memorise salient features – it is surprising how quickly you begin to feel more at home.

The clarity of the water enables the rare treat of eyeball navigation and a good lookout will be able to spot most dangers long before you hit them. Most of the rocks are covered with long growths of bright green weed that are usually visible on or near the surface at anything other than HW.

2. Ideally, choose a spell of fine settled weather, with neap tides, and arrive in daylight with ample time in hand to find a suitable berth. Do not be tempted to make a dash for the islands if there is any hint of deteriorating weather in the offing. You are far better off remaining on the mainland.

3. Try to visit the islands in June or July. If possible avoid August when they are at their busiest and the weather has a tendency to be less settled.

4. Have a more than adequate amount of ground tackle on board to cope with all eventualities. Most boats will normally have a CQR, Bruce or Danforth as their main anchor, but here you cannot afford to skimp on the size of your kedge(s). With the poor holding and fine sand

choose your anchorage not only with regard to the prevailing conditions, but also to what might happen within the next 12 hours. Before settling in overnight, be certain that you will be able to leave in the dark by working out an exit course to steer – at all states of the tide! Always have an alternative anchorage in mind before you need to find one.

In addition to the normal BBC shipping forecasts, Radio Cornwall shipping and inshore forecasts can be obtained in Scilly on FM 96.0. Following an announcement on VHF Ch 16 indicating which listening channel to select, Falmouth Coastguard transmits shipping forecasts for Scilly on VHF Ch 23 every four hours, commencing at 0140 UT.

If there is a serious likelihood of bad weather in the offing, and the timing permits, do not overlook the possibility of making a speedy return to the mainland before its onset. Remember that Mount's Bay can be dangerous to approach in heavy weather from the south-east and south and that the tidal dock at Penzance is only accessible from two hours before to one hour after local HW.

in many anchorages, I have found that my CQR does not always perform at its normal best and most local boatmen seem to favour a good sized Fisherman or Danforth. I would recommend one of each in addition to your normal ground tackle, with ample chain and warp of adequate weight.

Be sure you know how to use it all! Lower anchor until you feel it touch the ground, go astern and slowly veer the chain to lay it out along the bottom, allowing at least three times the anticipated depth at HW (five times the depth if using chain and warp). Belay the cable, go astern gently at first to ensure that the anchor bites, then increase the power to test the hold. If you feel the chain whilst doing this, you can tell if the anchor is biting – or not! If the chain or warp jumps and loses tension it has definitely not taken. Don't take a chance, but start again.

There is much sense in the old maxim that it is better to be safe than sorry and always lay a kedge. **Certainly, if you are leaving your vessel unattended for any length of time this is definitely recommended.**

5. Keep a careful watch on the weather and be constantly aware of any potential changes, particularly from the direction to which the wind is most likely to shift. Accordingly,

6. Once in the islands, don't hurry. Take life at a gentler pace and don't take chances, least of all with the tide. The tidal streams are very unpredictable in the close proximity to the islands and for short periods they can often attain much greater strength than indicated in the Admiralty chartlets and Pilot. Predicted tidal heights are particularly susceptible to the atmospheric pressure – during prolonged spells of high pressure they can sometimes be almost a metre less than anticipated, and remember, too, that the range of nearly 6m at springs will considerably reduce the amount of space in many anchorages. Conversely, with just a 2.3m range at neaps there is a lot more water available.

However, if you plan your moves on a rising tide, ideally after half flood, most of the trickier, shallower passages can be tackled with impunity. Try them once the ebb has set in and you've no one to blame except yourself when things go wrong!

Following the local trip boats is not recommended – their skippers know these waters intimately, many of their short cuts pass rocks within a hair's breadth and they seem able to skim over the shallows on little more than a heavy dew. Be particularly wary of the large Bryher ferry, *Firethorn*; in spite of her size, she draws little more than 2ft!

7. Do not impede local boatmen, fishermen or other commercial craft; they are earning a living, you are there for fun, and they do not take kindly to finding yachts lying on their moorings when they return after a hard day's work, or blocking the quay steps when trying to embark or disembark passengers. If you are in any doubt – ask!

8. Water is a valuable commodity in Scilly, and you will have to pay to obtain it alongside. Make sure you fill your tanks on the mainland. As food and booze (which is all freighted in by sea or air) is inevitably more expensive, it is also worth stocking up before you leave. Gas refills are only obtainable on St Mary's, so make sure you always have a spare.

9. A number of the uninhabited islands are important bird breeding areas. The following are closed to visitors between 15th April and 20th August: Annet, The Western Rocks, Crebewethan, Gorregan, Melledgan, Rosevear, Norrard Rocks, Castle Bryher, Illiswillgig, Maiden Bower, Mincarlo, Scilly Rock, Stony Island, Green Island (off Samson) and Men-a-vaur.

In addition Tean is closed on a voluntary basis between 15th April and 20th July, when ringed plovers and terns are nesting, and certain areas of other islands have clearly marked nesting sites, such as the southern end of Gugh which visitors are asked to avoid. Nesting and territorial birds, particularly gulls, can be extremely aggressive. They will attempt to ward off intruders with alarming swoops to the head that are potentially injurious and definitely frightening for smaller children and timid souls like me!

10. Beware pot buoys! They will be encountered both in the outer approaches and anywhere among the islands. With such a wide selection to choose from, wreck diving is also very popular and you should give any boat flying international code flag 'A' (vertical white with blue swallow tail) a wide berth.

As Cowper concluded: 'A stay of a few days in these bewildering islands should afford most people a good deal of pleasure. There is perpetual variety. Every rock and bay and hill offers some new view, and the contemplation of this decomposing heap of stones in the midst of the ever-vexed Atlantic must arouse a wondering curiosity, if not an enthusiastic admiration . . .'

Solitude in St Helen's Pool

PASSAGES
MAINLAND TO ISLES OF SCILLY

PASSAGES

SCILLY FROM THE SOUTH CORNISH COAST

**(For safety information, charts
and performance chart see:-
Passages – The Manacles to Land's End)**

Waypoints

1 **Manacles** (0.5M due E of buoy)
  50°02′·82N / 05°01′·14W

3 **Lizard**
  (turning point 3M due S of light)
  49°54′·62N / 05°12′·14W

6 **Runnel Stone**
  (0.5M SW of buoy)
  50°00′·89N / 05°40′·94W

8 **Wolf Rock**
  (2M due N of lighthouse)
  49°58′·74N / 05°48′·56W

9 **Wolf Rock**
  (2M due S of lighthouse)
  49°54′·74N / 05°48′·56W

10 **Crow Sound approach**
  (1M due E of Tolls Island)
  49°55′·72N / 06°15′·04W

  Hats south cardinal buoy
  (Crow Sound)
  49°56′·21N / 06°17′·14W

11 **St Mary's Sound approach**
  (4ca due S of Peninnis Head)
  49°53′·88N / 06°18′·23W

  Spanish Ledge east cardinal buoy
  (St Mary's Sound)
  49°53′·94N / 06°18′·86W

Scilly approach from the north: Round Island light, St Helen's and Men-a-vaur, right, with White Island distant left

Approaching Scilly from the east. At about eight miles off, these low lying islands are only just beginning to show and appear as one unbroken line.

Wolf Rock always provides a useful check on your progress

Given a well-found boat, suitable weather and preparation, the passage from the English mainland should pose no major problem. Given unsuitable weather it should not even be contemplated. On a clear day, from the high ground of Lands End the islands are often visible, but with the daymark on St Martin's rising to a mere 56m and the highest ground on St Mary's 48m, they normally do not begin to show from sea level until about 12 miles distant – often it will be a lot less. As you sail ever further away from the land and, it seems, far out into the Atlantic, the doubts do not take long to crowd in – it is always worth remembering that one tends to anticipate a landfall a lot sooner than it usually appears.

The sight of the all-white ferry *RMS Scillonian III* helps to dispel a bit of unease – she sails a direct course from the Runnel Stone to St Mary's, leaving Penzance Monday to Friday at 0915, and returning from St Mary's at 1630. Saturday sailings vary depending on the time of year, but from early June to the end of August the ship leaves Penzance at 1100 and returns from St Mary's at 1500. There are no Sunday sailings. Subject to the tide and weather, she makes her approach into the islands either through Crow Sound or St Mary's Sound.

The frequent British International helicopters are direct flights from Penzance to St Mary's or Tresco, and the Skybus flights to St Mary's are from Land's End and Newquay Airports, on the north Cornish coast. In the season, the odds are also very much in favour of there being other pleasure craft bound in either direction. . .

GPS will doubtless do much to boost the confidence but, as always, a conventional and regular DR plot should be maintained at all times. Radar will hopefully confirm the island's existence from afar and the Racons on Wolf Rock (Morse 'T' 10M), Bishop Rock (Morse 'T' 18M), Round Island (Morse 'M' 10M) and Seven Stones (Morse 'O' 15M) should prove invaluable.

In the event of fog, a sudden reduction in visibility or an unexpected deterioration in the weather, the option of aborting the passage and returning to a mainland port should never be overlooked, however frustrating it might seem. In any of these conditions, an approach to Scilly is risky at the very least and potentially extremely dangerous. With so many offlying rocks and unpredictable tidal streams, the fog signals should be regarded as a warning to stay well clear of the islands and not an invitation to attempt an approach: Round Island (Horn (4) 60s), Wolf Rock (Horn 30s), Longships (Horn 10s), Seven Stones (Horn (3) 60s) – do not confuse with Round Island), Bishop Rock (Horn Mo (N) 90s), Spanish Ledge buoy (bell), Runnel Stone (whistle) and Tater Du (Horn (2) 30s).

Do not be tempted to run for the islands in heavy weather in anticipation of finding shelter: the overfalls and heavy seas in the approaches during gale force conditions, particularly with wind against tide, could in themselves easily overwhelm small craft. Should you find yourself in trouble, all rescues in this area are co-ordinated by Falmouth MRCC VHF Ch 16 call sign *Falmouth Coastguard* (working Ch 67, MSI broadcasts on Ch 23). Lifeboats are based at Newlyn, Sennen, St Ives and St Mary's.

A clear spell of settled anticyclonic weather would seem to be the ideal, for then the odds are in favour of a good easterly breeze to whisk you out to the west. However, in such conditions, fine weather haze is more than likely to be prevailing and the visibility often much diminished.

Given the low lying nature of the islands, there is much to be said for a night passage, timed to arrive soon after daybreak, for this busy stretch of water is well lit with the Runnel Stone south cardinal buoy (Q(6) + LFl 15s), Carn Base west cardinal buoy (Q (9) 15s) and the lighthouses at Tater Du (Fl (3) 15s 20M), Wolf Rock (Fl 15s 16M), Longships (Iso WR 10s W16M R15/13M), Seven Stones Light float (Fl (3) 30s 25M), Round Island (Fl 10s 18M), Peninnis Light (Fl 20s 17M) and Bishop Rock (Fl (2) 15s 24M) – all of which should be visible long before you would normally pick up any detail in daylight.

Although a night entry into the islands is not recommended for a first time visit, it is feasible with due care using St Mary's Sound, which is lit by Peninnis lighthouse (Fl 20s 17M), Spanish

St Martin's daymark, looking north-west to Round Island

Approach to St Mary's Sound from south east, Spanish Ledges buoy, centre, Woolpack Point, St Mary's, right, with Samson in distance beyond

Ledge buoy (Q (3) 10s), Bartholomew Ledge beacon (QR), North Bartholomew buoy (Fl R 5s), Bacon Ledge buoy (Fl R 5s), the leading marks into St Mary's Pool, lower (Iso RW (vert) 2s), upper (Oc WR (vert) 10s), and the (Fl RWG 2s) sectored light on the outer end of St Mary's harbour wall.

Bound for Scilly from the south Cornish coast, you will most probably be making the passage direct from Falmouth or the Helford, a distance of just under 60 miles to St Mary's, or from Mount's Bay where it is about 36 miles from Newlyn to St Mary's. In both cases the timing will invariably revolve around the tidal considerations, and the need to arrive in the islands in daylight.

FALMOUTH BAY TO ST MARY'S

To carry a fair tide south and west from Falmouth Bay around the tidal gate of the Lizard, it is best to leave at about three hours after HW Falmouth (three hours before HW Dover). This will then ensure a fair tide for the next six hours which should get you well across Mount's Bay and hopefully clear of the mainland. (See: Passages, Manacles to Land's End – page 171).

The rhumb line course of 270°T from a point about three miles south of the Lizard to Peninnis Head, at the entrance to Saint Mary's Sound, is a distance of 43 miles and will take you two miles south of Wolf Rock, which lies seven miles south-west of the Runnel Stone, providing a useful check on the tidal set.

Wolf Rock lighthouse is a slender grey granite column with a helipad and it can often prove difficult to spot, particularly if it has the morning sun upon it. Give the lighthouse a berth of at least a mile for, although the rock only covers a small area, it creates strong tidal eddies and heavy overfalls immediately to the west in bad weather. Traditionally, the Wolf earned it curious name from its voracious appetite for passing ships, and the first attempt to mark it in 1791 was

a drole reflection of this. A 20ft iron mast was erected on the rock by Lieutenant Henry Smith, topped with a replica of wolf's head, its open jaws forming a sound box that produced a hideous wail as the wind blew through. As predicted, it vanished in the first winter storms and it was not until 1840 that a 46ft high stone beacon was erected by the Trinity House engineer, James Walker, who later masterminded the present lighthouse, a magnificent feat of engineering standing 110ft above MHW.

Although begun in 1862 using pre-formed interlocking granite blocks shipped from Penzance, the structure was not completed until July 1869 and was brought into service on 1st January 1870. Always regarded as one of the most difficult lights to relieve, it became the first offshore light to be fitted, in 1973, with a helipad. In common with most offshore lighthouses, it is now unmanned.

West of the Wolf you will encounter large vessels emerging from the **Land's End Traffic Separation Scheme** (TSS). The northbound traffic lane begins four miles west of the Longships, the southbound lane half-a-mile east of the Seven Stones light float. Both lanes are three miles wide with a two-mile wide separation zone, and are marked on Admiralty charts 1148 and 2565.

As with all TSS, **you must cross the traffic lane on a heading as near as practicable at right angles to the general direction of traffic flow**. This means that you must keep your vessel in full profile to the oncoming shipping with your fore and aft line at right angles to the traffic and not your track through the water. You must also cross the TSS as rapidly as possible; if your speed is less than three knots over the ground, motor.

In good visibility the islands will begin to appear as a seemingly arbitary jumble of jagged humps along the horizon, very confusing at first and bearing little resemblance to what you are probably expecting. Initially you are only seeing the highest ground – closer-to they take on a more identifiable shape, but remain confusing as the overlapping effect makes them appear as one continuous

Entering St Mary's Sound, Peninnis Head with Porth Cressa beach on left

land mass rather than separate islands. However, once you begin to identify the conspicuous landmarks, things rapidly slip into place.

The red and white horizontal striped daymark is on the NE corner of St Martin's, and should not be confused with the all-white lighthouse on Round Island, at the NW corner of the islands. The pyramid-shaped island of Hanjague, just east of St Martin's, is also very distinctive, particularly in early morning sunlight. This and the rest of the **Eastern Isles** soon begin to detach themselves.

St Mary's is most easily identified by the tall TV mast (FR vert) and the greater amount of visible greenery and trees. Approaching from the east, the sight of a prominent white lighthouse seemingly at the southern end of St Mary's can be confusing. This is not Peninnis light (a much more diminutive structure), but the old lighthouse on St Agnes immediately to the west of St Mary's. From this approach the two islands look as if they are one.

There are two main entry channels into St Mary's Road when approaching from the east – the northernmost via Crow Sound requires sufficient rise of tide as you will have to pass over Crow Bar (least depth 1m). This and the other shallows in the area tend to deter most first timers who usually sensibly opt for the deeper and better marked southern entrance through St Mary's Sound.

ENTRY THROUGH ST MARY'S SOUND

St Mary's Sound lies between St Mary's and Gugh/ St Agnes. Although nearly a mile wide, the navigable area is restricted by two groups of rocky shoals along its southern flank, the Spanish Ledges (least depth 0.9m) and the Bartholomew Ledges (least depth 0.6m), which effectively reduces the width of the sound to under two cables in places. Approaching from seaward, the entrance to the Sound is marked to port by the Spanish Ledges

BYB east cardinal buoy (Q (3) 10s), and to starboard by the small iron lighthouse structure on Peninnis Head (Fl 20s), which is fringed by low cliffs with distinctive and sculptural rock formations.

There is plenty of depth in the approach and in the sound, but care should be taken if arriving near HW to avoid the Gilstone (dries 4.0m) and lies four cables due east of Peninnis light. When the rock is submerged, if there is any sea running, both it and the Gilstone Ledges further inshore are normally visible from the seas surging and breaking around them. Keeping all of Menawethan (the easternmost of the Eastern Isles) well open of Newfoundland Point, the easternmost extreme of St Mary's, you will pass to seaward of the Gilstone. Turn into the Sound once Peninnis Light is bearing just north of west. Immediately west of Peninnis Inner Head, the entrance to Porth Cressa is easy to identify – a long, wide inlet, with a sandy beach and houses at its head and, if the weather is favourable, many boats anchored within.

From here the long straight line of the Garrison fortifications mirrors the line of low cliffs forming the coast. Close inshore, the Woolpack YB south cardinal beacon marking the Woolpack Rock (dries 0.6m) should be left on your starboard hand. The red Bartholomew Ledges beacon (QR) identifies these dangerous rocks (least depth 0.8m) at the inner end of St Mary's Sound – leave this and the North Bartholomew red can buoy (Fl R 5s) on your port hand before curving gently northwards into St Mary's Road.

If there is much ground swell from the west, as there invariably is, the sight of the sea breaking on the Bartholomew Ledges can be intimidating and, with a wind of any strength from the east or south-east against the tide, a surprisingly nasty sea can build up in St Mary's Sound.

The ingoing (NW) tidal stream begins at HW Dover –0310; the outgoing (SE) stream begins at HW Dover +0245 and attains a spring rate of nearly two knots and about three-quarters of a knots at neaps.

Approaching Crow Bar, Innisidgen on left, 'Hats' buoy and distant 'Crow Rock' beacon just left of yacht

In quiet conditions there are no further hazards from the North Bartholomew buoy as long as you keep at least a couple of cables off the south and west side of St Mary's. Although Woodcock Ledge is covered 2.7m, in common with most of the other submerged rocky ledges in the islands it can be a serious problem if there is any ground sea running, when the depth can be much reduced in the troughs, and dangerous if the seas are breaking. To safely avoid the Woodcock Ledge keep further out into St Mary's Road and do not begin to turn towards St Mary's Harbour until the anchorage is well open and you can see the inner end of the quay. (See: St Mary's Pool approach from south, page 212).

ENTRY THROUGH CROW SOUND

Crow Sound lies between the north eastern shore of St Mary's and south west of the Eastern Isles. Although wide at its mouth, any approach is

'Crow Rock' beacon coming onto transit with distant South Hill, Samson, will give the line of deepest water over Crow Bar

conditional on having sufficient rise of tide to pass over Crow Bar, which dries between 0.7m and 0.5m over much of its length, but has a narrow channel (least depth 0.8m) between its southern end and Bar Point on St Mary's. Watermill Cove, on the northern side of St Mary's, is a handy anchorage to wait for the tide.

When approaching from the east, if there is a sea running do not cut the corner past the Eastern Isles, but hold well to the south to avoid the shallower waters of the Ridge and Trinity Rocks. These can often kick up uncomfortable seas and they break heavily in bad weather.

With the north-east going tidal stream which begins HW Dover +0500, a race develops across the entrance to Crow Sound for a couple of hours and this can extend up to two miles offshore. In reasonable weather this seldom presents a problem, but with a strong wind against tide it can be dangerous to small craft. Races also form to the east of the Eastern Isles, off Menawethan and Hanjague.

Within Crow Sound, the streams are much weaker, rarely exceeding one knot at springs,

running (NW) into the Sound for three hours from HW Dover –0100, then out of the sound (ESE) for eight hours, beginning HW Dover +0200.

Once the Eastern Isles are well abeam on your starboard hand, you should be able to spot the unlit Hats YB south cardinal buoy about a cable ENE of Innisidgen, a low and jagged peninsula which rises to a distinctive conical rocky point. Pass just south of the Hats buoy, but do not edge too close to Innisidgen as there are a couple of offlying rocks (drying 1.3m and 1.3m). Instead, maintain a course parallel to the shore until the Crow Rock isolated danger beacon (Fl (2)10s) is well open of Bar Point, a long sandy beach backed by dunes and higher ground covered in trees.

You are now looking south-west down the full length of St Mary's Roads: Tresco, wooded and fringed with a long white sandy beach lies to starboard and in the far distance the two rounded green hills of Samson should be easy to spot. South Hill is the left hand of the two, and once Crow Rock beacon is centred on this you have the line of the deepest water over the bar.

Crow Rock is steep-to and can be passed on either side; from here on the depths begin to increase noticeably as you enter St Mary's Road. If beating, beware of the Pots (dries 1.8m) and Round Rock (dries 1.5m), which lie nearly half-a-mile off the southern shore of Tresco. When covered, they can be avoided by either holding Crow Rock beacon on a back bearing of 029°T, or ahead, by keeping the old lighthouse on St Agnes in transit with Steval, the low island on the distant westernmost point of St Mary's, to give a course of 209°T.

PASSAGE FROM MOUNT'S BAY

A departure from Mount's Bay has the advantage of not having to worry about the tidal gate of the Lizard. However, to maximise on the tide, it is probably best to push the foul tide out of Mount's Bay for an hour or so by leaving about three hours before HW Dover. By the time you reach the Runnel Stone it should be setting well to the SW, and then W for the next four hours, giving you a good shove on your way until two hours after HW Dover, when it will be running northwards.

To be able to depart at this time, you will have to be lying in Newlyn or moored or anchored off Penzance, Mousehole or St Michael's Mount as the tidal dock at Penzance does not open until two hours before local HW (HW Dover +0550). If you leave then you will have a foul tide for the next three hours and a strong tide setting you south for a further three.

PASSAGES

SCILLY FROM THE NORTH CORNISH COAST

Waypoints

12 **Cape Cornwall** (2M due west of summit)
50°07'·63N / 05°45'·71W
Longships (0.75M due W of lighthouse)
50°04'·04N / 05°45'·95W

13 **Seven Stones** (4M due S of light float)
49°59'·62N / 06°04'·34W
Seven Stones Light float:
50°03'·65N / 06°04'·37W

14 **Seven Stones** (4M due N of light float)
50°07'·62N / 06°04'·34W

15 **Round Island** (6ca due N of lighthouse)
49°59'·35N / 06°19'·40W
New Grimsby approach
(4ca NW Kettle Rock)
49°58'·43N / 06°21'·59W
Eastern Isles (6ca E of Mouls Rock)
49°57'·16N / 06°13'·64W
Crow Sound approach
(1M due E of Tolls Is)
49°55'·72N / 06°15'·04W

From the north Cornish coast, Padstow or St Ives are probable points of departure, aiming for a landfall on the north western side of the islands, most probably New Grimsby Sound. (See: Tresco (page 225) for approach and entry directions). It is about 70m from Padstow to New Grimsby, and slightly more to St Mary's. From St Ives the distance is about 40 miles.

If you are lying in the tidal basin at Padstow, you can conveniently leave about an hour after local HW (HW Dover –0550) and you should then carry a fair tide along the length of the north Cornish coast and beyond for the next seven hours, after which it will become north going from two hours after HW Dover.

From St Ives Bay, again leave an hour or so after local HW (HW Dover –0605) and you will have at least six hours mostly favourable tide. From Cape Cornwall the direction of the prevailing wind will most likely dictate your course to the islands and whether you will pass to the north or south of the

Inner approach to New Grimsby from north; Cromwell's Castle, Hangman Island and moorings clearly visible

Seven Stones, a large group of dangerous rocky ledges (drying up to 2.9m) nearly a square mile in extent 14 miles west of the Longships and seven miles NE of Round Island.

They are marked by a 12m high unmanned red light float (Fl (3) 30s 25M), anchored two miles to the north-east. This can provide a good check on the tidal set, although it is a lot less easy to spot than the lightship that formerly marked this reef, which attained international notoriety after the *Torrey Canyon* disaster in 1967. Whether bound north or south, the whole area should be given a suitably wide berth.

As with the passage from the south coast, you will have to traverse the Land's End TSS, and my preferred route is to hold closer to the coast and make a departure from the mainland a couple of miles north of the Longships, with a course to pass well south of the Seven Stones and a landfall on the NE side of the islands. Here, depending on the prevailing weather conditions, you can make the final decision on whether to enter by way of Crow Sound or St Mary's Sound, or northabouts by New Grimsby Sound or the North West Passage, (formerly known as the North Channel).

NORTH WEST PASSAGE, BROAD SOUND AND SMITH SOUND

As most visitors will be arriving from the Cornish mainland, these westernmost approaches are the least likely to be used and, due to the number of offlying dangers and strong tidal streams, they are best avoided by newcomers to the area. If they are to be attempted, good visibility and weather are essential.

The North West Passage, previously known as the North Channel on older charts, leads you in to the west of Bryher and Samson and the Northern Rocks, which have the smaller islands of Maiden Bower and Mincarlo at their extremity.

This passage has been much improved with the strategically located Steeple Rock YBY west cardinal buoy (Q (9) 15s) marking this dangerous and isolated hazard, which almost dries LAT just over a mile south-west of Mincarlo, and the Spencers Ledge YB south cardinal buoy (Q (6) + LFl 15s) at the south-western extreme of the rocky ledges extending from Samson and Great Minalto. Once past the buoy, you have a clear run across to St Mary's as long as you make due allowance to steer up clear of Woodcock Ledge as you close the island. This approach from the north-west is made on 127°T, and the black and white beacon on the islet of Tins Walbert (just off the the northern shore of St Agnes), in line with old St Agnes lighthouse, provides a useful transit.

The far western approach through Broad Sound is made just over a quarter of a mile to the north of Bishop Rock lighthouse on a course of 059°T. It is probably the least enticing of all the routes into the islands, heavy overfalls occur in bad weather over the whole area north and south of the Bishop Rock lighthouse and numerous unmarked rocks and ledges, some just awash at LAT, create large areas of breaking seas in heavy weather or ground swell. The transit of 'the summit of Great Ganilly island just open to north of Bants Carn on St Mary's' is extremely difficult to make out at this distance. Care must also be taken to allow for the tidal streams setting across your course. Round Rock BY north cardinal buoy will be left well over on your starboard hand to clear the northern end of the Western Rocks, with the Gunner YB south cardinal buoy to port. Both provide a good check on the tide which sets strongly across your track. You must then steer just to the north of the Old Wreck BY north cardinal buoy, from where it is a clear run into St Mary's Road.

Smith Sound, though deep, is narrow and fringed by many unmarked rocky shoals, making it a poor substitute for St Mary's Sound if approaching from the south. It should only be used with local knowledge.

ST MARY'S

Tides	HW Dover +0607
Range	St Mary's MHWS 6.0m–MHWN 4.3m, MLWN 2.0m–MLWS 0.7m
Charts	BA: 34, 883, 1148, 2565. SC5603. Stanford: 2 . Imray: C7
Waypoints	See Passages, Mainland to Scilly
Hazards	Pool and Bacon Ledges (lit). The Cow (unlit). No harbour offering all-weather shelter. Very busy in season, poor holding in anchorage
Overnight charge	St Mary's Harbour Authority mooring or anchoring £13

The largest and most fertile of the Isles of Scilly, St Mary's is also the most populated, its inhabitants variously dependent on farming, fishing, ship husbandry, pilotage and most recently, tourism. A blend of sheltered wooded and marshy valleys, tight clusters of daffodil fields surrounded by high evergreen windbreak hedges, and invigorating areas of bleaker, more windswept heathland, the island is criss-crossed with many deep hedged roads. Although it would seem impossible to get lost in such a small area, the virtual lack of signposts makes inland forays very interesting!

The coastal footpath is one of the best ways to explore, the views are splendid and for 10 gentle miles it winds past secluded coves, fine sandy beaches – frequently empty even in the height of summer – some memorable cliff and rock formations and a number of outstanding ancient burial chambers.

Old Town was the capital until Hugh Town began to develop after Star Castle and the garrison were built between 1593 and 1594 on the peninsula known as the Hue. This was part of Queen Elizabeth's continuing development of the chain of coastal fortifications begun by her father Henry VIII in anticipation of a Spanish invasion.

Scilly became an important Royalist outpost during the Civil War. Prince Charles, later Charles II,

St Mary's Harbour is the major hub of activity in the islands

St Mary's Harbour, early in the season. The visitors' moorings are on the left, RMS Scillonian III *is in her usual daytime berth on the quay and Porth Cressa lies on the upper right with Hugh Town in between. Bacon Ledge buoy on bottom right*

was billetted in Star Castle for nearly six weeks during March and April 1646, while his escape route to the Low Countries was planned via the Channel Isles. In 1667, after 118 years of military occupation, the army abandoned Scilly and the bemused inhabitants lapsed rapidly back into their hand-to-mouth existence of fishing, farming, smuggling and reaping the heaven-sent rewards, as the increasing amount of shipping resulted in ever greater numbers of shipwrecks. Between 1745 and 1796, 750 men died in the seas off Scilly from this cause alone.

The bay to the west of Hugh Town offered scant shelter and the Old Quay was built in 1601 to facilitate landing and give some extra protection to coasting vessels which dried out on the beach to discharge their cargoes. When Cowper visited the island in 1893, he commented on the need for a better breakwater linking the shore to the outlying Rat Island, in those days home to 'an infectious diseases hospital containing eight beds'. The New Quay was built just after the turn of the century, not only linking Rat Island to the shore, but extending to seaward beyond, making it accessible at any state of the tide.

St Mary's has long been the base for the mainland link with the off-islands. In 1920 the islanders formed their own Isles of Scilly Steamship Company, and in 1926 the first

Scillonian was built. Today the *RMS Scillonian III* carries on the tradition of carrying visitors, vital supplies and the mail. Additional cargo to the islands is shipped into St Mary's by the Steamship Company's other vessel, the pale blue *Gry Maritha*, from where it is distributed by smaller craft to the off-islands.

Visitors can arrive either by sea or air, but once in the islands, the colourful fleet of large open motor boats belonging to the members of the St Mary's Boatmen's Association becomes the primary form of transport. The Association was formed in 1958 and most of these sturdy waterborne charabancs were built prior to, during, or just after WWII, all of which are skipper owned, with each skipper being born and bred on St Mary's. The lack of a wheelhouse is no macho indulgence – their very special brand of eyeball navigation precludes any such interference with vision!

Visitor's to St Mary's in their own boats have a choice of three commonly used anchorages depending on the prevailing weather, two of which are adjacent to Hugh Town, the main commercial centre of the Isles of Scilly.

St Mary's Pool on the western side of Hugh Town is well sheltered from north-east through east to south, but becomes increasingly uncomfortable once the wind hooks much further to the west. Porth Cressa, on the south side of Hugh Town, is sheltered in winds from west through north to east. Watermill Cove on the northern side of the island, though distant from any facilities, provides excellent shelter from

Chapter 5

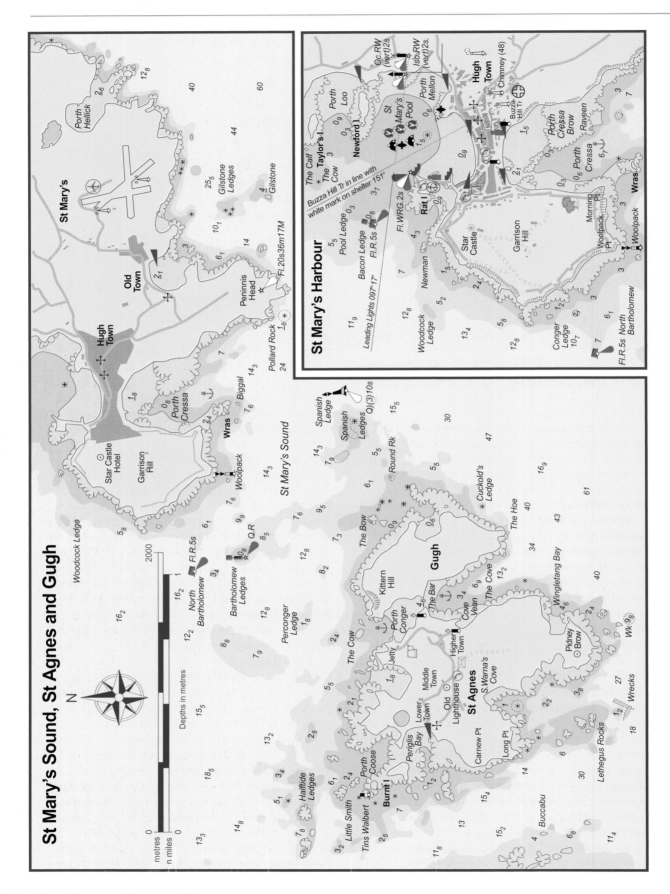

St Mary's Sound, St Agnes and Gugh

St Mary's Harbour

south through to west and is a particularly good retreat in strong south-westerlies.

As St Mary's possesses the only artifical harbour of any size in the islands, it is not surprising that most first time visitors head for the visitors' moorings and anchorage in St Mary's Pool. However, there are several factors that combine to make this option less attractive than it might initially appear.

Hugh Town – St Mary's Harbour – is first and foremost a commercial port, privately administered by the Duchy of Cornwall, which has owned the Isles of Scilly since 1337. The facilities are often stretched to the limit by the ever increasing annual influx of visiting craft. The demands on the near-sacred ground of the Quay are particularly heavy – the outer end is used daily by the RMS *Scillonian III* between 1145 and 1630, and the various steps along its length are very busy prior to the 1015 and 1400 trip boat departures, and during the late afternoon when the boats return to disembark their passengers.

The quay is also much used by local fishing boats and off-island supply boats; neither their skippers, the boatmen or the harbour staff take kindly to finding it or the steps impeded by yachts, the only exception being the innermost set of steps where the New Quay joins the Old Quay – these are reserved exclusively for visitors' dinghies. If all this is understood from the start a lot of potential problems can easily be avoided!

When both Harbour Master Jeff Penhaligon and the tide permit, it is possible to go alongside for short stays of up to an hour or so on the inner end of the quay to shop or pick up crew. If you have a problem such as an engine breakdown, it is also possible to dry out overnight in the inner berths by prior arrangement with the harbour master, provided there is space and no prevailing surge. The bottom is firm sand and, if you position yourself by one of the three good ladders, you will be able to get ashore at LW.

Normally, when the outer end of the pier is free of commercial activity, boats are allowed alongside between 0830 (0945 Saturdays) and 1130, or from 1630 to 1700 to take on water and fuel (diesel only – petrol is available nearby in cans). Here again, there is but one simple rule of thumb to keep everyone happy – ask before you make any attempt to berth alongside, either contact the Harbour Office on VHF Ch 16, 14; call sign *St Mary's Harbour*, or hail the harbour staff who are usually evident somewhere on the quay and will always do their best to help.

The second problem is the harbour itself which does not always guarantee the shelter or comfort that most visitors are probably anticipating. The large inner part is shallow and dries as far as middle steps on the quay at springs. The remaining area of water sheltered by the quay is entirely taken up with local moorings. None of these are to be used by visitors, even temporarily, and you should keep well clear of them – many of the moorings have very long floating pick-up warps just waiting to ensnare the unwary.

All visiting craft must therefore either lie on one of the 38 yellow visitors' moorings in St Mary's Pool, or anchor just inshore of them but you will soon discover that this part of the harbour is exposed to the west and an extremely dangerous lee shore in strong winds from the north-west. It also suffers badly if there is any ground swell running from the west or south-west, as there frequently is.

The holding is indifferent, mostly sand and weed, with the odd rocky patch, and to quote the Harbour Authority: '. . . . St Mary's Harbour is renowned for yachts dragging their anchors during gales, particularly when the wind is from the north-west. . . . if the weather deteriorates when you are in the harbour think of seeking alternative shelter early'.

The provision of visitors moorings in 1996 has to a great extent eased the problem, they are more than heavy enough to hold most normal sized yachts in gale force conditions, although the degree of onboard comfort will leave much to be desired!

The moorings cost £13 for one night, £25 for two nights and £35 for three nights, irrespective of the size of your boat, and as an inducement to use them you will be charged exactly the same at anchor. The good news, if you decided to linger, is that the fourth night is FREE; vessels calling for water fuel and stores will pay £6 for a stay of up to two hours.

The Harbour staff will usually be out to collect dues in the morning. However, when the weather permits, be warned that the moorings and anchorage are usually very crowded, often constituting a further problem in itself – during 2003 well over 3,000 yachts visited the port!

Nevertheless, Hugh Town is the only shopping centre of any size within the islands and the only place where fuel and water are available alongside. A visit will probably be necessary during most stays in Scilly, but personally I would simply recommend it for a temporary daytime stop and overnight only if the weather is settled and calm.

Chapter 5

ST MARY'S POOL
– APPROACH FROM SOUTH

The direct approach from St Mary's Roads is partially encumbered to the west by the rocky shallows of the adjoining Pool and Bacon Ledges (least depth 0.3m), which is indicated by the Bacon Ledge red can buoy (Fl R 5s). Here again, if there is any ground sea running, the potential danger of this hazard is much enhanced by the surge and seas breaking upon it. If the seas are breaking white on Newford Island and the shore to the north of St Mary's Pool, it will be very uncomfortable and you should seek an alternative anchorage. Even if you are only intending to go alongside for water or fuel, you will encounter considerable surge along the quay.

There are two transits to clear Pool and Bacon ledges. If approaching from the south-west, you will use the South Passage and you can begin to turn in toward the harbour once you have the two sandy beaches of Porth Thomas and Porth Mellon open of the outer end of the quay wall.

The beaches are separated by a scrub covered headland with a rocky foreshore, and careful scrutiny (binoculars are a definite help) will reveal the two leading marks, the lower, a post with large orange triangle topmark, and the upper, on the higher ground of Mount Flagon, a post with large orange 'X' topmark, just to the right of a prominent bungalow. These give a leading line of 097°T. They are not the easiest marks to pick out from a distance, particularly in poor light or if the morning sun is behind them. The lower one is particularly elusive when there is a forest of masts in the anchorage that lies immediately to seaward.

At night, the lower leading mark displays a light (Iso RW(vert) 2s), and the upper leading mark (Oc W R(vert) 10s). At the outer end of New Quay, the white sector (vis 100° – 130°) of

Visitors are only allowed to berth alongside St Mary's busy quay to take on fuel and water with the harbour master's permission at specified times

the (Fl RWG 2s) sectored light gives a clear passage past Bacon Ledge (Fl R 5s) if approaching from the NW.

ST MARY'S POOL VISITORS' MOORINGS AND ANCHORAGE

Give the outer end of the New Quay a wide berth to avoid the fairly constant stream of trip boats and everything else that seems inevitably to emerge from behind the harbour wall. If the *Scillonian III* or any other large vessel appears to be manoeuvring, keep well clear, and always adhere to **three-knot speed limit set throughout the harbour**.

The 38 visitors' moorings are ranged in five trots just east of the lifeboat mooring, while the anchorage lies further inshore, all within an area bounded by an imaginary line from the northern side of the life-boat slip to the lifeboat mooring (see chartlet). Depths on the seaward side are about 2m and reduce fairly steadily as you move inshore – if the moorings are all full, select a suitable berth according to size and draught

St Mary's Pool: South Passage leading marks

over which seas of any significant size will break. The leading line of 151°T between the Cow and the Bacon Ledge, known locally as the Middle Passage, has the Buzza Tower as the upper mark, which is prominent and easy to spot on the skyline, whereas the lower mark, a white painted beach shelter with a white stripe on the roof by the Town Beach, is much harder to see.

There is a third approach into St Mary's Pool known as the North Passage, inshore of the Cow and to seaward of the Calf Rock (dries 1.8m) off Taylor's Island, using a white painted mark on the eastern end of the Old (inner) Quay and a white painted window on the triangular shaped roof behind it. Unless you have seen these marks at close quarters and know exactly where and what you are looking for, I would not recommend the north passage for strangers – given the small distance saved it is far easier to use the middle passage.

FACILITIES

Hugh Town is the only town in Scilly and, though small, it is a busy, bustling place during the season, and even more so when the *Scillonian III* makes her daily appearance and the quay becomes a frantic mass of activity!

You can either land and leave your dinghy (on a good long painter) at the clearly marked steps by the inner end of the quay or, alternatively, anywhere on the beaches. This is often a far better ploy as the steps can become very crowded and dinghies can suffer if there is any surge.

Water and fuel can only be obtained alongside between the hours quoted above by arrangement with the harbour staff, who provide the hose. There is also a public tap outside the harbour office, which is situated upstairs and clearly marked at the seaward end of the Harbourside Hotel, the main building on the quay. However you obtain it, you will be charged 5p a gallon for water.

Diesel can be found at the outer end of the quay from Sibleys men, who are normally around during the morning period when yachts are permitted alongside. Otherwise you can find them to fill cans in the garage behind the Harbourside Hotel. Here petrol, oil, battery charging etc is also available, 0800 – 1200, 1300 – 1700 daily and 0800 – 1200 Saturdays.

Close by, in the area still known as Rat Island, you will find the Rat Island Sailboat Co and the Sail Loft & Canvas Shop sailmakers. Situated beneath the harbour office, the Harbour Authority's

as well as the space available, **but under no circumstances should you attempt to anchor to seaward of the life-boat mooring or the large red Customs buoy.** This area is used by the *Scillonian III* to turn into her berth – if you get in her way you will incur both the wrath of her master and the harbour master. Take care also to avoid the buoyed clusters of keep pots laid by local fishermen closer inshore along the fringe of Newford Island.

In southerly and easterly winds, if the Pool is overly crowded, Porth Loo, immediately to the north, is a viable alternative anchorage and also free of charge. Sound into a suitable spot midway between Newford Island and Taylor's Island, taking care to avoid the rocky ledges extending from both islands, but close enough inshore to keep off the eastern transit of the North Passage. The bottom is a mixture of sand, stone and weed and it is advisable to use a trip line.

ST MARY'S POOL – APPROACH FROM NORTH

Approaching from the north, particular care should be taken to avoid the Cow, an isolated rock (dries 0.6m) 1.5 cables west of Taylor's Island,

Leading marks

Middle Passage marks: Buzza Tower with white stripe on beach shelter roof

showers – four in total (£1 slotmeter) are in self-contained cubicles with WC and washbasin, open daily between 0800 and 1645, and until 2100 during July and August – invariably you will have to queue. Alternatively, check availability at the tourist office before walking up to the campsite beyond Star Castle where, for a similar price, you can shower in peace! Rubbish skips are located behind the Harbourside Hotel and there are also public toilets and a payphone on the quay.

It is but a short walk along the quay and past the Mermaid Inn to find all normal provisions within easy reach of Hugh Street, the main centre. Early closing is Wednesday, although most shops remain open during the season. They also tend to open earlier than on the mainland, usually between 0800 and 0830. The post office's hours are 0815 – 1700, but it closes at 1215 on Saturdays. The only banks – Barclays and LloydsTSB – are open weekdays from 0900 – 1600. Note that only Lloyds TSB has a cashpoint facility, although the Stop & Shop supermarket, open daily 0800 – 2200 and Sun 1000 – 1600, does offer a cashback facility.

Shops comprise a baker, two butchers, a newsagent, chemists, several gift shops, a good mix of cafés and pubs with appropriately nautical names. The Atlantic Inn, Bishop and Wolf, and the Mermaid all do food, as do a smattering of eating places – the Pilots Gig Restaurant (Tel: 422654) and the Galley (Tel: 422602). Hotels like Tregarthens (Tel: 422540) or the Star Castle (Tel: 422317) are also open to non-residents.

Beyond the Isles of Scilly Steamship Office, turn right into the Thorofare and behind the blue door opposite the RNLI shop you will find Southard Engineering, which also had the best stock of chandlery in the islands. Island Home Hardware in Garrison Lane is the only place in the islands where Calor and Gaz refills can be obtained.

The Tourist Information Centre is located in the old Wesleyan Chapel in Garrison Lane and a synoptic weather chart and forecast are displayed here daily as well as at the harbour office.

Follow the footpath around the head of Porth Cressa beach past the public WC and you will come to that other cruising essential, the launderette, which does service washes only, Mon – Sat 0900 – 1300, 1330 – 1700. Next door is a petrol station and Buccabu bike hire.

If you follow the Strand and continue onwards and over the hill behind the lifeboat station, you will eventually reach the Porth Mellon industrial estate, which might seem to be an unappealing sort of place until you enter the portals of the Isles of Scilly Wholesale Company. This undoubtedly has the best selection of fresh produce on the islands and much else to offer in the way of provisions. If this is your only destination, it is far quicker to land on Porth Mellon beach from the anchorage. Nike Marine Engineering is also based on the estate.

There is a fairly limited choice of things to do ashore, apart from the shopping and walks. In Church Street you will find an excellent museum with the fully rigged gig *Klondyke* as its centrepiece; those less inclined to use their legs and partial to the eccentric can opt for one of the entertaining guided bus tours of the island, but undoubtedly the best spectacle is the summer evening gig racing. Women crews race on Wednesdays, men on Fridays, usually starting at 2000 on the far side of St Mary's Roads off Nut Rock, and finishing off the end of the New Quay, which is an excellent vantage point. However, to get really close to the action, join one of the many trip boats which follow the race. Packed to the gunwales with screaming and fanatical supporters, this is one Scilly experience that you will never forget!

These elegant and racy clinker rowing boats are on average between 28 and 32ft long, with a beam of about 5ft and were once unique to Scilly. They evolved during the last century to take pilots off to ships, either from the land or towed behind the larger sailing pilot cutters for use as boarding boats in the open sea.

Their fine turn of speed meant that they were

Hugh Town, St Mary's Port Guide
Area telephone code: 01720

Harbour Master: Mr Jeff Penhaligon, Harbour Office, The Quay, Hugh Town, St.Mary's, Isles of Scilly. (Tel: 422768) Daily 0800 – 1700

VHF: Ch 16; 14. Call sign *St.Mary's Harbour*, office hours

Mail Drop: c/o Harbour Office

Emergency Services: Lifeboat in St Mary's. Falmouth Coastguard

Anchorages: St Mary's Pool – in specified area inshore of visitors' moorings, good shelter north-east through east to south, but subject to swell, often very crowded, holding poor. Dangerous in strong winds from west or north-west. Alternatives Porth Cressa or Watermill Cove, depending on weather

Mooring/berthing: 38 visitors' moorings in outer harbour. Berthing alongside quay only by prior arrangement with Harbour Master

Dinghy landings: Where indicated at inner steps on quay. On beaches

Marina: None

Charges: On visitors' mooring or at anchor, £13 one night, £25 two nights, £35 three nights, fourth night free

Phones: Public phone on quay and others in town

Doctor: Health Clinic (Tel: 422628)

Hospital: (Tel: 422392)

Churches: C of E, RC and Methodist in Hugh Town

Local Weather Forecast: Daily map and synopsis on board outside Harbour Office and at Tourist Information Centre

Fuel: Sibleys will provide diesel aboard alongside quay by prior arrangement with Harbour Master (0830 – 1130, Sat 0930 – 1200). Otherwise petrol and diesel in cans from Sibleys garages on the quay and at Porth Cressa

Water: Available alongside from hoses on quay by prior arrangement with Harbour Master only during fuelling times above, otherwise in cans from tap outside Harbour Office, all charged at 5p a gallon

Gas: Calor/gaz from Islands Home Hardware, Garrison Lane. (Tel: 422388)

Tourist Information Centre: Old Wesleyan Chapel (Tel: 422536)

Banks/cashpoints: Lloyds TSB (cashpoint) and Barclays in Hugh Street. Cashback facility at Stop and Shop supermarket

Post Office: Hugh Street

Rubbish: Bins on quay behind hotel

Showers/toilets: Toilets and showers beneath Harbour Office

Launderette: Porth Cressa

Provisions: Most normal requirements available.

Co-op supermarket open 0800 – 1000 daily, 1000 – 1600 Sundays

Chandlers: Southard Engineering (Tel: 422539)

Repairs: Ask at Harbour Office

Marine engineers: Southard Engineering (Tel: 422539). Nike Engineering (Tel: 422991) or ask at Harbour Office

Electronic engineers: None

Sailmaker: Rat Island Sailboat Co, Sail Loft & Canvas Shop (Tel: 422037) on quay behind Harbourside Hotel

Transport: Daily ferries from St Mary's to Penzance (except Sundays) and Skybus air connections to Land's End and Newquay airports (Tel: 0845 710 5555). British International helicopter service to Penzance (Tel: 01736 363871). British Rail connections at Penzance (Tel: 08457 484950)

Car hire: Sibleys (Tel: 422431)

Eating out: Good selection from fish and chips to pubs/restaurants/ bistros

Things to do: Museum. Excellent walks and beaches. Gig racing every Wednesday and Friday evening

Chapter 5

inevitably used for less lawful activities. In an attempt to reduce the amount of smuggling, the number of oars was limited to six by the Customs, whose boats they would otherwise outrun. Nevertheless, they regularly rowed and sailed (with a fair wind they could set a lugsail and small leg o' mutton mizzen) across to Brittany to collect contraband. Their handiness and the skill of their crews was also crucial to the other major activity in Scilly, saving life and salvage from shipwrecks.

The revival of interest in these fascinating craft began in the 1950s when the Newquay Rowing Club bought most of the surviving gigs in Scilly, including the 1812 built *Newquay*, the oldest in existence, refurbished them and began to race them. This generated new enthusiasm for racing

in Scilly, some of the boats were returned to the islands and new ones built, spurred on with annual visits by Newquay crews.

During the last 10 years, however, the whole sport has snowballed dramatically. New gigs and dedicated crews, both male and female, have emerged from just about every Cornish port, and there is a hotly contested calendar of racing events all around the coast with the highpoint, the World Pilot Gig Championship, held in Scilly every Spring.

PORTH CRESSA

When the weather permits – wind in the north-west, north or east and no ground swell from the south – Porth Cressa can be a more pleasant alternative to visit than St Mary's. However,

The position of these anchored yachts in Porth Cressa is a clear indication of how much of the bay is encumbered by drying rocks, invisible at high water!

although sheltered in westerly winds, if there is much swell it can become uncomfortable, particularly around HW. This is inevitably a popular anchorage and it can become overcrowded at times, as it is just as convenient for the town and free of any commercial activity. If you are lying at the seaward end of the bay, it is a long dinghy ride to get ashore at HW, or a scramble through rocks and weed at LW.

Be warned though – with any hint of a wind shift to the south-west, south or south-east, or a sudden onset of swell from this direction, do not linger. Porth Cressa can become worse than untenable more rapidly than you might predict, so seek an alternative anchorage at the earliest opportunity.

Approach and anchorage

Although the entrance to Porth Cressa opens immediately west of **Peninnis Inner Head**, if approaching from the east, care must be taken to avoid **Pollard Rock** (dries 1.8m) 100m due south of Inner Head, and it is best to hold on more to the west before steering up towards the **Wras**, the isolated rocky island on the western side of the entrance. If approaching from the west, keep well to the south of the Woolpack beacon to avoid a rock which dries 0.6m just under a cable south-west of the Wras. **Biggal Rock** (2.4m) is a visible outlyer just south of the Wras and, once this is abeam to port, you can begin a gradual turn into the bay.

The appearance of Porth Cressa is very deceptive at HW – there are extensive drying rocks all along the eastern side, the head of the bay, and the area between the Wras and Morning Point dries completely on big tides. If possible, a low water approach has much to recommend it as all the hazards will then be evident, notably **Fennel Rock** (dries 1.8m), which lies at the north-eastern corner of the large drying rocky base of

the Wras. Approach with care, keeping the Wras about 100m on your port hand and steering about NNW. Ahead **Raveen**, a 4.6m rocky islet, marks the outer edge of **Porth Cressa Brow** (dries up to 4.9m) on the east side of the bay; once this is abeam on your starboard hand, you can begin to sound for an anchorage, with the depth beyond this point rapidly reducing from 6m or 7m to between 3m and 2m. **Brow Breeze Rocks**, which dry 0.3m, extend across most of the head of the bay.

Although a number of underwater cables are indicated on the Admiralty chart, these are well covered and not normally a problem.

The bottom is mostly fine sand and the holding once again is indifferent. I would not leave a boat unattended here on a single anchor for any length of time except in the very calmest of weather.

WATERMILL COVE

This remote and pleasant anchorage at the northern end of St Mary's, just east of Innisidgen (see Crow Sound and St Martin's chartlet), is often almost deserted. It is an option if you are seeking somewhere less crowded, and is also handy when waiting for sufficient tide to cross Crow Bar. Its greatest value, however, is as a bolt hole in strong south-westerly weather when St Mary's Pool becomes very uncomfortable and Porth Cressa potentially dangerous.

In common with all anchorages in Scilly, Watermill has its limitations and, in winds of any strength from much north of west, can become uncomfortable once the western reef covers, unless you are of shallow enough draught to tuck right inshore. However, if there has been a blow from the south-west followed by the normal predictable wind veering to the north-west, it is not difficult to run back down under the lee of the eastern side of the island to the shelter of Porth Cressa, providing there is not too much swell from the south.

Although sheltered in southerly winds, swell will tend to work its way in from the east, particularly around HW, making it uncomfortable. Once the wind shifts anywhere from south-east through east to north-west, the cove becomes untenable and dangerous.

The coastal footpath to the west leads to the dunes and sandy beach at Bar Point, passing the Innisidgen burial chambers en route. The footpath to the east leads to the delightful beach at Pelistry Bay. Do not swim here when the sandy spit to Tolls Island is covered, as there are dangerous rip currents.

Porth Cressa, a couple of hours before HW, looking across to Garrison Hill. The Wras and smaller Biggal Rocks are on middle left, with Woolpack Point beyond. Isolated Raveen Rock and larger Porth Cressa Brow are just right of centre

Watermill Cove has a fine sandy beach at LW, and from here it is a pleasant and easy 45 minute walk to Hugh Town. The best route is to take the footpath from the beach to the lane, turn right at the head of the lane, continue past the duck ponds and follow the road up hill to Telegraph (public pay phone), then first right once you have passed Telegraph tower. This leads down to Porth Loo – whence follow a sandy footpath across the head of Porth Thomas and Porth Mellon beach and join the main road into town. Should you intend to return laden with provisions, Eric's Bus Service will conveniently drop you back at the duck pond!

Approach and anchorage

If approaching from the south or east, keep well to seaward to avoid the outlying rocks off Toll's Island and, if nearing towards LW, be wary of the outlying rock shown on the Admiralty chart as just awash LAT, well to seaward in the centre of the cove.

The cove is most easily located by the prominent pine trees on the fern covered hill overlooking the western side. Do not turn inshore until you have the sandy beach at its head on a south-westerly heading, but remember that at HW springs the beach is entirely covered. Alternatively, turn in once the distinctive sheer profile of Carn Wethers headland on the easternmost end of St Martin's is just open to the east of the conical island of Gt Ganinick to give a back bearing of 027°T.

Take particular care when approaching from the west. Keep up towards Hats YB south cardinal buoy and **do not cut the corner off Block House Point**, as the drying reef here extends much further to the north-east than you might imagine. Keep at least a cable offshore until the head of the cove is well open and you are onto the Carn Wethers back bearing. Nose your way in from here into a suitable depth – if you keep the highest, outer point of Innisidgen just open of the rocky islet off Block House Point, you should have between 5m and 3m at LAT.

Here the bottom is mostly sand and weed with some rock, so the holding is reasonably good. Closer inshore is a clear band of sand leading into the beach, fringed by weed-covered rocks. Although the shelter improves closer to the shore, the rocks limit the swinging room.

Avoid the wide south-eastern part of the bay, which is not only rocky but shallow almost as far to seawards as the small boat moorings in the south-eastern corner. Here there is a ruined gig house and small slipway which has a cunning low tide, sandy approach channel dug through the rocks, making it the ideal place to land by dinghy if you are heading for Pelistry Bay.

Watermill Cove is an attractive but much less used anchorage, which provides good shelter in south-westerlies

The Turk's Head Pub *is the prominent white building on the shore at Porth Conger, but it's probably time to leave as the north-westerly breeze begins to hook round into the bay . . .*

ST AGNES AND GUGH

Tides	HW Dover +0607
Range	St Mary's MHWS 6.0m–MHWN 4.3m, MLWN 2.0m–MLWS 0.7m
Charts	BA: 34, 883, 1148, 2565. SC5603. Stanford: 2 . Imray: C7
Waypoints	See Passages, Mainland to Scilly
Hazards	Many unmarked rocks and shallow ledges, Perconger Ledge, Cuckold's Ledge, Halftide Ledges, The Cow, (all unlit). No harbour offering all weather security
Overnight charge	None

'With this Mark you run in amongst many rocks terrible to behold . . .' still serves as a warning to those who have the good fortune to spot the old lighthouse on St Agnes from afar. Closer to, it is rarely long out of sight, standing proud on the low summit of this gentle island, as it justly deserves,

for this was the earliest offshore light to be established by Trinity House.

The coal braziers were fired up for the first time on 30th October 1680. They, and the Argand lights that succeeded them, continued to burn bright until 1911 when the lighthouse was deemed redundant after Peninnis Head light was built. Although the tower and its keeper's house are now a private home leased from Trinity House, they are still responsible for keeping this important navigational daymark gleaming white.

Although St Agnes and Gugh outwardly display similar physical characteristics to the rest of the inhabited islands, there is one fundamental underlying difference – they were never joined to the others, which were originally a single land mass until the sea levels rose during the Bronze Age. Leaving the waters of Scilly shallow and rock strewn, this gave rise to the legend that these are the last remaining fragments of the lost land of Lyonnesse, which once supposedly extended far west of Land's End.

Even today it is theoretically possible, on big spring tides (although in practice you would not have enough time), to make a low water circuit of most of the islands on foot, crossing via Crow Bar to Tresco and St Martin's, and across New Grimsby Sound to Bryher and Samson.

The inhabitants of St Agnes and Gugh form the most south-westerly community in the British Isles and, like the rest of the islands, their livelihood today is dependent on the tourist industry and a small amount of fishing, but sadly, due to the inroads of cheap foreign imports, increasingly less on the traditional flower farming. A century ago, the men of St Agnes were renowned worldwide as among the finest pilots in Scilly, capable of navigating ships from the western approaches as far north as Glasgow or as far east as Bremen.

This compact and attractive island is easy to explore in little more than a couple of hours.

Its central part is a dense and intimate patchwork of flower fields surrounded by high windbreak hedges, in marked contrast to the open moorland of Wingletang Down to the south. Here, in an inlet on the rocky and boulder strewn coast, you you might find terracotta

A fine overview of the Bar between St Agnes, top, and Gugh, bottom, with anchored boats in the Cove, left and an empty Porth Conger, right

beads from a wrecked Venetian trader in the sands surrounding Beady Pool.

Castella Down lies to the west and here the Troy Town stone maze will catch your eye. Laid out in 1729 on the low clifftop by the bored son of the lighthouse keeper, it provides an impressive if chilling foreground to a very different kind of maze – the off-lying rocks bordering Smith Sound, Annet, the Western Rocks and the distant finger of Bishop Rock lighthouse.

This light was built between 1852 and 1858 by Nicholas and James Douglass to the design of James Walker, and the team of workmen were billetted on the small island of Rosevear, where the remains of their cottages can be seen. Standing in one of the most exposed locations in the world, in 1874 the lighthouse was hit by such heavy seas that the lenses were broken, the structure was felt to 'reel and stagger', and the upper gallery was filled with sand! By 1887 the foundations had undergone major strengthening and the height increased by 40ft to 167ft (50.9m), making it the tallest lighthouse in Britain. In spite of this, in heavy gales, much of it is frequently hidden by the mountainous seas.

Periglis Bay, on the north-west corner of the island, provides a small natural but drying harbour for local boats, protected by Burnt Island and overlooked by the church and old lifeboat

Chapter 5

house which closed in 1920. To seaward of Burnt Island, there is a prominent BW beacon on the islet of Tins Walbert, one of the leading marks for the North West Passage.

Apart from two houses more reminiscent of somewhere on the eastern seaboard of Maine, the island of Gugh is virtually featureless. It is connected to St Agnes by a sand bar (except at HW springs) and is a heathy, heathery place with many rocky outcrops and several important megalithic remains, including the Old Man of Gugh, a 9ft standing stone, and Obadiah's Barrow. Today, some of the island's present inhabitants are likely to make a more immediate impression, as the southern end is home to a large colony of very aggressive gulls during the nesting season in early summer.

There are two possible anchorages depending on the direction of the prevailing wind and sea – the sand bar connecting Gugh to St Agnes normally separates them. This dries about 4.6m, and covers at springs when there is a noticeable tidal stream from north to south through the inlet, making bathing dangerous.

Porth Conger on the northern side of the bar is sheltered from north-east through south to west, but exposed once the wind edges any further north. The Cove on the southern side is well-sheltered from west through north to north-east, except around HW if the bar is covered, when fresh northerlies and north-westerlies can create quite a bit of chop. Although nominally sheltered from south-westerly and easterly winds, any swell will make itself increasingly felt, particularly towards HW. In the onset of winds from the south or south east, get out as soon as possible.

APPROACHES AND ANCHORAGE, PORTH CONGER

Approaching from the east, keep to the north of Spanish Ledges until **the Bow** (10m), an isolated island off the eastern side of Gugh, is abeam when it is safe to steer across for Kittern Rock (17m) on the northern end of Gugh. Keep about 100m off the rock and steer for the northern end of **the Cow** (St Agnes), leaving it several boat lengths to port to avoid the ledge extending to the north-west, before bearing round into Porth Conger and making an approach midway between Gugh and St Agnes. There is a short cut used by local boats in the narrow passage between the Cow, the Calf (St Agnes) (dries 1.2m) and the shore, which is best avoided by strangers.

Overlooked by the old lighthouse, these boats are enjoying a well-sheltered anchorage in the attractive surroundings of the Cove

Approaching from St Mary's, keep well to the west of the Bartholomew Ledges buoy and the North Bartholomew shoal, which breaks heavily if there is any sea running. So too does the **Perconger Ledge** (least depth 1.8m). If the visibility is good, the best plan is to use the leading line for St Mary's Roads – the daymark on St Martin's over the top of Creeb Island – until you can see the gap opening between Gugh and St Agnes. In the distance the **Hakestone** (2m) should be visible beyond the sand bar – if you keep this more or less on the centre of the bar it will give you a clear line in.

The deepest water lies north of the end of the jetty. Sound into a suitable depth and anchor well clear of the few local moorings and the approach to the jetty, which is in regular use. Close to the St Agnes shore there is a rocky patch, otherwise the bottom is clean fine sand, although the holding is indifferent. South of the jetty, in what looks to be the ideal and most sheltered place to anchor, depths reduce rapidly and much of this

flat sandy area dries at springs, making it ideal for bilge keelers.

APPROACH AND ANCHORAGE, THE COVE

The approach to the Cove will invariably be made from the east or north east. If arriving from St Mary's, the safest bet is to exit St Mary's Sound to the north east of Spanish Ledge buoy, and then steer south until Pidney Brow, the 13m hill on the southern end of St Agnes, is just open of **the Hoe**, the prominent rock on the southern tip of Gugh. This line keeps you in clear deep water past **Cuckolds Ledge** (dries 1.4m).

As you close the Hoe, which is steep-to, keep a couple of boat lengths to seaward and, once the Cove opens and you have the distant lump of the Cow lined up on the centre of the sand bar, you can steer straight up into the anchorage, leaving the **Hakestone** (2m) 50m or so on your starboard hand. The only real hazard in the approach is the **Little Hakestone** (dries 3m) on the south western corner of the entrance – as long as you keep up to the Hakestone this is not a problem, the entrance is over 300m wide and there is plenty of room.

In clear calm weather and once you have got your local bearings, it is possible to take a short cut to the south west of the Spanish Ledges by using the transit of Steval, the islet off the westernmost extreme of St Mary's, in transit with Hangman Island in New Grimsby Sound. This gives a back bearing of 344°T and takes you close to Round Rock (dries 1.2m) and the Brow Ledge which extends east from Gugh. Do not be tempted to cut the corner, but keep on this course until Pidney Brow is well open of the Hoe.

There will invariably be other boats at anchor in the Cove, so sound in towards the head of the inlet and select a suitable spot. The depths reduce gently the further north you proceed, with a mostly sand and weed bottom and reasonable holding. Ideally let go somewhere along the centre line of the inlet as the shoreline is very rocky on both sides (but easy to spot by the weed), except across the head of the bay where the bar forms a fine sandy beach that is excellent for swimming. The bar should be avoided when covered as the current can run hard across it.

Avoid Cove Vean – the inlet on the western side – which is rocky and dries almost to its mouth on big tides. Although the Admiralty chart shows a number of underwater cables running out of the Cove they are well buried and will not present a problem.

FACILITIES

If anchored in Porth Conger, do not leave dinghies tied alongside the jetty, which is busy with pleasure boats late into the evening, but land on the sandy beach/old slip immediately below the Turk's Head pub (Tel: 01720 422434), a particularly convivial watering hole where bar food and evening meals are available.

If anchored in the Cove, land by the St Agnes end of the Bar where the footpath leads up to join the concrete road. Turn right for the pub, or turn left and you will climb the gentle hill past two café/tea rooms and eventually reach the surprisingly well-stocked post office, general store and off-licence (Tel: 01720 422364), which can cater for most normal requirements. There is not usually a surplus of bread, but if you are lingering here for a while they will order this (and anything else you might need) from St Mary's on a daily basis.

Continue along the road towards the old lighthouse and you will find a public phone box; there is also a payphone in the Turk's Head. No water or fuel is available.

Chapter 5

TRESCO, BRYHER AND SAMSON

New Grimsby Sound is guarded by Cromwell's Castle on the Tresco shore, with Hangman Rock and Bryher beyond

Tides	HW Dover +0607
Range	St Mary's MHWS 6.0m–MHWN 4.3m, MLWN 2.0m–MLWS 0.7m
Charts	BA: 34, 883, 1148, 2565. SC5603. Stanford: 2 . Imray: C7
Waypoints	See Passages, Mainland to Scilly
Hazards	Many unmarked rocks and shallow ledges, large areas between islands dry. No harbour offering all weather security
Overnight charge	Tresco Estate mooring £13, at anchor £5

Those seeking expensive works of art, bottles of claret, exotic shrubs and flowers, or merely an attractive and sheltered anchorage need look no further than Tresco. The second largest island in Scilly, it is private and unique in that it is leased from the Duchy of Cornwall by the Dorrien-Smith family, the descendants of Augustus Smith, a Herefordshire land owner who took over the administration of the islands in 1834. Assuming the title of Lord Proprietor of all Scilly, his beneficial dictatorship lasted a remarkable 38 years until his death in 1872 and transformed their prosperity.

Based on Tresco, he built the house known as Tresco Abbey as his main residence and immediately began to establish the Abbey Gardens for which the island is internationally

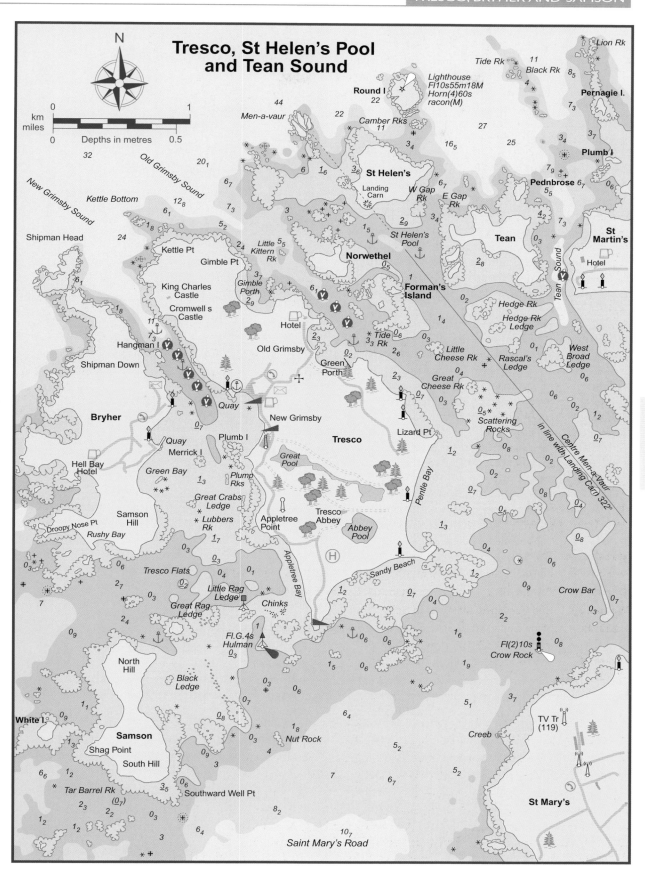

Tresco, St Helen's Pool and Tean Sound

N

km
0   1
miles
0   Depths in metres   0.5

Lighthouse
Fl10s55m18M
Horn(4)60s
racon(M)

Lion Rk

Tide Rk   11
Black Rk   8₅

Round I   4
22

Pernagie I.

Men-a-vaur   22   27   25   3₄   3₇

Camber Rks   11   Plumb I

3₄   16₅   7₉

St Helen's   Pednbrose 6₇

Landing   W Gap   E Gap   5₅
Carn   Rk   Rk

Norwethel   2₉   3₄   4₂   7₃

Kettle Bottom   Old Grimsby Sound   6₇   6₇   Tean   St
                                                                                Martin's

32   20₁   6₇   7₃   5₂   1₅   2₈   Hotel

New Grimsby Sound   12₈   5₅   St Helen's
                                        Little   Pool
                                        Kittern
24   18   6₁   Rk   0₅

Shipman Head   Kettle Pt   2₄   Forman's   Hedge Rk

Gimble Pt   3₇   Island   1₄   Hedge Rk
                        Gimble   Ledge

6₁   King Charles   Porth   6₁   0₂   West
        Castle   2₉   0₁   Broad
18   Cromwells   Hotel   Little   Rascal's   Ledge
        Castle   Tide   Cheese Rk Ledge
11   Hangman I   Old Grimsby Rk   2₆   Great   0₂   1₂
7₃   2₃   0₆   Cheese Rk   0₇
        Shipman Down   Green   0₃   0₇   0₂
                        Porth   0₂   Scattering
                                        2₃   Lizard Pt Rocks   0₅   0₈
Bryher   Quay   0₅
        Quay   New Grimsby   Tresco   1₂   0₇
        Merrick I   Plumb I   0₂   0₈
Hell Bay   Green Bay   Great   Pentle Bay 0₇   0₄
Hotel   Pool   1₃
        Plump
Droopy Nose Pt Rks   Tresco   0₄   0₅
        Great Crabs   Abbey   Abbey   1₂   0₆
Samson   Ledge   Appletree Pool   0₄   0₇
Hill   Lubbers   Point   Crow Bar
Rushy Bay   Rk   Sandy Beach 0₇   0₄   0₉   0₇
        1₇   1₂   0₈   0₃
7   Tresco Flats 0₃   0₄   0₁   0₇   0₄
        0₂   1₆
2₇   0₃   Little Rag   0₆   0₆   2₂   Fl(2)10s
        Ledge   Chinks   0₆   0₆   Crow Rock 0₈
2₄   Great Rag   1₅   1₆   1₉
        Ledge   1   Fl.G.4s
0₉   North   Hulman   0₃
        Hill   Black   0₃   0₆   7₃   TV Tr
1₁   0₉   Ledge   0₇   6₄   5₁   (119)
White I.   Samson   0₆   0₃   1₈ Nut Rock   5₂
1₃   Shag Point   0₉   4   Creeb
        South Hill   7   6₇   5₂
6₆   1₂   3₅   0₆   8₂
Tar Barrel Rk (0₇) Southward Well Pt   10₇
2₃   0₃   6₄   Saint Mary's Road   St Mary's
1₂   2₂   3

renowned. Today, the 17 acres of south facing terraces are a botanist's paradise, with subtropical plants from all over the world flourishing in this unique outdoor location. Crew members less interested in flora can ponder sagely on the collection of ship's figureheads and memorabilia salvaged from local shipwrecks housed in the *Valhalla* museum within the gardens.

On a wider scale, Smith did much to enhance the general well-being of the inhabitants and eventually managed to virtually wipe out the rampant smuggling to establish a well-ordered society. A fervent believer in education, he introduced the first compulsory schooling in the United Kingdom, established five shipbuilding yards and created a new industry – the cultivation of early flowers and potatoes – which have long been one of the commercial mainstays of the Isles of Scilly.

Tresco's economy today is based on the hyper-efficient management of tourism, and it even sports its own heliport with direct flights from Penzance. Although there is still a small amount of farming, the majority of the old workers' cottages are now converted into up-market self-catering holiday homes and timeshare properties. The luxurious Island Hotel, overlooking Old Grimsby on the eastern side of the island, is even more prestigious and would not look out of place in a Caribbean setting.

Apart from a few tractors and golf buggies, Tresco is blissfully car free, although the few miles of road seem at times to be positively overrun by small children on hired bicycles, of which there are nearly 300! It is, however, a quite intriguing island of two very distinct halves, both physically and spiritually.

The south-eastern end is low lying, heavily wooded in the vicinity of the Abbey Gardens and has two large reed fringed lakes, Great Pool and Abbey Pool, and a shoreline of magnificent white sandy beaches. The cottage-lined road that climbs the gentle hill between New Grimsby on the west side, Dolphin Town in the centre and Old Grimsby on the east forms a natural divide.

North of this, delightful walks along the coastal footpath soon take you back to nature in the raw, the untouched, windswept expanse of rock strewn heathland, gorse and heather of Castle Down, named after the gaunt granite remains of King Charles Castle. Built between 1550 and 1554, this was superseded in 1652 by Cromwell's Castle, which was better positioned to protect the entrance to New Grimsby.

New Grimsby Sound approach from north, Tresco on left, Bryher, right, with Shipman Head in foreground. Cromwell's Castle and Hangman Island are visible midway down the sound. St Mary's is in the far distance

Walking the rugged cliff top around the north-eastern end of the island, you can search for, and hopefully find, the island's best hidden attraction – the cave at Piper's Hole. It was, until recently, much easier to find as there was a steel ladder leading down into a gully where the narrow, rock-encumbered entrance lies. The ladder has now been removed, but those who explore beyond the entrance will find that the cave eventually opens into a much larger inner chamber where there is a shallow pool, its bottom composed of a horribly glutinous clay. A torch, some candles and a complete lack of claustrophobia are essential for the successful completion of this expedition!

For the visiting yachtsman, Tresco is best known for having the most protected anchorage in Scilly – New Grimsby Sound – which lies between the western side of the island and Bryher. This long narrow passage is for the most part little more than a couple of cables wide and much of it is now taken up with the Tresco Estate's 22 visitors' moorings. In high season the demand for these is

Round Island and the northern side of the islands. The soundings drop away fast and there are no offshore hazards more than a few cables from the main land masses, although if there is much wind or ground sea running from the west or south-west, the sight of seas breaking heavily along the rocky north-western shores can be somewhat daunting.

The tidal streams generally run at up to two knots at springs (and reputedly over four knots close inshore off Round Island), creating confused seas with wind against tide for several miles to seaward. Close to the entrance to the sound, overfalls can occur off Kettle Bottom Ledge from three to four hours after HW Dover.

Once Round Island is well on your port quarter, with the rounded humpback of St Helen's Island and the distinctive summits of Men-a-vaur abeam, hold a south-westerly course about a quarter of a mile from the shore and the northernmost point on Bryher, **Shipman Head**, will appear as a long, undulating and rocky promontory on your port bow.

This forms the western side of the entrance to New Grimsby Sound, so keep your distance off until you can see clearly into the Sound and can identify the two prominent marks within: **Cromwell's Castle**, a flat topped rounded stone tower is on the eastern side of the entrance, and the pyramid-shaped bulk of **Hangman Island** (16m) lies slightly further into the sound on the western side.

Though relatively narrow, the entrance to the Sound is deep and easy to enter as long as due care is taken to avoid **Kettle Bottom Ledge** (dries 3.2m), which extends two cables to the north-west of Tresco, forming a trap for the unwary who try to cut the corner. Normally, if there is any hint of ground sea, it is easy enough to spot from the ominous surge over it.

Once the steep western side of Hangman Island is bearing about 157°T, it is safe to steer inshore, but make due allowance for the tide which sets across the entrance in excess of two knots at springs, running east at HW Dover +0115 and west HW Dover –0510. Shipman Head is steep-to, and it pays to keep up to this side of the entrance before easing midway between Cromwell's Castle and Hangman Island in the final approach.

ANCHORAGES AND VISITORS' MOORINGS

Immediately south of Cromwell's Castle there is a deep water anchorage with depths ranging between 7m and 11m, mostly sandy bottom. Once

always heavy and the remaining anchorage space inevitably crowded, as it is the ideal base from which to explore both Tresco and Bryher.

New Grimsby Sound is perfectly sheltered in winds from south-west to west, and north-east through to south-east. Although safe, in strong winds from the north, particularly north-westerlies, and strong southerlies, it can become very uncomfortable and rough with wind against tide, particularly at springs. Nor too, is it entirely devoid of swell and, like just about every other anchorage in the islands, it can be quite rolly at times.

Old Grimsby Sound on the eastern side of the island is the best alternative anchorage on Tresco, and although shallower and more exposed, in fine weather it is often quieter and less crowded. The Tresco Estate has six visitors' moorings here. Depending on your position there is good shelter in all except easterly wind directions, but it is prone to swell in northerlies. Due to the many unlit hazards, neither New Grimsby nor Old Grimsby should be approached in darkness by strangers.

NEW GRIMSBY SOUND

Approach from north
Given favourable weather, the easiest approach to New Grimsby Sound is from seaward, by way of

The southern approach to New Grimsby looking across Tresco Flats to Bryher, where Green Bay lies just left of centre. Merrick Island and, nearest, Plumb Island are both conspicuous while New Grimsby Quay is in the sandy bay on the extreme right

Hangman Island is abeam, the depths rapidly reduce to between 3m and 4m. On the Tresco shore there is a prominent rocky outcrop, beyond which the 22 visitors' moorings extend southwards along the eastern side of the sound. If there is no indication that they have been reserved and you are happy to pay the £13 overnight charge, just pick one up – they are all good for up to 15 tons, maximum 15.2m (50ft), no rafting permitted. Should you wish to try and reserve one in advance, you can contact the harbour master, Henry Birch (Tel: 01720 422792 or mobile 07778 601237). Normally he will be out to collect your dues in the late afternoon.

If you prefer to anchor, either let go to the north of the moorings, clear of them along the Bryher side of the channel, or further to the south, but here you must take care – beyond the cluster of private moorings the depths reduce rapidly and there is little more than than 0.5m abeam of New Grimsby Quay. The overnight charge for anchoring is £5.

There are also two underwater power cables, clearly marked on both the Tresco and Bryher shores by triangular yellow boards which must be avoided.

Shallow draught boats can work their way closer inshore and anchor, although they will not be able to dry out as this is not permitted on Tresco except with the harbour master's prior agreement. Anchoring is prohibited inshore of a line from the end of the quay southwards to Plumb Island, as the quay is in constant use with trip boats and ferries and their approach must not be impeded. For this reason visitors are not allowed to lie alongside the quay except in very special circumstances with the harbour master's permission. **All dinghies must be left on the sandy beach** – you will find yourself very unpopular if you leave them alongside the quay or any of the steps.

If there are many boats at anchor, the restricted swinging room and convoluted tidal streams can cause problems. At springs they run at up to two knots from one hour before local LW to one hour after LW (HW Dover –0140 to +0140), and the flow is intriguing as the direction changes four times every 12 hours: SE from HW Dover –0010, NW from HW Dover +0125, SE from HW Dover +0415. and NW again from HW Dover –0340.

Approach from south across Tresco Flats

The southern approach to New Grimsby Sound from St Mary's Road is across **Tresco Flats**, an extensive area of drying sands, which is shallow and seems complicated at first glance.

As long as you do not attempt it on a falling tide and preferably wait until after half flood, it should not present a problem for boats of average draught. At MHWS you should easily carry 5m over the Flats or about 3.3m at MHWN. For boats drawing no more than 1.2m this approach can be made with care from about 2 hours after LW although deeper draught boats should wait at least until half flood.

When approaching from the direction of St Mary's, leave through the south passage and steer 340°T across St Mary's Road. The island of Samson, with its twin rounded hills, lies well away on your port bow, with Bryher beyond and the larger wooded bulk of Tresco, with its long white sandy beaches, to starboard.

The isolated Nut Rock (1.5m) is a useful and fairly visible outlier to the Tresco channel – leave this a couple of boat lengths to port. From here the Hulman Beacon, a rather spindly looking iron perch with a green triangular topmark (Fl G 4s) will be visible on your starboard bow – steer a course to leave this a good 30m on your starboard hand as the rocks extend well beyond the perch. On your port bow the Little Rag Ledge Beacon is another flimsy affair, topped with a red painted radar reflector; it was anticipated that this would also be lit by summer 2004. Do not steer directly for this, but make a gradual turn towards it to avoid the southernmost edge of the reef (dries 1.3m). Take care not to stray too far to starboard either, to avoid the isolated patch of the Chinks Rocks (dry 1.3m).

It sounds and looks more complicated than it really is. The water is disturbingly clear and as long as the light is good you will not only be able to see the darker areas of weed over the rocks and the clean sand beneath your keel, but even the crabs running around upon it!

Tresco's Appletree Bay, the long sandy beach backed by dunes on your starboard hand, is a

New Grimsby Sound, south approach nearing high water. The 'Hulman' beacon is on right, 'Little Rag Ledge' beacon is just visible left of centre and Hangman Island is distinctive in the distance on the far left

popular daytime anchorage when the weather permits, but it should be noted that yachts are not allowed to anchor within 150 yards of the beach, and in no circumstances are they allowed to dry out on the beach as this is in the direct line of the helicopter flight path into Tresco heliport. Any yacht that is considered to constitute a danger to the helicopter will be towed away!

Once Little Rag Ledge Beacon is abeam and there is enough rise of tide, you can proceed directly across Tresco Flats. This large sandy spit dries up to 1.7m in places and extends nearly a mile westwards from Appletree Point at the northern end of Appletree Bay. In the far distance you should now be able to spot two rocky islands in mid channel – the left hand one, Merrick Island, is the lowest (2.6m), while Plumb Island (7m) is on the right. Further beyond, the pyramid-shaped profile of Hangman Island (16m) is quite unmistakeable. Keep Merrick in front of Hangman, on about 340°T, and you will avoid the rocky ledges closer inshore off Appletree Point.

However, if you are doubtful whether you have sufficient depth over the Flats, deeper water will be found by swinging more to the west once you are past Little Rag Ledge beacon. Ahead, Samson Hill on the south end of Bryher has two small summits, steer for the left hand one on about 302°T for just over mile. Further away on your port hand, Yellow Rock is a small rocky islet midway between Samson and Bryher – once you have this abeam and bearing about 230°T, you can turn north-east. In good visibility the top of the distant Bishop Rock lighthouse over the centre of Yellow Rock gives a good idea of when to turn. The bottom is all sand so if you touch on a rising tide you will come to no harm.

The only real hazard is the isolated Lubbers Rock (dries 1.7m), which should be left on your port hand. As long as you can see the southern

Little Rag Ledge beacon   Hulman beacon

Old Grimsby Sound is an alternative anchorage on Tresco, or you can use one of the visitors' moorings. Looking north, the conical summit of Norwethal is distinctive on the right, and the Island Hotel is in the centre of the picture

end of the more distant island of Mincarlo open of Works Point, the southernmost tip of Bryher, you will clear this safely.

Beyond this point the Bryher side of the channel is fringed by Little Crab Ledge (dries 2.4m) and Great Crab Ledge (dries 5.3m, just covers at HW) – normally some of it can be seen as cluster of rock heads. On the Tresco side, the Plump Rocks dry 2.2m. As long as you keep the small white gabled building on New Grimsby Quay just open of Plumb Island, you will pass up the centre of the channel clear of all these hazards.

Finally, steer between Plumb Island and Merrick, where the deepest water will be found on this side of the channel, and once Merrick is abeam steer straight for the lower end of the moorings to avoid the only other hazard on the Bryher side of the channel, Queens Ledge (dries 2.5m).

OLD GRIMSBY SOUND

Approach, anchorage and visitors' moorings

With suitable weather and a quiet sea, the easiest approach to this alternative Tresco anchorage is, again, from seaward. Ideally, aim to make your approach soon after LW when most of the hazards will be easy to spot. Do not cut the corner off the isolated rounded rocky island known as Golden Ball if approaching from the north-east as there are several isolated off-lying rocks.

As with New Grimsby, hold a course mile to seaward until you can see clearly into the Sound- the island of Norwethal on the eastern side is a

good mark, as it has a very distinctive flat-topped rock formation at its highest point – and make your approach following the line of the Tresco shore, giving due allowance for the tide which can set strongly across the entrance.

For a first visit I would suggest visiting New Grimsby to begin with, and reconnoitering the entrance to Old Grimsby from the land. It is then but a short hop around the northern end of Tresco, taking care, of course, to avoid Kettle Bottom.

Once inside the entrance to the sound, Little Kittern Rock (dries 1.9m) is the biggest hazard, and lies on your port hand opposite the entrance to Gimble Porth, the sandy bay on your starboard hand, which can provide a pleasant temporary anchorage in the north-eastern corner. Merchant's Point is the rocky headland at the southern end of Gimble Porth – aim to pass 30m or so off this and maintain this offing. In the distance, on your starboard bow, the prominent ruined blockhouse overlooking the southern end of Green Porth will soon be in sight on a grassy headland, with the long sandy beach and dunes of Green Porth running round to the small pier that separates it from Raven's Porth.

Once this is open to starboard, you can anchor anywhere in mid-channel clear of the visitors' moorings where there are depths of just over 3m, with a sandy/weedy bottom. As in New Grimsby, the moorings cost £10 a night and it will cost £5 a night to anchor. The tidal stream can be strong here, up to two knots at springs, running south-east through the sound for eight hours beginning HW Dover –0210, and north-west for the remaining four hours.

Shallower draught boats can edge out of the tide and closer into Green Porth where there is generally better shelter and less swell, but no anchoring is permitted anywhere inside of a line drawn from Long Point to Blockhouse Point and take care to avoid the underwater cable which is indicated by the sign at the head of the beach and runs out of the bay to the south of the quay.

Leave your dinghy either on the beach or the quay; the long landing causeway at the northern end of Raven's Porth belongs to the hotel and is private.

If continuing further south, take care once Trafford Rock is abeam as the isolated trap of Tide Rock (dries 1.4m) lurks 100m to the SSW. To avoid it, bear over towards Block House Point once Middle Ledge is abeam.

Passage from Old Grimsby to St Mary's Road

With sufficient rise of tide it is possible to exit from Old Grimsby to the south and into St Mary's Road by following the Tresco shoreline beyond Block House Point. Cooks Rock (dries 4.3m), which lies about 150m due east of the point, is the only hazard. From here keep about 250m from the dunes backing the white sandy beaches until you are past Rushy Point, which has a post with a diamond shaped yellow sign marking an underwater cable.

From here you should be able to see Crow Rock beacon and beyond, on St Mary's skyline, the Telegraph Tower. Keep these in transit to give a course of 162°T and you should avoid all the rocky ledges off the south-eastern end of Tresco, most of which are likely to be covered, so a good lookout on the bow is advisable.

From Crow Beacon, bear away for St Mary's, keeping Steval and the old lighthouse on St Agnes in transit, to give a course of 208°T.

FACILITIES

Tresco Estate, and in particular its harbour master, Henry Birch, do everything they can to assist the visiting yachtsman in the friendly and helpful manner that has always been their hallmark. Water containers can be filled free of charge from the tap by the Quay Café, where there are also public toilets. Close by, the ever popular New Inn (Tel: 01720 422844), the island's only pub, sports a bar that was completely refurbished with prime pitchpine planks washed ashore during the winter of 1993. There is a good range of bar meals and basic showers are also available (£1) – enquire at the bar.

Diesel and petrol can be obtained in cans if you ask at the Estate Office, which is in the large complex of farm buildings on the southern side

of the bay, where the post office and public telephone are also located. (The PO is closed Weds pm, Sat pm and all day Sun). Rubbish must be left in bags in the trailer behind the Quay shop.

Tresco Stores and Off-licence (Tel: 01720 422806) has moved from its former location a short distance up the hill from the quay and is now situated by the Estate Office. The shop has a comprehensive selection of provisions and is open daily Mon – Sat 0830 – 1800, Sun 1000 – 1300. Should you need washing done, the Island Laundry, also by the Estate Office, can do a same day service if your laundry is delivered to them before 1200; they will also dry washing if required.

The Abbey Gardens (open daily 1000 – 1600, moderate admission charge) can be found a mile and a half away.

Continue up the road beyond the New Inn and a brisk five to 10 minute walk brings you to Old Grimsby, passing St Nicholas's C of E church en route. The smart Island Hotel (Tel: 01720 422883), overlooking the northern side of Old Grimsby Harbour, is open to non-residents for breakfast, lunch, dinner and bar. Showers are also available, along with freshly baked bread and wine/spirits off-sales.

BRYHER

Bryher is the smallest of the inhabited islands and has a sleepy charm all of its own, much enhanced by the interesting topography which gives the island its name, being Celtic for 'place of hills'. Fishing, flower growing and, increasingly, the tourist trade are the mainstay of the small population, but with limited accommodation ashore, it remains one of the least visited of the islands.

Like Tresco, it is an island of contrasts. Rushy Bay on the southern tip is a delightful white sandy beach with good bathing, the coastal footpath along the western side of the island provides a panoramic if somewhat chilling view of the Norrard rocks stretching away to the west, while a foray over the tight turf of Shipman Down affords a spectacular view of the aptly named Hell Bay, and a wild rock strewn path out towards Shipman Head.

Watch Hill, one of the highest points in Scilly, was formerly used as a lookout for shipwrecks and has some of the best views in the islands.

Green Bay anchorage

From the shoal draught yachtsman's point of view, Bryher is best known for Green Bay, an attractive and popular drying anchorage with excellent shelter from SSW through to north.

The easiest approach is immediately to the north of Merrick Island and south of Halftide bar, a higher bank which dries 2.8m. Keep up more towards the northern side of the bay and sound your way into a suitable spot where you will dry out on a mostly flat sandy bottom. Take care to avoid the Brow Ledge and Three Brothers Rocks which lie closer inshore on the south western corner of the bay.

FACILITIES

The promise of the grandly named settlement known as the Town belies the reality, for this is little more than a hamlet where you will find the Vine Cafe and a public telephone box. Though limited, the facilities on Bryher are surprisingly good, not least the Bryher Post Office and Stores (open 0900 – 1800 daily, 1000 – 1500 Sun in season). Renowned for Mrs Bushell's superb home baked pies, bread and pasties, no cruise to Scilly is complete without sampling them!

The international code flags S-H-O-P make it easy to spot from the anchorage, you can land in Kitchen Porth, or on the beach further to the south, but keep clear of the jetty on Bar Point which is in more or less constant use. This unassuming structure is probably the most famous jetty in the UK – its high speed construction was witnessed by thousands of TV viewers when it was built as one of the many frantic challenges faced by Anneka Rice!

The Fraggle Rock Cafe (Tel: 01720 422222) is

Green Bay, Bryher, is a popular and sheltered anchorage for boats able to take the ground

open throughout the day and also serves evening meals. Those in search of a pint can follow the signposts and stroll over to the bar in the Hell Bay Hotel (Tel: 01720 422947) on the western side of the island where meals are also available, in either the bar or the full works *à la carte* in the dining room.

Neither water nor fuel are available. However, limited chandlery, rigging and mechanical repairs can be obtained from Blue Boats on the foreshore (Tel: 01720 423095) and a good marine engineer, Steve Hulands aka Bryher Marine (Tel: 01720 423047 or mobile 07810 592487) is also on hand.

SAMSON

Today, barren Samson is the largest of the uninhabited islands, its sole residents aggressive gulls and timid black rabbits.

Burial cairns and ruined cottages are the only remaining evidence of the people who lived here, latterly in abject poverty, until the 1850s when Augustus Smith removed them to the larger islands and consigned Samson to cattle grazing and, briefly, a deer park. This proved a failure when the deer discovered they could wade across at low water to enjoy the lusher delights of Tresco!

The best landing is on the fine sandy beach at Bar Point on the north-eastern corner, where it is possible to anchor in settled weather midway between Puffin Island and Bar Point in about 1m, making a careful approach from Yellow Rock. This is very exposed at HW and is not somewhere I would recommend for anything more than a daytime stop.

St Martin's looking north-west to Tresco.

Labels on image: Bryher, Tresco, Tean Sound, St Helen's Pool, East & West Gap Rocks, Men-a-Vaur, Round Island

ST MARTIN'S TEAN SOUND AND ST HELEN'S POOL

Tides	HW Dover +0607
Range	St Mary's MHWS 6.0m–MHWN 4.3m, MLWN 2.0m–MLWS 0.7m
Charts	BA: 34, 883, 1148, 2565. SC5603. Stanford: 2 . Imray: C7
Waypoints	See Passages, Mainland to Scilly
Hazards	Many unmarked rocks and shallow ledges, large areas between islands dry. No harbour offering all weather security
Overnight charge	Tean Sound Hotel mooring £10

The north and north-eastern side of the Isles of Scilly is much less developed and less visited. St Martin's has a small population, both Tean, (pronounced *Tee-Ann*) and St Helen's are uninhabited, so for those seeking a quieter anchorage there are several possibilities, although the pilotage is more demanding.

ST MARTIN'S

Surrounded by extensive shallows and drying sands along its southern side and exposed rock-encumbered bays along its northern coast, the long narrow island of St Martin's has few anchorages suitable for deeper draught boats, with the exception of Tean Sound.

Fin keel boats of moderate draught will just be able to lie afloat at neaps in Higher Town Bay, whilst for those able to dry out comfortably the choice is marginally better, although very dependent on the prevailing weather. Although the bays on the northern side of the island look

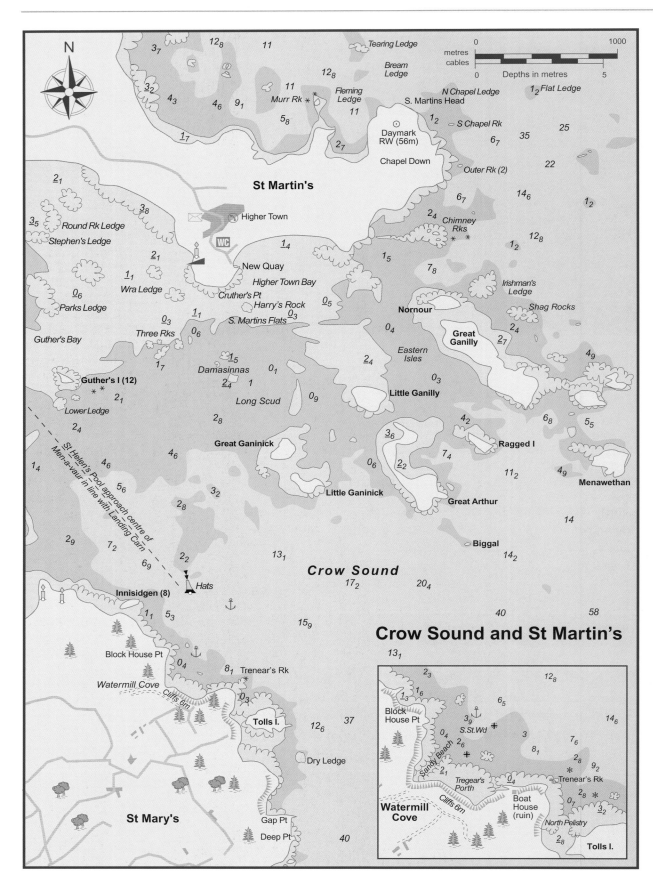

Crow Sound and St Martin's

enticing, the numerous rocky ledges make this an area that should only be explored with extreme caution in settled weather – all of which is a shame, as the island is very attractive.

A backbone ridge of granite forms a distinct division along its length – the northern side is wild heathland edged with some deep cliffbound coves, in marked contrast to the fields and softer agricultural scenery of its gently sloping southern flank, with an atmosphere in many ways reminiscent of rural Brittany, an impression that is further enhanced by the presence of the St Martin's Vinyard and Winery, which overlooks Higher Town Bay. Established in 1996, it produced its first vintage in 2000, a medium dry white, and the vineyard offers tours and tastings throughout the summer daily from 1000 – 1600. There is a small visitor centre and farm shop.

From the holidaymaker's point of view, the magnificent sandy beaches are the main attraction, and the island has also acquired something of a reputation for arts and crafts in recent years with several galleries and holiday sketching, painting and even paper making courses. The sailor, however, knows the island best for the splendid rocket-shaped red and white striped daymark, which stands 56m above sea level at the summit of Chapel Down, the north-eastern corner of the island. This was erected in 1687 by Thomas Ekin (the date inscribed on the tower is, curiously, incorrect) and it is well worth walking up to for the views from this vantage point.

APPROACH, ANCHORAGE AND VISITORS' MOORINGS, TEAN SOUND

Tean Sound is a narrow but mostly deep passage between the western end of St Martin's and the deserted neighbouring island of Tean. It can be entered from seaward at any state of the tide, but

St Martin's on the Isle Hotel and the visitors' moorings in Tean Sound looking to seaward

the approaches require considerable care as they are fringed with rocky ledges, and I would only recommend it in fair weather, good visibility and with an absence of swell. If there is a heavy ground sea running from the west or north-west, seas can break heavily across the approach, particularly between Pednbrose and Pernagie, making it potentially very dangerous.

Ideally, try to time your arrival fairly soon after LW when most of the off-lying hazards will be visible, notably Black Rock (6m) and its associated ledges which extend northwards to Deep Ledges (least depth 0.6m) and southwards to South Ledge (dries 1.4m). Together they form a line of reefs nearly a mile in length, but it is possible to enter either east or west of this hazard depending on the direction of your approach.

From the east, give all of the northern shore of St Martin's and White Island a reasonable berth until you have Lion Rock (8m) abeam to port. Keep a good 100m off this and its associated rocks and gradually ease round onto a heading of 180.3°T. This course can be confirmed by keeping the tall TV tower on the distant skyline of St Mary's just open of Goat's Point, the western-most point on St Martin's.

Once Pernagie Island (9m) is on your port quarter, you should edge more to port towards Plumb Island (13m) and its cluster of smaller islets to make sure you avoid Rough Ledge (dries 1.4m). This lies almost midway between Plumb Island and Pednbrose (12m), the prominent island immediately to the north of Tean which forms the western side of Tean Sound.

Keep about 100m off Tinkler's Point and about 50m off Goat's Point on St Martin's to avoid Thongyore Ledge, a nasty rocky shoal (dries 1.4m) on the starboard side of the channel.

From the west or north, keep up towards Round Island, taking care to avoid the Eastward Ledge (dries 2.9m) a cable to the NNE of the island.

From here identify Babs Carn, a rocky bluff on the west side of St Martin's which is easy to spot,

Higher Town Bay looking towards the Eastern Isles

and the small flat island of Pednbean (1.8m) which lies to the east of Pednbrose. This is more difficult to identify from afar, but Pednbean in transit with Babs Carn on 154°T gives you the best approach line, leading midway between Pednbrose and the Corner Rock (least depth 0.3m). Once you have Pednbrose abeam, steer more to port towards Tinkler's Point and the centre of Tean Sound.

The deepest water in the anchorage is taken up with seven moorings belonging to the St Martin's on the Isle Hotel (Tel: 01720 422092), call sign *Santa Marta* VHF Ch 16 or 12. Visitors are welcome to use these free of charge if they book for dinner at the hotel, otherwise a charge of £10 per night will be made. The bar and bar meals, or lunches are also available to non-residents, as well as showers on request.

Alternatively, anchor in the centre of the channel to the north or south of the moorings depending on the wind direction, but keep well clear of the end of the quay which is in regular use. Depending on your position, shelter can be found in winds from most directions except the north, and it can be exposed in southerly winds at HW. At springs the tide runs at up to two knots in the narrows, which often creates uncomfortable conditions with wind against tide and a risk of dragging as the bottom is mostly rocky, so a two anchor moor is definitely recommended.

In east or south winds an alternative anchorage can be found off Porth Seal, between Plumb Island and Tinkler's Point. There are sandy patches, but also boulders and heavy kelp closer inshore and it is advisable to use a trip line.

SOUTH APPROACH TO TEAN SOUND

This approach to Tean Sound lacks any good transits, but is easier than it looks on the chart. Once you have had a bit of practice it is a good exercise in eyeball navigation – provided you have reasonably good light.

Make the approach at about half flood and steer 005°T from Crow Rock beacon until Broad Ledge (dries between 4.3m and 5.3m) is on your starboard beam. From here leave West Broad Ledge (dries 2.5m, but beware 0.7m outlier on eastern side) to port and John Martin's Ledge (dries 3.9m) to starboard. Then, steer up for the moorings in the centre of Tean Sound. Even if covered, both rocky ledges will be easy to spot from the weed over them.

HIGHER TOWN BAY

Higher Town bay is sheltered from west through north to north-east and, although there are a few groups of rocks, with due care it is relatively easy to approach from Crow Sound, ideally after half flood.

If you have sufficient water over Crow Bar you can use the useful stern transit, keeping the Crow beacon in line with the middle of the distant jagged backbone of the Haycocks rocks on the northern end of Annet, which should give you a heading of about 048°T. This will take you well clear to the south of the distinctive Guther's Island with its twin flat topped rocks and rocky outliers, leaving the three **Damasinnas** (known locally as the Sinners) Rocks (drying between 2.4m and 1.5m) on your starboard hand and the **Three Rocks Ledges** (drying between 0.9m and 0.7m) to port. Here again, a good lookout on the foredeck will be able to spot both these hazards from the large amount of weed clinging to them.

As you draw abeam of Cruther's Point and the small landing quay, wait until you have the two boathouses on the dunes behind the beach open of the end of the quay before turning inshore – this will clear the last remaining hazard, the isolated Harry's Rock (dries 1.2m) a cable south-east of the quay.

Anchor anywhere in the western end of the bay, but keep clear of the approach to the quay which is used by the ferries. Do not leave dinghies tied to the quay, but you can land anywhere on the beach.

FACILITIES

Do not be misled by the enticing prospect of three towns, for here again these are little more than hamlets – Higher Town in the centre, Lower Town at the western end and Middle Town in between!

Lower Town has a handy fruit and veg shop, the Locker, with a limited selection of other provisions, open daily 0930 – 1730. Just above it on the hillside you will find the Seven Stones pub (Tel: 423560), which serves bar meals and is open for evening meals 1930 – 2100.

Middle Town has little more to offer than a public phone box, but Higher Town Post Office Stores and Off-licence (open 0900 – 1700 daily, closed for lunch, open for an hour on Sunday mornings) has a reasonable selection of tinned food, frozen produce, gifts and books, but no fresh food. There is, however, excellent fresh

The approach marks to St Helen's Pool from Crow Sound: the rocky landing carn centred between Men-a-vaur's distinctive peaks

bread at St Martin's Bakery, and if you're keen to emulate it you can even enrol on a bread making course! There is also a public phone, tea room and bistro crafts/gift shop.

There is no fuel available on the island. Water in small quantities (cans) can sometimes be obtained from the St Martin's on the Isle Hotel.

ST HELEN'S POOL

St Helen's Pool is an open roadstead fringed by Tean, St Helen's Island and Tresco. At one time this was the favoured bolt hole for larger vessels when St Mary's Roads became uncomfortable. On St Helen's island there is a legacy from the days of sail; the small ruined building, dating from 1756 and known as the pest house, was once an isolation hospital for disease-ridden seamen.

St Elidius' hermitage, the oldest Christian building in Scilly, and a small complex of excavated church buildings dating from the eighth to 12th century will be found nearby. Behind them a steep path leads to the heathery summit of the island from where there are spectacular views of St Helen's Pool, the lighthouse on Round Island and Men-a-vaur. Tean was inhabited until the latter part of the 18th century and was a centre for burning kelp for fertiliser. The remains of the few small cottages can still be found on the southern foreshore. The island is voluntarily closed between 15th April and 20th July when ringed plovers are nesting.

The total lack of facilities and sheer isolation of St Helen's Pool are its main attractions making it a quieter alternative to the more popular anchorages.

At low water, when the extensive reefs of Golden Ball Brow are uncovered to the north-west,

Foreman's Island — Men-a-Vaur in transit with Landing Carn — Old Man

they form a perfect natural breakwater and the virtually landlocked shelter in St Helen's Pool is excellent. At the top of the tide, however, if there is any swell, you are likely to feel it and it will pay to look around for a more comfortable berth further to the south, either east of Foreman's Island or west of Old Man, depending on the wind direction.

The tide through the Pool follows much the same pattern as in Old Grimsby, running south-east at up to two knots springs for nearly eight hours, beginning HW Dover –0040 then turning north-west for four hours.

There is however, plenty of depth, usually ample room and the holding is good. Although you will certainly feel fully exposed to the force of the wind in a blow, it will not generate a great deal of sea and this, in many ways, is as safe as any anchorage in Scilly in such conditions.

For boats able to dry out comfortably, West and East Porth on the southern side of Tean provide excellent shelter.

APPROACHES AND ANCHORAGE

St Helen's Pool can be approached in several differing ways. Firstly, from Crow Sound, which is shallow but straightforward with sufficient rise of tide; or from Old Grimsby, again shallow but easy with a rising tide; from St Mary's Sound towards HW; and from seaward from the north through the passage known as St Helen's Gap.

St Helen's Gap is deep enough in itself, but the inner shallow bank between it and the Pool means that you will again need sufficient rise of tide. The tide runs strongly across this approach and it is both narrow (about 300m wide) and

St Helen's Pool is a classic and more remote Scilly anchorage. Old Grimsby Sound and Green Porth, Tresco, can be seen beyond

flanked by rocky ledges, which leaves little room for mistakes.

Personally I would recommend one of the 'overland' approaches for a first visit. You can then reconnoitre St Helen's Gap for future reference, or alternatively leave that way.

St Helen's Pool from Crow Sound.

Wait until half flood before approaching from the vicinity of the Hats buoy in Crow Sound. Steer 322°T, which will take you past the distinctive Guther's Island, and more important, Higher Ledge (dries 4.0m), which should just still be showing. In the far distance ahead, to the left of the rounded island of St Helen's, the unmistakeable pointed summits of **Men-a-vaur** are the marks you now need – **get the Landing Carn, a prominent lump of rock on the western end of St Helen's, in line with the gap between the two highest summits on Men-a-vaur** and this 322°T transit will take you safely into the anchorage, passing between the Chinks Rocks (awash LAT) and Hunters Lump (dries 0.9m). This is the narrowest part of the approach,

St Helen's Pool north approach viewed from Tean, with East and West Gap Rocks in centre well uncovered at low water, and Round Island on right

proceed slowly with a lookout on the bow.

Once the impressive bulk of Hedge Island is abeam you are entering the Pool, which extends for nearly mile, with depths varying between 2.5m and 7m. If you intend to anchor close to St Helen's Island, beware the sandy spit (dries 2.9m) which hooks round to the south and west from the island, and sound in until the pest house ruin on the shore is bearing about north-east.

St Helen's Pool from Old Grimsby is a simple bit of eyeball navigation, ideally undertaken from half flood onwards. It is easiest if you pass south of Lump of Clay Ledge (dries 1.4m) and leave Little Cheese Rock several boat lengths to port before heading up towards St Helen's. Little Cheese (0.7m) is visible even at HW and when covered, the surrounding ledges are easy to spot from the weed on them.

St Helen's Pool approach from St Mary's Sound is more demanding and uses the same marks described in the southern exit from Old Grimsby – St Mary's Telegraph tower in transit with Crow Rock Beacon, 162°T. On this the Cones Rock (dries 0.6m) and Diamond Ledge will be left close to port, so keep a good lookout. You will then pass midway between Little Pentle Ledge (dries 2.8m) and West Craggyellis Ledge (dries

0.8m). Both will be covered, but Great Pentle Rock (1.7m), at the western end of the Pentle Ledge, gives you a good indication of when you have passed these hazards.

Once Lizard Point on Tresco is abeam, keep slightly to port to avoid Tea Ledge (dries 3.7m), the weed on which should be visible, and then ease over to starboard leaving Little Cheese Rock on your port hand and thence straight into the anchorage.

If you climb to the summit of St Helen's Island to take in the view (definitely best at low water), you you will be able to clearly see St Helen's Gap, the narrow (100m) passage out to the north between the West (0.9m) and East (2.3m) Gap Rocks. Although both are visible at HW, ledges extend beyond them for some distance, particularly to the north of the East Gap Rock.

St Helen's Pool from seaward

Keep up to Round Island, leaving it 200 – 300m to starboard, and then steer to leave Didleys Point, the eastern end of St Helen's, about 100m to starboard. The Gap Rocks should be clearly visible from here – steer to leave the West Gap Rock on your starboard hand until you are almost abeam of the East Gap Rock, at which point you should ease more to port, passing midway between the two. Keep this course to the SSW and do not be tempted to haul round too rapidly into the Pool or you will fall foul of the sand spit (dries 2.9m) which extends a good 200m from the island shore.

THE EASTERN ISLES

With calm weather and good visibilty, Admiralty chart 883 and considerable care, the more adventurous can make an interesting foray amongst the Eastern Isles. They offer a number of temporary daytime anchorages, depending on the prevailing conditions, and the chance of seeing a few seals along the way, particularly in the vicinity of Menawethan. It is, however, not an area I would recommend for an overnight stop other than in exceptionally settled weather.

The easiest approach is south of Biggal and to the east of Ragged Island, keeping over to the west side of Great Ganilly. There are several passage graves on the Arthurs, but Nornour is probably the most interesting of these now deserted islands for here, along the southern edge of the island, you will find the impressive excavated Bronze Age settlement for which the island is famous.

Chapter 5

Isles of Scilly Anchorages at a glance

WIND	SHELTER OPTIONS	COMMENT
North	St Mary's Pool	Good if closer inshore
	Porth Cressa	Very good in absence of swell
	New Grimsby	Good, but prone to swell
	Old Grimsby	Good
	St Helen's Pool	Good in lee of St Helen's
	The Cove	Very good, except when bar covered at HW
North East	St Mary's Pool	Very good
	Porth Cressa	Very good
	New Grimsby	Very good
	Old Grimsby	Good
	Porth Conger	Good, if well in
	The Cove	Good
	St Helen's Pool	Good in lee of Old Man
	Tean Sound	Good at south end
East	St Mary's Pool	Very good
	Porth Cressa	Very good
	Porth Conger	Very good
	The Cove	Good
South East	St Mary's Pool	Very good
	New Grimsby	Good
	Porth Conger	Very good, except at HW if bar covered
	Tean Sound	Good at northern end
South	St Mary's Pool	Very good
	Watermill Cove	Very good, but possible swell around HW
	Porth Conger	Very good except at HW if bar covered
	Old Grimsby	Good
	New Grimsby	Good, except towards HW, wind against tide
	St Helen's Pool	Good
South West	New Grimsby	Good, particularly at north end
	Old Grimsby	Very good
	Watermill Cove	Very good, but possible swell at HW unless well in
	Porth Conger	Very good
	The Cove	Good, if well in, but subject to swell
	St Helen's Pool	Good
West	New Grimsby	Very good
	Old Grimsby	Very good
	Watermill Cove	Very good, if well in
	Porth Cressa	Good, if well in, but subject to swell at HW
	Porth Conger	Good, if well in
	The Cove	Very good
	Tean Sound	Good
	St Helen's Pool	Good in lee of Norwethal
North West	Porth Cressa	Very good
	The Cove	Very good
	Old Grimsby	Good, if well in
	St Helen's Pool	Good, but swell likely around HW. Best towards south end of pool

PASSAGES
LAND'S END TO PENTIRE POINT

Favourable tidal streams

Land's End:

Bound west/north:	One hr after HW Dover
Bound south/east:	Five hrs before HW Dover

Passage charts for this sea area

BA: 2565 St Agnes Head to Dodman Point
1148 Isles of Scilly to Land's End
1149 Pendeen to Trevose Head
1156 Trevose Head to Hartland Point
1168 Harbours on the North Coast of
Cornwall
SC5603 is particularly useful

Imray: C7 Lizard Point to Trevose Head
C58 Trevose Head to Bull Point

Stanford: 13 Start Point to Padstow

French: 2218 Du Cap Lizard à Trevose Head

Safety information and weather

Initial announcement VHF Channel 16 then
switch to:

Falmouth Coastguard: VHF Channel 86 at 0140,
0540, 0940, 1340, 1740, 2340 UT

*Land's End from the south. Cape Cornwall is in the distance
with the Brisons on extreme left*

Cape Cornwall NCI station (Tel: 01736 787890)
St Ives NCI station (Tel: 01736 799398)
Stepper Point NCI station (Tel: 07810 898041)

Waypoints

1 **Longships** (0.75M due W of lighthouse)
50°04'·00N / 05°45'·95W

2 **Cape Cornwall**
(2M due W of summit chimney)
50°07'·63N / 05°45'·71W

3 **Pendeen**
(1M due NW of lighthouse)
50°10'·78N / 05°41'·27W
St Ives (West Pier head)
50°12'·78N / 05 28'·73W
Stones buoy 50°15'·64N / 05 25'·47W
Newquay (North Pier head)
50°25'·08N / 05°05'·19W

4 **Trevose Head**
(2M due NW of lighthouse)
50°32'·94N / 05°05'·31W
Padstow (just off St Saviour's Point)
50°32'·75N / 04°55'·92W

Chapter 6

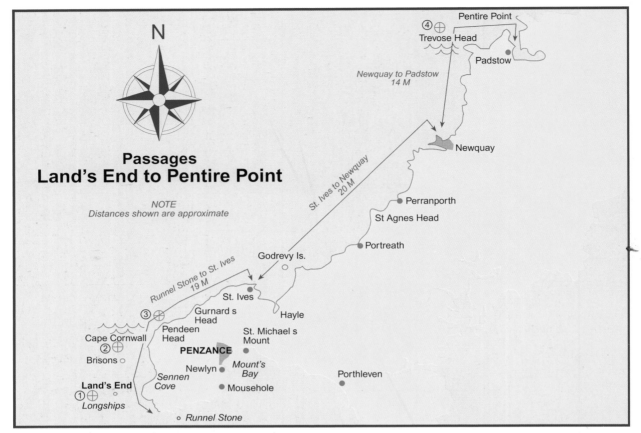

Passages
Land's End to Pentire Point

NOTE
Distances shown are approximate

As a cruising ground there is, sadly, little to recommend the North Cornish coast. In the prevailing south-westerly winds it presents an exposed and rugged lee shore with just a few drying harbours that cannot be guaranteed as places of refuge – an unwholesome combination and a natural deterrent for pleasure boating.

Rounding Land's End and bound up the Irish Sea, your course will soon take you well away from the coast, an offing that you should endeavour to maintain.

Although there is little real cruising potential on this dangerous stretch of coast, it has become increasingly used by yachts on passage to and from South Wales and the Bristol Channel to the Isles of Scilly and the West Country during the summer months. Most would, I'm sure, agree that it is an area they try to pass through as quickly as possible, waiting for the right conditions, and completing it in one leg. However, there will obviously be occasions when circumstances dictate a need to put in somewhere, or when in very settled weather and an offshore wind, a little bit of cruising can be contemplated, and it is for this reason that this short passage section is included.

LAND'S END TO ST IVES BAY

Land's End, the most westerly point in England, is not a particularly distinctive headland, being somewhat lost against the rest of this noble stretch of pinkish grey granite cliffs which rise to over 70m along one of the most rugged sections of coast in southern England. The prominent white Land's End Hotel and other buildings are all part of the privately owned Land's End tourist complex, and further to the north the famous First and Last House in England is high on the cliff top.

A mile offshore, the infamous **Longships** reef has claimed many ships and the tidal streams are strong and unpredictable in their vicinity. Although the north-going flood begins one hour after HW Dover, it does not turn north-east along the north Cornish coast until two hours later attaining over two knots at springs. Five hours before HW Dover, the ebb begins to run south-west back along the coast.

There is a convenient inshore passage between the Longships (Iso WR 10s W16M R15/13M) and the mainland, but **this should only be attempted in settled conditions, good visibility and never at night.**

The Longships looking east to Land's End and Armed Knight Rock, top right. Seas are breaking on Kettle's Bottom, centre, the inshore passage lies between this rock and the mainland. Whitesand Bay and Sennen, top left

Pass a quarter of a mile to seaward of Land's End, from where the Brisons, two conspicuous rocky islands to the north, provide the best transit. The highest point of the highest island (27m) should be kept just open to the west of the highest point of the low island (22m), a bearing of 001°T. Kettle's Bottom, forming the inshore, easternmost extremity of the Longships rocks, dries 5.2m, and Shark's Fin, the most northerly reef, dries 3.2m.

If passing to the west of the Longships give the whole area a good berth, and if bound up the coast maintain a course well north of east for just over a mile to clear the Shark's Fin. At night, the north-eastern red sector of the Longships covers all hazards along this section of coast and should

Longships inshore passage marks: Brisons high summit just open of low summit

not be entered until Pendeen lighthouse opens. With jagged rocks and breaking water to seaward, and the tall, lonely finger of the lighthouse with its precarious helicopter landing pad, this is a menacing stretch of water where you will probably feel little inclined to linger.

The large sandy sweep of Whitesand Bay forms a break in the cliffs, and the village and tiny harbour of Sennen Cove will be seen at its southern end with its lifeboat house, the most south-westerly station in England.

It was here in 1794/95 that Samuel Wyatt, the Trinity House architect, assembled, numbered and shipped the granite blocks to Carn Bras Rock to build the first Longships lighthouse, which was replaced in 1873 with the present structure by Sir James Douglas.

The keepers were often stranded here during winter storms and in 1966 it was one of the first lighthouses to receive much needed supplies by helicopter, the lantern house windows padded

The Longships from the west. Land's End, left,
Gwennap Head, right

out with mattresses in case the rotors touched!

There is a fair weather anchorage in offshore winds just off Sennen village, inside the Cowloe Rocks, but this is very exposed and cannot be recommended. Passing to the north of the Brisons the tidal streams run strongly past Cape Cornwall, a distinctive, cone-shaped headland, uniquely, the only cape in England. Topped by a conspicuous ruined chimney, this is one of the first indications of the extensive mining operations that once covered this stretch of coast. For the next 10 miles, the cliffs are dotted with old pumping houses, chimneys and other buildings, from which the underground workings extended far beneath the sea bed, in places well over a mile out into the Atlantic. Cape Cornwall also has an NCI lookout (Tel: 01736 787890).

The Vyneck is an isolated rock three cables north-west of Cape Cornwall – from here on a course a mile to seaward will clear all hazards except the overfalls which extend westwards from Pendeen Head, a bold headland. On it, the squat white lighthouse of Pendeen Watch (Fl (4) 15s 16M) looks out over the Wra, or Three Stone Oar, a group of small rocky islands just under a half mile offshore.

The coast follows a north-easterly direction from here on, a continuous unbroken line of impenetrable granite cliffs and one of the major sea cliff climbing centres in England. Along it, and in the approaches to St Ives Bay, a good lookout should be kept for pot and net buoys; in spite of the exposure of this coast, it is much worked by local boats.

ST IVES BAY TO TREVOSE HEAD

The drying fishing harbour of St Ives is tucked in behind St Ives Head at the south western corner of this four mile wide bay. There are drying moorings for visitors within the harbour; deeper draught vessels can anchor off in suitable offshore weather. An NCI station is located on St Ives Head (Tel: 01736 799398).

The rest of St Ives Bay is backed by the long sandy beach and extensive dunes of Hayle Towans, which stretch away to its far northern end where the lighthouse (Fl WR 10s W12M R9M) on Godrevy Island lies close inshore. Built in 1859, this was always a controversial siting for it gives little indication of the notorious reef, the Stones, which extends nearly a mile to the north-west of the island. A lightship or lighthouse on the outermost rock was the favoured option, but was turned down because of the cost. An area of strong currents, and drying rocks, many awash at HW, their outer limit is marked today by the Stones BY north cardinal buoy (Q) and the area is covered by the red sector of the Godrevy light 101° – 145°T.

The Sound, the inshore passage between Godrevy and the Stones, is half a mile wide and not recommended without local knowledge as there are overfalls, particularly with wind against tide, and the additional hazard of numerous pot buoys – this is no place to be caught with a fouled propeller if motoring. Pass well to seaward of the whole area.

Bound north from St Ives Bay, the flood begins about two hours after HW Dover, (two hours after local LW). **Bound south**, ideally leave around local HW, which will entail pushing the tide for the first hour, but will ensure a fair tide round Land's End and into Mount's Bay.

From the Stones buoy it is just over 17 miles to the next possible drying harbour at Newquay, along an impressive but unwelcoming stretch of coast; mostly high, crumbling cliffs, averaging between 40 and 75 metres in height. Along them there are numerous sandy coves and bays, such as Porthtowan and Perranporth, holiday resorts particularly popular with surfers thanks to the almost perpetual ground swell which produces ideal conditions for the sport. Numerous small rocky islets lie close inshore, but with the exception of Bawden Rocks, two small islands a mile north of St Agnes' Head, there are no off-lying dangers.

Unless heading for Newquay, the direct course to Trevose Head, just over 22 miles to the north-east, takes you safely two to three miles offshore. Inland, higher ground runs parallel to the coast, and a conspicuous feature is the large obelisk on the skyline south-east of Portreath.

Trevose Head lighthouse (Fl 7.5s 21M) is a prominent white tower on a precipitous headland with two large rocky islets, the Bull and Quies, nearly a mile to seaward. There is an inshore passage between them and the coast, but this should not be used without local knowledge and again the tide runs hard here. Give the islets and the headland a wide berth. From here Padstow Bay begins to open, with Pentire Point forming its distant northern extremity just over five miles away.

With no possible shelter in winds between south-west and north-east throughout this passage area, if the weather deteriorates and a blow looks likely, particularly from the south-west, the advice in the Admiralty Pilot 'to seek a good offing' is probably as sensible as you will get. Padstow is the only place where complete shelter will be found once you are inside the harbour. However, this is tidal and only accessible two hours either side of HW, and the Camel estuary on which it lies is approached over a bar that becomes very dangerous in strong onshore weather.

A decision to run for Padstow in deteriorating conditions should be considered very carefully, with particular regard to the state of the tide, aiming to arrive between half-flood and HW. With any ground swell, once the ebb commences, the shallow waters of Padstow Bay become very hazardous and unapproachable in strong winds from the north-west. The Stepper Point NCI station (Tel: 07810 898041) overlooks the approach

to the estuary and can always be contacted 0900 – 1800 in season for details of current weather and sea state.

In fog or poor visibility, additional aids to navigation along this section of coast are the Longships (Horn 10s), Pendeen (Horn 20s), Stones Buoy (Whistle) and Trevose Head (Horn (2) 30s).

Trevose Head from the west. Gulland Rock on left, Stepper Point, centre, and Pentire Point in far distance

The entrance to the River Camel viewed from Pentire Point, with Stepper Point on right and the houses of Trebetherick on left

Godrevy Lighthouse – the inspiration for Virginia Woolf's novel To the Lighthouse . . .

With surf breaking on Porthmeor Sands and the Tate Gallery on extreme right, St Ives' drying harbour is tucked well in behind St Ives Head. The Hayle Estuary is in the far distance

ST IVES AND NEWQUAY

Tides	HW Dover−0605
Charts	BA: 1168, SC 5603.4, 5603.5. Stanford: 13. Imray: C7
Hazards	**St Ives**: Harbour dries, exposed in onshore winds. Hoe Rock and conical green buoy to NE (both unlit), Carracks Rocks to SE (unlit)
Overnight charge	**St Ives**: Harbour Authority mooring £13 **Newquay**: Drying alongside £9.20

From a distance St Ives Head looks like an island and, when entering the bay, this should be given a good berth to avoid Carn Everis Rocks on its northern side, which dry 3m, and Hoe Rock on its north-eastern side, which dries 1.8m. In the closer approach an unlit conical green buoy

marks the end of the ruined outer pier and should be left to starboard. Smeatons Pier, which forms the eastern protective arm of the harbour, has a prominent but disused white lighthouse at its outer end. At night the pier head is marked by (2FG vert) lights; this and the shorter west pier (2FR vert), enclose a harbour which dries completely at LAT, but is normally accessible after half flood. It has a firm sandy bottom and there is a fleet of quite large fishing and trip boats based here during the summer months which lie on heavy fore and aft drying moorings or alongside

the quay. Shelter is good in south and westerly weather, but anything further north can send a considerable sea into the bay and causes a heavy swell within the harbour.

In favourable conditions, anchor about 100m south-east of the harbour entrance in about 3m, but watch out for the large number of buoys marking keep pots towards Porthminster beach.

Due to the increase in fishing boat activity and landing, it is no longer possible to berth overnight inside the outer end of Smeatons Pier, but high water permitting, deep keel boats can

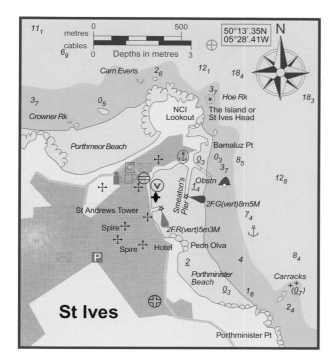

St Ives, launched on a trailer across the beach.

St Ives Bay stretches away to the north-east, backed by the extensive sand dunes and beach of Hayle Towans. Hayle, in the south-eastern corner, is a run-down, tidal harbour used by a few local fishing boats. Approached over a dangerous bar and tricky entrance channel through a large expanse of drying sands, it is not recommended for visitors.

NEWQUAY

In fair weather and ideally offshore winds, Newquay is a pleasant small drying harbour that is feasible for an overnight stop.

Midway between it and Godrevy, St Agnes' Head is prominent, 91m high, with steep cliffs, while inland the isolated St Agnes' Hill (200m) is covered in heather and gorse and surmounted by a beacon. This was another site of intensive tin mining activity in the 1800s, and several conspicuous ruins can be seen along the shore. Just north of St Agnes' Head, Trevaunance Cove was but one small port exporting tin and copper – it was frequently rebuilt between 1700 and 1920 as gales swept away the massive granite walls.

Closing the land from the south, East and West Pentire Points form the entrance of the Gannel, a silted-up river mouth creating a fine sandy beach, and Fistral Bay, renowned for surfing, leads up to Towan Head, the entrance to Newquay Bay, which has the large Atlantic Hotel prominent on its highest point.

Although there are no off-lying dangers, overfalls occur up to half a mile off Towan Head, and it is wise to give it a reasonable berth before turning into the bay, when the eastern extremities of Newquay's extensive hotels and houses will come into view along the skyline right down to the cliff-backed beaches. The harbour lies in the south-western corner of the town, hidden behind a headland, ENE of which the Listrey Rocks, least depth 0.5m and 1.2m, lie 300m offshore. Keep well out into the bay before heading in towards the harbour walls as they come into view.

The whole of the inner part of the bay dries at LWS and the harbour is normally only accessible for average draught boats three hours either side of local HW (HW Dover –0604). If waiting for the tide, anchor off in the bay, which is well sheltered from the south and west. The entrance is 23m wide between the north and south quays, and the isolated jetty in the centre of the harbour dates from 1870 when it was originally linked to the

berth here temporarily, if space is available, for short stays to replenish stores or in emergencies. However, bilge keelers or boats able to take the bottom are well catered for, with six drying visitors' moorings in the harbour just off the prominent Woolworths store on the waterfront. The charge is £13 per night. The harbour master, Mr Steve Bassett, will help with any problems. His office is on the pier (Tel: 01736 795018) and he normally works on VHF Channel 12, although VHF Channel 16 is also usually monitored when the harbour office is open. Fresh water is available on the piers, while Calor and Camping Gaz can be had from the Fishermen's Co-operative. Fuel, however, is not easily obtainable.

During the season the town reels under the assault of tourists, its picturesque narrow streets and alleyways, harbour and wide sandy Porthmeor Beach on the seaward side of St Ives Head providing all the essentials of a seaside holiday. In spite of a certain amount of inevitable commercialism, the town retains much of its unique atmosphere, a factor that has made it a popular haunt of artists for many years, even more so with the arrival of the Tate Art Gallery's western outpost which overlooks Porthmeor.

All other normal requirements can be found, such as banks, post office and provisions, and there are many cafés, pubs and restaurants. A very handy toilet and public shower block is in the car park just behind the harbour front. There are road and main line rail connections. A lifeboat is stationed at

A visit to Newquay's small drying harbour should only be considered in fair weather and offshore wind

shore with a wooden bridge carrying a railway track, which came down to the harbour through a tunnel to facilitate the loading of copper ore and china clay brought overland by rail from Par.

There were once four shipbuilding yards around Newquay and, at the height of its prosperity in the mid 1800s, nearly 150 trading vessels were owned in the port. The last cargo of clay was exported in 1921 and the last inward cargo (manure!) was discharged by the ketch *Hobah* in 1922.

Visitors normally berth alongside the inner end of the south quay, where there is a clean, hard, sandy bottom, and you will dry clear of the local fishing boats lying on heavy fore and aft moorings in the middle of the harbour, which suffers from a surge if there is much swell.

Harbour Master Captain Malcolm Gater is very helpful and is usually around 0830 – 1700 in the summer. His office is on the south pier (Tel: 01637 872809). Charges are £0.92 per metre per night, and water and diesel are available from him on request. Public toilets are close by, as is the licensed clubhouse of the Newquay Rowing Club where temporary membership is available, thus saving the trek up into town for a pint! These dedicated enthusiasts own several beautifully restored Scilly pilot gigs, including the oldest

one still afloat, *Newquay*, built in 1812.

Newquay is one of the largest holiday resorts in Cornwall and, the Surfing Capital of Britain, its lively main centre is a short walk from the busy harbour. All normal requirements are available, such as post office, banks, provisions, launderettes, pubs, cafés and restaurants. It has road, rail and air connections.

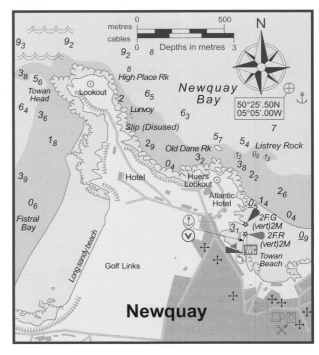

PADSTOW

Tides	HW Dover−0550
Range	MHWS 7.7m–MHWN 5.5m, MLWN 2.6m–MLWS 0.8m
Charts	BA:1168, SC: 5603.5. Stanford:13. Imray: C7, C58
Waypoint	North Pier End 50°32'51N / 04°56'17W
Hazards	Gulland, Newland, Gurley, Chimney and Roscarrock Rocks (all unlit) and many pot buoys to seaward. Wreck west of Stepper Point (unlit). Doom Bar and much of river and outer harbour dries. Buoyed channel (lit) but liable to change. Approach can be dangerous in onshore wind and sea. Busy tidal fishing port
Overnight charge	Harbour Authority, at anchor or alongside £12

It is 13 miles from Newquay to the mouth of the River Camel, and Padstow lies two miles upstream. This is a most attractive estuary, a spectacular area of golden drying sands, with a shoreline of low cliffs, fine sandy beaches and rolling dunes providing some lovely walks.

In 1989, as part of a flood prevention scheme, a hydraulic bottom hinged gate was installed in the entrance of the formerly drying inner harbour, making it possible to lie afloat here, and this has not only resulted in a steady increase in visiting pleasure craft, but also ongoing improvement to shoreside facilities.

Flanked by clean yellow sand, the final approach channel to Padstow is clearly visible on the right. Visitors lie afloat in the inner harbour, which is accessible for two hours either side of HW

However, the mouth of the river is restricted by the Doom Bar, a large sandbank drying at low water and, during strong onshore winds or heavy seas, this lives up to its melancholy name, particularly around low water when the sea can break right across the entrance – conditions that are not always obvious from seaward. With care though, the River Camel is not difficult to enter in daylight and yachts of normal draught will have ample water from half-flood onwards.

The attractive Camel estuary looking to seaward with the Doom Bar just beginning to uncover on left. Newland Island is in the centre, with Pentire Point on right

The approach at night is relatively straightforward once you have located Stepper Point light (LFl W 10s), which only has a four mile range, being only 12m above sea level.

Note, however, that the shore lights of Trebetherick and Polzeath on the eastern side of the entrance are by far the most dominant feature from seaward and should not be mistaken for the lights of Padstow, which are far less visible and do not really begin to emerge until you are well into the river.

APPROACHES

The approach from the north or south is unmistakable. Trevose Head, four miles to the west, is a steep 80m high headland, which rises above the surrounding hinterland, giving it the appearance from a distance of being a separate island. In addition, the Bull and Quies, prominent large rocks, lie a mile to the west.

The lighthouse is on the north-western corner of the headland and dates from 1847; Padstow lifeboat house is on the north-eastern side of the headland in Mother Ivey's Bay, re-sited here in 1967 after the original station at Hawkers Cove inside the mouth of the estuary fell prey to the encroachment of the Doom Bar. This bar, according to local legend, was created by a mermaid, shot by a local man who thought she was a fish. Cursing him with her dying breath, she threw up a handful of sand which turned into the Doom Bar, vowing that 'henceforth the harbour should be desolate!'

Tidal streams run strongly off Trevose – over two knots at springs – particularly between the rocks and the headland and you should keep to seaward of the Quies before heading up into Padstow Bay, passing inside Gulland Rock, a prominent rocky island 28m high, where again the stream can run strongly.

There are several isolated hazards further inshore; Gurley Rock (least depth 3m) and Chimney Rock (2.3m) are not normally a problem to boats of average draught, but worth remembering near low water, particularly if there is any ground swell running. Stepper Point, a bold and rounded grassy headland, footed with cliffs, forms the south side of the river mouth and is easily identified by the large stone daymark, like a truncated factory chimney. There is an NCI

Padstow approach channel at low water, showing proximity to the shore. The Pool lies beyond

lookout (Tel: 07810 898041) high up at its eastern extremity, and almost at sea level the harbour approach light on an iron pillar (L Fl 10s 4M).

Three cables WNW of the daymark there is a dangerous wreck, almost awash at LW, so give the headland a wide berth and head up towards Pentire Point, another bold headland forming the north-eastern arm of the bay, with the distinctive island of Newland, a pyramid 35m high, half a mile to the north-west. Approaching from the north, it is best to keep well to seaward of Newland, as Roscarrock, a rock with least depth of 0.8m, lurks three cables west of Rumps Point, the north-eastern corner of Pentire. The brig *Maria Asumpta* was disastrously wrecked here in May 1995.

THE RIVER CAMEL TO PADSTOW

Enter the river on a flood tide, ideally no earlier than three hours before local HW (HW Dover –0550) and do not attempt it in any ground swell from the north-west, or if breaking water can be seen.

The Doom Bar, a large expanse of drying sand, fills the south-western corner of the river mouth, and opposite, the houses of Trebetherick sprawl along the low cliffs. These are fringed with rocky ledges, and the channel between them and the

sands runs due south, with the western end of Pentire Point providing a useful back bearing.

Depths reduce quickly from 3m to a least depth of 0.8m two cables north of the first channel buoy, Greenaway, a red port hand can (Fl (2) R 10s), while Doom Bar, two cables further south, is a conical green starboard hand buoy (Fl G 5s). At low water the channel is a cable wide and depths vary between 2m and 0.4m as far as St Saviour's Point, known locally as *Ship-me-pumps*, a quarter of a mile downstream of the harbour.

A prominent monument stands on this rocky headland and a red and green middle ground buoy (Fl R 5s) abeam of it, where the channel divides. The main channel to the harbour lies to starboard of the buoy, while the river bears away towards the village of Rock on the eastern shore. Just south of the buoy, there is the Pool, with an average depth of 3m and a number of local moorings in it. It is possible to anchor clear of them, if waiting for sufficient water to get into the Inner harbour, although at springs the tide can run hard, between four and five knots at times, on both the flood and ebb.

A large area of drying sandbanks fills the centre of the river and the narrow approach channel to Padstow also dries almost completely at springs. Hold tight to the western shore and leave the green beacon with triangular topmark close on your starboard hand, (Fl G 10s). Pass the green

Kettle Rock buoy (QG) to starboard and just short of the harbour entrance leave the red Town Bar can (Q R) to port. The outer pier ends are marked with (2FR vert) and (2FG vert) port and starboard.

Proceed under power and watch out for fishing boats under way, particularly in the harbour mouth, where the main stream runs strongly at right angles to the entrance. South Dock, the commercial harbour, lies immediately to port, a long narrow, drying basin, but yacht borne visitors should continue straight ahead through the tidal gate into the Inner Harbour, which is open two hours either side of HW, day and night, weekends and Bank Holidays. The maximum depth within the harbour is usually maintained at three metres, although more water can be retained to accommodate deeper draught boats if the berthing master is informed on arrival. Visitor charges (the same whether you anchor in the river or lie alongside) are £1.20 per metre per night.

The impressive new harbour office, built in 2000, is close by on South Quay and incorporates an amenity block with showers, toilets and laundry with 24 hour access by pin code/keypad. The showers are included in your berthing fee and the laundry is operated by pre-pay tokens available from the harbour office (open 0800 – 1700 weekdays, and two hours before and after HW, every tide). You should try to report by VHF before arrival, or as soon as you have berthed. Visitors are requested not to leave vessels unattended for any length of time without first consulting the harbour master.

The Harbour Commission sometimes has visitors' moorings available in the river for vessels up to 12m. To check either call *Padstow Harbour* (VHF Ch 16; 12, during office hours) or telephone ahead for availability.

FACILITIES

This is a small, unspoilt town, with attractive and colourful old buildings lining the quayside. Popular with holidaymakers, Padstow has managed to avoid much of the overt commercialism of some of the other north Cornish resorts.

Formerly a vital port for north Cornwall, exporting tin, copper, slate, granite, china clay and grain, and importing coal, salt and timber, it was also important as a shipbuilding centre. By the beginning of this century, however, commercial trade had dwindled steadily with the silting of the Doom Bar and the advent of road

Visiting boats lie afloat in Padstow's secure and attractive inner harbour, which is accessed through a tidal gate

and rail transport, and it would seem that the mermaid's wish had been fulfilled, for little more than a small fishing fleet remained.

However, in recent years this has grown considerably, evidence of the resurgence in prosperity. Pot and net boats land vast quantities of shellfish here, as a look in the sizable wet tanks on the Fish Quay will reveal, and large beam trawlers also work out of the port. Coasters occasionally discharge cargoes of fertiliser and roadstone and the resident sand dredger, *Sandsnipe*, lands about 100,000 tons a year, mostly for agricultural use.

The prominent red brick building on the north side of the harbour was formerly a warehouse – today it houses additional visitors' showers, toilets and a laundry, accessed 24 hours by the same pin code, and the Tourist Information Centre.

The town's facilities incorporate an HSBC, Lloyds TSB and Barclays bank, all with cashpoints, provisions, including a Spar (open late and on Sundays) and a Tesco supermarket on

Rick Stein's Café offers simpler, cheaper fare and, should you be out of luck, there's always a choice of several good fish and chip shops! Other possibilities are Brocks Restaurant (Tel: 532565) or Margots (Tel: 533441).

The walks out towards Stepper Point and beyond are a delightful way to work up an appetite or thirst, with an abundance of fine sandy beaches en route. Alternatively, head inland and explore the Camel Trail, which follows the course of the old railway line to Wadebridge, beyond which Padstow was linked to the main rail network until it fell victim to Dr Beeching's axe in 1966. It's an attractive and gentle riverside walk as long as you are prepared to run the gauntlet of the myriad of cyclists! If you'd rather join them than be at their mercy, bikes can be hired at the beginning of the trail.

However, much of the pleasure boating activity in the estuary, particularly dinghy sailing, is centred on Rock, on the opposite shore. Here there are several deeper pools and a large number of local moorings as well as some drying Harbour Commission moorings also available for visitors, athough these tend to be hired on a weekly basis for people holidaying in the area. Rock is a much quieter little village, with many holiday homes, and is linked to Padstow by the Harbour Commissioners *Black Tor* pedestrian ferry, which runs continuously between 0800 and 1950. If you are lying in the Pool, the ferry can be hailed to take you ashore.

Rock Sailing Club has a fine clubhouse, an old converted grain warehouse on the quay with excellent facilities. Visitors are welcome to use the bar and showers, and snack meals are also available. The sand dunes and clean beaches running seaward from Rock towards Brea Hill are most attractive, and those seeking a longer walk should head out through Trebetherick and Polzeath to the distant heights of Pentire Point, with its fine views of the estuary and the rugged coast beyond.

The Camel, once a busy waterway, is still navigable on a good tide as far as Wadebridge, about five miles inland where yachts can dry out alongside Commissioner's Quay. However, this definitely needs some local knowledge or reconaissance in the dinghy, as the channel is tortuous and unmarked.

the outskirts of the town, to which a free courtesy bus runs from the harbour three times a week (see harbour office for times).

Chandlery, Calor and Camping Gaz are available through the harbour master, as well as diesel and petrol if you leave your cans outside the harbour office at 0900 or 1600. Alternatively diesel can be obtained alongside the South Pier when the tide permits, while all the berths in the inner harbour are equipped with water and electricity (£1 and £5 card meters).

As a popular holiday town, there is a plethora of quayside cafés, no shortage of pubs, notably the London Inn, Old Custom House and Old Ship, all of which have good pub menus, and a number of restaurants catering for all tastes and prices, including the celebrated Seafood Restaurant (Tel: 532700), owned by the well-known television chef and author Rick Stein. Inevitably, here, reservations well in advance are essential.

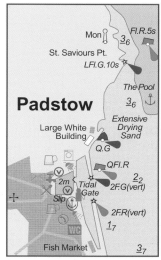

Padstow Port Guide

Area telephone code: 01841

Harbour Master: Captain Trevor Platt, Harbour Office, Padstow, PL28 8AQ (Tel: 532239. Fax: 533346) Mon – Fri, 0800 – 1700.
E-mail: infor@padstowharbour.fsnet.co.uk
Website: http://www.padstow-harbour.co.uk

VHF: Ch 16, working 12, call sign *Padstow Harbour*, office hours and two hours either side of HW

Mail Drop: c/o Harbour Office

Emergency Services: Lifeboat at Trevose Head. Falmouth Coastguard

Anchorages: The Pool, a quarter mile downstream of Padstow. Drying, clear of moorings at Rock

Moorings/berthing: Inner harbour, afloat at all times, access through tidal gate two hours either side of local HW, day and night, weekends and Bank holidays. Harbour Commission moorings in river sometimes available on application

Charges: £1.20 per metre per night

Water Taxi: Regular ferry Padstow to Rock will pick up from boats in the Pool

Marina: None

Phones: On quay

Doctor: (Tel: 532346)

Hospital: Treliske, Truro (Tel: 01872 250000)

Churches: All denominations

Local Weather Forecast: Harbour Office

Fuel: Harbour Master can arrange diesel and petrol in cans. Diesel alongside seaward side of South Pier when tide permits

Gas: Calor/Gaz from Harbour Office

Water: On quay

Tourist Information Centre: Red brick building, north side harbour, (Tel: 533449)

Banks/cashpoints: Barclays, Lloyds TSB and HSBC all have cashpoints

Post Office: Duke Street

Rubbish: Bins on quay

Showers/toilets: In Harbour Office, and red brick building, North Quay. Public toilets on quay. Toilets/showers, Rock Sailing Club

Launderette: In Harbour Office and red brick building, North Quay

Provisions: Most normal requirements. Spar open till 2130, and Sundays. Tesco on outskirts of town

Chandler: Limited selection at Rigmarine, South Quay,

(Tel: 532657). Harbour Office can usually assist

Repairs: A J England, (Tel: 532418). Chapman & Hewitt (Tel: 01208 813487).G B Smith & Son (Tel: 01208 862815)

Marine engineers:Techon Marine (Tel: 533114). Padstow Auto Marine (Tel: 532994). G B Smith & Son (Tel: 01208 862815). Reynolds Marine (Tel:533955)

Electronic engineers: Marconi Marine (01326 312855).

Transport: Buses via Bodmin (Tel: 01208 79898) connect with mainline railway at Bodmin Parkway (Tel: 08457 484950). Newquay airport (Tel: 01637 860551) flights to London and other UK destinations

Car Parking: Large car park on South Quay

Yacht Club: Rock Sailing Club, The Quay, Rock, Wadebridge PL27 6LB (Tel: 01208 862431)

Eating out: Good pubs, cafés and restaurants in both Padstow and Rock

Things to do: Local museum in Padstow. Guided tours of Prideaux Place, (stately home). Excellent beaches, swimming and walking

Padstow outer harbour

INDEX

A

Abbey Gardens 224, 229
Abbreviations and symbols 15
Admiralty Charts 10
Airport, Newquay 202
Amsterdam Point 154
Anchor Stone 63
Annet 219
Anstey's Cove 26
Anthony Passage 108
Appletree Point 227
Aquarium, The National Marine 103
Asparagus Island 174
Atkins, Evelyn and Babs 124
Aubrey de Selincourt 19, 51
August Rock 164, 166
August Rock buoy 122, 168
Aveton Gifford 86
Avon, River 72, 84
Axe, River 24
Axe Yacht Club 25
Axmouth harbour 24

B

Babbacombe Bay 26
Babs Carn 233
'Bacon Ledge' buoy 212
'Bag', the 80, 81
Balcombe Creek 82
Baltic Wharf Boatyard 65
Banjo Pier 125
Bantham 86
Bar Point 206
Barbican 101, 103, 104, 105
Barn Pool 98
Barnabas 189
Bartholomew ledges 204
Basking shark 173
Bass Point 173
Bass Rock 77
Batson Creek 78
Bayard's Cove 56, 61
BBC 61
BBC Local Radio Stations 12
Beady Pool 219
Bearings 10
Beer Head 25
Beer Roads 25
Beesands 29
Beggars Island 108
Belloc, Hilaire 130
Bellows and Field 119
Berry Head 19, 21, 26, 27, 51, 55, 56
Bigbury Bay 71, 84
Bigbury-on-Sea 72
Biggal 237
Biggal Rock 216
Bight, the 35
Bishop Rock lighthouse 202, 207, 219, 227
Bizzies 121
Black Head 141, 173, 176
Black Rock 122, 145

Black Rock Point 109
Blackness Point 64
Blackstone Point 55
Blackstone, The 77
Block House Point (St Marys) 217
Blockhouse Point (Tresco) 229
Blyth, Chay 63, 106
Boa, The 174
Boatmen's Association, St Mary's 209
Boatyard, Calstock 113
Boatyard, Gweek Quay 170
Boatyard, Mashford 98, 107
Boatyard, Multihull Centre Services, 107
Boatyard, Weir Quay 113
Bodinnick 136
Bodinnick ferry 136
Bolt Head 69, 70, 75
Bolt Tail 69, 80, 84
Bosahan Cove 167
Bosahan Point 167
Bovisand 98
Bovisand, Fort 97
Bow Creek 64
Bow, The 178, 220
Brazen Island 135
Bridge, The 98
Bridport 21, 22
Brisons 241
Bristol Channel 240
Brit, River 22
Britannia, HMS 57
Britannia Royal Naval College 57
British International helicopters 202
Brixham 21, 27, 50
Broad Ledge 234
Broad Ledge, West 234
Broad Sound 198, 207
Brow Breeze rocks 216
Bruce anchor 198
Brunel Tower 35
Bryher 195, 207, 219, 224, 229
Budleigh Salterton 25
Bull and Quies 243, 248
Bull Hill Bank 35
Buoyage 9, 15
Burgh Island 72, 84
Buzza Tower 213

C

Cadgwith 173, 176
Calamansack 169
Calf (St Agnes), The 220
Calf Rock 213
Calstock 110, 113
Camel, River 247
Camel Trail 251
Cannis Rock 120, 139
Cape Cornwall 242
Car Croc 122, 166
Cargreen 112
Carick Carlys Rock 158
Carn Base 174, 187

Carn Wethers 217
Carr, Frank 69
Carrick Roads 144, 154
Carricknath 154
Castella Down 219
Castle Down 224
Cattewater 102
Cawsand 97, 98
Cawsand Bay 73, 97
Cellar Bay 89
Channals Creek 158
Chapple Rocks 75
Charles, Fort 79
Charlestown 140
Charmouth 23
Chart Datum 10
Chartlets 10
Checkstone Ledge 33
Chesil beach 21
Chichester, Sir Francis 98
Chimney Rock 193, 248
Chinks Rocks 227, 236
Church Cove 173
Cliff House 77, 79
Clovelly Bay 102
Clyst, River 36
Coastguard, Brixham 8, 133
Coastguard, Falmouth 8
Coastguard Maritime Rescue Co-ordination, Falmouth 145
Coastguard, Portland 8
Cobb, the 24
Cobbler Channel 101, 102
Cockle Sand 35
Collapit Creek 82
Compass Cove 57
Cones Rock 237
Conger Rock 33
Cornwall oyster fisheries 166
Cothele House 113
Cothele Quay 113
Cove, The 220
Coverack 172, 176
Cow (St Agnes), The 220
Cow, The 213, 221
Cowlands Creeks 160
Cowper, Frank 46, 80, 195, 200
CQR anchor 198
Crab Ledge, Great 228
Crab Ledge, Little 228
Craggan Rocks 173
Cremyll 98, 99
Cremyll ferry 97
Cromwell's Castle 224, 225
Crow Bar 205, 216, 219
Crow Rock 206
Crow beacon 229
Crow Sound 202, 204, 205
Cruising Club, Island 80
Cuckolds Ledge 221
Culdrose, RNAS 123
Custom House Quay 147, 149, 150
Customs 14

D

D Day landings 79
Damasinnas 234
Dandy Hole 109
Danforth anchor 199
Dart Harbour and Navigation Authority (DHNA) 57, 63
Dart, Lake of the 64
Dart, River 21, 55
Dart Valley Trail 62
Dartmouth 28, 60, 69
Dartmouth Castle 57
Dartmouth day beacon 28
Dartside Quay 64
Dava Rocks 176
Dawlish 26
Dawlish Warren 31, 34
Den Point 43
Dennis Head 166
Depths 9
Devon Yawls 40
Devonport 100, 106
Diamond Ledge 237
Distances 9
Dittisham 63
Dodman Point 8, 116, 117, 119, 120
Dodman Point Gunnery Range 120
Dolphin Town 224
Doom Bar, The 247, 248, 249
Dorrien-Smith 222
Douglas, Sir James 241
Downend Point 28, 118, 128
Drake, Sir Francis 99, 106
Drake's Island 95, 98, 99
Drug Smuggling Action Line 14
Drum 121
Drying Heights 9
du Maurier, Daphne 135, 136, 137, 164, 167
Duchy Oyster Farm 169
Duncannon 64
Durgan 166

E

East Exe buoy 31
Eastern Blackstone 28, 56
Eastern Isles, The 204, 205, 237
Ebb Rocks, Eastern and Western 89
Eddystone lighthouse 73, 106, 118
Edward's Rock 87
Elberry Cove 27
Emergencies 8
English Channel 19, 175
English Heritage 145
English Riviera 27, 45
Erme, River 72, 86
Exe Estuary, The 25, 30
Exe, River 25, 30
Exeter 37, 40
Exmouth 26, 30, 33, 34
Exmouth Bar 31
Exmouth Dock 33

F

Fal, River 122, 144
Falmouth 119, 144, 147, 203
Falmouth Bay 122, 166, 203
Falmouth Bay & Estuaries
conservation initiatives 154, 167
Falmouth Classics 151
Falmouth Docks 145
Falmouth Harbour
Commissioners' 147
Falmouth Working Boats 135
Fastnet 94, 102
Fennel Rock 216
Ferry Boat Inn (Dart) 63
Ferry Boat Inn (Helford) 167
Ferry Inn 78
First and Last House 240
Fishcombe Cove 27
Fisherman anchor 199
Fisherman's Cove 77
Fisher's Nose 101
Flag Officer, Sea Training
Operations Room 121
Flagstaff, Devonport 95
Flat Owers Bank 64
Fleet Mill Reach 65
Flushing 151, 152, 166
Fowey 117, 118, 119, 128, 130
Fowey Classics 135
Fowey Gallants 135
Fowey lighthouse 130
Fowey Regatta Week 135
Frenchman's Creek 164, 167, 170
Frogmore 82
Frogmore Creek 81, 82
Froward Point 28

G

Galmpton Creek 64
Gap Rocks 237
Gear Rock 183, 186
Gedges rocks 122, 166
Gerrans Bay 121
Gig racing 214
Gigs 246
Gillan Creek 122, 166
Giles, Morgan 80
Gilstone 204
Gimble Porth 228
Glendurgan Gardens 167
Global Maritime Distress and
Safety System (GMDSS) 10
Goat's Point 233
Godrevy Island 242
Golant 137
Golden Ball 228
Golden Ball Brow 235
Golden Cap 23
Gorran Haven 120, 143
Goss, Pete 65
GPS 12
Grahame, Kenneth 130, 134
Great Ganilly 237
Great Hogus reef 191
Great Molunan 153
Great Pentle Rock 237
Green Bay 229
Green Porth 228
Greenbank 150

Greenbank Quay 150
Greenway Quay 64
Gregory Rocks 71
Greystone Ledge 71
Gribbin Head 119, 120, 139
Grove Point 20
Gry Maritha 209
Gugh 195, 218, 220
Gull Rock 121, 174
Gulland Rock 248
Gunfacts 13, 121
Gunwalloe 174
Gurley Rock 248
Guthen Rocks 176, 191
Guther's Island 236
Gwavas Lake 188
Gweek 166, 170
Gwennap Head 174
Gwineas Rocks 120, 142

H

Hakestone 221
Hakestone, Little 221
Half Moon Battery 145
Hall Walk 137
Hallsands 29
Halton Quay 113
Halwell Point 81
Ham Reach 65
Ham Stone 71
Hamoaze 95, 106
Hangman Island 225, 227
Hanjague 204, 205
Harbour Authority, Exeter City 38
Harbour Authority, Truro 159
Harbour Authority, Yealm 88
Harbour, Sutton 101, 103
Harbour Taxi, Salcombe 81
Harry's Rock 235
Hats buoy 206, 217
Hayle 245
Hayle Towans 242
Hedge Island 237
Heights above sea level 11
Helford, River 122, 164, 203
Helford Passage 167
Helford Point pontoon 169
Heliport, Penzance 185
Hell Bay 229
Helston 166
Helston buoy 122
Herring 127
Herzogin Cecilie 71, 80
High House Point 82
Higher Gurrow Point 64
Higher Ledge 236
Higher Town Bay 233, 234
Hilaire Belloc 70
Hillsea Point 72
Hoe (Plymouth) 106
Hoe, The (Scilly) 221
Holes Hole 113
Home Reach 65
Hope Cove 71, 84
Hope's Nose 27
Huers' huts 178
Hugh Town 209, 211
Hulman Beacon 227
Hunters Lump 236

I

Ince Point 108
Inner Froward Point 55
Innisidgen 206, 216
Inshore Waters Forecasts 12
Irish Sea 175
Island, the 80
Isles of Scilly 195
Isles of Scilly, anchorages
at a glance 238
Islington Wharf 153

J

'J' class 151
James, Dame Naomi 61
Jennycliff Bay 98
John Martin's Ledge 234
Jupiter Point 108

K

Kettle Bottom Ledge 225
Kettle's Bottom 241
Kilcobben Cove 173
Kingsand 97
Kingsbridge 78, 82
Kingsbridge ferry 74
Kingswear 56, 57, 61, 62
Kingswear Castle 57
Kittern Rock 220
Kynance Cove 174

L

Lamorna Cove 194
Lamouth Creek 160
Lamp Rock 130
Landing Carn 236
Land's End 172, 174, 195, 202,
239, 240, 242
Land's End Hotel 240
Land's End Traffic Separation
Scheme (TSS) 196, 203, 207
Lantic Bay 118
Lath Rock 121
Lead Stone 26
Lerryn 137
Limebury Point 75, 80
Lincombe 81
Lion Rock 233
Liskeard 126
Listrey Rocks 245
Little Cheese Rock 237
Little Kittern Rock 228
Little Pentle Ledge 237
Little Rag Ledge Beacon 227
Little Trigg rocks 180
Lizard, The 119, 123, 172, 173, 174,
179, 180, 203, 206
Lizard lighthouse, The 173
Loe Bar 174, 180
Loe Beach 159
Loe Pool 181
Long Point 229
Longroom Port Control 95
Longships 172, 202, 240
Looe 117, 124
Looe, East 126
Looe Island 117, 124, 128
Looe luggers 127
Looe, River 124

Looe, West 126
Lostwithiel 135
Low Lee shoal 174, 186
Lower Town 235
Lowest Astronomical Tide - LAT 9
Lowland Point 172, 176
Lubbers Rock 227
Luggers 127
Lugo rock 154
Lump of Clay Ledge 237
Lyme Bay 20, 21, 55
Lyme Regis 21, 23
Lyme Regis Sailing Club 24
Lympstone 35
Lynher, The 107
Lyonnesse 218

M

Mabel Shoal 81
Maer Rocks 33
Maggotty Bank 160
Maiden Bower 207
Mallard Shoal 101
Malpas 160
Manacle buoy 123, 172
Manacle Point 123
Manacles, The 123, 176
Marazion 175, 191
Mare, the 178
Maria Asumpta 249
Marina, Brixham 52, 54
Marina, Dart 60
Marina, Darthaven 60
Marina Developments Ltd 102
Marina, Falmouth 152, 153
Marina, Mayflower International
98, 99
Marina, Noss-on-Dart 60
Marina, Port Pendennis 148
Marina, Queen Anne's Battery
98, 101, 102
Marina, Southdown 107
Marina, Sutton Harbour 98, 103
Marina, Torquay 47, 49
Marina Village, Millbay 106
Marina, Mylor Yacht Harbour 155
Marinecall forecast 13
Maritime Museum, Exeter 37
Mary's Rocks, West and East, 87
Maurier, Daphne du 130
Mawnan Church 167
Mayflower 104, 186
McMullen, RT 46, 180
MDL 106
Men-a-vaur 225, 235, 236
Menawethan 204, 205
Merchant's Point 228
Merrick Island 227
Mevagissey 120, 131, 139, 141
Mewstone, the 28, 55, 70
Mewstone, Great
72, 75, 89, 94, 95
Mewstone Ledge 89
Mewstone, Little 70, 75
Middle Back 64
Middle Passage 213
Middle Town 235
Middleton, EE 61, 62
Midmain 125
Mill Bay 77, 79, 80

Millbay Docks 95, 97
Millbrook 107
Millbrook Lake 107
Mincarlo 207
Misery Point 89, 90
Mitchell, Percy 143
Mixtow Pill 137
Mont St Michel 190
Moonraker of Fowey 127, 134
Morris Rogue 27
Mount Batten 101, 104
Mount Batten breakwater 101
Mount Batten Centre, The 101
Mount Edgcumbe Country Park 98
Mount Flagon 212
Mount Wise 100
Mountamopus 174
Mount's Bay 172, 174, 190, 192, 199, 203, 206, 242
Mousehole 145, 174, 190, 192, 206
Mouthstone Ledge 89
MRCC, Falmouth 202
Muhlhauser, George 61
Mullion Island 174, 179, 180
Museum, Falmouth Maritime 148
Museum, Lifeboat House 80
Museum, National Maritime 113
Museum, Overbecks 80
Museum, Topsham 39
Museum, Valhalla 224
Mylor 151
Mylor Bridge 156
Mylor Creek 154, 156
Mylor Pool 154, 156
Mylor Yacht Harbour 154, 155

N

Nare Head 121
Nare Point 122
National Coastwatch Institution 8
National Lighthouse Centre 182
National Trust 7, 159, 181
Naval Dockyard 95
Needles 20
Ness Pole sand 43
Ness, the 26
New Grimsby Quay 226
New Grimsby Sound 197, 206, 219, 224
New Grimsby Sound - Approach from north 225
Newford Island 212, 213
Newland 249
Newlyn 145, 174, 175, 186, 190, 192, 203, 206
Newquay 245
Newton Ferrers 91
Nimble Rock 28
Normandy short stay visitors' pontoon 78
Nornour 237
North Bartholomew shoal 220
North Channel, The 198, 207
North Cornish coast 172
North Cornwall 8
North Passage 213
North Quay 148
Northern Rocks 207
Norwethal 228

Noss Mayo 91
Nut Rock 214, 227

O

Obadiah's Barrow 220
Old Grimsby Sound 197, 225, 228
Old Man of Gugh 220
Onedin Line 61, 140
Orcombe Point 26, 31
Ore Stone 26
OSGB36 datum 10
Outer Penzeath rock 191

P

Packet ships 150
Padstow 206, 243, 247
Padstow Bay 243
Padstow Harbour 250
Paignton 27
'Palmerston's Follies' 98
Pan, The 158
Par 120, 140
Parn Voose Cove 173
Peak Rock 128
Pedn Billy point 169
Pednbean 234
Pelistry Bay 216
Penarrow Point 155
Penberth 174
Pencarrow Head 118
Pendeen Head 242
Pendeen lighthouse 241
Pendeen Watch 242
Pendennis Castle 145
Pendennis Point 122, 145
Pendennis Shipyard 147
Peninnis Head 203, 204, 218
Peninnis Light 202
Penlee Point 72, 97, 174, 187
Penryn 153
Penryn quay 153
Pentewan 141
Pentillie Castle 113
Pentire Point 239, 243, 249, 251
Pentire Points, East and West (Newquay) 245
Penzance 145, 174, 175, 182, 184, 190, 191, 199, 202, 206
Penzance Harbour lighthouse 183
Penzer Point 192
Perconger Ledge 220
Percuil River 154
Periglis Bay 219
Pernagie Island 233
Perranporth 242
Picklecombe 98
Pidney Brow 221
Pier & Harbour Company, St Mawes 154
Pier, Prince of Wales 149
Pighole Point 64
Pilchards 127
Pill Creek 159
Piper's Hole 224
Place House 155
Plumb Island 227, 233
Plump Rocks 228
Plym, River 101

Plymouth 72, 94, 186
Plymouth Breakwater 95
Plymouth Hoe 100
Plymouth Sound 72, 95
Plymouth, The City of 105
Plymouth Waterfront Walk 105
Polca Rock 124, 128
Pole Sands 30, 31
Polgwidden Cove 167
Polkerris 139
Pollard Rock 216
Polperro 118, 124, 127
Polridmouth Cove 137
Polruan 131, 135, 137
Polwheveral Creek 170
Polzeath 248, 251
Ponsence Cove 167
Pont Pill 133, 137
Pontoon, Brixham Town 54
Port guide:
  River Exe 41
  Torquay 49
  Brixham 54
  River Dart 67
  Salcombe 83
  River Yealm 93
  Plymouth 114
  Fowey 138
  Falmouth 162
  Penzance 185
  Newlyn 189
  St Mary's 215
  Padstow 252
Port Navas 169
Port Navas Creek 167, 169
Port Pendennis 148
Porth Conger 220
Porth Cressa 204, 209, 215
Porth Cressa Brow 216
Porth Loo 213
Porth Mellin 174
Porth Mellon 212
Porth Saxon 167
Porthcurno 174
Porthleven 174, 179, 181
Porthmellin Head 121
Porthmellon 143
Porthmeor Beach 245
Porthoustock 123
Porthscatho 121
Porthtowan 242
Portland Bill 18, 19, 21
Portland Bill inshore passage from the west 20
Portland Race and how to avoid it 19
Portland Race, passage inside 20
Portlemouth, East 78, 80
Portlemouth ferry 77
Portreath 243
Portwrinkle 117
Poundstone 75
Powderham Castle 35
Powderham Sand 36
Prawle Point 70, 80
Predannack Head 174, 181
Punch's Cross 119
Punch's Cross rock 130
Pye, Peter and Anne 127, 134

Q

Quay, Albert 131
Quay, Custom House 149
Quay, Polruan 130, 135
'Quay Punts' 150
Queens Ledge 228
Quiller-Couch, Sir Arthur 137

R

Ragged Island 237
Raleigh, Sir Walter 150
Rame Head 71, 72, 94, 117
Raney, the 124, 128
'Range', the 56
Ranneys, the 118, 124
Rat Island 209, 213
Readymoney Cove 130, 137
Regatta Week, Falmouth 151
Restronguet 158
Restronguet Creek 156, 158
Retreat Boatyard, the 40
Rill Point 174
RMS *Scillonian III* 184, 202, 209, 211
Rock 249, 251
Roscarrock 249
Rosemullion Head 122, 166
Rosevear 219
Rough Ledge 233
Round Britain and Ireland Race 102
Round Island 202, 204, 207, 235
Roundwood Quay 160
Rowing Club, Newquay 215, 246
Royal Marine Training Camp 36
Royal Naval College 61
Royal Naval Dockyards 106
Ruan Creek 160
Rule of twelfths' 11
Rumps Point 249
Runnel Stone 174, 202, 206
Rushy Bay 229
Rushy Point 229

S

Sailing Association (POFSA), The Port of Falmouth 151
Sailing Club, Exe 34
Sailing Club, Helford River 168, 169
Sailing Club, Looe 126
Sailing Club, Penzance 185
Sailing Club, Restronguet 155
Sailing Club, Rock 251
Sailing Club, Saltash 110
Sailing Club, St Mawes 155
Sailing Club, The Fowey Gallants 134
Sailing Club, The Quay 109
Sailing Club, Topsham 40, 41
Sailing Club, Torpoint Mosquito 107
Salcombe 69, 74
Salcombe Bar 74, 77
Salcombe yawls 40, 80
Salmon netsmen 113
Saltash 107, 110
Saltstone Beacon 81
'Salty', the 44

Samson 206, 207, 219, 227, 230
Sandhill Point 75
Satellite Derived Position Note 10
Schooners 78
Scillonian III 212
Scoble Point 77, 81
Sconner Lake 109
Season Point 89
Seaton 25
Sennen Cove 241
Seven Stones 202, 207
Shaggles Sand 35
Shagstone 72, 94, 95
Shaldon 44
Shambles 20
Shambles Bank 19
Sharkham Point 28
Sharks 126
Shark's Fin 241
Sharpham House 65
Sharpitor Gardens 80
Ship Canal, Exeter 37
Shipman Down 229
Shipman Head 225
Shipping Forecasts 12
Shipyard Ltd, Squaresail 140
Shoalstone Point 27
Sidmouth 25
Silver Pit 35
Singlehanded Transatlantic 102
Site of Special Scientific Interest 75
Skerries 29
Skybus 202
Slapton Ley 28, 79
Slapton Sands 28
Slimers, Outer and Inner 89
Smalls Cove 77
Smith, Augustus 222, 230
Smith Sound 198, 207, 219
Snapes Point 81
Soar Mill Cove 71
South Hams 75, 82
South Passage 212
South Sands 80
South Wales 240
Southdown 107
Southdown Lake 107
Southpool Creek 79, 81
Spanish Ledges 204
Spernan Shoals 173
Spratt sand 43
Spy Glass Point 118, 128
St Agnes 195, 204, 218
St Agnes' Head 242, 245
St Alban's race 20
St Anthony 166
St Anthony Head 122, 145
St Anthony light 121, 122
St Austell Bay 120, 139
St Catherine's Point 130
St Clement's Island 187
St Clement's Isle 174, 192
St German's River 107, 108, 109
St German's Quay 109
St Helen's Gap 236, 237
St Helen's Island 225, 231
St Helen's Pool 235, 236
St Ives 206, 244
St Ives Bay 206, 242
St Ives Head 244
St John's Lake 107

St Just 158
St Martin's 195, 202, 204, 219, 231
St Martin's on the Isle Hotel 234
St Mary's 195, 202, 204, 208
St Mary's Pool 197, 211, 216
St Mary's Pool - approach
   from north 213
St Mary's Pool - approach
   from south 212
St Mary's Road 214, 226
St Mary's Sound 202, 204, 236
St Mawes 145, 149, 154, 156, 167
St Mawes Castle 154
St Michael's Mount 174, 183, 190
St Saviour's Point 249
Staddon Heights 97
Staddon Point 96
Stanfords Chart Folios 10
Star Castle 208
Starcross 35
Starcross Fishing and
   Cruising Club 35
Starehole Bay 71
Start Bay 28, 29, 69
Start Point 18, 21, 29, 56, 69, 80, 119
Start Point lighthouse 28
Start Rocks 29
Start, the 19, 21
Steam Railway,
   Paignton and Dartmouth 57
Steamer Quay 66
Steeple Rock 207
Steer Point 92
Stepper Point 248, 251
Stepper Point light 248
Steval 206
Stoke Gabriel 64
Stonehouse 98
Stones, The 242
Straight Point 25, 31
Straight Point Range 31
Subfacts 13
Sunbeams 151
Sunny Cove 77
Sutton Harbour 100, 101, 103
Sutton Pier 103
Sutton Pool 105
Swanpool Beach 122

Talland Bay 128
Tamar, River 95, 110
Tamar road bridge 112
Tater Du 174, 202
Tavy, River 112
Taylor's Island 213
Tea Ledge 237
Team Phillips 65
Tean 231
Tean Sound 197, 233, 234
Teign estuary, The 26, 42
Teign, River 42
Teignmouth 26, 42, 43, 44
Temptress 7, 170
Tern IV 63, 140
Thatcher Rock 27
The Wind in the Willows 130, 134
Thongyore Ledge 233
Three Rocks Ledges 234

Three Stone Oar 242
Thurlestone rock 72
Tiddy 109
Tide Rock 229
Tides 10
Todden, the 178
Tolcarne Creek 159
Toll Point 166
Toll's Island 217
Tolverne Point 159
Tom Kneebone ledge 192
Topsham 26, 31, 37, 38, 39
Topsham Quay 37, 39
Tor Bay 26, 45
Torbay Royal Regatta 47
Torpoint 107
Torpoint ferry 95
Torquay 21, 27, 45, 46
Torrey Canyon 207
Totnes 65, 66
Towan Head 245
Town Quay 161
Town Quay, Fowey 130
Transatlantic races 94
Trebetherick 248, 251
Trefusis Point 152
Trelissick House 159
Tresco 195, 202, 206, 219, 222, 235
Tresco Abbey 222
Tresco Estate 225, 229
Tresco Flats 226
Trevaunance Cove 245
Trevose Head 243, 248
Trevose Head lighthouse 243
Trinity House 182, 218
Trout's Boatyard 38
Troy Town stone maze 219
Troys 135
Truro River 159, 160
Truro, City of 161
Tuckenhay 64
Turf Hotel 37
Turnaware Bar 159
Turnaware Point 159
Twostar 102
Tywardreath Bay 139

Udder Rock 118
Uganda 160

Variation 10
Veryan Bay 121
Voge Rock 173
Voose, the 167
Vrogue Rock 173
Vyneck, The 242

Waddeton Point 64
Wadebridge 251
Wareham Point 82
Warren Point 33, 109
Warren, the 26
Watch Hill 229
Water taxi, Exe 33
Water taxi, Fowey 134, 138
Water taxi Helford 168
Water taxi, Yealm 93

Waterhead Creek 81
Watermill Cove 205, 209, 216
Watersports Association,
   Falmouth 149
Waypoints 10
Weather and Forecasts 11, 12, 13, 14
Wells Rock 86
Wembury Bay 72, 89
Wembury Church 89
West and East Porth 236
West Bay 22
West Country Rivers 6
West Craggyellis Ledge 237
Western Blackstone Rocks 57
Western Rocks 198, 219
Weymouth 20
WGS shifts 10
WGS84 datum 10
Whelps, The 121
White Island 233
Whitehouse Point 130
Whitesand Bay 117, 241
Whitestrand Quay 78
Wingletang Down 219
Wiseman's Pool 136, 137
Wolf Rock 77, 202
Wolf Rock lighthouse 175, 203
Woodcock Ledge 205
Working Boat Association,
   Falmouth 151
Working Boats 151
World Pilot Gig Championship 215
Worth, Claud 63, 140, 143, 167, 169
Worth, Tom 167
Wra, the 242
Wras 216

Yacht Club, Brixham 53
Yacht Club, Cargreen 112
Yacht Club, Dartmouth 58
Yacht Club, Mylor 156
Yacht Club of England,
   Royal Western 102
Yacht Club, Port Navas 169
Yacht Club, Royal Dart 57
Yacht Club, Royal Fowey 131, 133
Yacht Club, Royal Plymouth
   Corinthian 100
Yacht Club, Royal Torbay 46, 47
Yacht Club, Salcombe 77
Yacht Club, Starcross 35
Yacht Club, The Royal Cornwall 150
Yacht Club, The Royal Dart 58
Yacht Club, Yealm 92
Yacht Club, The Royal Tor Bay 48
Yacht Clubs 14
Yacht Harbour Association 60
Yacht Harbour, Mylor 155
Yacht Harbour, Torpoint 107
Yacht Haven, Plymouth 98, 100, 102, 104
Yacht Haven, Visitors' 147
Yealm Head 89
Yealm, River 72, 88

Zone Point 122